379 .2630973 R136h
Raffel, Jeffrey A
Historical dictionary of
school segregation and
desegregation : the American

D0075626

HISTORICAL DICTIONARY OF SCHOOL SEGREGATION AND DESEGREGATION

THE AMERICAN EXPERIENCE

JEFFREY A. RAFFEL

379.2630973
R136h

GREENWOOD PRESS 1/99
WESTPORT, CONNECTICUT • LONDON

CUYAHOGA COMMUNITY COLLEGE
METRO CAMPUS LIBRARY

Library of Congress Cataloging-in-Publication Data

Raffel, Jeffrey A.
    Historical dictionary of school segregation and desegregation :
the American experience / Jeffrey A. Raffel.
      p. cm.
    Includes bibliographical references and index.
    ISBN 0–313–29502–6 (alk. paper)
    1. Segregation in education—United States—History—
Encyclopedias. 2. School integration—United States—History—
Encyclopedias.
    LC212.52.R34   1998
    379.2'63'0973—dc21   98–11102

British Library Cataloguing in Publication Data is available.

Copyright © 1998 by Jeffrey A. Raffel

All rights reserved. No portion of this book may be
reproduced, by any process or technique, without the
express written consent of the publisher.

Library of Congress Catalog Card Number: 98–11102
ISBN: 0–313–29502–6

First published in 1998

Greenwood Press, 88 Post Road West, Westport, CT 06881
An imprint of Greenwood Publishing Group, Inc.

Printed in the United States of America

The paper used in this book complies with the
Permanent Paper Standard issued by the National
Information Standards Organization (Z39.48–1984).

10 9 8 7 6 5 4 3 2 1

This book is dedicated to my mother, Renée, whose strong beliefs in equality live within me, and my father, George, whose interest in my work serves as a continuing inspiration to me.

CONTENTS

PREFACE

School segregation and desegregation have been at the center of conflict and have aroused the passions of Americans for many decades. This reference volume is an attempt to bring some rationality to a subject loaded with emotion. Herein brief essays describe the over 270 key court decisions, people, types of school desegregation plans, legislation, organizations, terms and concepts, and reports and publications that have played a significant role in the history of this topic. Entries are included in alphabetical order. This comprehensive reference work should prove helpful to students studying this topic: teachers of black history, the sociology of education, and related fields; scholars conducting research in this field; and practitioners involved in the school desegregation process. I believe that they will be aided by having all this material in one volume in a convenient form.

I have attempted to be inclusive in determining the entries. The volume covers school segregation and desegregation in postsecondary as well as elementary and secondary education. The geographical area, however, is limited to the United States. The time period covers the topic from before the Civil War through the latest court decision at the time of the writing of this book. Given the historical development of the battle for school desegregation, however, the focus is on the last 50 years. The length of each item is related to its importance in the history of school segregation and desegregation, not necessarily the entry's importance on other dimensions. Thus the U.S. Constitution is a brief entry, despite its importance to the nation, while the Fourteenth Amendment, the concept of separate but equal, and *Plessy v. Ferguson* (1896) are given more space.

Of course, I could not include all possible entries. Lines have to be drawn. I was most conscious of drawing them at the following places. This volume is not a historical dictionary of civil rights; the efforts of those who braved sit-ins and freedom rides are not included here, except where they had a direct bearing on school desegregation. Nor have I included all the court decisions relating to affirmative action, a related but far broader topic than the concern here. I have included material on affirmative action as it has been implemented in postsecondary institutions (as opposed to employment). Nor could I include entries relating more generally to African-American education rather than my more specific topic. I did include "classic" writings that have had historical impact, such as the Coleman Report, but I decided to wait for the judgment of history on recent books on school desegregation, such as David Armor's *Forced Justice* (1995) and Gary Orfield and Susan Eaton's *Dismantling Desegregation* (1996). Despite a list of significant individuals suggested by Charles Willie, I limited the number of people entries to the 50 or so who in my view have had the greatest sustained impact on the topic. Specifically, I included those individuals who had a great influence over defining national law in school desegregation and the implementation of the law, central figures in a landmark case or event, those who devoted their careers to school desegregation and had an impact during their lifetime, and major spokespersons of views on segregation and desegregation. I thus included presidents, Supreme Court justices, lawyers, federal judges, and academics. The latter proved the hardest category within which to draw lines. I included those educators and researchers whose research had an impact on cases and the national public debate around the issue. This criterion generally led me to exclude academics who wrote one good book or individuals involved in one legal case. I also had to limit the number of court decisions to the most significant, not all that related to the topic. While I did include a few Court of Appeals and state court decisions, generally I limited the selection of court decisions to those from, or reviewed by, the U.S. Supreme Court. I did not include every court decision on every school desegregation case.

At the end of each item I have listed bibliographic material to help readers with any follow-up research. These are listed chronologically, the most recent first. I have, where possible, included the most recent, comprehensive source, along with "classics" where appropriate. Generally, I have listed at least three further sources; for the most important entries I have included up to six. I have cited books and journal articles rather than newspaper articles or dissertations. Works listed in the General Bibliography at the end of the volume are cited in the entry references by the author's last name, title, and date.

Cross-references that are also separate entries in this dictionary have been noted with an asterisk directly after their appearance in the text of individual entries. Court decisions are sometimes referred to in the text of entries by the last name of the plaintiff in the case as well as the year of the decision, for example, *Brown* (1954) for *Brown v. Board of Education* (1954) and *Bakke* (1978) for *Regents of the University of California v. Bakke* (1978).

I have tried to be as complete as possible in stating the facts about each entry, for example, including birthplaces or the full names of actors in the court cases. I have also endeavored to describe the issues of controversy where appropriate, laying out the arguments made by those with different opinions.

The Chronology following the Introduction will give the reader a brief historical overview of segregation and desegregation in the United States since 1787. The General Bibliography at the volume's end includes many significant references for individual entries plus some additional references that helped me to compile this book. A bibliography organized by place, that is, city or school district, will help readers interested in particular cases of school desegregation. The Geographical Bibliography is not a comprehensive listing of all material on each case, but it should provide a good starting point for those seeking more information on school desegregation in particular cities and places. Those seeking short articles about desegregation in various places should also refer to the journal *Integrated Education* (now *Equity and Excellence in Education*), the *Southern Education Report*, published by the Southern Education Reporting Service, and reports of the U.S. Civil Rights Commission.

While a historical dictionary can provide the reader with much useful information about a major historical topic, some material gets lost in the entry method of discourse. While I cannot totally make up for this loss, I fill in some information to make the volume more complete and helpful in the Introduction, where I designate stages of school segregation and desegregation history, note some overarching issues in this history, and identify some recent trends and issues in the field.

During the historical span that this book covers the words *Negroes, blacks*, and *African Americans* have been used to refer to this racial group. I have decided to use the word *blacks* except where I am using a direct quote or paraphrasing a speaker or writer. While one might argue that the term *Negro* is appropriate given the historical period covered by this volume, or that *African American* should be used because of its currency, *black* stands in juxtaposition to the term *white*, the term used herein to refer to Caucasians, and was in use for an important phase of the desegregation battle. For similar reasons, I refer to Hispanics rather than Latinos.

I received much help in writing this book, and I gratefully thank those who helped me. Cathy Dennis, Sarah Keifer, and Lesley McKnight served as able research assistants. I especially thank Cathy for her good cheer in tracking down obscure references, Sarah for happily surfing the Internet to locate helpful source material, and Lesley for spending hours in the library correcting errors of omission I made previously. Brett Levy helped to construct the chronology with painstaking detective work in several libraries. Jen Bowdle Collins was an excellent research assistant in the latter stages of this effort, locating needed sources at the library, on the Internet, over the telephone, or wherever she could obtain the needed information. Diana Simmons translated my scrawl into manuscript corrections and reorganized computer files into a complete manuscript.

David Armor, Gary Orfield, Charles Willie, David Garrett, Jennifer Hochschild, and Leslie Goldstein read sections of the manuscript and provided me with helpful and sage advice as well as encouragement. Christine Rossell did likewise, but she also went beyond the call of duty in making scores of detailed suggestions that greatly improved this work. Dorry Ross and Rose Bosler were immense helps in creating the index. I thank them all and, of course, take full responsibility for this work and any errors of omission or commission.

While hundreds of people, too numerous to thank here, have expanded my knowledge about school segregation and desegregation over my years of active involvement in this topic, I have learned a great deal more through my reading and research in compiling this book. I thus owe a debt of thanks to George Butler and Greenwood Press for conceiving of this volume and asking me to write it. I thank my friend and dean, Dan Rich, for encouraging me to accept this task in the midst of my administrative assignment and for strongly supporting me along the way. The College (now School) of Urban Affairs and Public Policy at the University of Delaware has been my academic home for over 25 years and remains a splendid place for me to conduct my work.

Finally, I thank my immediate family for their support. My wife Joanne has observed me as this effort changed from a project to an obsession, and I thank her for her patience. While my children have left the nest, they remained as inspirations for me as I wrote this book: Allison for her energy and panache, Lori for her endurance and storytelling ability, and Ken for his analytical ability and computer savvy. I also thank our most recent family additions, Tom and David, my sons-in-law, who both served as examples of the rewards that follow hard work.

INTRODUCTION

Understanding today's controversies over school desegregation requires an understanding of yesterday's roots of school segregation. While this volume provides descriptions of people, events, court decisions, legislation, and other entries that help to establish this foundation, a different type of presentation and analysis is necessary for comprehending the flow of the history of school segregation and desegregation.

STAGES OF SCHOOL DESEGREGATION

A number of authors have set forth helpful stages of school segregation and desegregation. They revolve around a similar set of key events. Samuel Myers (1989) has set out the broadest framework. Myers specifies four stages of the education of blacks in the United States:

1. *Prohibition* of the education of blacks before the Civil War. South Carolina adopted the first compulsory illiteracy law in 1740 making it a crime to teach slaves to write; other southern states followed.

2. *Development* of education for blacks after the Civil War with the establishment of the Freedmen's Bureau, which helped to found schools for blacks throughout the South, and many historically black colleges and universities (HBCUs).

3. *Segregation* following the *Plessy v. Ferguson* Supreme Court decision of 1896, which established the principle of separate but equal as constitutional and kept blacks in inferior schools for decades.

4. *Desegregation* following the 1954 *Brown* Supreme Court decision, which overturned the *Plessy* decision and the separate but equal principle, and the Civil Rights Act of

1964, which provided the federal government with the enforcement tool to effect school desegregation.

Wilkinson (1979) divides Myers's last stage, the desegregation stage, into four periods:

1. *Absolute defiance* (1955–1959) from the *Brown* remedy decision to the end of Virginia's attempt to defy the Supreme Court and maintain segregated schools through massive resistance.

2. *Token compliance* (1959–1964) from the end of massive resistance to the passage of the Civil Rights Act of 1964.

3. *Modest integration* (1964–1968) from the Civil Rights Act of 1964 to the 1968 *Green* U.S. Supreme Court decision, in which the Court ruled that freedom-of-choice plans, supposedly allowing black and white students to select their schools, had to be effective in desegregating or racially balancing the district's schools.

4. *Massive integration* (1968–   ) from *Green* on.

If Wilkinson were writing today, he would probably add a fifth period, perhaps calling it "limitations to busing," from the first *Milliken* decision (1974), in which the U.S. Supreme Court limited the power of courts to order school desegregation in metropolitan areas, to the present. During this phase opposition to busing seemed to slow, if not reverse, the direction of the courts and school desegregation.

These two conceptualizations of stages after the Civil War are based upon four critical events of the history of school segregation and desegregation: *Plessy v. Ferguson* (1896), *Brown v. Board of Education* (1954), the Civil Rights Act of 1964, and *Green v. County School Board* (1968). Three were decisions of the U.S. Supreme Court, one an act of the U.S. Congress.

While the *Plessy* and *Brown* decisions are well known to most, and the Civil Rights Act of 1964 is familiar to many, because it helped to turn the promise of school desegregation into reality by placing enforcement responsibility in the executive branch of the federal government, the impact and meaning of the *Green* decision is less well understood. Conservatives view this decision as a turning point, the movement from *color-blind* to *color-conscious* decisions. It was in the *Green* decision that the U.S. Supreme Court, reviewing school desegregation implementation in a small rural county in eastern Virginia, changed its stance from insisting on antidiscrimination, assigning students to schools without regard to their race, to desegregation, requiring schools to be racially balanced. Conservatives (e.g., Wolters, 1984) see this as a move from the principle of *color blindness*, assigning pupils to schools without regard to race, to *affirmative action*, using race as a factor in student assignment. Liberals view this decision as a turning point because the Court went from accepting desegregation plans that had no practical effect to plans that would, in the language of *Green*, "work now." Thus Kujovich (1992:219), quoting Justice Lewis Powell in *Keyes* (1973), concludes that *Green* transformed *Brown*'s "concept of state neutrality . . . into the present constitutional doctrine requiring affirmative state action to desegregate school systems" in those school districts where the state had previously created segregation, and Armor (1995:7) states, "In short, these later decisions changed the meaning of desegregation from prohibiting forced segregation to requiring forced integration. Instead of embracing race-neutral remedies, which the original *Brown* decision seemed to do, the federal courts ultimately sanctioned race-conscious policies wherever remedies were imposed."

Perhaps the most interesting point was made by constitutional law scholar Philip B. Kurland (1994). He notes that there is both "irony and justice" in the fact that the delay in implementation of racially neutral school assignment caused by segregationists after the *Brown* decision ultimately led to a frustrated Court deciding in *Green* to raise the bar and require racial balancing of schools. Kurland quotes Thurgood Marshall's oral argument to the Court in *Brown* as exemplifying the position of the NAACP Legal Defense Fund that government neutrality was the objective: "Then I think whatever district lines they draw, if it can be shown that those lines are drawn on the basis of race or color, then I think they would violate the injunction. If lines are drawn on a natural basis, without regard to race or color, then I think that nobody would have any complaint" (420).

The *Milliken* decision should be included as a fifth critical event for those now dividing the history of school desegregation into phases. The U.S. Supreme Court's 5–4 decision to disallow the desegregation of the Detroit schools with the surrounding suburban school districts marked the beginning of the limiting of school desegregation and busing. The construction of this major hurdle to metropolitan school district plans began an era that includes a series of court decisions that specify how to end formal school desegregation plans.

Efforts to divide the history of desegregation are not limited to elementary and secondary education. Dentler, Baltzell, and Sullivan (1983) proposed the following eras in higher education:

First era (1636–1865): Blacks had no opportunity for higher education, except at 4 schools formed after 1850.

Second era (1866–1915): With the spur of the Morrill Act, a network of 40 black institutions was developed, de jure segregated, poor, but influential in building a foundation for black education.

Third era (1916–1930): Blacks entered white graduate and professional schools, but segregation also hardened.

Fourth era (1931–1954): Rising tide of successful civil rights litigation won by the NAACP opened access for blacks at white state universities.

Fifth era (1955–1973): De jure segregation ended, the Civil Rights Act of 1964 was passed, the *Adams* decision (1973) forced the executive branch to implement *Brown* in higher education, and college attendance among blacks expanded.

They concluded that at the time of their writing (early 1980s) a sixth era was unfolding, "a swinging back, a reversal of the expansionary, optimistic, equalizing trends of the 1955–1973 era" (9–10) to a time when issues were more complicated with the "dragon" of state-imposed segregation "slain." Thus in the history of the desegregation of higher education, as in the development of the desegregation of elementary and secondary education, the *Brown* decision also plays a critical role. But U.S. Supreme Court decisions specific to higher education, such as *McLaurin* (1950), *Sipuel* (1948), and *Sweatt* (1950), are also significant.

EVALUATING SCHOOL DESEGREGATION

While there is almost universal agreement that school segregation sanctioned by law was bad, there is still great disagreement over whether school desegregation has been good; that is, there is certainly much disagreement about the impact of the *Brown* decision and the decisions that were constructed on the legal foundation established by *Brown*. There are several reasons for this.

First, the criteria on which one judges school desegregation are not well defined and accepted by all. Specifically, one question surrounding much of the debate over school desegregation is whether it "works." But there is no agreement on the dimensions on which to judge desegregation's impacts. Here the statement of Mayer et al. (1974: xviii) is helpful: "Nor is it clear what 'works' means—better racial attitudes, high academic achievement, later lives of more opportunity, a more democratic America?"

Armor (1995:4) writes that the "harm and benefit thesis" has been critical to the ongoing debate over the success or failure of school desegregation. This thesis "holds that school segregation is harmful and school desegregation is beneficial to the educational and social outcomes of schooling." Armor's statement of this thesis has two components. The first argues that segregated schools are harmful to the educational, psychological, and social development of minority children. This is in part a result of the reinforcement of negative stereotypes and resultant reduction of self-esteem. The second component of this thesis assumes that desegregation has the opposite effect, that it boosts minority self-concept and achievement while improving race relations.

Armor (1995:70) concludes that studies after *Swann* (1971) suggest that "modern research tends to find that effects are not uniform but vary from one study (and presumably one set of conditions) to another." Results of many studies do not indicate that school desegregation will boost minority achievement or self-concept, nor does desegregation necessarily result in improved race relations. There is a consensus that desegregation does not affect white achievement, which gives comfort to some but, according to Armor, makes it hard to justify busing plans to whites. Studies of black achievement resulting from school desegregation do not show consistent positive effects; while some reviews of the literature are optimistic, many are not. Crain, Braddock, and colleagues (see Schofield, 1995, for a summary of this work) have focused not only on test scores but also on "life chances"—overcoming isolation from middle-class opportunities and networks, those that can open doors to college and careers. Thus the Census Bureau reported in September 1996 (Holmes, 1996) that the same ratio of whites and blacks aged 25 to 29 (86.5 percent of blacks and 87.4 percent of whites) held high-school diplomas in March 1995, an indication of equal "life chances," although the income and college-graduation gaps between blacks and whites remained. Wells and Crain (1994) thus argue that more sociological research, focusing on breaking the cycle of segregation and permitting minority students to access high-status institutions, is needed to supplement research with a psychological perspective, concentrating on the "hearts and minds" of minority children.

One way to view this research literature is offered by Henderson et al. (1996). Noting the mixed, if not disappointing, established effects of school desegregation plans, the authors argue that "desegregation cannot be treated as if it were a uniform program in all racially mixed schools. . . . Rather desegregation is a complex process and needs to be studied cautiously" (165). They suggest that school desegregation has effects that "may vary with type of students, type of school, type of community, SES (socioeconomic status), gender, and other related factors" (166). Hochschild (1984) adds type of desegregation plan to this important list of variables. Therefore, focusing simply on the demographics of a desegregated situation will not reveal the potential impact of a particular situation. Schofield's (1995) careful and comprehensive review of the effects of school desegregation on elementary and secondary students reaches similar conclusions.

Those who judge school desegregation using the criterion of equal results are sure to be disappointed with its effects, for no one could argue that blacks or Hispanics have achieved equality of income or status in America today. But those whose standard is equal opportunity could well point to the removal of explicit state-sanctioned laws that once limited minority attendance at most of our nation's southern public schools and postsecondary educational institutions. Certainly, conservatives would argue that with the elimination of de jure barriers to minority attendance the courts have fulfilled the ideal of color blindness, and this success should not lead down the path to color consciousness.

The second reason for disagreement over the extent to which school desegregation has been successful relates to the scope of the concept as well as its effects. The effects of school desegregation cannot simply be added up after reviewing the literature on how a particular plan had an effect on individuals, for example, student achievement, intergroup attitudes, or college attendance, that is, a reductionist view of policy impacts. In this arena the whole is greater than the sum of its parts. School desegregation as an antidiscrimination strategy was the vanguard of the civil rights movement and has affected more than children changing schools or achievement-test scores. School desegregation has affected the relation of blacks to whites in American society.

The reductionist analysis of desegregation effects, while important and helpful, misses the major impact of the *Brown* decision. Muse (1964:38), in his chapter on "Negrophobia," offers one impact of the *Brown* decision. He writes, "For most white Southerners the essential jolt in the *Brown* decision was its simple recognition of the fact that Negroes are citizens of the United States. . . . The Negro minority was not quite part of the 'public' in the South. . . . [A] 'Southerner' in common parlance was emphatically a white person." Consider also the mirror image of this conclusion. Jack Greenberg (1994), former chief legal counsel of the NAACP Legal Defense Fund, concludes that the school desegregation decisions spurred the black assertion of rights that fueled the civil rights movement.

Wilkins (1996:16) also takes a broad view, noting the tremendous effects that the decision to end state-sanctioned discrimination in public schools had on America:

The social change caused by *Brown* was enormous. In the post-*Brown* world, much school desegregation was accomplished and virtually all the public spaces in the rest of society were desegregated as well. The civil rights movement forced the federal government to move both legislatively and administratively in its behalf. Blacks moved into positions undreamed of in the pre-*Brown* world—chairman of the Joint Chiefs of Staff, president of Planned Parenthood, quarterback in the National Football League, president of the National Education Association, mayors of major cities, bank tellers, police chiefs, and professionals in institutions ranging from newspapers to investment banking firms.

Wirt's recent (1997) book on changes that have occurred to the social, political, and economic system of Panola County, Mississippi, since the *Brown* decision is an excellent example of taking a more macro view. But not all global views are positive. Neuborne (1996:201) laments:

When I began as a civil rights lawyer in the 1960s, there was a naiveté. . . . The world seemed simpler then; the assumption was that if we could only remove the legal chains that bound people into apartheid, then equality would inevitably and inexorably follow. We assumed that what was stopping equality in this nation was not deep wellsprings of racism and deep economic inequality, but an artificial impediment caused by law, and if we could just get rid of the impediment, equality would then follow. . . . But I must confess to you that the task is much more complicated than any of us understood in the 1960s.

Neuborne notes that they thought that they were at the end of a journey, but it was really the beginning.

Thus to judge the broad effects of *Brown* requires a standard of comparison. There is a major conflict, however, even over the broad standard. Specifically, does one judge the effects of the *Brown* decision by comparing the post-*Brown* era to the *past* or to the *ideal*? The former leads to a positive view, the latter to a negative one. While the *Brown* decision led to a positive change in the status of blacks in the nation, it did not lead to full equality. Thus Wilkins's view is positive because he compares the status of blacks in his day to the period before 1964, but Neuborne's view is more negative because he compares the status of blacks today to the ideal of full equality.

The reasons for the lack of full realization of the dream and ideal are varied and contentious. Some would argue that the strategy was wrong. Others would contend that the courts were not forceful enough. Many would suggest that the vestiges of segregation and America's apartheid remain and cannot be fixed by legal decisions, that white attitudes and behaviors and/or black response to years of discrimination must be modified. Dismantling apartheid was a necessary, but insufficient, condition for full equality. Thus interpreting the past is difficult. Discerning the future, especially in the context of the past, is even harder.

FUTURE OF SCHOOL DESEGREGATION

Most analysts agree that in the last two decades school desegregation has been slowed and may have reached its peak. The Supreme Court has reaffirmed that racial balance is a temporary remedy, that de facto segregation does not require a remedy, and that the dual systems can achieve unitary status requiring nondiscrimination but not racial balance. One reads increasing numbers of newspaper articles about courts backing off and decrease in support for race-based policies, for example, judges declaring districts unitary or allowing deviation from mandatory school desegregation plans. Court orders have recently been lifted in Denver, Buffalo, Dallas, Savannah, and Wilmington, Delaware, and in many other districts school boards are considering returning to court to end them (e.g., Prince George's County, Maryland, and Duval County, Florida) or are ending their voluntary plan (Seattle). The number of blacks in segregated schools is high, and problems with desegregating large cities are continually documented. For example, Kunen (1996) cites the fact that one-third of black students in the nation now attend schools where the enrollment is 90–100 percent minority (black, Hispanic, Indian, Asian). There are more black children in segregated schools today than in 1954 (Carter, 1996).

Rossell and Armor (1996:270) have tracked the degree of school desegregation over time with "the largest national sample and most complete data base ever assembled." Before *Green* "substantial majorities" of blacks and whites in the North and South were enrolled in one-race schools (i.e., over 90 percent of either race). With *Green* this began to change, and *Swann* (1971) accelerated the pace, especially in the South. Using the index of dissimilarity to measure racial imbalance (the degree to which minority and majority students are found in the same proportions in the average school as in the district overall), they find that a substantial reduction in racial imbalance occurred from 1968 to 1974, and a more modest reduction resulted until the early 1980s. Another modest reduction continued until the last data-collection period. Interracial exposure, however, the average percentage of whites in the schools of minority students, showed an improvement from 1968 to 1974, but then the trend reversed. They argue that the loss of whites in large school districts, with some of the loss due to mandatory desegregation plans, has made it harder to desegregate schools.

Some have argued that we will never see more desegregation, especially with the increasing percentage of minority students in the nation. Brown (1996:46) concludes, "To state it bluntly, we have already seen the maximum amount of integrated public schools that we are likely to see in our lifetime." Orfield sees the latest racial segregation numbers as the beginning of a historic reversal. Orfield (Kunen, 1996) predicts that by 2020 half of the nation's school population will be nonwhite, and they will be even more isolated from whites than they are today.

Not surprisingly, pessimism about these trends abounds. Ellen Condliffe Lagemann, coeditor of a recent book (Lagemann and Miller, 1996:1) reviewing the significance of the *Brown* decision, writes that "today, it is difficult to write with hope about the prospects for racial justice and equality in the United States." Columnist Tom Wicker titled his 1996 book *Tragic Failure: Racial Integration in America.*

TODAY'S ISSUES

The present volume, it is clear, has been written in a period of rethinking and reevaluating of school desegregation. Both blacks and whites are rethinking issues. This rethinking is manifested in a variety of ways.

Black leaders, divided on the importance of desegregation (in contrast to upgrading black institutions) as a tool to reach equal status since the time of Booker T. Washington and W.E.B. Du Bois, are increasingly questioning the degree to which school desegregation should be the focus of their efforts. School desegregation historically has been a means to the end of equal opportunity; litigation was pursued to enhance educational opportunities for black children (Willie, 1989). But a recurring question in the history of school segregation and desegregation has been whether blacks need to "sit next to whites" to succeed in school. Can you have separate schools that are equal? One argument is that since the reason that whites separate blacks is to lower black resources, that is, to provide them with differential treatment, separation is doomed to fail. Orfield and Eaton (1996) have argued that of course black students do not learn more from sitting next to white students, but moving from a school isolated in poverty into a school with middle-class values and resources helps. Of course, the original argument was that blacks are stigmatized and psychologically harmed when they are separated by law.

Despite the argument that separate schools are never equal, some black leaders are calling for schools that would serve only black students or even black students of one gender only. Black immersion academies, which could more directly address the specific needs of young black males, are offered as a solution to the poor achievements and life experiences of too many black young men.

While it has not changed its official position, even the NAACP was rethinking its position on school desegregation at its June 1997 national convention.

It must be recognized that desegregation at the postsecondary level is quite different from school desegregation at the elementary and secondary level (Amaker, 1988). In higher education attendance is not mandatory and students are not limited to attendance areas or districts. Busing is certainly not an issue, for no transportation is provided. As noted earlier, there is a strong desire among blacks to maintain historically black institutions. Some parallels are significant. Black state institutions have been underfunded vis-à-vis their white counterparts, and the *Brown* decision has been applied to both levels, albeit with different remedies and levels of success.

One dilemma for advocates of desegregation thus occurs as the school desegregation decisions and logic are applied on the postsecondary level. If black schools at the elementary- and secondary-school level were eliminated through desegregation, what should happen to historically black colleges and universities? Kujovich (1992) has analyzed the relation of the nation's higher-education institutions to its elementary- and secondary-education schools as a system of discrimination and limited opportunity. In the elementary and secondary arena the U.S. Supreme Court demanded in the *Green* decision that desegregation plans dismantle black schools and desegregate the student bodies. If *Green* were followed in higher education, would this destroy black colleges, institutions that are believed to have helped the disadvantaged?

Preer (1982) has also analyzed the legal and educational paradoxes of higher-education desegregation. She juxtaposes two concerns: "the need to overturn legally enforced segregation and the need to maximize educational opportunities for black students" (1). The first is a legal question and the second an educational policy question. She asks: How do you fight for historically black schools while opposing segregation? To what extent is there a comparison to elementary and secondary desegregation and legal precedent at this level of education? Preer discusses the conflict between the NAACP Legal Defense Fund strategy, focused on desegregation, and the National Association for Equal Opportunity in Higher Education (NAFEO) view, concerned for the preservation of historically black colleges and universities (HBCUs). Preer's dilemma has not been resolved, even with the most recent U.S. Supreme Court decision in *United States v. Fordice* (1992). Kaplin (1985:520) has specified a good outline of the challenges ahead at the higher-education level:

As the history of the *Adams* litigation makes clear, the desegregation of higher education is very much an unfinished business. . . . Its completion poses knotty legal, policy, and administrative enforcement problems and requires a sensitive appreciation of the differing missions and histories of traditionally black and traditionally white institutions. . . . The challenge is for lawyers, administrators, government officials, and the judiciary to work together to fashion solutions consonant with the law's requirement to desegregate yet serving to increase rather than limit the opportunities available to minority students and faculty.

   Arguments and actions about school segregation and desegregation become more important as the stakes are rising in line with the increasing percentage of black and minority students in our nation. From 1972 to 1992 the percentage of black students in the nation's public schools increased by 2 percent and the percentage of Latinos increased by 89 percent. White enrollment decreased by 14 percent (Orfield, 1993). The socioeconomic status of many minority students is not high. For example, Thompson (1996) provides an analysis of the most recent census to highlight the status of black college students in the nation. A majority (52 percent) of black youth live in single-parent–headed households, compared with 18 percent of whites. If nothing else, this will present tremendous financial challenges for black youth to attend college and postsecondary education. Black students entering college are twice as likely as whites to have a deceased parent (10.1 percent vs. 4.4 percent) or to have divorced parents (44.3 percent vs. 20.4 percent). These students are also twice as likely to have a parent who has not completed high school and three times as likely to have an unemployed father or income under $20,000 annually.

   Thus the issues of school segregation and desegregation will not disappear. Indeed, their importance will grow as the percentage of American schoolchildren who are minority increases in the decades ahead. Any solutions will be found in a more complex legal, social, political, and educational world. Understanding the roots of the issues and the basic terms and concepts, landmark court decisions, significant legislation, types of frequently used plans, influential writings, active organizations, and important people in the field of school segregation and desegregation may not be sufficient for developing solutions, but such knowledge will certainly be necessary for any resolution.

CHRONOLOGY

1787

September 17: Constitutional Convention adopts U.S. Constitution in Philadelphia.

1837

February 25: Cheyney College, the first historically black college, is established in Pennsylvania.

1849

November: Massachusetts Supreme Court decides *Roberts v. City of Boston*.

1865

March 3: U.S. War Department establishes the Freedmen's Bureau.

1866

April 6: Civil Rights Act of 1866 granting citizenship to blacks is passed over President Andrew Johnson's veto.

1868

July 20: Fourteenth Amendment to the U.S. Constitution ratified.

1873

April 14: U.S. Supreme Court decides *Slaughterhouse Cases*.

1875

March 1: President Grant signs the Civil Rights Act of 1875.

1877

January 26: Deadlock broken as Compromise of 1877 establishes procedure to resolve Tilden-Hayes presidential election.

1883

October 15: U.S. Supreme Court decides the *Civil Rights Cases*, judging the Civil Rights Act of 1875 to be unconstitutional.

1886

May 10: U.S. Supreme Court decides *Yick Wo v. Hopkins*.

1890

August 30: Congress passes Second Morrill Act, providing grants to states for separate but equal land grant institutions.

1895

September 18: Booker T. Washington delivers the Atlanta Compromise Address at the Cotton States and International Exposition.

1896

May 18: U.S. Supreme Court decides *Plessy v. Ferguson*.

1899

December 18: U.S. Supreme Court decides *Cumming v. Richmond County Board of Education*.

1900

November 3: The first installment of Booker T. Washington's *Up from Slavery* is published in *Outlook* magazine, before its 1901 book release by Doubleday.

1903

April 18: W.E.B. Du Bois's *The Souls of Black Folk* is published.

1905

July 11–13: Niagara Movement, a precursor to the NAACP, is formed.

1908

November 9: U.S. Supreme Court decides *Berea College v. Commonwealth of Kentucky*.

1909

February 12: NAACP founded on 100th anniversary of Lincoln's birthday.

1915

June 21: NAACP wins its first case before U.S. Supreme Court; *Guinn v. United States* decision makes the "grandfather clause" illegal.

1919

April 9: Commission on Interracial Cooperation is founded in Atlanta.

1927

November 21: U.S. Supreme Court decides *Gong Lum v. Rice.*

1930

May 7: U.S. Senate defeats John Johnston Parker's nomination for the U.S. Supreme Court.

1934

October 16: Charles Hamilton Houston named special counsel to the NAACP.

1938

December 12: U.S. Supreme Court decides *Missouri ex rel. Gaines v. Canada.*

1939

October 11: NAACP Legal Defense and Education Fund is founded, with Thurgood Marshall as special counsel.

1944

January 6: Southern Regional Council is granted a charter in Atlanta, succeeding Commission on Interracial Cooperation.

January 26: Gunnar Myrdal's *An American Dilemma* is published by Harper and Brothers.

April 24: United Negro College Fund is established.

1947

October 29: President Truman's Committee on Civil Rights releases *To Secure These Rights.*

1948

January 12: U.S. Supreme Court decides *Sipuel v. Oklahoma State Board of Regents.*

February 8: Southern Regional Education Compact is signed by 14 states trying to avoid desegregation of state higher-education institutions.

1950

June 5: U.S. Supreme Court decides *Sweatt v. Painter* and *McLaurin v. Oklahoma State Regents.*

1952

January 12: University of Tennessee becomes the first major southern university to admit blacks.

1953

October 5: Earl Warren is sworn in as Chief Justice of the U.S. Supreme Court after nomination by President Dwight D. Eisenhower.

December 8–9: Reargument in *Brown I* takes place before U.S. Supreme Court over the meaning of the Fourteenth Amendment.

1954

January 29: Gordon Allport publishes *The Nature of Prejudice* by Addison-Wesley.

May 17: U.S. Supreme Court decides *Brown v. Board of Education I* and *Bolling v. Sharpe* ("Black Monday").

July 11: First white citizens' council organized in Indianola, Mississippi.

1955

April 11–14: Reargument in *Brown II* takes place before U.S. Supreme Court over implementation of *Brown I*.

May 31: U.S. Supreme Court decides *Brown v. Board of Education II*.

July 15: U.S. Fourth Circuit Court of Appeals decides *Briggs v. Elliott*.

November 28: James Jackson Kirkpatrick, editor of the *Richmond News Leader*, advocates "interposition" to stop school desegregation.

December 1: Rosa Parks refuses to give up her seat to a white passenger on a Montgomery, Alabama, bus, beginning the boycott.

1956

March 12: Southern Manifesto, signed by over 100 southern congressmen, denounces the *Brown* decisions.

March 12: U.S. Supreme Court decides *Florida ex rel. Hawkins v. Board of Control*.

August 27: A 27-day special session of the state legislature starts in Virginia to try to stop school desegregation and the NAACP.

August 30–September 17: Antidesegregation protests occur against efforts to desegregate schools in Mansfield, Texas; Clinton, Tennessee; and Sturgis and Clay, Kentucky.

1957

September 9: President Eisenhower signs Civil Rights Act of 1957, establishing U.S. Commission on Civil Rights.

September 24–25: Arkansas Governor Orval Faubus announces on television his activation of the National Guard in Little Rock. President Eisenhower sends 101st Airborne Division to Little Rock.

1958

September 29: U.S. Supreme Court decides *Cooper v. Aaron*.

1959

June 26: Prince Edward County Board of Supervisors adopts a budget without funds for public schools, thereby closing its schools rather than implementing school desegregation.

1960

February 1: Wave of sit-ins at segregated lunch counters, led by black college students, begins in Greensboro, North Carolina, and spreads throughout the South.

October 19: Martin Luther King, Jr., and approximately 50 other blacks are arrested at New Orleans sit-in, leading to efforts by Robert Kennedy to free King and John Kennedy calling Coretta Scott King to offer sympathy for her jailed husband.

November 14: New Orleans closes its schools rather than implement school desegregation.

1962

September 20: Mississippi Governor Ross Barnett stops James Meredith from registering at the University of Mississippi.

September 30: President Kennedy federalizes the Mississippi National Guard and sends 300 federal marshals to ensure James Meredith's admission to the university.

1963

January 14: Governor George Wallace of Alabama declares, "Segregation now . . . segregation tomorrow . . . segregation forever" in his inaugural address.

June 11: President Kennedy issues proclamation commanding Alabama's Governor George Wallace not to obstruct justice at the University of Alabama, federalizing the National Guard, and calling for new laws to ensure justice.

June 12: Medgar Evers, NAACP Mississippi field secretary, is assassinated in Jackson, Mississippi.

August 28: Martin Luther King, Jr., gives "I have a dream" speech at March on Washington.

September 15: Four black children are murdered in Sunday-morning bombing of Sixteenth Street Baptist Church in Birmingham, Alabama.

November 22: President Kennedy is assassinated in Dallas; Lyndon B. Johnson is sworn in.

1964

May 22: President Lyndon Johnson unveils Great Society.

May 25: U.S. Supreme Court decides *Griffin v. County School Board of Prince Edward County.*

July 2: Congress passes the Civil Rights Act of 1964. President Johnson signs the act, establishing the Office for Civil Rights and greater enforcement powers for the federal government.

August 14: Mississippi becomes the last state to desegregate at least one school district (Biloxi).

1965

February 21: Malcolm X is assassinated in New York City mosque.

April: Office of Education in the Department of Health, Education, and Welfare issues the first desegregation guidelines.

April 11: Elementary and Secondary Education Act is signed by President Johnson.

June 4: President Lyndon Baines Johnson delivers speech at Howard University commencement pledging to bring blacks into America's mainstream.

August 11–21: Race riots in Watts area of Los Angeles leave 35 dead.

August 18: Governor John Volpe signs Massachusetts Racial Imbalance Act as Massachusetts becomes the first state in the nation to enact legislation in support of school desegregation.

October 3: Meeting between Mayor Richard Daley of Chicago and President Johnson leads to rescinding of Department of HEW/Office of Education fund cutoff.

November 8: President Lyndon Baines Johnson signs the Higher Education Act of 1965, which includes a title helping Historically Black Colleges.

1966

March: Office of Education issues revised desegregation guidelines requiring school integration.

July 1: Coleman Report (*Equality of Educational Opportunity*) published.

September 26: METCO, a voluntary school busing program, begins busing minority students to suburban schools in the Boston metropolitan area.

December 29: U.S. Court of Appeals, Fifth Circuit, decides *United States v. Jefferson County Board of Education*.

1967

February 9: *Racial Isolation in Public Schools* report issued by U.S. Commission on Civil Rights.

May 1–October 1: Riots in Cleveland, Newark, Detroit, New York, Chicago, and Atlanta.

August 30: Senate confirms Thurgood Marshall as the first black member of the U.S. Supreme Court.

1968

March 2: Kerner Commission reports that nation is headed toward two communities, "one white, one black, separate and unequal."

April 4: Martin Luther King, Jr., is assassinated in Memphis.

May 1: Mexican American Legal Defense and Educational Fund is established.

May 27: U.S. Supreme Court decides *Green v. County School Board of New Kent County.*

September 9: New York City's United Federation of Teachers strikes over school decentralization and community control.

November 5: Richard M. Nixon is elected President as his Southern Strategy succeeds.

1969

June 23: Warren Burger is sworn in as Chief Justice of the U.S. Supreme Court.

September 9: Operation Exodus begins sending children in buses to empty seats in Boston schools to desegregate.

September 14: City University of New York system adopts open enrollment for fall 1970.

October 7: National Association for Equal Opportunity in Higher Education (NAFEO) is founded.

October 19: NAACP sues the Department of Health, Education, and Welfare to enforce federal school desegregation guidelines.

October 29: U.S. Supreme Court decides *Alexander v. Holmes.*

1971

April 20: U.S. Supreme Court decides *Swann v. Charlotte-Mecklenburg Board of Education.*

July 28: Fifth Circuit Court of Appeals *Calhoun v. Cook* decision permits the Atlanta Compromise.

1972

March 17: President Nixon submits message to Congress summarizing "Student Transportation Moratorium Act" and "Equal Educational Opportunities Act" to limit busing.

May 21: David Armor releases his study of school desegregation in six cities: "The Evidence on Busing" is published in *The Public Interest.*

June 23: President Nixon signs Education Amendments of 1972, which include limits on busing and $2 billion for desegregating schools in the Emergency School Aid Act.

1973

June 12: U.S. Court of Appeals (D.C. Circuit) decides *Adams v. Richardson.*

June 21: U.S. Supreme Court decides *Keyes v. Denver School District No. 1.*

1974

January 21: U.S. Supreme Court decides *Lau v. Nichols.*

April 23: U.S. Supreme Court declares *DeFunis v. Odegaard* moot.

July 25: U.S. Supreme Court decides *Milliken v. Bradley I.*

August 21: Congress passes Equal Educational Opportunities Act of 1974 with the revised Esch Amendment.

September 12: Boston school desegregation begins with protests, violence, and boycott.

1976

June 7: U.S. Supreme Court decides *Washington v. Davis.*

June 28: U.S. Supreme Court decides *Pasadena City Board of Education v. Spangler.*

December 4: Congress passes Byrd Amendment to limit busing.

1977

January 25: U.S. Supreme Court decides *Newbury Area Council v. Board of Education of Jefferson County, Kentucky.*

June 27: U.S. Supreme Court decides *Milliken v. Bradley II.*

December 9: Congress passes Eagleton-Biden Amendment to Labor-HEW Appropriations Act of 1978 to limit busing.

1978

June 28: U.S. Supreme Court decides *Regents of the University of California v. Bakke.*

September 11: Metropolitan interdistrict desegregation plan is implemented in New Castle County, Delaware.

1980

May 5: Department of Education begins as cabinet department as requested by President Jimmy Carter.

August 8: President Jimmy Carter signs executive order establishing White House Initiative Office on Historically Black Colleges and Universities.

1983

May 24: U.S. Supreme Court decides *Bob Jones University v. United States.*

1986

September 26: William H. Rehnquist is sworn in as U.S. Supreme Court Chief Justice.

November 11: President Reagan and congressional representatives reach agreement to extend life of U.S. Commission on Civil Rights.

1991

January 15: U.S. Supreme Court decides *Board of Education of Oklahoma City v. Dowell.*

February 26: Detroit Board of Education approves all-male school to try to overcome problems of young black men.

1992

March 31: U.S. Supreme Court decides *Freeman v. Pitts*.

June 26: U.S. Supreme Court decides *United States v. Fordice*.

1994

October 20: President Clinton signs the Magnet Schools Assistance Program, a part of the Elementary and Secondary Education Act.

October 27: U.S. Court of Appeals, Fourth Circuit, decides *Podberesky v. Kirwan*.

1995

June 12: U.S. Supreme Court decides *Missouri v. Jenkins*.

July 20: University of California Board of Regents votes to end affirmative action on its campuses.

1996

March 18: Fifth Circuit Court of Appeals decides *Hopwood v. State of Texas*.

July 9: Connecticut Supreme Court orders the desegregation of the Hartford schools in *Sheff v. O'Neill*.

November 5: California voters vote in favor of Proposition 209, limiting affirmative action.

A

ABILITY GROUPING. The placement of students with purportedly similar abilities or attainment into the same classroom, educational program, or instructional group. The placement may range from temporary groups in individual classrooms to setting up long-standing different classes and programs in individual schools. Where placement by ability is more permanent and classes are based on this placement, the practice is called tracking. At the secondary level the term is used to describe the assignment of students to levels of classes such as vocational, general, college prep, honor, or AP (advanced placement) or to a recommended four-year plan based on a student's post–high-school plans, college prep or academic, vocational, or general. At the elementary level this practice is generally called ability grouping, and students are placed into fast, average, or slow groups within classes or in separate classes. About one-quarter of the nation's school districts use cross-classroom ability groups.

Meier, Stewart, and England (1989) define academic grouping as the generic term encompassing four components: ability grouping, curriculum tracking, special education, and compensatory education.* Thus ability grouping is primarily for elementary-school students as they are sorted by ability into groups in separate classrooms or within-classroom groups such as the "bluebirds, robins, and sparrows" for reading, math, and spelling. "Curriculum tracking generally is a secondary school practice and involves the assignment of students by ability and/or interest to different classes, or 'tracks' of study that usually have different curricula (e.g., college-bound, general business, vocational)" (23). Special education is for students who are not considered able to benefit from the regular curriculum, and thus the students are placed in a special curriculum of special education classes. Finally, compensatory education programs, based on the cultural-deprivation theory ''that poor school performance is the result of a deprived home and/or neighborhood environment'' (23), are remedial programs aimed at the educationally and economically disadvantaged.

Ability grouping may interfere with school desegregation* when placement into groups is related to race. Researchers have consistently found that race is highly related to placement; blacks are more likely to be placed in lower-ability groups, and ability grouping is thus a component of second-generation problems* of school desegregation. According to Oakes in Wheelock (1992), ''In the last decade, the NAACP Legal Defense Fund,* the ACLU [American Civil Liberties Union*], and the Children's Defense Fund have all identified tracking as the most important 'second generation' segregation issue'' (xi). The Civil Rights Division* has also targeted tracking practices, as have more mainstream groups such as the National Governors' Association, the Carnegie Corporation, the College Board, and the National Education Association. Meier, Stewart, and England argue that academic grouping practices are antithetical to school integration* because school integration requires equal treatment and academic grouping requires differentiating students.

Ability grouping is viewed by many educators and parents as necessary to ensure that brighter students will not be held back in their education by slower learners. The assumption is that teachers have to teach to least able learners in a classroom, and therefore more advanced learners will be disadvantaged by heterogeneous classes. Many also believe that slow learners will be better able to learn if they are grouped together so that material can be directed to their level. It is also believed that they will develop a more positive self-concept if they are not placed with faster learners who outshine them in class. Teachers favor ability grouping to lessen the degree of heterogeneity in their classrooms and thus to help make teaching more manageable. Ability grouping and tracking also allow students to be trained for careers most appropriate for their abilities, for example, college for the educationally able and vocational work for those with more limited academic talents. A meta-analysis of studies of tracking and ability grouping by Kulik and Kulik (1991) found that these approaches did increase the self-esteem* of low-achieving students, but not achievement.

Several criticisms of ability grouping have been made. Some argue that ability grouping is racially discriminatory and leads to resegregation.* Minorities are two to three times as likely as whites to be assigned to lower-ability tracks and classes for the educable mentally retarded. Others argue that ability grouping is educationally harmful, not helpful. Students in the lower groups are not provided with the curriculum that they need to succeed in life and are not given the same-quality teachers and resources as those in the higher groups. Placement in lower groups reduces self-esteem and leads to a self-fulfilling prophecy—less is expected of these students, less is offered to these students, less is sought by these students, and less is accomplished by these students. It is also argued that ability grouping misidentifies or misclassifies many students. Questions have also arisen about the extent to which the skills now needed for different careers are really different in kind.

Among the criticisms of tracking are that those in the lower tracks receive fewer and less adequate resources than those in higher tracks, tracking becomes a self-fulfilling prophecy as student and teacher expectations are lowered, and the curriculum of lower tracks impedes progress toward college success. Others argue that the best teachers are assigned to the higher tracks and the least experienced to the lower tracks. Higher-order thinking skills are more likely to be demanded of the higher tracks. Those in the lower tracks are working with peers with lower motivation, which becomes a further detriment to their education. Many errors take place in assignments to tracks, thus compounding these problems. Those who believe that every child can master all the worthwhile educational goals see tracking as a means to limit too many children from achieving their full educational potential.

Opponents of ability grouping argue, with some research support, that not only is race related to placement in lower tracks, it is a cause of such placement because of teacher expectations that vary by student race. One example of tracking related to race is the placement of black students in educable mentally retarded (EMR) special education tracks. For example, in 1990, when blacks were 16 percent of national enrollment, their percentage of the EMR enrollment was about twice that. The national Educational Longitudinal Survey of 1988 found that African-American, Latino, and native American eighth graders had twice the chance of whites to be in a remedial math course.

Jeannie Oakes, a researcher and critic of tracking, has concluded that "no group of students has been found to benefit consistently from being in a homogeneous group" (1985:7). Oakes offers a helpful set of dimensions to differentiate across an array of tracking policies and practices in secondary schools: "*extent*, the proportion of the total number of classes that were tracked at the school; *pervasiveness*, the number of subject areas at the school that were tracked; *flexibility*, whether students were tracked subject by subject or across more than one subject on the same criteria; *mobility*, the amount of student movement up and down track levels; and the *locus of control*, who makes the decisions about where students belong" (49).

Critics of ability grouping and tracking have called for "detracking." The most favored approach is cooperative learning, where students are placed in small heterogeneous groups, given a group assignment toward a common goal, and taught to support and learn from each other. The product is judged against a set standard of success. However, few school districts or schools have rejected ability grouping and "detracked."

See also **Hobson v. Hansen**.

References: Leon Lynn and Anne Wheelock, "Making Detracking Work" and related articles, *Harvard Education Letter* 13, no. 1 (January–February 1997): 1–10; Wheelock, *Crossing the Tracks* (1992); James A. Kulik and Chen-Lin Kulik, "Ability Grouping and Gifted Students," in *Handbook of Gifted Education*, ed. N. Colangelo and G. Davis

(Boston: Allyn and Bacon, 1991); Eva Wells Chunn, "Sorting Black Students for Success and Failure: The Inequity of Ability Grouping and Tracking," in *Black Education*, ed. Smith and Chunn (1989), 93–106 (originally published as a special issue of the *Urban League Review*, Summer 1987, Winter 1987–1988); Meier, Stewart, and England, *Race, Class, and Education* (1989); Oakes, *Keeping Track* (1985); David Kirp, "Schools as Sorters: The Constitutional and Policy Implications of Student Classification," *University of Pennsylvania Law Review* 121, no. 705 (1973): 710–17, excerpted in Yudof et al., *Kirp and Yudof's Educational Policy and the Law* (1987), 595–99.

ADAMS V. CALIFANO. See *Adams v. Richardson*.

ADAMS V. RICHARDSON, 480 F.2d 1159 (D.C. Cir. 1973). U.S. Court of Appeals* decision that ordered President Richard M. Nixon's* Department of Health, Education, and Welfare* (HEW) (Office of Education*) to take "appropriate action to end segregation in public educational institutions receiving federal funds." This decision had a major impact on the federal government's role in elementary- and secondary- as well as postsecondary-school desegregation.* The Nixon administration had abandoned the use of the threat of cutting off federal funds to local school districts as provided by the Civil Rights Act of 1964.* Instead, it relied upon voluntary compliance. This was consistent with Nixon's Southern Strategy,* a political strategy based on lax enforcement of civil rights* and movement away from busing* and affirmative action* to garner votes and support in the South.*

The NAACP Legal Defense Fund* (LDF) brought suit in October 1970 against Secretary of HEW Elliot Richardson on behalf of 22 families who claimed to suffer from the state segregation* and 2 other parties who claimed that their federal tax monies were being illegally allocated to the ten states (Arkansas, Florida, Georgia, Louisiana, Maryland, Mississippi, North Carolina, Oklahoma, Pennsylvania, and Virginia) that had failed to desegregate their higher-education systems. The suit charged the federal government with failing to properly enforce Title VI of the Civil Rights Act of 1964, which prohibits discrimination on the basis of race, color, or natural origin in jurisdictions receiving funds for federal educational programs. HEW had failed to force school districts to desegregate; scores were not in compliance with the *Swann** (1971) decision.

On November 16, 1972, federal District Court* Judge John H. Pratt found HEW guilty of "benign neglect," subverting the 1964 Civil Rights Act. He ordered HEW to quickly issue rules and regulations that would lead to the withholding of federal funds if they were not followed. HEW appealed immediately, and the U.S. Court of Appeals for the District of Columbia heard the case *en banc*, that is, with all of its eleven judges. But for the first time in history a group of black educators dissented. In an *amicus curiae** brief the National Association for Equal Opportunity in Higher Education* (NAFEO), an organization of the presidents of the historically black colleges and universities*

(HBCUs), argued that Pratt's decision should be overturned. They argued that the HBCUs should not be undermined by the federal decision and that desegregation at the higher-education level did not necessarily have to follow the precedents at the elementary and secondary level, where all schools were desegregated and many black schools were closed.

The U.S. Court of Appeals upheld the District Court's decision in this June 1973 unanimous decision. The court, however, did not specify what standards HEW should apply to recalcitrant school districts. Judge Pratt had concluded that HEW had stopped enforcing the law, allowing school districts that continued to delay desegregation and failed to correct de jure racial imbalance* to escape sanctions. The Court of Appeals decision generated HEW activity, but not much enforcement. President Nixon's opposition to enforcement, based on his political strategy, clashed with the court's demands. The court did make special note of HBCUs, requiring that state plans take into account the special problems and situations of HBCUs. Desegregation could not result in a decreasing of the proportion of black students enrolled in a state's higher-education system, nor could it result in the destruction of public HBCUs. HEW accepted eight plans from the ten states (Louisiana refused to submit a plan; Mississippi's was judged unacceptable), but the LDF went back to court to challenge these plans.

In *Adams v. Califano* (1977) Judge Pratt found that six states were still not in compliance. HEW did offer new criteria in the summer of 1977. HEW established four criteria for desegregation compliance and filed them with the court: (1) disestablishment of the dual system,* (2) desegregation of student enrollment, (3) desegregation of faculty, administrative staffs, nonacademic personnel, and governing boards, and (4) submission of plans and monitoring. Using these criteria, the court called for strengthening the black schools in the state systems and increasing black enrollment at white institutions. A year later HEW concluded that five of the six states still at issue had complied, but North Carolina had presented a plan that "offered no realistic promise" of desegregation. By 1982 a consent decree* between the federal government and the University of North Carolina, spurred on by conservative Senator Jesse Helms of North Carolina and President Ronald Reagan's* Department of Education* (formerly the Office of Education) officials, had been considered by the federal courts. The case dragged on, and in 1987 Judge Pratt dismissed the case, ruling that the plaintiffs no longer had legal standing. The ruling was overturned later in the year, but in 1990 the case was finally dismissed.

This was a landmark case in higher-education school desegregation law. Ten states were affected; states were declared to have maintained segregated colleges and universities; the court found that the federal government had been delinquent in implementing the law, and an immediate remedy was ordered. In essence this was a judgment that ten southern states had not followed the requirements of the *Brown* (1954) decision and the subsequent legislation to enforce the decision in their colleges and universities. The *Adams* decisions sought to increase access to higher education for blacks in the states named in the decisions, to increase black participation and completion of college in historically white public institutions, and to strengthen and improve historically black institutions.

References: William T. Trent, "Student Affirmative Action in Higher Education: Addressing Underrepresentation," in *The Racial Crisis in American Higher Education*, ed. Altbach and Lomotey (1991), 107–33; John B. Williams III, *Desegregating America's Colleges and Universities* (1987); Yudof et al., *Kirp and Yudof's Educational Policy and the Law* (1987); Leonard L. Hayes, "The Adams Mandate: Is It a Blueprint for Realizing Equal Educational Opportunity and Attainment?" in *The Impact of Desegregation on Higher Education*, ed. Smith, *The Impact of Desegregation on Higher Education* (1979), 195–206; Marcus and Stickney, *Race and Education* (1981); Orfield, *Must We Bus?* (1978).

AFFIRMATIVE ACTION. Efforts that take into account membership in protected groups (race, sex, disability, and national origin) to remedy and prevent discrimination* in the awarding of admission to universities and professional schools, jobs, and other social goods and services. At the postsecondary level most colleges and universities have made conscious and deliberate efforts to bring qualified people in underrepresented groups into educational institutions and jobs from which they have been largely excluded. Originally a remedy to deal with discrimination against blacks, the concept of affirmative action was later targeted at women and other groups (e.g., the disabled, Hispanics). The federal government began these efforts under the Civil Rights Act of 1964.* In 1965 President Lyndon B. Johnson* signed Executive Order 11246, which prohibited federal agencies from contracting with firms that were not committed to affirmative action. Such efforts now include requiring certain businesses and educational institutions that are recipients of federal funds to develop and implement acceptable affirmative action programs. These efforts are monitored by the Office of Federal Contract Compliance and the Equal Employment Opportunity Commission (EEOC). Colleges and universities have adopted affirmative action programs in admissions, hiring, and financial aid.

Proponents of affirmative action argue that it is needed to right the wrongs of the previous period of discrimination and to ensure a diverse society. But affirmative action has generated much criticism. The major criticisms and responses are as follows.

Opponents argue that affirmative action is "reverse discrimination," usually harming young white males. They contend that as implemented, affirmative action has moved beyond working hard to find qualified minority or female applicants (outreach) to selecting unqualified or less qualified minority or female applicants over those more qualified for admission or a position. They argue that too many times quotas have been set that require a certain number of minorities to be chosen, and that this leads to less qualified minorities being chosen over more qualified whites. Opponents of affirmative action vigorously oppose systems that give minorities or women extra points in the selection process or treat applicants of different backgrounds separately in the selection process. Critics of affirmative action argue that selection should be "color blind," that individuals should be chosen on their individual merits, and that this is true nondiscrimination. Critics charge that affirmative action is designed to reward individuals because they belong to a particular group, not because of their individual qualifications and experience. Thus critics compare affirmative action to the 1968 *Green** decision, in which the U.S. Supreme Court* moved from requiring the removal of discrimination to requiring school desegregation* through racial balancing.*

Proponents counter that affirmative action is not reverse discrimination but rather alters the biased practices that favored white males in the past. Affirmative action restructures the status quo that favors white males. For example, white males are much more likely to take advantage of networking to receive jobs. While some whites may feel discriminated against, they are really feeling the loss of the privileged access they have historically enjoyed. Proponents maintain that affirmative action does not have to be a quota system. Affirmative action should take race and sex into account in selection decisions for admissions, hiring, or contracts. Normally it is implemented as flexible, temporary means that are means of inclusion, not exclusion, as were historical quotas used to exclude or limit the number of certain groups. Affirmative action should not be a means to admit incompetent applicants, but rather a means to find qualified applicants who have been previously excluded and to help recruit, retain, and promote women and minorities. Qualifications not related to the success of applicants should be dropped or modified. Proponents also argue that it is not enough to be "color blind" when discrimination has led to unequal results. Affirmative action is therefore necessary to make up for previous discrimination, that is, to make the victims whole. Proponents point out that while discrimination lasted for hundreds of years in the United States, making discrimination illegal and positive steps such as affirmative action have been in effect for only a few decades. Thus a longer time period is needed to reverse the centuries of discrimination. Furthermore, when opponents charge that unqualified people are given preference in affirmative action programs, they often define qualifications too narrowly or include "qualifications" that are not relevant to the particular position and are actually "pretexts" for rejection and exclusion, for example, requiring a high-school degree for jobs that do not really require a high-school education. One advocate has used the analogy of forming an orchestra. You would begin by identifying a set of virtuoso musicians, but you would not use a selection process that could result in selecting all violinists. You would be seeking qualified musicians, including violinists, oboists, and trumpeters, who would play well together.

In 1995 the Board of Regents of the University of California voted to end affirmative action at all of its campuses. California Governor Pete Wilson had pushed for this, and a majority of the board, despite a last-minute plea from civil rights* leader Reverend Jesse Jackson, agreed. The criticism of the state system's affirmative action policy had been that it relied on quotas and was a form of reverse discrimination leading to an overemphasis on race in decisions and discussions. In 1996 voters in the state voted in favor of the California Civil Rights Initiative (Proposition 209*), which would ban all gender- and race-based preferences in public jobs, contracts, and education. In December 1996 a federal judge blocked enforcement of this initiative while she considered its constitutionality, but the Court of Appeals* overturned her decision in April 1997 and allowed the implementation.

Affirmative action has been used to describe the U.S. Supreme Court's requirement since the *Green* decision that school districts that had de jure segregation* have the obligation to take affirmative action to desegregate their schools. This obligation is interpreted as requiring racial balance in the schools rather than simply removing barriers to where black students may attend school, that is, a race-neutral assignment plan.

See also **DeFunis v. Odegaard; Hopwood v. State of Texas; Podberesky v. Kirwan; Regents of the University of California v. Bakke**.

References: Christopher Edley, Jr., *Not All Black and White: Affirmative Action, Race, and American Values* (New York: Hill and Wang, 1996); Andrew Hacker, "Goodbye to Affirmative Action?" *New York Review of Books* 43, no. 45 (July 11, 1996): a27; *Britannica Online* (1996); *Dissent* 42, no. 4 (Fall 1995); Jost, "Rethinking Affirmative Action" (April 28, 1995); Bernard Schwartz, *Behind Bakke: Affirmative Action and the Supreme Court* (New York: New York University Press, 1988); Sindler, *Bakke, DeFunis, and Minority Admissions* (1978).

AFRICAN-AMERICAN IMMERSION ACADEMIES. Schools serving only black males created to deal with the special needs of African-American black males and the crisis that black males face in the United States. African-centered schools exist in public school systems in Atlanta, Cleveland, Detroit, Kansas City, Milwaukee, Oakland, Washington, D.C., and other cities. In some cities the courts have viewed such schools as the modern results of the rejected separate but equal* principle.

The status of black males has been viewed as so marginal in American society that black males may be an "endangered species." Black males are disproportionately represented in negative educational categories such as students with low grades, suspensions and expulsions, and assignment to remedial education courses. Employment, income, and crime statistics indicate that this low success rate does not change after schooling. For example, over 40 percent of federal and state prisoners are black men, while they comprise only 6 percent of the total population.

While the motive for the separation of black males is unlike the intent of the segregationists before *Brown** (1954), the courts have not looked favorably upon African-American immersion academies for black males. In 1991 a federal court in Detroit granted a preliminary injunction to stop the assignment of black males to a school proposed by the Detroit Board of Education. The American Civil Liberties Union* of Michigan and the National Organization for Women Legal

Defense and Education Fund challenged the establishment of the school because of the exclusion of girls; the court agreed, and the district had to abandon its plans. Miami's plan was abandoned after the Department of Education* objected, and Milwaukee went to immersion academies for both sexes (and open to whites) on advice of counsel. The NAACP* and Urban League have also expressed concern about such academies, fearing a return to segregation* and an endorsement of the separate but equal philosophy that took so long to repudiate.

Advocates of immersion schools for black males argue that the negative social stereotype of black males as lazy, lustful, ignorant, aggressive, and prone to criminal acts is hard to overcome in regular schools. They contend that current schools have clearly failed this group, as manifested by the failure rate of black male students. They therefore conclude that there is a need to segregate black males so that educators can help them to overcome the negative stereotypes others hold and too many incorporate into their own minds. Advocates argue that the city schools are segregated anyway or that school desegregation* has not helped black students overcome the negative effects of American culture.

Some communities have established enrichment programs for black males outside of the regular school day. In Raleigh, North Carolina, for example, 11- and 12-year-old boys are mentored by black school-district employees. Such programs focus on goals such as male bonding, building self-esteem,* developing academic values and skills, and providing a safe haven from peer-group culture. Program evaluations are not yet available to allow an analysis of the educational effect of such academies.

References: Christine J. Faltz and Donald O. Leake, "The All-Black School: Inherently Unequal or a Culture-based Alternative?" in *Beyond Desegregation*, ed. Shujaa (1996), 227–52; Debra Viadero, "A School of Their Own," *Education Week* 16, no. 7 (October 16, 1996), 27–31; Kai Alston, "Community Politics and the Education of African American Males: Whose Life Is It Anyway?" in *The New Politics of Race and Gender*, ed. Catherine Marshall (Washington, DC: Falmer Press, 1993), 117–27; Kevin Brown, "Do African American Males Need Race and Gender Segregated Education? An Educator's Perspective and Legal Perspective," in *The New Politics of Race and Gender*, ed. Catherine Marshall (Washington, DC: Falmer Press, 1993), 107–16.

ALEXANDER V. HOLMES COUNTY BOARD OF EDUCATION, 396 U.S. 19 (1969).

U.S. Supreme Court* decision ordering the immediate desegregation* of 30 rural Mississippi school districts after rejecting the Nixon* administration's request to delay school desegregation* for one year. The Fifth Circuit Court of Appeals* had granted a motion to delay implementation of school desegregation plans.* The NAACP* and the federal government, which had worked together toward passage of the Civil Rights Act of 1964,* were on opposing sides for the first time in the modern civil rights* era in this case. The Court decided that the school districts must be desegregated "at once" and "operate now and hereafter only unitary schools," thus abandoning the *Brown II** (1955) notion of all deliberate speed.*

References: Orfield and Eaton, *Dismantling Desegregation* (1996); Greenberg, *Crusaders in the Courts* (1994); Jones, *From Brown to Boston: Desegregation in Education, 1954–1974*, vol. 2 (1979), 1462–63.

ALL DELIBERATE SPEED. Phrase in the U.S. Supreme Court's* *Brown II** (1955) opinion, written by Chief Justice Earl Warren,* to describe the required pace of implementation of its landmark decision, a decision that tolerated delay and obstruction throughout the South.* Justice Felix Frankfurter suggested the phrase, thinking that Justice Oliver Wendell Holmes had first used the term. Frankfurter had thought that the term came from English Chancery law. The original source, however, was not Holmes but a poem, "The Hound of Heaven," written by Francis Thompson (1859–1907) in 1893: "But with unhurrying chase / And unperturbed pace / Deliberate speed, majestic instancy." Holmes had used the term "with all deliberate speed" in a previous court case (*Virginia v. West Virginia*, 220 U.S. 1 [1911], but it had no clear legal meaning. Critics contended that the South placed more emphasis on "deliberate" than "speed" and that these ill-chosen words fostered state and school-district delays in desegregating schools. The phrase certainly was an oxymoron, an expression of two words that are contradictory. The Court wanted its decision implemented but was trying to provide some flexibility to U.S. District Courts* to accomplish school desegregation.* The Court "shunned further reliance on the notion" (*Oxford Companion*) in *Griffin v. County School Board of Prince Edward County** in 1964 when Justice Hugo Black concluded for the Court that "there has been entirely too much deliberation and not enough speed. The time for mere 'deliberate speed' has run out." The Court then "repudiated the phrase" in *Green v. County School Board of New Kent County** in 1968.

References: Safire, *Safire's New Political Dictionary* (1993); Hall, *Oxford Companion* (1992); Wilkinson, *From Brown to Bakke* (1979); Kluger, *Simple Justice* (1975); Greenberg, *Race Relations and American Law* (1959).

ALLPORT, GORDON WILLARD (born November 11, 1897, Montezuma, Indiana–died October 9, 1967, Cambridge, Massachusetts). An American psychologist with an expertise in personality who wrote the significant book *The Nature of Prejudice** in 1954. He spent almost his entire career at Harvard University after receiving his B.A., M.A., and Ph.D. there. He was president of the American Psychological Association in 1937 and editor of the *Journal of Abnormal and Social Psychology* for over a decade.

Works about: Dejnozka and Kapel, *American Educators' Encyclopedia* (1991), 20; John F. Ohles, ed., *Biographical Dictionary of American Educators*, vol. 1 (Westport, CT: Greenwood Press, 1978), 30; *Who's Who in the East* (Chicago: Reed Reference Publishing, 1974), 12–13.

Works by: *The Nature of Prejudice* (Cambridge, MA: Addison-Wesley, 1954).

AMERICAN CIVIL LIBERTIES UNION (ACLU). A private voluntary organization dedicated to civil rights* and civil liberties, often working through the courts by using test cases, that joined the NAACP* in several major school desegregation* federal court cases. The ACLU was a key member of the civil rights coalition during the fight for equality in schools and other areas of American life. While the NAACP Legal Defense Fund* (LDF) led the fight at the U.S. Supreme Court* level, the ACLU joined many cases, including *Brown* (1954), with *amicus curiae* (friend of the court) briefs. ACLU lawyers also planned legal strategy with the LDF. A number of ACLU affiliates, for example, ACLU-Delaware and the Southern California ACLU, were leaders in local battles to secure equal educational opportunity* and school desegregation. The ACLU took a leading role in northern and western cases in the 1970s.

The ACLU was founded in January 1920, arising out of the efforts of the National Civil Liberties Bureau to defend conscientious objectors and civil liberties more generally during World War I. The ACLU's role in the famous *Scopes v. State of Tennessee* case in 1926, when it challenged a Tennessee law prohibiting the teaching of evolution, brought it to national prominence. The ACLU has been a major defender of controversial groups such as Nazis, Communists, and even the Ku Klux Klan* in support of the principle of free speech.

Litigation, public education, and lobbying have been the major tools used by the ACLU in working to achieve its goals. Many of the landmark U.S. Supreme Court cases have been won by the ACLU, including cases concerning free speech, church-state relations, criminal procedure, and civil rights. The ACLU has a national office in New York City, a Washington office focusing on legislation, and a network of affiliates and chapters across the 50 states. There were 1,000 members in 1920; in 1996 the ACLU had 275,000 members and a staff of 125.

References: Hall, *Oxford Companion* (1992); Samuel Walker, *In Defense of American Liberties: A History of the ACLU* (New York: Oxford University Press, 1990); Norman Dorsen, "American Civil Liberties Union," in *The Guide to American Law: Everyone's Legal Encyclopedia* (St. Paul: West Publishing, 1984) vol. 8, 215–16; Orfield, *Must We Bus?* (1978).

AN AMERICAN DILEMMA. A massive study (over 1,400 pages) of the condition of the Negro in American society and the relation of the Negro to the larger American society by Swedish social economist Gunnar Myrdal* written for the Carnegie Foundation and published in 1944. It is formally titled *An American Dilemma: The Negro Problem and Modern Democracy.*

The major conclusion of the study was that the status of the Negro in America violated the American ideal, and thus at the heart of the "Negro Problem" was an American dilemma, "the ever-raging conflict between, on the one hand, the valuations preserved on the general plane which we shall call the 'American Creed,' where the American thinks, talks, and acts under the influence of high national and Christian precepts, and, on the other hand, the valuations on specific planes of individual and group living, where personal and local interests; economic, social, and sexual jealousies; considerations of community prestige and conformity; group prejudice against particular persons or types of people; and all sorts of miscellaneous wants, impulses, and habits dominate his outlook'' (xxi). These struggles go on across people and, more importantly, within single individuals. The creed includes the ideal of "the essential dignity of the individual human being, of the fundamental equality of all men, and of certain inalienable rights to freedom, justice, and a fair opportunity'' (4). Negroes and other Americans believe in the creed, but "the Creed is not lived up to in America'' (4). Myrdal called the treatment of Negroes America's greatest failure but also its greatest opportunity.

This study provided documentation of the poor quality of black schools and the lack of equality of black to white schools in the South.* Myrdal argued that full equality of a dual system* would ruin the finances of southern states. He noted the dilemmas of black leaders and the NAACP.* The fight for equality led to the establishment of and support for black professional schools, which perpetuated the dual system. Topics in this most comprehensive volume included racial beliefs, population and migration, economic inequalities, the Negro and agriculture, the Negro in business and other white-collar occupations, housing, economic discrimination, politics and the Negro, the inequality of justice, segregation* and discrimination,* social stratification, protest, and the Negro church and schools.

Myrdal was 40 years old when he was selected to direct this study. He was chosen in part because he was not an American and could give the issue a fresh examination. He consulted with some of the leading black scholars of the day, for example, W.E.B. Du Bois,* but steered clear of hiring them, again to avoid preconceived notions. The research team included more than 100 scholars, assistants, and consultants. Egerton (1994) concludes that the volume was most impressive for four reasons: the mountain of facts documenting "the depth and breadth of white racism," the documentation of the mistaken view of white superiority, the stating of the conflict between the strong American creed for equality and opportunity and these prejudices,* and the discussion of the moral dilemma that resulted from these inconsistencies.

David Armor (1995:62–63) notes the thesis of a vicious cycle in the book. From the report, "White prejudice and discrimination keep the Negro low in standards of living, health, education, manners, and morals. This, in turn, gives support to white prejudice. White prejudice and Negro standards thus mutually 'cause' each other.'' Thus if black standards, for example, in employment, could be raised, prejudice would decrease.

See also **Busing; Desegregation;** *The Nature of Prejudice;* **Race Relations; Status Differential**.

References: Armor, *Forced Justice* (1995); Egerton, *Speak Now against the Day* (1994); Gunnar Myrdal, *An American Dilemma: The Negro Problem and Modern Democracy* (New York: Harper and Brothers, 1944).

AMERICAN MISSIONARY ASSOCIATION (AMA). Congregationalist-supported organization, founded in Buffalo, New York, in 1846, that worked with the freedmen to help establish schools for blacks in the South.* The AMA, which sought the nonviolent abolition of slavery in the United States, sent missionaries into the South and founded 7 black colleges and 13 normal schools in the decade from 1861 to 1870. It financially supported 170 black colleges by 1870. AMA educators had to confront hostility and violence in their work. Today, state and local educational agencies have absorbed most of the 500 schools established by the AMA. Six of the 10 surviving colleges founded by the AMA remain affiliated with the New York City body.

References: Jones-Wilson et al., *Encyclopedia of African-American Education* (1996); Clara Merritt DeBoer, *His Truth Is Marching On: African Americans Who Taught the Freedmen for the American Missionary Association, 1861–1877* (New York: Garland, 1995); Joe Martin Richardson, *Christian Reconstruction: The American Missionary Association and Southern Blacks, 1861–1890* (Athens: University of Georgia Press, 1986); Augustus Field Beard, *A Crusade of Brotherhood: A History of the American Missionary Association* (Boston: Pilgrim Press, 1909; New York: Kraus Reprint, 1970).

AMICUS CURIAE. Friend of the court, a person or organization filing a legal brief with the court, one who does not have a direct interest in the case but who has an interest in the legal doctrine resulting from the case. Such friends of the court usually side with one of the parties to the suit. Their briefs, usually filed in appellate courts in "public interest" cases, can bring important legal points to the forefront as well as analyses of the potential impact of a decision. In school desegregation* cases the American Civil Liberties Union* and the Solicitor General of the United States have been participants at the U.S. Supreme Court* level as *amici curiae*. The Eisenhower* administration, for example, supported school desegregation as an *amicus curiae* in the 1954 *Brown v. Board of Education** case. In the *Bakke** (1978) case more than 50 *amicus curiae* briefs were submitted.

References: Hall, *Oxford Companion* (1992); Erwin N. Griswold, "Amicus Curiae," in *The Guide to American Law: Everyone's Legal Encyclopedia* (St. Paul: West Publishing, 1984), vol. 8, 236–37; Greenberg, *Judicial Process and Social Change: Constitutional Litigation Cases and Materials* (1977).

ANCILLARY PROGRAMS. Compensatory education* programs implemented with school desegregation plans* to help minority students achieve the status that they would have achieved if a dual system* had not existed. Ancillary programs may also be ordered as an alternative when a desegregation* plan leaves many minority students without a desegregated school situation because the school system is overwhelmingly minority and racially balancing all schools is thought to be counterproductive. They may also be ordered in school systems with plans that are able to racially balance all schools. In *Evans v. Buchanan** (1975), the Wilmington metropolitan case, for example, the court ordered special classes and assistance for minority children in reading and ordered the hiring of human-relations specialists in order to facilitate the transition to desegregated schools. In *Milliken II** (1977), the Detroit decision that followed after the U.S.

Supreme Court* had denied a metropolitan school desegregation plan to the segregated city children, the U.S. Supreme Court ruled that the ordering of ancillary programs by a federal court was permissible. The inclusion of compensatory education programs, in-service training programs for school personnel, and special guidance and counseling programs was opposed by the state, which feared the cost of such programs, on the grounds that since the constitutional violation involved student assignments, such ancillary programs exceeded the scope of the violation. The Court ruled that such programs were permitted to overcome past violations so that minority students could be helped to achieve what they would have achieved absent the violation. Feldman, Kirby, and Eaton's research indicates that at least in the four school districts studied the additional resources did not eradicate educational deficits of minority children or create equal educational opportunity.*

References: Orfield and Eaton, *Dismantling Desegregation* (1996); Joseph Feldman, Edward Kirby, and Susan E. Eaton, *Still Separate, Still Unequal: The Limits of the Milliken II Educational Compensation Remedies* (Cambridge, MA: Harvard Project on School Desegregation, April 1994); Betsy Levin, "School Desegregation Remedies and the Role of Social Science Research," *Law and Contemporary Problems* 42, no. 1 (Autumn 1978): 1–36.

ARMOR, DAVID J. (born November 11, 1938, Long Beach, California). A prominent researcher and participant in the battles over school desegregation* and busing* since his writing of a much-quoted 1972 article on the effects of busing; an expert witness on behalf of several school boards opposing school desegregation orders. David Armor received his B.A. with highest honors from the University of California at Berkeley in 1961 and his Ph.D. from Harvard in 1966. He served as an assistant professor of sociology at Harvard from 1965 to 1970 and as an associate professor from 1970 to 1973. Armor then returned to California as a senior social scientist at the Rand Corporation in Santa Monica from 1973 to 1982. He served as president of his consulting firm, National Policy Associates, Inc., from 1981 to 1986 and returned to this role after serving as acting assistant secretary of defense from 1986 to 1989.

He served on the Los Angeles School Board from 1985 to 1986 and was the Republican nominee for Congress from California's 23rd District in 1982. Armor was appointed as senior fellow at the Institute for Public Policy, George Mason University, in 1994.

Armor has been actively engaged in school desegregation research for over 30 years. Most recently he wrote *Forced Justice* (1995), a comprehensive book analyzing recent court cases and research on the effects of school desegregation. Armor served on the Coleman Report* staff and from 1966 to 1971 continued to reanalyze the Coleman data. He studied racial isolation for the U.S. Commission on Civil Rights* and evaluated METCO,* a voluntary metropolitan school desegregation program in the Boston metropolitan area, in his 1972 *Pub-*

lic Interest article. Armor began testifying as a witness against mandatory busing plans in the 1970s. His 1978 article on "White Flight and the Future of School Desegregation" while he was at Rand questioned the efficacy of school desegregation plans that led to a loss of white students. Armor was involved in metropolitan school desegregation court cases such as the Kansas City and Atlanta cases. In the 1980s and 1990s Armor was involved in designing plans in Savannah–Chatham County, Georgia, Worcester, Massachusetts, Knox County, Tennessee, and Baton Rouge, Louisiana. Armor has testified as an expert in cases where defendants sought to have their districts declared a unitary system,* including Norfolk, Virginia, Muskogee and DeKalb counties, Georgia, Wilmington, Delaware, Tampa–Hillsborough County, Florida, St. Louis, Topeka, Kansas, and Dallas, Texas.

Works about: *Who's Who in America* (Chicago: Reed Reference, 1994), 111.

Works by: with Christine H. Rossell, "The Effectiveness of School Desegregation Plans, 1968–1991," *American Politics Quarterly* 24, no. 3 (July 1996): 267–302; *Forced Justice: School Desegregation and the Law* (New York: Oxford University Press, 1995); "Why Is Black Achievement Rising?" *Public Interest*, no. 108 (Summer 1992): 65–80; "White Flight and the Future of School Desegregation," in *School Desegregation*, ed. Walter G. Stephan and Joe R. Feagin (New York: Plenum Press, 1980); "The Evidence on Busing," *Public Interest*, no. 28 (Summer 1972): 90–126.

ARMOUR V. NIX, 446 U.S. 930 (1980). U.S. Supreme Court* affirmation of lower-court decision that Atlanta's school district was not responsible for the segregated housing in the metropolitan area, and thus a metropolitan school desegregation plan* was not required. The plaintiffs, led by the Atlanta American Civil Liberties Union,* had argued that the segregated demographic structure of the Atlanta metropolitan area was built upon, according to Orfield and Eaton (1996), "many decades of explicit residential discrimination,* first expressed in formal segregation* laws, then in planned construction of racial borders, in formal agreements between the city's white and black leaders about segregated housing for blacks" (301), and in the administration of numerous governmental programs. While the U.S. District Court* did find numerous ways that the government had caused racial segregation in housing, it built upon David Armor's* survey evidence and concluded that "why people live where they live can never be fully explained." Furthermore, the court reasoned that the fair-housing law that now existed would break the link between historical discrimination and contemporary segregation. Furthermore, since the school district was not responsible for the acts of discrimination in housing that did occur, it could not be held responsible for remedying their effects. This decision thus had the effect of closing off the argument that housing segregation in metropolitan areas should be remedied by school desegregation.* In conjunction with the *Milliken I** (1974) decision, this ruling limited the potential court acceptability of metropolitan school desegregation.

References: Orfield and Eaton, *Dismantling Desegregation* (1996); Gary Orfield and Carole Ashkinaze, *The Closing Door: Conservative Policy and Black Opportunity* (Chicago: University of Chicago Press, 1991).

ATLANTA COMPROMISE. An agreement between the Atlanta NAACP* and the Atlanta school board that called for hiring more black administrators in the city schools, including the superintendent, in return for not desegregating the Atlanta public schools. While the federal court gave its approval to the settlement, the national NAACP and the NAACP Legal Defense Fund* opposed this compromise and threw out the leadership of the local office.

The Atlanta school desegregation* case began in 1958 when the school district was 70 percent white, but as the case dragged on, the district became 79 percent black by the 1973–1974 school year. Viewing the desegregation* of the city schools as futile, in 1973 the Atlanta branch of the NAACP accepted a compromise whereby its demands for busing* were dropped and a majority of the top administrative positions in the city school district went to blacks. The compromise was approved by the District Court* in *Calhoun v. Cook* (1975). The plan left 59,000 black students, a majority of the school system, in schools 90 percent black. Following the compromise, a group of black parents asked the American Civil Liberties Union* to intervene to work for metropolitan school desegregation, but the U.S. District Court judge did not rule for the parents, and the judge's decisions were affirmed at the U.S. Supreme Court* level.

References: "*Calhoun v. Latimer*," in *Encyclopedia of African-American Education*, ed. Jones-Wilson et al. (1996), 75–76; Alton Hornsby, Jr., "Black Public Education in Atlanta, Georgia, 1954–1973: From Segregation to Segregation," *Journal of Negro History* 76 (1991): 21–47; Gary Orfield and Carol Ashkinaze, *The Closing Door: Conservative Policy and Black Opportunity* (Chicago: University of Chicago Press, 1991); Alonzo A. Crim and Nancy J. Emmons, "Desegregation in the Atlanta Public Schools: A Historical Overview," in *School Desegregation Plans That Work*, ed. Charles Vert willie (Westport, CT: Greenwood Press, 1984), 149–62; Orfield, *Must We Bus?* (1978).

ATLANTA COMPROMISE ADDRESS. Speech to the Atlanta Cotton States and International Exposition made by Booker T. Washington* on September 18, 1895, that called for blacks to be accommodating to whites, to build their industrial skills, and to not challenge the system. Washington argued that "our greatest danger is that in the great leap from slavery to freedom we may overlook the fact that the masses of us are to live by the productions of our hands, and fail to keep in mind that we shall prosper in proportion as we learn to dignify and glorify common labor and put brains and skill into the common occupations of life." Washington went on to conclude, that "the wisest among my race understand the agitation of questions of social equality is the extremist folly, and that progress in the enjoyment of all the privileges that will come to us must be the result of severe and constant struggle rather than artificial forcing" (Kluger, 70).

References: Michael W. Williams, *The African American Encyclopedia*, vol. 6, 1656–58 (1993), 1656–57; Marcus and Stickney, *Race and Education* (1981); Kluger, *Simple Justice* (1975).

AYERS V. ALLAIN. See United States v. Fordice.

AYERS V. FORDICE. See United States v. Fordice.

AYERS V. MABUS. See United States v. Fordice.

AYERS V. WALLER. See United States v. Fordice.

B

BAKKE. See Regents of the University of California v. Bakke.

BELL, DERRICK A. (born November 6, 1930, Pittsburgh, Pennsylvania), civil rights* lawyer, author, and activist who has taken strong personal stands on civil rights issues that have impacted his career, has been a pioneer in positions never before held by blacks, and has been an advocate for black advancement.

Bell's father, who ran a small garbage-collection business, had left school after sixth grade. Bell received an A.B. in political science from Duquesne University in 1952. He then enlisted in the U.S. Air Force and reached the rank of second lieutenant. He received his law degree from the University of Pittsburgh Law School after his air force service. He was the associate editor of the law review and graduated fourth in his class, the only black student in the class.

Bell worked in President Dwight D. Eisenhower's* Department of Justice* from 1957 to 1959 as a staff attorney and was the only black attorney among 1,000 lawyers, but resigned when he was told that he had to decide between his membership in the NAACP* and his position. He became the executive secretary of Pittsburgh's NAACP from 1959 to 1960 and then was hired by the NAACP Legal Defense Fund* (LDF), serving as a staff lawyer from 1960 to 1966. He worked on school desegregation* cases in Mississippi and helped to get James Meredith* admitted to the University of Mississippi. In 1966 Bell returned to the federal government as Deputy Director of the Department of Health, Education and Welfare's* (HEW) Office of Civil Rights*. He resigned a year later to accept his first academic position as director of the Western Center on Law and Poverty for 1968–1969. He was appointed as Harvard Law School's first black law professor in 1969, formally as a lecturer and then as a professor from 1971 to 1980. As a Harvard law professor teaching civil rights law, he was also a critic of the LDF, charging that the organization focused too much on desegregation* to the detriment of quality education for blacks. He became dean of the University of Oregon Law School in 1981 but resigned in 1985 when the school refused to hire an Asian-American woman whose candidacy he supported. He returned to Harvard, but in 1987 he organized a sit-in when two professors failed to receive tenure because of what he believed were ideological reasons. In 1990 he announced that he was taking an unpaid leave from his $125,000 position until the school added a woman of color to the tenured faculty, which at that point consisted of 60 people but no black woman. After two years Harvard advised Bell that his leave was completed and his tenure was revoked. Bell became the Distinguished Weld Visiting Law Professor at New York University in 1991.

Works about: *Who's Who among African Americans, 1996/97*, 9th ed. (Detroit: Gale Research, 1996), 97; Greenberg, *Crusaders in the Courts* (1994); *Current Biography Yearbook 1993* (New York: H. W. Wilson Company, 1993), 44–48.

Works by: *Faces at the Bottom of the Well: The Permanence of Racism* (New York: Basic Books, 1992); *Shades of Brown: New Perspectives on School Desegregation* (New York: Teachers College Press, 1980); *Race, Racism, and American Law* (Boston: Little, Brown, 1973).

BELTON V. GEBHART, 91 A.2d 137 (1953). One of two Delaware school desegregation* cases first decided by the state Chancery Court in Delaware and later consolidated under the 1954 landmark *Brown v. Board of Education** decision. In suburban Claymont, north of Wilmington, Delaware, black children could not attend the local high-school complex but had to be bused to downtown Wilmington's Howard High School. There was also evidence that Howard High School's teachers were less educated and there was a higher student/teacher ratio than at Claymont High School; the curriculum and extracurricular activities were also somewhat more limited at the black school. Ethel Belton and seven other black parents from Claymont tried to have their children admitted to Claymont High School but were turned down.

Chancellor Collins Seitz of the Delaware Chancery Court visited the schools in question and was convinced that the schools were unequal. He also concluded that his lower court could not overturn the U.S. Supreme Court* precedent set by *Plessy v. Ferguson** (1896) and *Gong Lum v. Rice** (1927) establishing the principle and legitimacy of the separate but equal* doctrine. But Seitz did rule that because the state had failed to provide equal education, the state had to admit the black students in question to the superior schools, that is, the white schools. Thus Seitz was the first judge to order that black elementary or secondary students be admitted to a white school. The case was appealed by the state of Delaware to the U.S. Supreme Court and was consolidated under *Brown v. Board of Education.*

See also **Evans v. Buchanan**.

References: Greenberg, *Crusaders in the Courts* (1994); Wolters, *The Burden of Brown* (1984); Kluger, *Simple Justice* (1975).

BEREA COLLEGE V. COMMONWEALTH OF KENTUCKY, 211 U.S. 45 (1908). The first U.S. Supreme Court* case on desegregation* in higher education and the only such case that reinforced the separate but equal* doctrine of *Plessy v. Ferguson** (1896) in higher education. The small Berea College had had a racially mixed student body since its inception (1855). In 1904 Kentucky passed the Day Law, which allowed the teaching of members of both races simultaneously only if they were taught at least 25 miles apart. In a 7–2 decision the U.S. Supreme Court upheld the state's right to pass laws to regulate state-chartered private institutions on the basis of race, for example, to pass laws that prohibited interracial marriage, to require separate coaches for train transportation as upheld in *Plessy v. Ferguson*, and therefore to segregate the college. Thus the nation's highest court condoned mandating segregation* even in private higher education in this decision. In 1950 the law was amended, and blacks were again enrolled at Berea College.

References: Preer, *Lawyers v. Educators* (1982); Greenberg, *Judicial Process and Social Change: Constitutional Litigation Cases and Materials* (1977); Kluger, *Simple Justice* (1975).

BICKEL, ALEXANDER M. (born December 17, 1924, Bucharest, Romania– died November 7, 1974, New Haven, Connecticut). Scholar and law professor who as clerk to the U.S. Supreme Court* Justice Felix Frankfurter helped to rewrite the memo in the 1954 *Brown v. Board of Education** case requiring the rearguing of the case to consider the intent of the framers of the Fourteenth Amendment.* Bickel researched the intent of the framers of the amendment for Frankfurter, who passed his memo on to the remainder of the Court.

Bickel came to the United States in 1938. He graduated from the City College of New York in 1947 and from Harvard Law School, where he edited the *Harvard Law Review*. He became Frankfurter's clerk during the Court's 1952 term. The delay caused by the reargument allowed the Court, led by Chief Justice Earl Warren,* to form a consensus. Bickel's research led to the Court's conclusion that the debates over the Fourteenth Amendment* could not determine the *Brown* decision. After his clerkship Bickel taught at Yale Law School, where he advocated judicial self-restraint, writing his most influential book, *The Least Dangerous Branch: The Supreme Court at the Bar of Politics* (1962).

Works about: Hall, *Oxford Companion* (1992).

Works by: *Politics and the Warren Court* (New York: Harper and Row, 1965); *The Least Dangerous Branch: The Supreme Court at the Bar of Politics* (Indianapolis: Bobbs-Merrill, 1962, 1986).

BILINGUAL EDUCATION. Providing students who do not speak English at home with instruction in their native language while their English skills improve. Bilingual education has become a major symbolic and programmatic thrust for Hispanic and Latino advocates, many of whom see it as the remedy for inequality in education, analogous to desegregation* and civil rights* for blacks, and also seek to preserve their culture and language. Most bilingual programs seek to help students in a transition to the regular school program.

Title VII of the Elementary and Secondary Education Act of 1965* provided the first federal recognition of the need for programs for students from non-English-speaking backgrounds. In 1968 Congress passed the Bilingual Education Act to help encourage and fund programs that taught students in their native language while helping them achieve proficiency in English. On May 25, 1970, the Department of Health, Education, and Welfare* (HEW) issued guidelines that established the need for special assistance to students who had deficiencies in English and set the stage for bilingual programs throughout the nation. In *Lau v. Nichols** (1974) the U.S. Supreme Court* unanimously supported the HEW regulation's purpose.

In America's cities students from many backgrounds receive bilingual education. In New York City, for example, most bilingual students are Spanish speakers, but bilingual programs are also offered for students in Chinese, Haitian, Creole, Russian, Korean, Arabic, Vietnamese, Polish, Bengali, French, Urdu, and Albanian. The Department of Education's* Office of Bilingual Education and Minority Languages Affairs oversees the distribution of over $100 million for bilingual programs across the country, including professional development and school district–higher education cooperative ventures.

Since bilingual programs require a critical mass of students to make it efficient to provide the program, bilingual advocates may find themselves in conflict with those who seek school desegregation,* that is, a dispersal of minority students. Advocates of bilingual education also have to confront those who favor assimilation over the segregation of those with a different culture. Critics of bilingual education advocates argue that they are really calling for a bicultural program that will isolate non-English-speaking children. Whatever the arguments for and against, many school desegregation plans* require and specify in detail bilingual education programs for language-minority students in the district. Bilingual education is often juxtaposed to English as a second language (ESL) programs that offer intensive remedial instruction only in English.

Schnaiberg's March 1997 review of the status of research on bilingual education lists several barriers to useful research on this topic:

- The emotional nature of the issues and the threat that negative findings about the effects of bilingual education will lead advocates to cast the author as racist or anti-Hispanic are deterrents to research.

- Those funding the research generally have a position on the issue.

- Money for research on this issue is scarce.

- The definition of bilingual education and the nature of programs using this label vary tremendously; for example, some use fully certified instructors, while others use non-certified personnel with limited proficiency in English or the students' native tongue.

- There are various definitions of success in these programs, from speed of entering the mainstream of schooling to the development of fully bilingual graduates.

- The mobility of bilingual students makes longitudinal studies difficult to implement.

- The great range of students in bilingual programs, varying in socioeconomic and educational as well as ethnic background, makes it difficult to generalize about any program.

As a result of these barriers, questions such as what program components work best with limited-English students under what conditions are not easily answered.

References: Lynn Schnaiberg, "The Politics of Language," *Education Week* 16, no. 23 (March 5, 1997): 25–27; *Catalog of Federal Domestic Assistance, 1996*; Stephen Krashen, "Bilingual Education," in *Encyclopedia of Educational Research*, ed. Alkin (1992), 119–23; Yudof, Kirp, and Levin, *Educational Policy and the Law* (1992); Christine H. Rossell and J. Michael Ross, "The Social Science Evidence on Bilingual Education," *Journal of Law and Education* 15, no. 4 (Fall 1986): 385–419; J. Llanes, "The Sociology of Bilingual Education in the U.S.," *Journal of Education* 163 (1981): 72–84; Peter D. Roos, "Bilingual Education: The Hispanic Response to Unequal Educational Opportunity," *Law and Contemporary Problems* 42, no. 1 (Autumn 1978): 111–40.

BILINGUAL EDUCATION ACT OF 1968. Title VII of the Elementary and Secondary Education Act, the first national legislation to help minority students with their English-language skills. The act, signed by President Lyndon B. Johnson,* authorized funds to support educational programs to assist students who were poor and educationally disadvantaged. Latino students, who had been segregated and had not received much language development in segregated schools, were the target group of this legislation. This was grant-in-aid legislation; no action of state or local school officials was required. After the Supreme Court's* 1974 *Lau** decision, requirements were created under Title VI of the Civil Rights Act of 1964.* Under the Office of Bilingual Education and Minority Languages Affairs of the Department of Education,* local educational agencies or in some cases postsecondary institutions and nonprofit organizations may receive funds for projects to establish, operate, or improve bilingual education* and related programs. In fiscal year 1995 over $117 million was obligated for this effort.

References: *Catalog of Federal Domestic Assistance, 1996*; Contreras and Valverde, "The Impact of *Brown* on the Education of Latinos" (1994); Herbert Teitelbaum and Richard J. Hiller, "Bilingual Education: The Legal Mandate," *Harvard Educational Review* 47, no. 2 (May 1977): 138–70.

BLACK MONDAY. Term given by segregationists to May 17, 1954, the date of the U.S. Supreme Court* *Brown v. Board of Education** decision. Circuit Judge Tom Brady's pamphlet, *Black Monday*, became the handbook of the White Citizens' Council movement in Mississippi.

See also **Massive Resistance**.

References: Frank T. Read, "Judicial Evolution of the Law of School Integration since *Brown v. Board of Education*," in *Law and Contemporary Problems* 39, no. 2 (1975): 7–49; Muse, *Ten Years of Prelude* (1964).

BLACK NATIONALISTS. Those who seek to form all-black organizations and push for black control of institutions with means ranging from community control* of school districts to limiting adoptions of black children to black families. Charles Hamilton drew a distinction in 1972 between the black nationalist and the black integrationist. The integrationist believes that we must move beyond eliminating segregation* to achieving integration,* that is, officials must take affirmative action* to ensure that the races will be integrated. Remedies would include school busing* and the integration of housing, for example, public housing projects in white neighborhoods. Exclusive reliance on voluntary means is insufficient. The black nationalist believes that the goal should be black control of the key political, economic, social, and educational institutions that exist and affect black communities. Nationalists push for all-black organizations and argue, for example, that blacks do not need to sit next to whites to learn in school and should not be forced to leave their neighborhoods to be bused to white schools. Nor should blacks have to make their plea to white organizations and leaders.

The Marcus Garvey movement was a precursor of the 1960s nationalist movement. Thousands of blacks rallied to the back-to-Africa cause under Garvey in the early 1920s. Subsequently W.E.B. Du Bois* advocated black economic nationalism. According to Hamilton, the movement from integration to nationalism resulted from several factors, including disappointment with the pace of integration and change, the politicization in the aftermath of several long hot summers in the late 1960s, the killings and trials of militants such as the Black Panthers and Angela Davis, and the increased interest in Africa and opposition to the Vietnam War.

See also **Black Power**.

References: Levy, *Documentary History of the Modern Civil Rights Movement* (1992); Cashman, *African-Americans and the Quest for Civil Rights, 1900–1990* (1991); Derrick Bell, "The Case for a Separate Black School System," in *Black Education*, ed. Smith and Chunn (1989), 136–45; Charles V. Hamilton, "The Nationalist vs. the Integrationist," *New York Times Magazine*, October 1, 1972, reprinted in *The Great School Bus Controversy*, ed. Mills (1973), 297–310; John H. Bracey, August Meier, and Elliott Rudwick, eds., *Black Nationalism in America* (Indianapolis: Bobbs-Merrill, 1970).

BLACK POWER. Slogan articulated in the late 1960s by those seeking black control over the development and institutions of the black community, to instill pride in blacks, and to counter the acceptance of negative white stereotypes. This need for black independence was articulated most successfully by Malcolm X* and Stokely Carmichael (who first brought public attention to the slogan in June 1966); other advocates were H. Rap Brown, Huey Newton, Bobby Seale, and Eldridge Cleaver. Integration* and assimilation were rejected, and in their place black institutions devoid of white help or support were advocated. Organizational advocates included the Student Nonviolent Coordinating Committee (SNCC) and the Congress of Racial Equality (CORE). Black power advocates argued that black pride must be heightened, and the slogan became "Black is beautiful." The slogan had a peaceful side, the advocacy of black institutions and influence, and a dark side, implying black violence and guerrilla warfare. Brown, who followed Carmichael at SNCC, told audiences to "get you some guns" during the summer of city riots in 1967. The movement itself developed into the anti–Vietnam War protests of the late 1960s and early 1970s. The call for black power was built upon Marcus Garvey's nationalistic movement in the 1920s and W.E.B. Du Bois's* call for black pride. William H. Watkins (1996) discusses black nationalists,* pan-Africanists, and separatists as related ideologically and emerging from the experience with the international slave trade and European colonialism to lay the foundation for today's radical reformers and critical theorists. He highlights W.E.B. Du Bois in his analysis.

References: William H. Watkins, "Reclaiming Historical Visions of Quality Schooling: The Legacy of Early 20-Century Black Intellectuals," in *Beyond Desegregation*, ed. Shujaa (1996), 5–28; Safire, *Safire's New Political Dictionary* (1993); Vincent P. Franklin, *Black Self-Determination: A Cultural History of African-American Resistance* (Brooklyn, NY: Lawrence Hill Books, 1992); William L. Van Deburg, *New Day in Babylon: The Black Power Movement and American Culture 1965–1975* (Chicago: University of Chicago Press, 1992); Marger, *Race and Ethnic Relations* (1991); Stokely Carmichael and Charles V. Hamilton, *Black Power: The Politics of Liberation in America* (New York: Random House, 1967).

BOARD OF EDUCATION OF OKLAHOMA CITY V. DOWELL, 498 U.S. 237 (1991). Decision of the U.S. Supreme Court* that helped to define the conditions under which a school district may be declared a unitary system,* specifically whether the district implemented the court order in good faith and eliminated the vestiges of school segregation,* as outlined in the *Green** (1968) decision, "to the extent practicable." The Court accepted the argument that the Oklahoma City school district, which had previously been judged to be unitary, no longer had to desegregate its schools and could return to neighborhood schools,* even if these would be segregated.

In 1972 the U.S. District Court* ordered a school desegregation plan* for the Oklahoma City public schools. The "Finger Plan" called for students in kindergarten to attend their neighborhood schools, children in grades one through four to attend formerly all-white schools, children in grade five to attend for-

merly all-black schools, and students in the higher grades to be bused to integrated schools. In integrated neighborhoods at all grade levels students would
stay in their neighborhood school.

In 1977 the U.S. District Court* found that the school district had achieved
unitary status, a decision that was not appealed. In 1984 the board adopted a
student reassignment plan under which some desegregated schools would return
to segregated schools in grades one through four to alleviate busing* burdens
on young black students. Since more neighborhoods had become integrated,
black students had to travel farther, that is, past integrated areas, to attend desegregated schools. After the District Court denied a motion to reopen the case,
the Tenth Circuit Court of Appeals* ruled that the case could be reopened. The
District Court then found that the original plan was no longer workable, the
board had complied for over a decade, and the new plan was not developed
with discriminatory intent.* The Court of Appeals again reversed the District
Court's decision, arguing that the board had the affirmative duty not to take any
action that would impede desegregation.* This created a difference in stances
between the Tenth Circuit and the Fourth Circuit ruling in the Norfolk case
(*Riddick v. School Board of Norfolk, Virginia** [1986]). In 1986 the U.S. Supreme Court declined to hear the appeal from the Tenth Circuit decision.

After taking the case after another appeal in 1991, the U.S. Supreme Court's
slim majority (Justice William Rehnquist* wrote the opinion, and Justices White,
O'Connor, Scalia, and Kennedy joined) noted that "from the very first, federal
supervision of local school districts was intended as a temporary measure to
remedy past discrimination.*" Desegregation decrees "are not intended to operate in perpetuity." The Supreme Court put great weight on the board's compliance with the original court order over the years and the board's promise to
comply with the law. The case was remanded to the District Court to determine
if the board had complied in good faith with the desegregation order and if "the
vestiges of past discrimination had been eliminated to the extent practical." To
accomplish the latter, the Supreme Court stated that the District Court should
examine the *Green* (1968) factors—student assignments, faculty, staff, transportation, extracurricular activities, and facilities. If the district had achieved
unitary status, then the District Court should judge the student reassignment plan
only on whether it met the standard of the Fourteenth Amendment's* equal
protection clause.* Justice Thurgood Marshall* dissented, noting the legacy of
resistance by the board and calling for a higher standard before judging a district
unitary. He sought to require the district to remove and continue to eliminate
any message of racial inferiority.

In this important decision the Supreme Court emphasized that desegregation
orders should not be viewed as permanent. The Court maintained that the tradition of local control over schools is a most significant one in the United States,
and federal orders should displace local control only as long as necessary to
remedy past discrimination.

References: Orfield and Eaton, *Dismantling Desegregation* (1996); Wolters, *Right Turn* (1996); Armor, *Forced Justice* (1995); Abernathy, *Civil Rights and Constitutional Litigation* (1992).

BOB JONES UNIVERSITY V. UNITED STATES, 461 U.S. 574 (1983). The first U.S. Supreme Court* case to deal with the issue of whether the federal government could refuse to grant tax-exempt status to a religious school because of its discriminatory practices. In November 1970 the Internal Revenue Service (IRS) started to inform private, sectarian colleges that it had changed its policy for granting tax exemptions based on the *Green** (1968) decision. Bob Jones University in Greenville, South Carolina, was on this list, as was Goldsboro Christian School in Goldsboro, North Carolina. Both had at one time refused to admit blacks, although Bob Jones University began permitting the admission of blacks in 1971, but both did not allow black students to date whites. (Bob Jones University had retained its tax-exempt status from its inception in 1927 until 1970.) In 1977 the IRS sued Bob Jones University for unpaid taxes, and in 1978 the U.S. District Court* decided in favor of Bob Jones University, basing its decision on the freedom of religion clause of the U.S. Constitution* and the meaning of the tax law. In 1980 the Fourth Circuit Court of Appeals* reversed this decision. Both schools appealed to the nation's highest court. On January 8, 1982, the Reagan* administration decided to support the university before the U.S. Supreme Court, believing that the IRS did not have the legal authority to revoke tax-exempt status on the grounds of discriminatory actions. With the U.S. government abandoning its case against Bob Jones University, the U.S. Supreme Court, in a highly unusual move, asked black attorney William Coleman, Jr., to enter the case as a friend of the court (*amicus curiae**). The Court, in an 8–1 decision, supported the IRS policy, concluding that the IRS is empowered to set rules to enforce a policy against racial discrimination* in education. The Court decided that it was not enough for a school to be a religious institution; it must also confer public benefit in a manner consistent with public policy, in this case, desegregation.* Chief Justice Warren Burger* wrote the opinion; Justice William Rehnquist* was the lone dissenter.

References: Wolters, *Right Turn* (1996); Grossman, *The ABC-CLIO Companion to the Civil Rights Movement* (1993); Detlefsen, *Civil Rights under Reagan* (1991); David Whitman, *Ronald Reagan and Tax Exemptions for Racist Schools* (Cambridge, MA: Center for Press, Politics, and Public Policy at the Kennedy School of Government, Harvard University, 1984).

BOLLING V. SHARPE, 347 U.S. 497 (1954). Washington, D.C., case decided on the same day as the *Brown** decision and applying a different principle but reaching the same conclusion that segregated schools are unconstitutional. Black children had been denied admission to white schools in Washington, D.C. In the *Brown* decision the U.S. Supreme Court* ruled that the Fourteenth Amendment* prohibits states from maintaining segregated schools. The *Bolling v.*

Sharpe 9–0 opinion, written by Chief Justice Earl Warren,* concluded that the U.S. Constitution* would therefore require no less of the federal government. According to the opinion, the due process clause of the Fifth Amendment implicitly did not permit racial discrimination* in a manner analogous to the equal protection clause* of the Fourteenth Amendment. Thus the Court concluded that school segregation* was not permissible in the nation's capital, even though its schools were not segregated by state law. The Court used reasoning it had announced in the 1944 decision *Korematsu v. United States*, that under the Fifth Amendment classifications based on race were constitutionally "suspect" and would be subjected to "most exacting scrutiny."

The city's schools were segregated by laws passed by Congress. While the black and white schools were more equal than in southern states, per student expenditures in 1947 were $160.21 for whites and $120.52 for blacks. The leader of a boycott of a black overcrowded school, Gardner Bishop, met civil rights* attorney Charles Houston* at an NAACP* meeting. Houston agreed to submit a case to desegregate the Washington schools, and Bishop called off the boycott.

Unlike the other southern school desegregation* cases, the argument could not be made under the Fourteenth Amendment because the amendment barred states, but not the Congress or federal government, from denying equal protection. Houston's legal strategy was to push the district by filing suits calling for equalization of facilities. But as his heart condition worsened, Houston and Bishop turned to James Nabrit,* who sought to attack segregation more directly. When John Philip Sousa Junior High School opened in Washington on September 11, 1950, Bishop asked that the 11 students, including 11-year-old Spottswood Thomas Bolling, Jr., who accompanied him, be admitted. When this request was denied, Nabrit filed suit against the school board and its president, C. Melvin Sharpe. The suit did not contest or request equalization but rather challenged segregation based on the due process clause of the Fifth Amendment. The U.S. Supreme Court considered this case in the context of *Brown*, although it issued a separate opinion from *Brown*.

References: Greenberg, *Crusaders in the Courts* (1994); Witt, *Congressional Quarterly's Guide to the U.S. Supreme Court* (1989); Wolters, *The Burden of Brown* (1984); Kluger, *Simple Justice* (1975).

BRADDOCK, JOMILLS HENRY, II (born November 8, 1942, Jacksonville, Florida). Sociologist whose work has focused on the factors that affect black student achievement* and life success. Braddock, a graduate of Jacksonville University (1969), received his M.S. and Ph.D. in sociology from Florida State University (1971, 1973). After a period at the University of Maryland as an assistant professor in the Sociology Department (1973–1978), Braddock became an associate professor and then professor at Johns Hopkins on a part-time basis while he played a leading role in the university's educational sociology research centers. In 1992 he was named a professor and chair of the Department of

Sociology at the University of Miami, Florida. Braddock's published works include about 50 studies of race relations,* ability grouping,* equality of educational opportunity, sports and race, and correlates of academic performance of black students. His most well known research, conducted with Robert Crain* and James McPartland, investigates the long-term consequences of school segregation* on the employment and integration* of black students into American society. Braddock has been an active academic participant in discussions of school integration* in academic circles, presenting many papers on the topic at national conferences, while also working with national agencies such as the Department of Education* and serving as an expert witness in court cases, for example, Wilmington, Delaware, and federal hearings.

Works by: with R. L. Slavin, "Why Ability Grouping Must End: Achieving Equity and Excellence in American Education," *Journal of Intergroup Relations*, 20, no. 1 (1993): 51–64; "School Desegregation and Black Assimilation," *Journal of Social Issues* 41 (1985): 9–22; with R. L. Crain and J. M. McPartland, "A Long-Term View of School Desegregation: Some Recent Studies of Graduates as Adults," *Phi Delta Kappan* 66, no. 4 (1984): 259–64.

BRADLEY V. RICHMOND, VA. SCHOOL BOARD,

462 F.2d 1058 (4th. Cir. 1972), affirmed by an equally divided Court, 412 U.S. 92 (1973). Case that maintained the separation of the city and suburban school districts in the Richmond metropolitan area as the U.S. Supreme Court* voted 4–4, with Justice Lewis Powell,* former president of the Richmond Board of Education and member of the Virginia state board, not participating. "The judgment is affirmed by an equally divided court."

U.S. District Court* Judge Robert R. Merhige, Jr., wrote a 325-page opinion ordering that the city's predominantly black schools join with the schools of suburban Henrico and Chesterfield counties. His analysis of the Richmond and Virginia situation was based in part on the state's role in enforcing the segregationist policies of the Federal Housing Administration and Veterans' Administration racial segregation* policies in housing. There would be 104,000 students in the new district, with 78,000 bused, 10,000 more than under the old pupil assignment plans. The U.S. Court of Appeals* overruled Judge Merhige, focusing on whether the three local districts involved had met their constitutional obligations, and the Supreme Court, by the tie vote, affirmed its decision.

References: Armor, *Forced Justice* (1995); Zirkel, Richardson, and Goldberg, *A Digest of Supreme Court Decisions Affecting Education* (1995); Bolner and Shanley, *Busing* (1974).

BRENNAN, WILLIAM JOSEPH, JR.

(born April 25, 1906, Newark, New Jersey–died July 24, 1997, Washington, D.C.). Associate justice of the U.S. Supreme Court* from 1956 to 1990 who was the architect of many of the Warren Court's* landmark decisions and later a forceful proponent of liberty and equality on the Burger Court* and the Rehnquist Court.*

Brennan was appointed to the Court by President Dwight D. Eisenhower* during his reelection campaign in 1956. One of eight children of Irish Catholic immigrants, Brennan was a Democrat whose father was a labor leader and municipal reformer. Brennan graduated from the Wharton School, University of Pennsylvania, and Harvard Law School. In the 1930s he practiced law. During his World War II army service Brennan worked for the Under Secretary of War (Robert P. Patterson), earning the Legion of Merit. He returned to private practice after the war but was soon involved in the state court system, serving on the state supreme court.

Brennan wrote the opinion in *Cooper v. Aaron** (1958), fashioning the U.S. Supreme Court's response to massive resistance* in the South* in the Little Rock case. He became quite close to Chief Justice Earl Warren,* meeting weekly with him to consider cases and plan strategy. Brennan became a coalition builder and shaper of opinions on the Court. He became a target of Court critics who opposed judicial activism.

Works about: Linda Greenhouse, "William Brennan, 91, Dies; Gave Court Liberal Vision," *New York Times*, July 25, 1997, 1; *Britannica Online* (1996); Hunter R. Clark, *Justice Brennan: The Great Conciliator* (Secaucus, NJ: Carol Publishing Group, 1995); Peter H. Irons, *Brennan vs. Rehnquist: The Battle for the Constitution* (New York: Alfred A. Knopf, 1994); Hall, *Oxford Companion* (1992); Friedelbaum, "Justice William J. Brennan, Jr."(1991).

BRIGGS DICTUM. See Briggs v. Elliott.

BRIGGS V. ELLIOTT, 132 F. Supp. 776 (1955). Decision concerning school segregation* in Clarendon County, South Carolina. This case is significant for two reasons, originally as one of the four cases consolidated under the *Brown v. Board of Education** decision, and later as a critical case in decisions concerning the implementation of the *Brown* decision. Fourth Circuit U.S. Court of Appeals* Judge John J. Parker's* (1955) opinion concluded that the U.S. Supreme Court's* *Brown* decisions required that no state could deny the right to attend any school on the basis of race, but the Court did not take away the freedom of people to decide what school to attend. "The Constitution, in other words, did not require integration." According to this opinion, the Court forbids discrimination* but not segregation caused by voluntary actions of individuals, that is, de facto segregation.* (See *United States v. Jefferson County Board of Education* [1966] for the opposite viewpoint.) Over a decade later the U.S. Supreme Court in *Green v. County School Board of New Kent County** rejected this *Briggs* Dictum (or Parker Principle) and required school integration,* not simply nonracial assignments. To conservatives the abandonment of the *Briggs* Dictum in *Green* was the federal judiciary's most significant move from color blindness to color consciousness.

Clarendon County had a dual school system where in 1949–1950 the average expenditure per white student was $179 and the average per black student was

$43. Most of the 61 schools serving blacks were falling down, and the black schools were worth only one-third as much as the 12 white schools that schooled one-third as many students. The white children were in classes of almost half the number of students of those of the black children. The white schools had regular toilets; the black schools only had outhouses.

This case required NAACP Legal Defense Fund* counsel Thurgood Marshall* to decide between arguing for enforcement of the separate but equal doctrine,* an argument he was likely to win before sympathetic U.S. District Court Judge J. Waties Waring, or fighting the doctrine and the segregation laws directly, an argument that would first have to be made to a three-judge panel likely to include Waring, Parker, and an unfavorable third judge. Marshall decided to fight the segregation laws head-on. Robert McCormick Figg, Jr., representing the state, realized that the schools for blacks were not equal, and at the beginning of the court proceedings he acknowledged the inequality. He then asked for time for the state to bring the schools for blacks to a level equal to those for whites with its $40-million building program, but this delay was not permitted.

The three-judge panel concluded that the county could maintain separate schools if it improved the black schools. The court thus distinguished this case from *Sweatt** (1950) and *McLaurin** (1950). The latter cases had been at the graduate- and professional-school level where education was not compulsory and professional contacts were most important. Furthermore, according to the panel segregation was established by state law, and since no constitutional rights were being violated, these laws should stand. Judge Waring dissented, arguing, "Segregation is per se inequality" (*Briggs v. Elliott*, 98 F.Supp. 529 [1951]).

References: Kenneth W. Goings, *The NAACP Comes of Age: The Defeat of Judge John J. Parker* (Bloomington: Indiana University Press, 1990); Wolters, *The Burden of Brown* (1984); Kluger, *Simple Justice* (1975).

BROWN, LINDA CAROL (now Linda Brown Thompson) (born 1943, Topeka, Kansas). Daughter of the first plaintiff listed in the landmark U.S. Supreme Court* *Brown v. Board of Education** decision of 1954. In 1951 Linda Brown was 7 years old when her father, Rev. Oliver L. Brown, became the lead plaintiff of 12 in the Topeka case, *Brown v. Board of Education*. She and her two sisters and her family lived in a poor, mostly white part of town. Her father was a welder for the Santa Fe railroad and a part-time assistant pastor. She attended the Monroe School for "colored" students despite living much closer to the white Sumner School (21 blocks away versus 3½ blocks). She took the bus to her school, but her father wanted her to walk to her neighborhood school.* He was approached by the local NAACP* to participate in this famous case.

In 1979 Linda Brown Thompson became a plaintiff in the case's reopening, charging, with the help of the American Civil Liberties Union,* that the existence of 13 racially segregated schools violated the famous 1954 ruling in the case. She sought desegregated schools for her son and daughter. In 1988 she and other members of the family started the Brown Foundation, which awards scholarships and has worked on a multicultural curriculum for the public schools, as a memorial to the plaintiffs in the suit.

Works about: William Celis III, "Aftermath of '54 Ruling Disheartens the Browns," *New York Times*, May 18, 1994, 1, B7; Wolters, *The Burden of Brown* (1984); Kluger, *Simple Justice* (1975).

Works by: "Foreword," in *Eliminating Racism, Profiles in Controversy*, ed. Phyllis A. Katz and Dalmas A. Taylor (New York: Plenum Press, 1988), xi–xiii.

BROWN. See **Brown v. Board of Education of Topeka, Kansas**.

BROWN V. BOARD OF EDUCATION OF TOPEKA, KANSAS. Includes the landmark U.S. Supreme Court* decisions known as *Brown I** (1954) and *Brown II** (1955) or combined as *Brown*. In unanimous 9–0 decisions the U.S. Supreme Court ruled that school segregation* by law (de jure segregation*) was unconstitutional (*Brown I*) and set the parameters for the desegregation* of the schools (*Brown II*). The first decision, on the merits or the violation, overturned the rule of the *Plessy v. Ferguson** decision (1896), which had permitted separate but equal* institutions by race. The second decision, on the remedy or relief, led the way, however slowly, for the desegregation of the South's* schools. *Brown I* and *Brown II* are discussed separately in this volume.

This case consolidated several cases from four states with the following full titles: *Oliver Brown, et al. v. Board of Education of Topeka, Shawnee County, Kansas, et al.; Harry Briggs, Jr., et al. v. R. W. Elliott, et al.* (from South Carolina); *Dorothy E. Davis, et al. v. County School Board of Prince Edward County, Virginia, et al.*; and *Ethel Louis Belton, et al. v. Francis B. Gebhart, et al.* (from Delaware). Chief Justice Earl Warren* wrote the opinion. *Spottswood Thomas Bolling, et al. v. C. Melvin Sharpe, et al.* (from Washington, D.C.) was a related decision announced the same day.

See also **Belton v. Gebhart; Bolling v. Sharpe; Briggs v. Elliott; Bulah v. Gebhart; Davis v. County School Board**.

References: Wolters, *The Burden of Brown* (1984); Wilkinson, *From Brown to Bakke* (1979); Kluger, *Simple Justice* (1975).

BROWN V. BOARD OF EDUCATION (BROWN I), 347 U.S. 483 (1954). Landmark U.S. Supreme Court* decision declaring school segregation* unconstitutional, certainly the most significant U.S. Supreme Court decision on race, education, and equal opportunity. This case consolidated four separate school desegregation* decisions before the Court, cases from Kansas (*Brown v. Board of Education*, Topeka, Kansas), South Carolina (*Briggs v. Elliott**), Virginia (*Davis v. County School Board**), and Delaware (*Belton v. Gebhart**). "In each instance, (black schoolchildren) have been denied admission to schools attended by white children under laws requiring or permitting segregation according to race.'' In three cases a federal panel denied relief to the plaintiffs, but in Delaware Chancellor Collins Seitz ordered that the students be admitted to white schools because the court accepted the argument that the white schools were superior, not equal, to the schools for blacks. The set of cases became known as *Brown* because the *Brown* case was first on the list.

According to Kluger, ''At its first full-dress consideration of *Brown*, then, the Supreme Court of the United States was of several minds as to whether, how, and when it ought to strike down state-imposed segregation in the nation's schools'' (1975:613). But the justices were in agreement that the decision had to be a careful and, if at all possible, unanimous one. Thus after hearing arguments on the five cases on December 9–11, 1952, the Court, spurred on by Justice Felix Frankfurter, asked for a reargument on five questions, in part to give it more time for considering the weighty issues before it, building a court consensus, and allowing the South to prepare. Among the questions were what the understanding was that the Congress and states that ratified the Fourteenth Amendment* had about the outlawing of public school segregation and, if the Court ruled in the plaintiffs' favor, how the decision should be implemented. Reargument took place on December 8–9, 1953, with the NAACP* arguing that the Fourteenth Amendment had been aimed at achieving equality for blacks, the states arguing that desegregation was not required by this amendment, and the United States, as a friend of the court (*amicus curiae**), asserting that segregated education could not be continued under the Fourteenth Amendment.

The new Chief Justice, Earl Warren,* led the Court in reaching its unanimous decision. He believed that the only remaining justification for segregation was a belief in the inferiority of blacks, a notion that he could not support. Despite the initial concerns and perhaps even opposition of several members of the Court, they reached agreement that school segregation should be declared unconstitutional under the equal protection clause* of the Fourteenth Amendment and that the South* ought to be given time to adjust to their decision. Chief Justice Warren shaped the written decision to maintain unanimity among the justices. To help do this, he did not include any accusatory language about school segregation and the South and acknowledged that school segregation was also a northern problem.

The Court concluded that the history of the Fourteenth Amendment did not resolve the question before it. Moreover, the role of public education had changed from the time of the *Plessy** ruling, when the Court had concluded that facilities that were separate but equal* were constitutional, to a more sophisticated and important system in modern life. The Court, citing cases including *Sweatt v. Painter** (1950), recognized that these four school desegregation cases involved more than the question of whether tangible factors, such as buildings, curricula, and qualifications and salaries of teachers, were equal across white and black schools. The plaintiffs had contended that ''segregated public schools are not 'equal' and cannot be made 'equal' and that hence they are deprived of the equal protection of the laws.'' The Court accepted the plaintiffs' argument.

"We come to the question presented: Does segregation of children in public schools solely on the basis of race, even though the physical facilities and other 'tangible' factors may be equal, deprive the children of the minority group of equal educational opportunities? We believe that it does." The Court ruled that separate but equal schools were inherently unequal because segregation by law has a detrimental effect upon black children. They agreed with the court's statement (but not final decision) in the Kansas case that "the policy of separating the races is usually interpreted as denoting the inferiority of the Negro group. A sense of inferiority affects the motivation of a child to learn. Segregation with the sanction of law, therefore, has a tendency to retard the educational and mental development of Negro children, and to deprive them of some of the benefit they would receive" in a nonsegregated school system. Separating children in grade and high schools from others of similar age and qualifications because of race "may affect their hearts and minds in a way unlikely to ever be undone." Among the evidence cited was work done by Kenneth Clark* indicating that black children identified with white dolls. The Court stated that "modern authority" supports the finding that separate is not equal, and therefore "any language in *Plessy v. Ferguson* (1896) contrary to this finding is rejected." It concluded that "in the field of public education 'separate but equal' has no place."

The Court requested further arguments on relief or remedy because of the variety of local circumstances involved across these cases (and others to follow). Thus the need for *Brown II.**

The specifics of the *Brown* suit in Topeka were as follows. While its secondary schools were desegregated, Topeka had 4 elementary schools for black children and 22 elementary schools for white children. While the black schools were generally on a par with the white schools, which were somewhat newer, black children had much further to go to their schools and were often bused past their white neighborhood schools.* The NAACP attorneys presented evidence in court that segregation by law (de jure segregation*) created a sense of inferiority in black children. The U.S. District Court* ruled that since the black and white schools were essentially equal, under the precedents of *Plessy* and *Gong Lum** (1927), the court could not rule that segregation was unconstitutional. But the opinion of the U.S. District Court did make a key finding of fact that would be of great help when the case reached the U.S. Supreme Court: "Segregation of white and colored children in public schools has a detrimental effect upon the colored children. The impact is greater when it has the sanction of the law, for the policy of separating the races is usually interpreted as denoting the inferiority of the Negro group. A sense of inferiority affects the motivation of the child to learn." Segregation with the sanction of law, therefore, has a tendency to retard the educational and mental development of Negro children and to deprive them of some of the benefits they would receive in a racially integrated school system.

The immediate reaction to the *Brown I* decision was, not surprisingly, quite mixed. The NAACP's lead lawyer, Thurgood Marshall,* predicted that within five years school segregation would be eradicated; the governor of Virginia stated that "I shall use every legal means at my command to continue segregated schools in Virginia."

The Supreme Court's opinion in the four cases was short, only 11 pages, and tailored to maximize the chances for peaceful implementation. The decision had an impact on far more than schools. As Wilkinson concluded (1979:49): "After *Brown*, public beaches and buses, golf courses and parks, courtrooms and prison cell-blocks began to open to black and white alike. *Brown* was the catalyst that shook up Congress and culminated in the major Civil Rights acts of the century, one opening restaurants, hotels, and job opportunities to blacks, the other making black voters a new southern and national political force." Burt Neuborne in Lagemann and Miller offers six visions of the meaning of the *Brown* decision:

1. Vision of triumph; *Brown* as achievement. . . . *Brown* is not just an education case. *Brown* is an apartheid case and as an achievement it is extraordinary. . . . *Brown* marks the end of an eleven year legal battle. . . .

2. *Brown* as an aspiration, [as a] . . . benchmark for decency. . . .

3. *Brown* as a catalyst which started other movements, e.g. women's and gays' movement toward egalitarianism. . . .

4. *Brown* as a failure since the decision did not integrate the schools nor bring about a world of fairness. . . .

5. *Brown* as a challenge to close the gap, to keep our own identities without remaining separate. . . .

6. *Brown* as promise, setting the standard. (1996:204)

David Armor* raises three questions about the *Brown* decision: (1) Does the decision relate solely to de jure segregation or also to de facto segregation,* that is, action not brought about by state action? (2) To what extent is the decision based on causing psychological harm, and therefore, does the decision also apply where there is no state-imposed segregation? That is, if the decision is based on the harm that happens to black students as a result of segregation, whether such segregation is caused by governmental actions or other causes, would not school segregation require a remedy whatever the cause of segregation? (3) What remedies are therefore appropriate, and to what extent does the answer depend on the answers to the first two questions?

Brown I has been criticized for several reasons (see Wasby, D'Amato, and Metrailer, 1977). First, the opinion was not clear. Second, the opinion was not adequately built upon precedents. Third, the opinion was judicial legislation. Fourth, the Court relied too much on social science. Fifth, the Court did not adequately deal with the implementation of its decision. Kluger (1975), for example, offers that instead of basing the decision on social science evidence the Court could have used four alternative reasons to outlaw school segregation. The Court could have concluded that the Fourteenth Amendment's purpose was to remove all state-imposed discrimination.* Alternatively, the Court could have concluded that racial classification laws must be justified, and school segregation laws had not and could not be justified. Third, the Court could have reasonably decided that the separate but equal doctrine had been abused in practice and could no longer be adhered to; separate was never equal in practice. Finally, the Court could have based its argument on a rejection of the *Plessy* notion that segregation stamped blacks with a badge of inferiority only because they viewed it that way, certainly a conclusion hard to maintain in the 1950s. But whatever the Court could have done, there is no question that it raised the nation's consciousness about school segregation and forced Americans to confront this issue.

References: Yudof et al., *Kirp and Yudof's Educational Policy and the Law* (1987); Neuborne, "*Brown* at Forty: Six Visions" (1996); Armor, *Forced Justice* (1995); Wolters, *The Burden of Brown* (1984); Wilkinson, *From Brown to Bakke* (1979); Wasby, D'Amato, and Metrailer, *Desegregation from Brown to Alexander* (1977); Kluger, *Simple Justice* (1975).

BROWN V. BOARD OF EDUCATION (BROWN II), 349 U.S. 294 (1955). The remedy decision of the landmark *Brown v. Board of Education** case, in which the U.S. Supreme Court* decided that "school authorities have the primary responsibility for elucidating, assessing, and solving these problems; the courts will have to consider whether the action of school authorities constitutes good faith implementation of the governing constitutional principles." That is, the U.S. District Courts* were given the responsibility for judging the school desegregation plans* of local and state school authorities. This decision went to considerable length to spell out the kinds of problems that would face the implementors, including the physical condition of the school plant, the school transportation system, and revision of school districts and school attendance areas. The Court called upon District Courts to "enter such orders and decrees consistent with this opinion as are necessary and proper to admit to public schools on a racially nondiscriminatory basis with all deliberate speed the parties to these cases."

This implementation decision, calling for states to implement school desegregation* with all deliberate speed,* has received as much criticism as the first *Brown* decision (*Brown I**) received praise. The court's implementation plan was neither precise nor likely to be effective, given its dependence on local and state officials and federal District Court judges. States had established school desegregation plans based on desegregating one grade each year. The Court ruled that school desegregation must take place "now." However, the desegregation of the South* did not occur until the implementation of the Civil Rights Act of 1964.* Little desegregation of the schools in the South occurred from 1954 through 1964. Massive resistance* to the enforcement of the Court's order took place.

According to Wasby, D'Amato, and Metrailer (1977) *Brown II* has been criticized for several reasons. First, the Court made a decision that allowed too long for desegregation to be implemented; second, the Court failed to establish clear and precise guidelines to shape what was necessary; and third, the Court focused too much on compliance and not enough on the moral principle involved. Finally, the Court provided the southern states with a list of reasons to delay. Specifically, the Court failed to set a date to end school segregation.* Nor did it require the school boards to submit a school desegregation plan* within a fixed number of days. The Court was clearly responding to the concern that its decree be implemented in the hostile South.

References: Yudof et al., *Kirp and Yudof's Educational Policy and the Law* (1987); Wolters, *The Burden of Brown* (1984); Wilkinson, *From Brown to Bakke* (1979); Wasby, D'Amato, and Metrailer, *Desegregation from Brown to Alexander* (1977); Kluger, *Simple Justice* (1975).

BULAH V. GEBHART, 91 A.2d 137 (1953). One of two Delaware school desegregation* cases first decided by the state Chancery Court in Delaware and consolidated under the landmark case *Brown v. Board of Education** (1954). In the Wilmington suburb of Hockessin the schools were segregated. Sarah Bulah brought suit so that she would not have to drive her daughter Shirley two miles to a one-room school for "colored" students but so that Shirley either could be bused to that school or could walk to the neighborhood school.* After a series of letters to state officials she was informed that "since the State Constitution requires separate educational facilities for colored and white children, your children may not ride on a bus serving a white school." When she asked Harvard Law School graduate and black attorney Louis Redding to help, he said that he would help her to gain admission for her daughter to the white school, but not to get her daughter on the bus to ride to the colored school.

Chancellor Collins Seitz of the Delaware Chancery Court visited the schools at issue and was convinced that the schools were unequal. He also concluded that his lower court could not overturn the U.S. Supreme Court* precedent set by *Plessy v. Ferguson** (1896) and *Gong Lum v. Rice** (1927), establishing the principle and legitimacy of the separate but equal* doctrine. But he did rule that because the state had failed to provide equal education, the state had to admit the black students in question to the superior schools, that is, the white schools. Thus Seitz was the first judge to order that black elementary or secondary students be admitted to a white school. The case was appealed by the state of Delaware to the U.S. Supreme Courts and was consolidated under *Brown v. Board of Education*.

See also **Evans v. Buchanan**.

References: Greenberg, *Crusaders in the Courts* (1994); Wolters, *The Burden of Brown* (1984); Kluger, *Simple Justice* (1975).

BURDEN OF PROOF. A legal concept referring to the necessity of proving disputed facts. Generally, in a lawsuit the party bringing the suit, the plaintiff, has the obligation to prove its case, and the defendant has the burden of rebutting the evidence. In school desegregation* cases the burden of proof may rest on the defendant or the plaintiff depending on whether it is a violation hearing (plantiff's burden) or a postconviction hearing on any school issue including unitary* status (defendant's burden). Whether the plaintiff has to prove discrimination* or the defendant has to prove nondiscrimination may have a major impact on the court's decision.

In *Washington v. Davis** (1976), for example, the U.S. District Court* had to consider whether a verbal-skills test used by the Washington, D.C., police department was in violation of the U.S. Constitution.* Because black recruits had a higher failure rate than whites on this test, plaintiffs argued that the test was discriminatory and violated the Fourteenth Amendment.* The U.S. District Court did conclude that the differential success rate warranted shifting the burden of proof to the defendants; that is, the police department had to show that the test was job related and not discriminatory in intent. The District Court then concluded that the department had offered sufficient proof. Ultimately the U.S. Supreme Court* decided that to be judged unconstitutional, a governmental act had to be discriminatory in effect *and* intent. That is, those arguing that a given act was unconstitutionally discriminatory had to prove that the governmental action led to a disparate impact* and was intentionally aimed at doing so. The latter is much harder to establish than the former and thus poses a difficult hurdle for those trying to prove that segregation* is unconstitutional in a given school district. Where a district has been found to have de jure segregation,* the burden of proof is on the school district to show that its actions did not have a segregatory intent. Disproving a negative is quite difficult. Where a district has subsequently been declared unitary, the burden of proof shifts back to those challenging the board's actions.

References: Armor, *Forced Justice* (1995); Yudof, Kirp, and Levin, *Educational Policy and the Law* (1992); *The Guide to American Law: Everyone's Legal Encyclopedia* (St. Paul: West Publishing, 1984), 190–91; Gatti and Gatti, *New Encyclopedic Dictionary of School Law* (1983).

BURGER, WARREN EARL (born September 17, 1907, St. Paul, Minnesota–died June 25, 1995, Washington, D.C.). Fifteenth Chief Justice of the U.S. Supreme Court* (1969–1986) during the era when the Court accepted the validity of busing* to achieve school desegregation* and built upon the Warren Court's* major decisions on school desegregation. With a reputation for conservatism, Burger led the Court to a centrist position in a number of areas, including civil rights,* where his Court validated busing as an instrument to achieve school desegregation.

Warren Burger, one of seven children of Swiss and German parents, grew up on a farm outside St. Paul, Minnesota. Burger was editor of his high-school paper, was president of the student council, and earned several letters in sports. After high school Burger sold insurance and went to night school at the St. Paul College of Law (now William Mitchell College of Law), earning a degree with high honors in 1931. He taught on the faculty of the law school for 12 years while practicing law and then served as a partner in a St. Paul law firm for another 10 years. His legal practice focused on corporate, probate, and real-estate issues. He was active in civic affairs, serving as president of the Junior Chamber of Commerce, the first president of the St. Paul Council on Human Relations, and a member of the Governor's Interracial Commission.

Burger was active in state politics working for Governor Harold Stassen. He attended the Republican conventions in 1948 and 1952, where he was Stassen's floor manager. He helped Dwight D. Eisenhower* to receive his first presidential nomination in 1952 and was named Assistant Attorney General in charge of the Civil Division of the Department of Justice* in 1953. In 1955 President Eisenhower nominated him for the U.S. Court of Appeals* for the District of Columbia, and he joined this court in 1956, where he served until 1969. Burger received national attention from those in the legal profession for his conflicts with civil libertarians on this influential court. Burger was the leader of the court most favorable to police, prosecution, and judges.

Burger was nominated by President Richard Nixon* to the position of Chief Justice of the U.S. Supreme Court on May 21, 1969, to turn the Court in a more conservative direction. Burger was sworn in on June 23, 1969. He brought to the Court his judicial experience, his siding with law enforcement and opposition to the judicial activism of the Warren Court, and a career free of ethical questions.

Burger did not succumb to political pressure on civil rights and criminal law as Nixon had hoped. Under his leadership the Court continued to support school desegregation, although perhaps in a more cautious way. He wrote the *Swann v. Charlotte-Mecklenburg Board of Education* decision (1971), which was the Supreme Court's first decision allowing busing. But Burger was also the author of the majority opinion in *Milliken v. Bradley I** (1974), which halted metropolitan school desegregation in the Detroit area and, by precedent, throughout the nation.

Burger retired in 1986 after 17 years as Chief Justice to chair the commission planning the bicentennial celebration of the U.S. Constitution* (1987). He died at age 87 of congestive heart failure.

Works about: *Britannica Online* (1996); *Current Biography Yearbook 1995* (New York: H. W. Wilson Company, 1995), 615; Linda Greenhouse, "Warren E. Burger Is Dead at 87; Was Chief Justice for 17 Years," *New York Times*, June 26, 1995, 1; Bernard Schwartz, *The Ascent of Pragmatism: The Burger Court in Action* (Reading, MA: Addison-Wesley, 1990).

BURGER COURT. The U.S. Supreme Court* under the leadership of Chief Justice Warren Burger* from 1969 to 1986 that decided a number of school desegregation* cases, such as *Swann v. Charlotte-Mecklenburg Board of Education* (1971), requiring extending the *Brown** decision to northern and urban school districts. Chief Justice Burger was appointed by President Richard M.

Nixon* to turn the Court in a more conservative direction, but the Chief Justice led a court that increased the scope of *Brown*, requiring school busing* in urban southern school districts and school desegregation in some northern school districts.

In *Brown I** (1954) and *Brown II** (1955) the Warren Court* had declared school segregation* established by state law unconstitutional and had called for school desegregation with all deliberate speed.* It had not taken an active role in desegregation, leaving actions to remedy segregation to the federal District Courts,* until its ruling in the *Green** (1968) case. In *Green* the Warren Court had declared that school districts that had been segregated by law (de jure segregation*) had the affirmative duty to convert to a unitary system* and do so with a plan that would work immediately. The *Green* decision had been based on the two-school situation of rural New Kent County, but it was the Burger Court that applied the *Green* principles to the urban South.*

In *Alexander v. Holmes County Board of Education** (1969) the Burger Court rejected the Warren Court's concept of all deliberate speed and declared that the time for school desegregation was "at once." In *Swann v. Charlotte-Mecklenburg Board of Education* the Burger Court decided that the schools of Charlotte-Mecklenburg were segregated and that the transfer of pupils out of their neighborhood school* attendance areas, that is, busing, was not only permissible but also a necessary component of the remedy. In the *Keyes v. Denver School District No. 1** (1973) decision the Burger Court concluded that even though a school district was never segregated by a statute calling for segregated schools, it might be unconstitutionally segregated by law (de jure segregation) because of the school board's race-based decisions in school construction and drawing of school attendance boundaries.

In its *Milliken v. Bradley** (1974) decision the Burger Court, in a 5–4 vote, did establish a major barrier to metropolitan school desegregation and busing by ruling that the desegregation of Detroit's segregated public schools did not require the involvement of the surrounding suburban school districts. The Chief Justice wrote that "the scope of the remedy is determined by the nature and extent of the constitutional violation," and since the suburban districts had not been proven to have caused the city schools' segregation, they did not have to be included in the remedy.

The Burger Court also dealt with a key case on affirmative action* in universities. In *Regents of the University of California v. Bakke** (1978) the Burger Court developed a complicated response to a challenge to the University of California at Davis Medical School's admissions process. Three opinions were written, with Justice Lewis Powell's* swing vote agreeing with Justices William Brennan,* Byron White, Thurgood Marshall,* and Harry Blackmun that admissions programs with racial criteria did not necessarily violate the equal protection clause* of the Fourteenth Amendment* or Title VI of the Civil Rights Act of 1964,* while agreeing with Justices Burger, John Paul Stevens, Potter Stewart, and William Rehnquist* that the fixed quota system was not legal. Powell concluded that a school could take race into account in its admissions decisions but could not specify a fixed number of members of a particular race to admit.

The Burger Court is sometimes referred to as the Nixon Court because President Richard Nixon appointed four of the justices: Burger, Blackmun, Powell, and Rehnquist, three of whom replaced liberal judges who had been part of the majority against whom Nixon ran. The Burger Court took a position belying its conservative origins in the 1973 *Roe v. Wade* decision restricting limits on abortion. In the Pentagon Papers case, *New York Times Co. v. United States* (1971), the Court came down against prior censorship by the government of the press. Not surprisingly, analysts have found it difficult to categorize the Burger Court on the conservative-liberal or activist–self-constraint dimensions.

The Burger Court faced a great expansion in workload as the number of cases continued to grow. In the first year of the Warren Court it disposed of 1,293 cases, and in Warren's last term it had 3,117 cases. The Burger Court went from 3,357 cases in its 1969 term to 4,289 cases in its 1985 term.

The members of the original Burger Court were the following:

Hugo L. Black (1937–1971, appointed by President Franklin D. Roosevelt)

William O. Douglas (1939–1975, appointed by President Roosevelt)

John Marshall Harlan (1955–1971, appointed by President Dwight D. Eisenhower*)

William J. Brennan, Jr. (1956–1990, appointed by President Eisenhower)

Potter Stewart (1958–1981, appointed by President Eisenhower)

Byron R. White (1962–1993, appointed by President John F. Kennedy*)

Thurgood Marshall (1967–1991, appointed by President Lyndon B. Johnson*)

Later members were the following:

Harry A. Blackmun (1970–1994, appointed by President Richard M. Nixon)

Lewis F. Powell, Jr. (1971–1987, appointed by President Nixon)

William H. Rehnquist (1971–, appointed by President Nixon)

John Paul Stevens (1975–, appointed by President Gerald Ford)

Sandra Day O'Connor (1981–, appointed by President Ronald Reagan*)

In *A History of the Supreme Court* Bernard Schwartz argues that Chief Justice Burger was not a leader and consensus builder like Chief Justice Earl Warren, and the Burger Court spoke more as a collection of individuals than as a unanimous body. The split vote and several opinions needed to decide *Bakke* illustrate this tendency, especially in contrast to the Warren Court's unanimous *Brown* decision shaped and written by Earl Warren. Despite President Nixon's hopes, the Burger Court never reversed a Warren Court decision, and while it narrowed the scope of some decisions, it widened the application of others.

References: Schwartz, *A History of the Supreme Court* (1993); Lamb and Halpern, *The Burger Court* (1991); Bernard Schwartz, *The Ascent of Pragmatism: The Burger Court in Action* (Reading, MA: Addison-Wesley, 1990); Herman Schwartz, ed., *The Burger*

Years: Rights and Wrongs in the Supreme Court, 1969–1986 (New York: Viking, 1987); Bernard Schwartz, *Swann's Way: The School Busing Case and the Supreme Court* (New York: Oxford University Press, 1986); Paul Brest, "Racial Discrimination," in *The Burger Court*, ed. Blasi (1983), 113–31; Lee, *Neither Conservative Nor Liberal* (1983).

BUSING. The mandatory assignment of students away from their neighborhood school* or previously assigned school for the purpose of school desegregation.* Busing is a school desegregation technique based upon the transportation of pupils to a new school or school they have not previously attended for the purpose of desegregating schools. Court-ordered busing is a subset of busing to achieve school desegregation. Busing, especially court-ordered busing, is the center of the objections that many have toward school desegregation and the involvement of the courts and federal government in public education. Critics argue that busing has failed because white enrollment loss (white flight*) due to such plans reduces the interracial contact that was planned, and parental involvement in the schools, a necessary ingredient for student success in school, is greatly reduced as school assignments are separated from residences. Supporters counter that busing is often the only means to accomplish school desegregation because many whites will not attend schools with many black students without being forced to and that white enrollment loss is generally not due to busing but to other factors and can be minimized in the longer run with metropolitan school desegregation plans.*

The U.S. Supreme Court* in *Swann v. Charlotte-Mecklenburg Board of Education* (1971) ruled that busing was permissible as a remedy where a school system has de jure segregation.* District Courts* are allowed to order busing, but only under restrictive conditions. They must be remedying a constitutional violation, and busing has to be shown to be a feasible, reasonable, and workable remedy that will not threaten the educational process or the health of students involved. The remedy may not exceed the scope of the violation and must be designed to return the plaintiffs to the status they would have had but for the violation. After a busing plan is implemented, the court cannot require constant changes to maintain a particular racial balance in the schools. Nor do such orders last forever. Once a school district is declared unitary,* the District Court may end its order and return control to the local school board.

Technically, busing generally involves the use of one of two pupil assignment techniques, pairing* or clustering* (combining two or more schools with different racial makeups in different parts of the school district) or satellite zoning (assigning pupils from one geographical area with a particular racial composition to a school with a different racial composition). The school attendance areas may be contiguous or noncontiguous. Noncontiguous zones are more likely to be used in larger school districts and to require longer bus rides. Because the student assignment plan leaves students with no choice of school, such plans are considered mandatory plans.*

Efforts to limit busing have been made in Congress along four different paths.

First, bills have been introduced to prohibit the Department of Health, Education, and Welfare* (HEW) (now the Department of Education*) from using federal funds to require busing. Congress amended the 1968 HEW Appropriations Act with a provision that prohibited HEW from using funds to bus students, force assignment to particular schools, or close schools in conflict with parental choice as a means to overcome racial imbalance.* The purpose of this and later restrictions was to protect freedom-of-choice* plans from HEW interference. In 1976 Congress passed the Byrd Amendment,* over President Gerald Ford's veto, which prohibited the use of funds to require "directly or indirectly, the transportation of any student to a school other than the school which is nearest the student's home." HEW continued to require busing, so Congress passed the Eagleton-Biden Amendment* to the Labor-HEW Appropriations Act of 1978. This act prohibited the federal government from using federal funds to require busing beyond the nearest school to implement school desegregation plans* based on pairing or clustering of schools or building new school facilities.

Second, bills to prohibit the Department of Justice* from initiating or joining suits leading to busing have been considered. The House passed such a restriction in 1979 and 1980, but the provisions were dropped in conference committees both times. In 1980 Congress passed an appropriations act that again would have prohibited the Justice Department from bringing suits that would lead to busing, but President Jimmy Carter* vetoed the bill because this provision would have Congress dictating to the President that he could not use certain remedies required to implement constitutional guarantees. Carter reasoned that the provision violated the separation of powers doctrine.

Third, bills to restrict the federal courts' authority to order busing have been considered. Some bills have called for limiting the power of the lower courts to order busing, while others would eliminate the lower courts' jurisdiction in any case involving public schools. Most of the bills would remove federal jurisdiction in any decision requiring attendance at a public school based on race. While many such bills have been introduced, only two have been passed, both quite weak. The Education Amendments of 1972* postpone busing orders until all appeals are exhausted or the time for appeals has passed, but the U.S. Supreme Court ruled that this restriction does not apply in de jure segregation* cases and is thus inapplicable to virtually all cases in the United States. The Esch Amendment* to the Equal Educational Opportunities Act of 1974 placed busing as the remedy of last resort and restricted busing to the closest or next-closest school. But the amendment also contained a provision that affirmed the federal courts' authority to fully enforce the Fifth and Fourteenth Amendments* to the U.S. Constitution,* thus negating the effect of this bill.

Finally, resolutions proposing antibusing constitutional amendments have been offered. During the Ninety-second Congress more than 50 such proposed constitutional amendments were considered in hearings. None, however, were passed by Congress.

These efforts to reverse the busing remedies that have followed the *Swann* decision are of questionable constitutional status. Congress does not have the power to limit an individual's constitutional right to equal protection, and some bills face the problem of violating the separation of powers principle. Since constitutional amendments require a two-thirds vote in each body of Congress and then ratification by three-fourths of the states, the likelihood of limiting busing orders through such restrictive action is limited.

The U.S. Supreme Court's *Milliken I** (1974) decision greatly limited the use of busing as a remedy in metropolitan areas. In this decision the Court ruled that school boundaries could be crossed in a remedy only where the suburban districts or the state had taken action to segregate students. Given the great extent of racial segregation in metropolitan areas coterminous with city boundaries, *Milliken I* served to greatly restrict the possibility of a busing remedy.

The term *busing* is primarily used by opponents of mandatory school desegregation plans to achieve school desegregation. Busing, especially in the phrases "forced busing" and "massive busing," became a code word for opposition to racial balance and desegregation affecting whites. Advocates of school desegregation generally do not use this term. They view "busing" in its more generic form, the transportation of students to school. They therefore ask what all the fuss is about, given that approximately half of the nation's schoolchildren ride a bus to school. (Another significant percentage ride on public transportation.) For example, Mayer et al. (1974) point out that in 1973, when the busing issue was beginning to reach its peak of conflict, about 20 million students were regularly bused to school at public expense. Logistically this involved over one-quarter of a million buses traveling over two billion miles at a cost of almost two billion dollars. Few students (estimated by the U.S. Commission on Civil Rights* as about 5 percent) were bused for desegregation purposes during the 1966–1975 decade. The traditional form of busing has helped to consolidate school districts, transport students to school for better resources, and increase safety in traveling to school. In addition, desegregation advocates argued that these same buses had been used to bus black students past white schools to segregated schools miles from their homes.

Opponents of busing argue that busing for the purpose of school desegregation, because it moves children from their neighborhoods, is undesirable or wrong. That is, desegregating neighborhoods is viewed differently from transporting pupils across regular school attendance areas. Some busing opponents have argued that school desegregation is quite a different concept from busing. Desegregation requires the elimination of laws and policies separating the races, but busing is viewed as moving beyond removing such barriers to attempt to achieve racial balance* through mandatory means. This is a strategy of integration.*

One variant of busing is two-way busing, in which students are bused from white schools to black and from black schools to white. Whites are more negative about such plans because of their fears of violence in poor black neighborhoods and their concerns about the educational quality of black schools. A significant number of black parents are concerned with busing their children out of their neighborhoods because of their fear of the treatment their children will receive in white schools.

Public opinion surveys have generally shown that while support for school desegregation is wide and growing, support for busing is limited. In 1996 Gary Orfield* reported that a *USA Today*/Cable News Network Gallup Poll taken on the 40th anniversary of the *Brown** (1954) decision indicated that 87 percent of Americans viewed the decision as right. This percentage was up from 63 percent in the early 1960s. In the South* the change was most significant, from the 81 percent who thought the *Brown* decision was wrong in 1954 to the 15 percent who reported a similar judgment 40 years later. But three-quarters of the white population across the nation oppose school busing, at least as described in public opinion polls as analyzed by Christine Rossell* in 1995. While a majority of blacks have supported busing, black opinion is split, with a substantial minority (and in 1975 a slight majority) opposing busing. The wording of questions has a major impact on the measurement of public support for busing. Busing as an abstract policy transporting students across school-district lines receives far less support than transportation as the only policy that can further desegregation. Similarly, the attitudes of parents of children bused are far less negative than those of the general public.

One perplexing issue relating to busing is why the public supports the principle of school desegregation but opposes busing to achieve it. Rossell's 1995 analysis summarizes a number of explanatory theories. Mary Jackman argues that Americans accept the principles of integration and equal educational opportunity* because of their consistency with democratic values, but they reject actual efforts to implement these principles because of their support for the status quo and their current economic, social, and political dominance. This superficial tolerance argument suggests that opposition to implementation is opposition to the loss of whites' advantaged positions. This is contrasted with symbolic racism* and value theory. The symbolic racism explanation offers that individuals remain racists but know how to respond in a positive and acceptable way in surveys and in public discourse. They thus appear more favorable than they are when confronted with an action plan. Seymour Lipset argues that Americans' support of the principle of individual freedom runs into conflict with genuine beliefs in equal opportunity and racial integration. Compulsory policies, such as quotas and mandatory busing, are therefore opposed, while the principles are upheld. David Armor* prefers a personal cost-benefit explanation for white flight and white behavior and attitudes. For example, whites know that their children will not benefit from busing and also recognize the costs in time and distance from home.

References: Gary Orfield, ''Public Opinion and School Desegregation,'' in *Brown v. Board of Education*, ed. Lagemann and Miller (1996), 54–70; Rossell and Armor, ''The Effectiveness of School Segregation Plans, 1968–1991'' (July 1996); Rossell, ''The Convergence of Black and White Attitudes on School Desegregation Issues during the Four Decade Evolution of the Plans'' (January 1995); Douglas, *School Busing* (1994); Keynes and Miller, *The Court vs. Congress* (1989); Orfield, *Must We Bus?* (1978); Mayer et al., *The Impact of School Desegregation in a Southern City* (1974); Mills, *The Great School Bus Controversy* (1973).

BYRD AMENDMENT. An amendment to the fiscal year 1976 Labor-HEW appropriations bill that prohibited the Department of Health, Education, and Welfare* (HEW), now the Department of Education,* from withholding federal funds from local school districts that were segregated to force a student to be bused beyond his neighborhood school* because of race. Senator Robert C. Byrd, Democrat of West Virginia, proposed this amendment to the $36-billion HEW appropriation on September 19, 1975. The amendment passed on September 24, with the Senate voting 51–45 in favor. Congress ultimately passed this amendment over President Gerald Ford's veto. The amendment specifically prohibited the use of funds to require "directly or indirectly, the transportation of any student to a school other than the school which is nearest the student's home." HEW and President Jimmy Carter's* Attorney General, Griffin Bell, continued to require busing,* however, using court interpretations that indicated that busing to alleviate de jure school segregation* was different from that to overcome racial imbalance* and maintaining that paired* or clustered* schools could be treated as a single school for pupil assignment purposes. In 1978 Congress passed the Eagleton-Biden Amendment* to plug this loophole.

References: Amaker, *Civil Rights and the Reagan Administration* (1988); Yudof et al., *Kirp and Yudof's Educational Policy and the Law* (1987); Metcalf, *From Little Rock to Boston* (1983).

C

CARTER, JAMES EARL, JR. (born October 1, 1924, Plains, Georgia). As governor of Georgia Jimmy Carter was the architect of the Atlanta Compromise,* which gave blacks control of the Atlanta schools while avoiding busing,* and as the 39th president of the United States he established the federal Department of Education.* As a leader of the New South,* Carter brought many blacks and minorities into his state and federal administrations.

Jimmy Carter grew up in Archery, Georgia, the son of a politically active peanut farmer who served as a state legislator. Carter attended Georgia Southwestern College and the Georgia Institute of Technology and received his B.S. from the U.S. Naval Academy in 1946. In the navy Carter rose to the rank of lieutenant (senior grade) and worked under Admiral Hyman Rickover in the nuclear submarine program. In 1953, following his father's death, he returned to Plains to run the family peanut farm operations. Here Carter served as chairman of the county school board. He was elected to the Georgia State Senate in 1962 and reelected in 1964. Carter lost the 1966 gubernatorial primary but won in 1970 and became the 76th governor of Georgia on January 12, 1971. His inaugural address included the phrase "The time for racial discrimination* is over." He was instrumental in state government hiring blacks and women.

Carter started campaigning nationally in 1974 and won the Democratic nomination for President on the first ballot at the 1976 convention. He was elected President on November 2, 1976, defeating incumbent Republican President Gerald R. Ford with 51 percent of the vote. Carter served from January 20, 1977, to January 20, 1981, as the 39th President of the United States. Under his leadership the Department of Education was created in 1980. Carter was defeated in his reelection bid by Republican Ronald Reagan* in 1980, winning only 41 percent of the popular vote.

When Carter ran for President, concerns about his positions on civil rights* were paramount, given his origins not only in the Deep South* but in a part of Georgia known as hostile to blacks. On the other hand, Carter had the support of Martin Luther King's* father and civil rights activist Andrew Young. But Carter further led civil rights advocates to doubt his support when on the day he won the Wisconsin primary he talked about "ethnic purity" in a discussion of the role of the federal government in changing residential neighborhoods. As President, Carter appointed Drew Days III as Assistant Attorney General for Civil Rights and Eleanor Norton as Chairman of the Equal Employment Opportunity Commission. Both were the first blacks to head their respective agencies, and both had been nationally known and recognized civil rights advocates. Days, for example, had been a lawyer at the NAACP Legal Defense Fund.* Carter's appointments to the federal bench were also supportive of the civil rights movement.* In his first three years he appointed more blacks, Hispanics, and women than all previous administrations had done before him. Some important school desegregation* cases were filed by the Department of Justice* during Carter's presidency, including the Indianapolis metropolitan school desegregation case.

Works about: *Britannica Online*; Office of Public Information, the Carter Center, carterweb@emory.edu (July 22, 1995); O'Reilly, *Nixon's Piano* (1995); Norman C. Amaker, "The Faithfulness of the Carter Administration in Enforcing Civil Rights," in *The Presidency and Domestic Policies of Jimmy Carter*, ed. Herbert D. Rosenbaum and Alexej Ugrinsky (Westport, CT: Greenwood Press, 1994), 737–45.

Works by: *Negotiation, the Alternative to Hostility* (Macon, GA: Mercer University Press, 1984); *Keeping Faith: Memoirs of a President* (New York: Bantam Books, 1982).

CITIZENS' COMMISSION ON CIVIL RIGHTS. This commission defines itself as a "bipartisan group of former officials who have served in the federal government in positions with responsibility for equal opportunity. It was established in 1982 to monitor the civil rights* policies and practices of the federal government and to seek ways to accelerate progress in the area of civil rights." The 16 members in 1996 included William Taylor, former staff director of the U.S. Commission on Civil Rights* (USCCR), Theodore M. Hesburgh, former chair of the USCCR, Elliot Richardson, former Attorney General of the United States, and Roger Wilkins, former director of the Community Relations Service.* The commission is headquartered in Washington, D.C., and has issued several reports on the status of federal civil rights activity in education as well as housing, voting, employment, and hate crimes.

References: Jaszczak, *Encyclopedia of Associations* (1996), 2063; *Washington Information Directory, 1995–1996* (Washington, DC: Congressional Quarterly, 1995), 511; Corrine M. Yu and William L. Taylor, eds., *New Challenges: The Civil Rights Records of the Clinton Administration Mid-Term* (Washington, DC: Citizens' Commission on Civil Rights, 1995); Susan M. Liss and William L. Taylor, eds., *New Opportunities: Civil Rights at a Crossroads* (Washington, DC: Citizens' Commission on Civil Rights, 1993); Reginald C. Govan and William L. Taylor, eds., *One Nation Indivisible: The Civil Rights Challenge for the 1990s* (Washington, DC: Citizens' Commission on Civil Rights, 1989).

CIVIL RIGHTS. Rights of personal liberty guaranteed in the U.S. Constitution* to each individual as a member of American society, such as the right to equal treatment before the law in areas such as education, housing, public accommodations, and criminal justice. Civil rights are often juxtaposed with civil liberties, which are individual actions without government restriction, such as freedom of speech, press, and religion. Thus civil rights are based on the concept of equality granted under the law, and civil liberties are based on individual freedoms. The scope of a civil right is defined not only by a nation's constitution and laws but also by the interpretation of these. In the United States the term *civil rights* has become associated with the black movement for equal rights, the civil rights movement.* Civil rights for blacks and other groups (women, Indians, gays, the handicapped) have been enhanced through the legislative, judicial, and executive actions resulting from this movement.

References: Safire, *Safire's New Political Dictionary* (1993); Cashman, *African-Americans and the Quest for Civil Rights, 1900–1990* (1991); ''Civil Rights,'' in *American Educators' Encyclopedia*, by Dejnozka and Kapel (1991), 105; David M. Walker, *The Oxford Companion to Law* (Oxford: Clarendon Press, 1980), 224–25.

CIVIL RIGHTS ACT OF 1866. The first civil rights* act, passed during Reconstruction, this bill was aimed at destroying the Black Codes, which the states of the South* had passed to convert the newly freed slaves back into indentured servitude. The bill was passed over the veto of President Andrew Johnson. The act, and debates over the act, played a role in the *Brown** rearguments in helping to understand the intent of Congress in passing the Fourteenth Amendment.*

References: Greenberg, *Crusaders in the Courts* (1994); Earl M. Maltz, *Civil Rights, The Constitution, and Congress, 1863–1869* (Lawrence: University Press of Kansas, 1990); Kluger, *Simple Justice* (1975).

CIVIL RIGHTS ACT OF 1875. This law was declared unconstitutional by the U.S. Supreme Court* in 1883 in the *Civil Rights Cases,** thus leaving the way open for Jim Crow* laws in the South.* The law declared that all had equal access to accommodations, public conveyances, and places of public amusement such as theaters. The earlier attempt to guarantee blacks desegregated schools in this bill had failed to pass Congress.

References: Abraham and Perry, *Freedom and the Court* (1994); Greenberg, *Crusaders in the Courts* (1994); Grossman, *The ABC-CLIO Companion to the Civil Rights Move-*

ment (1993); William Gillette, *Retreat from Reconstruction, 1869–1879* (Baton Rouge: Louisiana State University Press, 1979); Kluger, *Simple Justice* (1975).

CIVIL RIGHTS ACT OF 1957. The first civil rights* bill since Reconstruction, this act created the U.S. Commission on Civil Rights* and changed the Civil Rights Section into the much stronger Civil Rights Division* in the Department of Justice,* to be directed by an assistant attorney general. This bill was advocated by the Eisenhower* administration and Attorney General Herbert Brownell and was enacted with the support of House Speaker Sam Rayburn and Senate Majority Leader Lyndon B. Johnson.* As a result of this act and subsequent legislation in 1964, 1965, and 1968, the Civil Rights Division grew from a staff of 29 lawyers and 30 clerical workers to a staff of more than 400 by 1980, with the caseload increasing from 143 at the end of 1957 to 2,300 by mid-1982.

References: O'Reilly, *Nixon's Piano* (1995); Abraham and Perry, *Freedom and the Court* (1994); Duram, *A Moderate among Extremists* (1981).

CIVIL RIGHTS ACT OF 1964. The most comprehensive civil rights* legislation in U.S. history, this act provided the federal government with strong enforcement powers in civil rights, including the authority to withhold federal funds and file suits against segregated school districts; it is generally credited with being the most significant instrument that led to the desegregation* of the South's* schools. The act gave the Attorney General the authority to file school desegregation* suits on behalf of private citizens who were victims, or the parents of victims, of racial discrimination* in public schools or colleges (Title IV). Moreover, the act also empowered the Department of Health, Education, and Welfare* (HEW), now the Department of Education,* to withhold federal funds from school districts or colleges that continued to discriminate (Title VI). Thus with this legislation school desegregation efforts were shared between the courts and the federal government; the political burden of desegregation was now shared, and the inevitability of school desegregation was established.

The act was passed in response to the assassination of President John F. Kennedy* during the beginning of the Lyndon B. Johnson* presidency. The bill had been developed by Kennedy's administration, in part as a response to the problems encountered by civil rights advocates in Birmingham, Alabama, in May 1963, and had been submitted to Congress on June 19, 1963. Johnson maneuvered the omnibus bill through Congress despite a southern filibuster following Kennedy's untimely death. Johnson signed the bill on July 2, 1964.

The legislation was quite comprehensive. Title I prohibited a number of southern practices to limit black voting, including the use of overly strict literacy tests. Title II was the most controversial part of the bill, guaranteeing blacks equal access to public accommodations such as hotels, motels, restaurants, and places of amusement. Title III gave the Attorney General the authority to file suits for the desegregation of public facilities other than public schools. Title

IV required the U.S. Office of Education* to provide technical assistance to school districts developing school desegregation plans,* including establishing desegregation assistance centers,* and authorized the Attorney General to file suits to force school desegregation. Title V increased the powers of the U.S. Commission on Civil Rights* and extended its life for another four years. Title VI, which became the most influential section of the act, authorized the cutting off of federal funds where discrimination was evident. Title VII established the Equal Employment Opportunity Commission and outlawed job discrimination. Title VIII obliged the U.S. Census Bureau to collect voting statistics by race. Title IX authorized the Department of Justice* to intervene in civil rights cases. Title X established the Community Relations Service* to serve as a force for mediation. Title XI spelled out the powers of the Attorney General in civil rights cases.

While the congressional and public debate focused on the legislation's public accommodations section, it was the section on withholding federal funds that ultimately proved to be the most far-reaching and effective provision. Title VI gave the federal government the authority to withhold federal funds from school districts that did not comply with HEW school desegregation guidelines. The Office for Civil Rights* (OCR) collected data on the status of desegregation in individual school districts. The OCR was given the responsibility to investigate complaints of discrimination brought to it by individuals and groups, and the Attorney General was given the power to bring suit in federal court against segregated school districts. School districts and universities were given time to voluntarily comply with OCR regulations. When compliance is not achieved, OCR initiates an administrative hearing or may refer the matter to the Department of Justice for the initiation of court proceedings.

Title VI required nondiscrimination in any program that received federal funds. Any such program found to be discriminatory could lose its federal funding. This covered most public schools and colleges as well as many private institutions of higher learning. Under this provision, according to John Williams III (1987, p.x) over time "19 states have been found guilty of operating de jure* segregated higher education facilities." The states are Alabama, Arkansas, Delaware, Florida, Georgia, Kentucky, Louisiana, Maryland, Mississippi, Missouri, Ohio, Oklahoma, Pennsylvania, North Carolina, South Carolina, Tennessee, Texas, Virginia, and West Virginia. Specifically, the Office for Civil Rights of the Department of HEW was given the responsibility for conducting compliance reviews in higher education, which it did in 1968 and 1969. During this period it requested plans from ten states found to be in noncompliance. With the election of Richard M. Nixon,* enforcement was relaxed, although this was successfully challenged in the *Adams v. Richardson** (1973) suit.

This law thus provided desegregation forces with the power of the federal government in investigations of segregation,* enforcement by the Attorney General, and the threat of withholding funds. This act added to the threat of court orders to end segregation the threat of administrative orders or guidelines from federal executive agencies and the loss of federal funds for noncompliance.

This law had a major impact on school desegregation. In 1965, the first year of enforcement, almost every rural school district in the South began desegregating. (Note that the passage of the Elementary and Secondary Education Act of 1965,* which was the first general education support program and which had a funding formula that favored poorer southern school districts, provided ammunition for the enforcement of the Civil Rights Act of 1964.) The following year faculty desegregation began, and the expectation was that desegregation would be completed by the fall of 1969. In the decades following the passage of the Civil Rights Act of 1964 the Justice Department initiated over 500 school desegregation suits, and the Department of Health, Education, and Welfare brought 600 more actions. HEW guidelines called for all grades to be desegregated by the fall of 1967. This action alone led to more desegregation than the ten years of previous court action.

Title IV of the act provides for desegregation assistance centers to aid the technical planning process. Twenty-six desegregation assistance centers existed by 1974, mostly at universities. They focused their activities on human-relations training for school personnel and educational changes to help the school desegregation process. The act also called for the Commissioner of Education to conduct a survey to determine the status of equal opportunity among various racial and ethnic groups in the nation. This resulted in the Coleman Report,* published in 1966.

While the legislation played a very significant role in desegregating the schools of the South, implementation of the legislation involved some problems. The threat of a cutoff was more useful as a threat than in its application. In essence it is an all-or-nothing device; either a district is discriminating or not. The cutoff thus would often hurt the students most in need of help and cause a public backlash against the agency that stops the funds and the very program established to aid those in need.

The legislation contained two restrictions. The act defined desegregation as "the assignment of students to public schools and within such schools without regard to their race, color, religion, or national origin, but 'desegregation' shall not mean the assignment of students to public schools in order to overcome racial imbalance.*" In another section the legislation included another limitation: "Nothing herein shall empower any official or court of the United States to issue any order seeking to achieve a racial balance* in any school by requiring the transportation of pupils or students from one school to another or one school district to another in order to achieve such racial balance, or otherwise enlarge the existing power of the court to insure compliance with constitutional standards." The authors and supporters of these restrictions hoped to forestall busing* remedies. The federal courts interpreted these restrictions as a limit on actions to overcome de facto school segregation,* but not state-imposed or de jure school segregation.

Gary Orfield,* in his detailed book (1969) on the implementation issues that followed the passage of this bill, describes the struggle between constitutional rights, as expressed by the U.S. Supreme Court* in *Brown** (1954) and by

Congress in this act, and the decentralized structure of power in the nation. This struggle moved to the federal bureaucracy, the courts, and meeting rooms of appropriations subcommittees with the passage of this bill. For example, Orfield describes the conflict between the U.S. Office of Education and Mayor Richard Daley* of the city of Chicago over a cutoff of funds to the Chicago public schools. Mayor Daley forced the Office of Education to back off from its funds cutoff.

References: Robert D. Loevy, ed., *The Civil Rights Act of 1964: The Passage of the Law That Ended Racial Segregation* (Albany: State University of New York Press, 1997); John B. Williams III, *Desegregating America's Colleges and Universities* (1987); Charles Whelen and Barbara Whelen, *The Longest Debate: A Legislative History of the 1964 Civil Rights Act* (Cabin John, MD: Seven Locks Press, 1985); Marcus and Stickney, *Race and Education* (1981); Orfield, *Must We Bus?* (1978); Beryl A. Radin, *Implementation, Change, and the Federal Bureaucracy: School Desegregation Policy in H.E.W., 1964–1968* (New York: Teachers College Press, 1977); Orfield, *The Reconstruction of Southern Education* (1969).

CIVIL RIGHTS CASES, 108 U.S. 3 (1883). These cases combined five challenges to the Civil Rights Act of 1875,* which was aimed at helping blacks become full citizens of the United States by making it a federal crime to deny blacks access to hotels, theaters, or transportation. The U.S. Supreme Court* found that the law was unconstitutional on the ground that the Fourteenth Amendment* only applied to state action and did not permit the regulation of the private actions of individuals. This decision greatly limited the rights of blacks in individual states. Only Justice John Marshall Harlan* dissented.

References: Nowak and Rotunda, *Constitutional Law* (1995); Abraham and Perry, *Freedom and the Court* (1994); Grossman, *The ABC-CLIO Companion to the Civil Rights Movement* (1993); Kluger, *Simple Justice* (1975).

CIVIL RIGHTS COMMISSION. *See* **U.S. Commission on Civil Rights**.

CIVIL RIGHTS DIVISION (CRD). Component of the U.S. Department of Justice* formed by the Civil Rights Act of 1957* to enforce federal antidiscrimination statutes. The CRD enforces federal statutes prohibiting discrimination* on the basis of race, sex, handicap, religion, or national origin. The division enforces the Civil Rights Acts of 1957, 1960, 1964,* and 1968 along with the Voting Rights Act of 1965 as amended in subsequent years and other legislation in the disabilities and additional areas. The Justice Department has the authority to go to court to obtain an order to desegregate a public school or public college.

The division, which in 1995 had 252 attorneys and 295 paralegal and support personnel, is directed by the Assistant Attorney General for Civil Rights. The CRD is located in Washington, D.C.; it has no regional offices. The division is significantly involved in filing *amicus curiae** (friend of the court) briefs in federal court cases, especially where the case has implications for enforcement responsibilities. For example, the division participated as *amicus curiae* in the U.S. Supreme Court* in the *Missouri v. Jenkins** (1995) case, arguing that the schools in Kansas City had not been desegregated and that it was appropriate to use test scores as one indication of the success of school desegregation.* The CRD has major enforcement responsibilities and as such develops model regulations, policies, and enforcement standards and procedures and provides technical assistance and training to improve the compliance efforts of other federal agencies.

The CRD has an Equal Opportunities Section that enforces federal statutes that prohibit public school officials from discriminating, many emanating from *Brown v. Board of Education** (1954) and subsequent decisions. The division's work covers elementary and secondary as well as higher education. The division works toward traditional school desegregation plans,* as well as dealing with second-generation problems.* For example, the division investigated complaints filed in Randolph County School District in Alabama. It found that black high-school students were consistently assigned to remedial classes and white students to advanced classes. The school district agreed to correct this problem. The division has played a role in the enforcement at the higher-education level, including the *United States v. Fordice** (1992) case. The division's work may result in court orders or consent decrees.* Its efforts are not limited to school desegregation issues; it has played a lead role in sex discrimination cases, including the challenge to Virginia Military Institute's male-only admissions policy.

As of 1995 the CRD had hundreds of open school desegregation cases, many of which have been inactive for 12 years according to the Citizens' Commission on Civil Rights.* Brannan (in Yu and Taylor) argues that this office needs to define a set of criteria to use to determine if districts have met unitary status,* consistent with the *Freeman v. Pitts** (1992) and *Board of Education of Oklahoma City v. Dowell** (1991) cases. Landsberg (1996) reports that in 1996 the CRD had only 13 attorneys working to enforce *Brown* and related decisions, not nearly enough to monitor the hundreds of court orders and consent decrees while reviewing higher-education segregation* and discrimination by sex and disability. However, overall funding for the CRD and the number of staff overall have been increasing under the Reagan,* Bush, and Clinton administrations, from \$16.5 million and a staff of 405 during fiscal year 1981 to almost \$60 million and a staff of 569 in fiscal year 1994.

References: *Catalog of Federal Domestic Assistance, 1996*; Brian K. Landsberg, "The Federal Government and the Promise of Brown," in *Brown v. Board of Education*, ed. Lagemann and Miller (1996), 27–36; Civil Rights Division, Department of Justice, *Civil Rights Division: Activities and Programs* (Washington, DC: Civil Rights Division, June 1995); Yu and Taylor, eds., *New Challenges* (1995); Liss and Taylor, eds., *New Opportunities* (1993); Govan and Taylor, eds., *One Nation Indivisible* (1989); Orfield, *Must We Bus?* (1978).

CIVIL RIGHTS MOVEMENT. Intense protest activity during the period from the *Brown v. Board of Education** decision in 1954 through about 1970 by individuals and groups to expand the rights of black citizens in the United States. The U.S. Supreme Court's* decision to overturn *Plessy v. Ferguson** and remove a major legal impediment to equality, the separate but equal* doctrine, led to demonstrations for equal treatment under the law. On December 1, 1955, Rosa Parks refused to move to the back of a bus in Montgomery, Alabama, thus inspiring a massive boycott of the public bus system in that southern city and widespread boycotts, sit-ins, and freedom rides throughout the South* to protest segregation.* The Reverend Martin Luther King* became the leader of the Montgomery boycott and rose to national prominence in the civil rights movement. The U.S. Supreme Court under Chief Justice Earl Warren* played an active role in the early 1960s in overturning local laws as unconstitutional, including the law requiring the Montgomery buses to be segregated. After the 1963 March on Washington and the assassination of President John F. Kennedy,* Congress passed the Civil Rights Act of 1964* and the Voting Rights Act of 1965. The civil rights movement resulted in increasing equality of opportunity and equal justice for blacks through judicial decisions such as *Brown*, executive actions such as presidential executive orders, and legislative actions such as the Civil Rights Act of 1964. The advocacy and success of this movement ultimately led to similar efforts by other minorities such as Indians, gays, women, and handicapped individuals and groups. The movement ended in the late 1960s with the assassination of Martin Luther King and the rise of black power.*

Characterized by *Britannica Online* as "a revolution in race relations," the civil rights movement generated much violence. In 1962, for example, the conflict over the admission of James Meredith* to the University of Mississippi led to a night of rioting and the death of two people. In the summer of 1964 three young civil rights workers became martyrs to the cause after being murdered by the Ku Klux Klan* in Mississippi.

References: *Britannica Online* (1996); Jones-Wilson et al., *Encyclopedia of African-American Education* (1996); Hall, *Oxford Companion* (1992); Levy, *Documentary History of the Modern Civil Rights Movement* (1992); Kluger, *Simple Justice* (1975).

CLARK, KENNETH BANCROFT (born July 24, 1914, Panama Canal Zone). Black psychologist whose landmark research on black children's self-concept played an important role in school desegregation* court cases and was cited by the U.S. Supreme Court* as part of Footnote 11* in the *Brown v. Board of Education** ruling in 1954. Clark and his wife's "doll test," where black children were asked to select among black and white dolls to respond to questions about their feelings, led to their conclusion that black children had a self-hatred brought on by school segregation.*

Clark was born as a U.S. citizen in the Panama Canal Zone. Clark's mother took him and his two-year-old sister to the United States when he was five years old. His father, a passenger agent with the United Fruit Company, vigorously objected to the move, and his parents eventually divorced. Clark's mother took a job as a seamstress in a New York City garment-district sweatshop, where she became a leader in the International Ladies' Garment Workers Union. After attending public schools in Harlem in New York City, Kenneth Clark received his A.B. in psychology from Howard University in 1935 and his M.S. in psychology (1936) and Ph.D. in experimental psychology (1940) from Columbia University. He met Mamie Phipps as an undergraduate at Howard, convinced her to change majors from mathematics to psychology, and after graduation taught her in an abnormal psychology course. She began the study of black children's self-identity that was to be the focus of their research after their marriage in 1938. They began publishing their work in the *Journal of Social Psychology* in 1939.

Kenneth Clark served in the psychology department of the City College of New York from 1942 to 1975, including his terms as a professor, 1960–1970, and Distinguished University Professor, 1970–1975. In 1975 Clark was named professor emeritus. Clark served as a consultant to the NAACP Legal Defense Fund* beginning in 1950. From 1939 to 1941 Clark worked with Gunnar Myrdal* on the research that led to *An American Dilemma.** Clark was president of the Metropolitan Research Center from 1967 to 1975 as well as president of consulting firms from 1975 on. Clark is the author or coauthor of eight books, including *Dark Ghetto* (1965), which examined the effects of residential segregation, and *Prejudice and Your Child* (1955), based on his report utilized by the U.S. Supreme Court. Clark served as a member of the New York State Board of Regents for over 20 years (1966–1986). He has been recognized by many national awards and honors, including his selection as the president of the American Psychological Association in 1970–1971 and honorary degrees from Princeton University, Johns Hopkins University, the City University of New York, and North Carolina State University.

Clark, while a young assistant professor of psychology at the City College of New York, was asked to testify in the *Briggs** (1955) case by NAACP* lawyer Thurgood Marshall.* Clark's research, completed with his wife, Mamie Phipps Clark, who had by this time earned her Ph.D. in psychology from Columbia University, examined the effect of segregation on the self-image of black children using projective tests. Clark traveled to Clarendon County and tested 16 black children. He presented the children with white and black dolls, identical except for color, and 10 of the children reported their preference for the white over the black doll. Nine picked the white doll as the "nice" one, and 11 chose the black doll as the "bad" one. Seven chose the white doll as looking like them. These results were similar to earlier work the Clarks had done. Marshall sought to have placed on the record the damages that occur from school segregation, and Clark's testimony provided evidence that segregation harms black children. In his testimony Clark argued that discrimination,* prejudice,* and segregation had caused the black children to have feelings of inferiority and confusion in self-image. Clark's testimony was cited by the Court in Footnote 11 in the *Brown v. Board of Education* decision as evidence of the harmful effects of school segregation.

John W. Davis,* who represented South Carolina before the U.S. Supreme Court in the *Briggs* case, was critical of Clark's testimony because of his finding that black children's self-image was lower in the North, where schools were not de jure segregated,* than in the South,* where they were segregated by law. (One could argue that segregation that exists that is not required by law is more harmful than segregation forced by legislation.) Kluger (1975) notes that Clark's testimony was hardly attacked in the *Briggs* trial, but could have been vulnerable to criticisms of the small sample size, fuzzy definitions, and inadequate specification of the causal variable, that is, to what degree the cause of low self-esteem* was school segregation, more general segregation, prejudice, discrimination, or other factors.

Kenneth Clark has taken an active role in helping minority youth in New York City. In the spring of 1954 Clark charged that de facto school segregation* existed in a number of New York City public schools. After denials, an investigation supported his charges and did lead to system reforms. Clark helped to specify the reforms that were needed. In 1962 Clark spearheaded the organization of Harlem Youth Opportunities Unlimited (HARYOU) and was named chairman. The organization worked to reduce unemployment, dropouts, and delinquencies among the area's youth and received significant funding through the poverty program. In 1967 Clark established the Metropolitan Applied Research Center (MARC), a nonprofit corporation in Washington, D.C., that assisted the school district with programs for improving student performance. In 1975 Clark left teaching and, with his family, founded a consulting firm (Clark, Phipps, Clark, and Harris, Inc.) that worked with corporations on their racial policies and affirmative action* hiring policies.

Works about: Greenberg, *Crusaders in the Courts* (1994); *Who's Who in America* (Chicago: Reed Reference, 1994), 676; Grossman, *The ABC-CLIO Companion to the Civil Rights Movement* (1993); Marcus and Stickney, *Race and Education* (1981); Kluger, *Simple Justice* (1975); *Current Biography Yearbook 1964* (New York: H. W. Wilson Company, 1964), 80–83.

Works by: *Dark Ghetto: Dilemmas of Social Power* (New York: Harper and Row, 1965); *Prejudice and Your Child* (Boston: Beacon Press, 1955).

CLUSTERING. A common technique in school desegregation plans* involving the reassignment of students at two or more schools to different grades at these schools to desegregate the schools. For example, when two schools are involved (pairing* schools), a K–5 black school and a K–5 white school are reassigned so that all pupils are assigned to one school for K–2 and the other for grades 3–5. In clustering this same reassignment is done with three or more schools, for example, pupils from three schools are reassigned to schools serving grades

K–1, 2–3, and 4–5. Further details depend on school capacity, school suitability for different grade levels, and the demographic characteristics of the students in the area. In some instances students in all but one grade (e.g., K–5) are assigned to one school and those in the single grade (e.g., grade 6) are assigned to the second school. This is called a grade center, in this specific example a 6th-grade center.

Since city schools generally have far greater capacity than suburban schools, when this technique is applied in a metropolitan plan,* several suburban schools are generally clustered with a single city school. This results in city black students often being assigned to suburban schools for many more years than their suburban white counterparts being assigned to city schools. This approach is generally not used at the high-school level so that high schools can offer the full grade-level range.

"Satellite zoning*" refers to the use of this technique where the school attendance areas are not contiguous. This technique is necessary where there are large black and white residential areas and pairing or clustering only adjacent schools is not possible. Satellite zoning may allow for an equalization of travel times across schools. David Armor* (1995) also calls this pocket or island zoning; Gordon Foster* (1973) calls it "skip zoning."

References: Armor, *Forced Justice* (1995); Rossell, "The Convergence of Black and White Attitudes on School Desegregation Issues during the Four Decade Evolution of the Plans" (January 1995); Richard A. Pride and J. David Woodard, *The Burden of Busing: The Politics of Desegregation in Nashville, Tennessee* (Knoxville: University of Tennessee Press, 1985); Hughes, Gordon, and Hillman, *Desegregating America's Schools* (1980); Gordon Foster, "Desegregating Urban Schools: A Review of Techniques," *Harvard Educational Review* 43, no. 1 (February 1973): 5–36.

COLEMAN, JAMES SAMUEL (born May 12, 1926, Bedford, Indiana–died March 25, 1995, Chicago, Illinois). Prominent sociological researcher whose works, including the Coleman Report* on student achievement* and his report on white flight,* have been at the center of the school desegregation* debate for over 30 years. Coleman received his B.S. from Purdue University in 1949 in chemical engineering. He changed fields and earned his Ph.D. from Columbia University in sociology in 1955. Coleman became a research associate at the Bureau of Applied Research at Columbia University from 1953 to 1955 and then assistant professor at the University of Chicago from 1956 to 1959. He switched his academic career between the University of Chicago and Johns Hopkins University as associate professor and then professor at Johns Hopkins from 1959 to 1973 and professor at the University of Chicago from 1973 on.

Coleman was a member of the President's Science Advisory Committee (1970–1972) and the author of over 30 major books and reports, including *The Adolescent Society* (1961) and several works on mathematics in sociology. He was a Guggenheim fellow at the Russell Sage Foundation. Coleman received much national recognition, as manifested by several honorary degrees, including those from Purdue, the State University of New York, and the Free University of Berlin.

Coleman was the lead author of the so-called Coleman Report in 1966, which reported on the school achievement of a large sample of American majority and minority schoolchildren. The report indicated that while social background played the major role in determining student achievement, school desegregation could help to change this determination. As Wolters notes (1996:343), one article even called him "The Scholar Who Inspired Busing.*" But nearly a decade later, Coleman indicated second thoughts about desegregation, or at least busing. Coleman's opposition to busing was signaled by his desegregation report on white flight issued in 1975, which indicated that desegregation increased the separation of blacks and whites rather than bringing them together. In Coleman's eyes busing had increased white flight from cities, and city school systems had been unresponsive and inadequate in maintaining discipline. In the 1980s Coleman's work focused on the degree to which student achievement was greater in private and parochial schools than in public schools.

Coleman's work was always central to the issues of school desegregation and always provoked controversy. Some members of the American Sociological Association tried to have Coleman expelled because of his 1975 work on white flight; the movement failed, and Coleman was elected president of the association in 1991. Coleman died of prostate cancer at age 68 at the University of Chicago hospital.

Works about: Wolters, *Right Turn* (1996); "James Coleman, Author of Landmark Education Studies, Dies," *Education Week* 14, no. 8 (April 5, 1995): 15; Robert D. McFadden, "Dr. James Coleman, 68, Dies; Worked to Help Foster Busing," *New York Times*, March 28, 1995, B11; *Who's Who in America* (Chicago: Reed Reference, 1994), 720.

Works by: *Equality and Achievement in Education* (Boulder, CO: Westview Press, 1990); with Sara D. Kelly and John A. Moore, *Trends in School Segregation, 1968–73* (Washington, DC: Urban Institute, August 1975); James S. Coleman et al., *Equality of Educational Opportunity* (Washington, DC: U.S. Government Printing Office, 1996).

COLEMAN REPORT. The popular title of the 1966 study *Equality of Educational Opportunity* based on a 1965 survey of 600,000 students in segregated and desegregated schools commissioned by the Office of Education* as required in the Civil Rights Act of 1964* (Section 402, Title IV). The survey was conducted by the National Center for Educational Statistics in the Office of Education with consultants and contractors. The survey was to document the "lack of equal educational opportunities* for individuals by reason of race, color, religion, or national origin in public educational institutions at all levels in the United States." It was assumed that educational resources would be demonstrated to be inferior for blacks and other minority groups, and that this would explain lagging minority achievement on standardized tests. Using tests of verbal ability, reading comprehension, and arithmetic skill, James Coleman* and his associates attempted to determine the role of various school and home factors, including school desegregation,* on student achievement.* The report was referred to as the Coleman Report after the project's director, a professor at Johns Hopkins University at the time. The Coleman Report focused on four questions: (1) the extent of segregation of six racial and ethnic groups (blacks, native Americans, Asian Americans, Puerto Ricans, Mexican Americans, and whites); (2) the extent of equal educational opportunity as measured by tangible factors such as textbooks and libraries; (3) student performance on standardized tests; and (4) the relationship between student achievement and school variables.

The Coleman Report established the level of school segregation* in the United States. The report showed that a dozen years after *Brown** whites still went to schools almost exclusively with whites and a majority of blacks went to schools that were majority black. It showed, for example, that even in the North 72 percent of black first graders attended predominantly black schools.

The report shook experts who expected to have documentation of the discrepancies between black and white students on school facilities and resources (expenditures, teacher backgrounds, equipment, textbooks), especially in the South.* Surprisingly, the Coleman Report found that there were few differences, and those that existed might favor blacks or whites.

The gap between black and white student achievement was documented. Black students were two to six years behind white students in reading, verbal, and mathematics performance throughout the nation. But the report also showed that black achievement was closer to white achievement in first grade than in later grades, suggesting that changing school policies would have a limited impact on the black-white achievement gap.

The major finding of the Coleman Report was that home environment explained far more of the differences in achievement than did differences in school resources. Black and white schools did not differ markedly in facilities or services. The differences that were found did not explain much of the achievement gaps between the races. Coleman and colleagues concluded that the inequalities of school achievement were primarily a function of children's homes, neighborhood, and peer environment, not school resources. The researchers did determine that the educational aspirations and backgrounds of other students at a school impacted achievement, and that blacks achieved more in desegregated schools.

The data generated by this study were severely criticized and carefully reanalyzed by several other researchers. Among the criticisms were that this was a cross-sectional, not experimental, design. The report did not prove that increased resources would not help disadvantaged students. Other critics argued that the most significant school factors were not investigated, for example, curriculum and school programs. Despite the criticisms, this report provided ammunition for desegregation advocates and inspired policy research for years afterward.

References: Armor, *Forced Justice* (1995); Armor, ''The Evidence on Busing'' (Summer 1972); Frederick Mosteller and Daniel P. Moynihan, eds., *On Equality of Educa-*

tional Opportunity (New York: Random House, 1972); James S. Coleman, "The Concept of Equality of Educational Opportunity," *Harvard Educational Review* 38 (1968): 7–22; Coleman et al., *Equality of Educational Opportunity* (1966).

COLUMBUS BOARD OF EDUCATION V. PENICK, 443 U.S. 449 (1979). U.S. Supreme Court* decision that reaffirmed its decision in *Keyes** (1973) that given proof that purposeful school segregation* had been adopted in a substantial portion of a school district, a presumption was created that the school board had indeed either practiced systemwide segregation or tolerated segregation effects. Thus districtwide relief in the form of school desegregation* was warranted. If the district had been segregated when *Brown** was decided, the board had the affirmative obligation to desegregate the district's schools. This decision came after decisions that had slowed school desegregation, that is, *Milliken v. Bradley** (1974) and *Pasadena City Board of Education v. Spangler** (1976).

References: Armor, *Forced Justice* (1995); Hall, *Oxford Companion* (1992); Dimond, *Beyond Busing* (1985).

COMMISSION ON INTERRACIAL COOPERATION. *See* **Southern Regional Council**.

COMMUNITY CONTROL. The transfer of authority from the central school bureaucracy to community-elected leaders in various parts of large city school districts initiated in the 1960s, a strategy often resulting from frustration with the lack of progress in school desegregation* as well as frustration with low achievement, attendance, and graduation rates of minority students. The assumption was that community control would shift the locus of control to more sensitive and responsive school officials and that the values and needs of minority groups would be better met and equal educational opportunity* would be more likely to be achieved. Thus the community-control and decentralization movement was based on a critique of bureaucracy integrated with democratic theory and black power* and black nationalism.*

Community control had its origin in New York City, where the Ford Foundation played a leading role. In November 1967 the Mayor's Advisory Panel on Decentralization issued its report, generally referred to as the Bundy Plan after its chairman, McGeorge Bundy, then Ford Foundation president. The report called for dividing the huge New York City School District into 30 to 60 districts with boards composed of parent-elected representatives and mayoral appointees. The boards would be given final authority over budget, curriculum, and personnel decisions. Despite intense educator opposition, three small demonstration districts were established, including one in Ocean Hill–Brownsville. The state legislature limited the authority of these new districts to the selection of the superintendent and a few other specified powers and left the remaining powers to the discretion of the city school board. In Ocean Hill–Brownsville the governing board of teachers, administrators, and black and Latino parents took actions that led to the dismissal of several teachers who were viewed as antiboard. When the board refused to reinstate the teachers, the teachers' union called a citywide strike. A bitter conflict ensued, and the board was ultimately dismantled. Thus in New York City community control resulted in tremendous political and racial conflict involving the teachers' union (the United Federation of Teachers, an American Federation of Teachers affiliate), the Council of Supervisory Organizations, and black community leaders.

Proponents of community control sought more accountability of school administrators to their minority communities, more parent and community participation in decision making, greater innovation, a better match between the needs of the community and the school curriculum, more job opportunities for community residents in their schools, greater development of community leaders, increased legitimacy of the school as an institution, and higher student achievement.* Opponents feared a return to patronage, corruption, and increased school segregation,* all of which occurred to some extent. Few would argue that community control was the panacea for educational change and improvement for minorities in New York City.

After studying decentralization and community control in five large school districts (New York City, Detroit, Chicago, Dade County, Florida, and Los Angeles), Lewis and Nakagawa argue that "decentralization 'solves' the American Dilemma* by subordinating African Americans in the competition for educational resources while legitimizing that subordination in terms of equality and power" (1995:xi). That is, blacks gain control of urban schools, but the major resources, now in the suburbs, have been separated from their grasp. The American Dilemma became bureaucratized as the "demand for racial equality was transformed into the demand to reorganize bureaucratic decision making" (6). Thus the disadvantaged are given a voice in government, but the role of the elites is preserved. Tensions are reduced; the status quo remains. They also point out that while the community-control movement led to black involvement in formerly all-white school bureaucracies in the 1960s, the 1990s movement has divided the poor in cities from the black middle class who now control the school bureaucracies.

Lewis and Nakagawa also question several assumptions of the movement. First, it was assumed that individual mobility would result from an improved school bureaucracy, but the labor market and residential segregation make this a more complicated relationship. Second, it was assumed that school governance would affect student achievement, but this has not been established. Third, it was assumed that power and authority could be transferred through legislative action, but bureaucracy and power are not that easily shifted. Finally, it was assumed that parents would participate in the new political system, but parents have not shown this increased commitment.

Community control should be differentiated from school decentralization. School decentralization may involve changes in governance or administration. In the former, power is shifted to subdistricts of the school district and to parents; in the latter, administrators of geographical subunits increase their authority. Critics of school decentralization have argued that administrative but not governance decentralization took place in districts such as New York City and Detroit in the reforms of the 1960s. The parents and community representatives did not gain influence over the schools, nor did the day-to-day activities and processes in the schools in decentralized districts change or improve.

References: Lewis and Nakagawa, *Race and Educational Reform in the American Metropolis* (1995); Orfield, *Must We Bus?* (1978); Alan A. Altshuler, *Community Control: The Black Demand for Participation in Large American Cities* (New York: Pegasus, 1970); Mario D. Fantini, Marilyn Gittell, and Richard Magat, *Community Control and the Urban School* (New York: Praeger, 1970); Henry Levin, ed., *Community Control of Schools* (New York: Clarion, 1970); Maurice R. Berube and Marilyn Gittell, eds., *Confrontation at Ocean Hill–Brownsville* (New York: Praeger, 1969).

COMMUNITY RELATIONS SERVICE (CRS). An office of the U.S. Department of Justice,* originally established under Title X of the Civil Rights Act of 1964,* which assists "communities in preventing and resolving disputes, disagreements, and difficulties arising from actions, policies, and practices that are perceived to be discriminatory on the basis of race, color, or national origin" in education, business, and public accommodations, according to the 1996 *Catalog of Federal Domestic Assistance.*

The CRS was originally placed in the U.S. Department of Commerce with the expectation that it would focus on racial conflicts over public accommodations, which had been the most controversial aspect of the Civil Rights Act of 1964, but the agency was moved to the Justice Department in 1966 by President Lyndon B. Johnson* to strengthen the operation and coordinate civil rights* programs. Members of the CRS staff utilize the processes of mediation, conciliation, technical assistance, and training techniques in communities to help them resolve their conflicts. Using conciliation, the CRS attempts to improve communications among the parties in a conflict. Through mediation the CRS attempts to obtain an oral or written agreement to settle disputes. The CRS provides technical assistance in community meetings, task forces, and conferences. CRS has conducted training in conflict-resolution techniques and has produced resource materials on this and related topics. The CRS does not take sides in such conflicts but rather works toward helping the parties in a dispute reach their own agreement. In fiscal year 1995 the CRS reported working on 1,404 cases requiring its conflict-prevention and resolution services. Not only has the CRS played a role in resolving disputes, it also has tried to prevent problems by working with minority groups and media in local communities to change the treatment of minorities by the media and to build constructive police-community relations. The CRS works through ten regional offices.

During the 1969–1970 school year the CRS was given a significant increase in staff to assist in the peaceful desegregation* of the schools in the South* following the U.S. Supreme Court's* order to proceed without delay. Between

August 1970 and February 1971 the CRS assigned 47 professionals who helped 492 school districts in 409 counties in 9 states in the South. The CRS created biracial parent councils as part of its effort in a number of communities. In Boston U.S. District Court* Judge W. Arthur Garrity* called on the CRS to help achieve peace, and the CRS helped to establish multiracial parent and student councils, a school security force, and an improved curriculum. In general, CRS's activities in school desegregation* cases have included the following activities: public safety and school security, citizen involvement, improved discipline codes, conciliation of disputes, identifying outside sources of assistance, providing liaison among affected parties, agencies, and institutions, training for police and school personnel, and improving communications. In the mid-1970s the CRS was active in working on issues relating to the Hispanic community.

In its early years the CRS almost exclusively handled conflicts among blacks and whites. In 1983, however, the CRS was given the responsibility for providing Cuban and Haitian refugees humanitarian assistance, placement, and resettlement services under Title V of the Refugee Education Assistance Act of 1980 and an executive order. In 1995 the Republican House majority tried to drastically cut the CRS, but Attorney General Janet Reno's strong support saved the agency.

References: *Catalog of Federal Domestic Assistance, 1996; Community Relations Service Annual Report* (for fiscal year 1993), 30th Anniversary (Washington, DC: Community Relations Service, U.S. Department of Justice, 1994); Deborah Lutterbeck, "The Mediators," *Common Cause Magazine* 20, no.1 (Spring 1994): 28–33; Community Relations Service, Department of Justice, and the National Center for Quality Integrated Education, *Desegregation without Turmoil: The Role of the Multi-racial Community Coalition in Preparing for Smooth Transition* (New York: National Conference of Christians and Jews, 1976); Ben Holman, "Desegregation and the Community Relations Service," *Integrated Education* 13, no. 1 (1975): 27–29.

COMPENSATORY EDUCATION. Educational programs that aim to compensate for the inadequate educational background of students caused by economic and social problems or restrictions by offering them an enriched educational experience. Such enrichment has included smaller class size, additional reading instruction, tutors, textbooks, computers, and other special equipment. Compensatory programs have been viewed as alternatives to school desegregation* and as components of ancillary programs* to prepare black students for school desegregation or to help black students who cannot be involved in school desegregation plans.* While the focus of compensatory education programs has been at the elementary and secondary levels, higher-education programs have also been adopted.

The educational programs of the federal War on Poverty were built on the premise of the need for compensatory education to help the millions of children in poverty whose educational achievement was low. These programs, begun in the 1960s, include Head Start and Title I (formerly Chapter 1) of the Elementary and Secondary Education Act of 1965* as well as the Job Corps, Upward Bound, and the Neighborhood Youth Corps. These programs have been evaluated many times and have been found to have had some limited success in increasing the achievement of disadvantaged, and frequently minority, pupils. The increase in student achievement* of blacks on standardized tests, including the National Assessment of Educational Progress, over the last two decades has been credited in part to compensatory education programs. David Armor,* however, has argued that the black improvement is due to rising socioeconomic levels rather than compensatory education (or school desegregation), which does not seem to have a large-enough effect to explain the great improvement. In 1997 the results of a longitudinal study of 27,000 students indicated that over a four-year period Title I students gained no more in achievement than those who did not receive Title I services.

Compensatory education is criticized for several reasons. Some criticize its premise, that government needs to ''compensate'' for cultural deprivation. Critics maintain that the fault lies not in the culture of students but the failures of schools or of society, which forces parents to socialize their children in ways to survive in their subordinate status. Others maintain that compensatory education offers more of the same instead of reforming the education system that is failing students. Still others argue that school desegregation is needed to ensure that students receive an appropriate education.

See also **Milliken v. Bradley (Milliken II)**.

References: Armor, "Why Is Black Achievement Rising?" (Summer 1992); Edward L. McDill, "Compensatory Education," in *Encyclopedia of Educational Research*, ed. Alkin (1992), 208–21; John U. Ogbu, "Social Stratification and the Socialization of Competence," in *Readings on Equal Education* 7 (1977–1979), ed. Barnett and Harrington (1984), 1–20; Benjamin S. Bloom, Allison Davis, and Robert Hess, *Compensatory Education for Cultural Deprivation* (New York: Holt, Rinehart, and Winston, 1965).

COMPROMISE OF 1877. The name given to an alleged agreement between the national government and the southern states under which the federal government purportedly agreed to end the military occupation of the South,* concluded efforts to transform southern society, and allowed white supremacy in the region in return for southern support for the Union, national supremacy, and the presidential election of Rutherford B. Hayes over Samuel J. Tilden. (Tilden had won more popular votes but had not received a majority of electoral votes, and the election outcome, disputed in several states, was held up in Congress.) This ended Reconstruction and, with the U.S. Supreme Court's* decision in *Plessy v. Ferguson*,* led to the segregated South. Gillette (1979) argues that no such deal was made and that the end of Reconstruction by this time was inevitable.

References: Thomas R. Dye, *Understanding Public Policy*, 7th ed. (Englewood Cliffs, NJ: Prentice Hall, 1992); William Gillette, *Retreat from Reconstruction, 1869–1879* (Baton Rouge: Louisiana State University Press, 1979); C. Vann Woodward, *Reunion and Reaction: The Compromise of 1877 and the End of Reconstruction* (New York: Doubleday Anchor Books, 1956).

CONSENT DECREE. In the context of school desegregation,* a negotiated agreement among parties in a school desegregation or higher-education suit that the court accepts as a settlement of the suit. The most significant consent decrees for the desegregation of elementary and secondary education were adopted in Atlanta, Georgia, and St. Louis, Missouri. In the Wilmington, Delaware, metropolitan area the two antagonists' agreement was attacked by the state's legislature and was judged unacceptable by U.S. District Court* Judge Sue Robinson, so that a consent decree overturning the original court order could not be issued. At the university level the consent decree between the University of North Carolina and the federal government followed over a decade of wrangling in federal court. The negotiated settlement included the university's agreement to increase its outreach to in-state black students and ease transferring from two-year community colleges to the university. Consent decrees are viewed as alternatives to costly conflictual courtroom litigation, but the issue of adequate court monitoring of implementation is significant.

See also **Atlanta Compromise**.

References: Wolters, *Right Turn* (1996); Raymond Wolters, "The Consent Order as Sweetheart Deal: The Case of School Desegregation in New Castle County, Delaware," *Temple Political and Civil Rights Law Review* 4, no. 2 (Spring 1995): 271–99; James J. Prestage and Jewel L. Prestage, "The Consent Decree as a Tool for Desegregation in Higher Education," in *Black Education*, ed. Smith and Chunn (1989), 158–75; Amaker, *Civil Rights and the Reagan Administration* (1988); Lloyd Anderson, "The Approval and Interpretation of Consent Decrees in Civil Rights Class Action Litigation," *University of Illinois Law Review*, no. 3 (1983): 579–632; Dentler, Baltzell, and Sullivan, *University on Trial* (1983).

CONSTITUTION. *See* **U.S. Constitution**.

CONTACT THEORY. A theory developed in Gordon Allport's* book *The Nature of Prejudice*.* The essence of his theory was that "prejudice* . . . may be reduced by equal status contact between majority and minority groups in the pursuit of common goals." Prejudice reduction was even more likely if it was "sanctioned by law, custom, or local atmosphere," that is, by institutional supports, and if the contact between the groups was in the service of a common goal or task. Thus contact in an interracial setting in schools could break the vicious cycle of prejudice, discrimination,* segregation,* and inequality described by Gunnar Myrdal* in *The American Dilemma*.*

References: Armor, *Forced Justice* (1995); Hawley and Jackson, *Toward a Common Destiny* (1995); Allport, *The Nature of Prejudice* (1954).

CONTROLLED-CHOICE PLAN. A school desegregation plan* that combines elements of mandatory plans* and voluntary plans* and is based upon parental choice of a child's school assignment, with a backup mandatory plan if enough parents do not make a choice to further school desegregation.* Controlled-choice plans may be court ordered or developed by school boards. These plans were first adopted in the early 1980s as a compromise between mandatory plans, which assign every student to a school, and voluntary plans, which allow every student to remain at his or her neighborhood school.* Parents must rank their school choices for their child and are not guaranteed their neighborhood schools. School-district officials then try to give first choices while also achieving school desegregation objectives. In its purest form this plan involves no attendance zone; parents and students have a choice of all schools serving the appropriate grade level. Districts assign students to schools based on parental/student choice, racial balance,* and capacity.

The advantage of controlled-choice plans is that voluntarism and choice are the central elements of the plan and forced busing* is utilized only as a last resort. Proponents have noted the high percentage of parents and students who receive their top choice of school assignment. However, it has been estimated that 10–30 percent of children do not receive their first choice in such plans, and others choose to leave the public schools before determining how they fared. Christine Rossell's* empirical analysis of 20 school districts with more than 30 percent minority enrollment, which included 8 districts with a controlled-choice plan, indicates that controlled-choice plans lead to less white flight* than mandatory plans but more than voluntary plans. They also do not lead to as much interracial exposure (as measured on the index of interracial exposure*) as do voluntary plans. A major problem that controlled-choice plans have to face is their complicated school assignment procedures. Rossell argues that "in short, as far as parents are concerned, controlled choice plans have too much control and not enough choice" (1995:69). She also questions the claim that controlled-choice plans will lead to educational reform because the limitations on choice to achieve school desegregation will not force poor schools to change due to enrollment loss. If students fail to choose a particular school, it is not allowed to open empty. Rather, students are mandatorily assigned so as to both fill it and desegregate it.

Controlled-choice plans have been implemented in Boston, Cambridge, Holyoke, Lowell, Lynn, and Worcester, Massachusetts; San Jose, California; and Yonkers, New York. The number of such plans in Massachusetts is due to the advocacy of controlled-choice plans by two state officials.

References: Charles Willie and Michael Alves, *A New Approach to School Desegregated Education and School Improvement* (Providence, RI: Desegregation Assistance Center of Brown University, 1996); Christine H. Rossell, "Controlled-Choice Desegregation Plans: Not Enough Choice? Too Much Control?" *Urban Affairs Review* 31, no. 1 (September 1995): 43–76; Rossell, "The Convergence of Black and White Attitudes on School Desegregation Issues during the Four Decade Evolution of the Plans" (January

1995); Charles Glenn, "Controlled Choice in Massachusetts Public Schools," *Public Interest* 103 (Spring 1991:88–105); Michael J. Alves and Charles V. Willie, "Controlled Choice Assignments: A New and More Effective Approach to School Desegregation," *Urban Review* 19, no. 67 (1987): 67–88.

COOPER V. AARON, 358 U.S. 1 (1958). Unanimous U.S. Supreme Court* decision (9–0, Chief Justice Earl Warren* writing for the Court) concerning the implementation of school desegregation* in Little Rock, Arkansas, that established the principle that local community resistance or the threat of violence could not be used as an excuse to delay a school desegregation plan.* This case involved one of the most notorious incidents of resistance to the 1954 *Brown* * decision, the battle over desegregating Central High School in Little Rock, Arkansas.

The Little Rock Board of Education had announced that it would comply with the *Brown* ruling three days after the decision. In May 1955 the board approved a school desegregation plan to begin in the fall of 1957 at the high-school level and desegregate all schools by 1963. The NAACP* challenged the plan as being too slow, but the U.S. District Court* upheld it. Seventeen black students were carefully chosen to enter Central High School. Half dropped out before the September 1957 start of school, leaving nine students.

The desegregation plan upset a good portion of the community. The White Citizens Council* placed ads in the local newspaper citing the evils of school desegregation such as integrated love scenes in school dramatic performances and integrated showers and rest rooms. Governor Orval Faubus,* elected as a moderate, appeared on television the night before school was to open to announce that he had activated the Arkansas National Guard to stop the black children from entering the school. Faubus said that public disturbances were imminent, and he believed that order could not be maintained if desegregation was implemented. If the children were admitted, "Blood would run in the streets." (Greenberg* states that "there had been no evidence to support this fear of violence" [1994:229].) Faubus thus received national publicity for his actions and greatly inflamed the situation. A hostile white crowd formed at the school and taunted the children as they approached. The children were turned back by Faubus's National Guard.

Federal Judge Ronald N. Davis requested that the Department of Justice* collect information about those defying the court order, including the governor. On September 4 Faubus called President Dwight D. Eisenhower* to request his cooperation and understanding in defying the order, and the next day the President informed Faubus by telegram that he would honor his oath to support and uphold the Constitution,* that the Justice Department had begun an investigation, and that he expected the governor, other state officials, and the National Guard to comply and cooperate.

The President was told that the governor was anxious to get out of the morass and sought a meeting with the President. On September 14 Governor Faubus met with President Eisenhower in the President's vacation office in Newport, Rhode Island. President Eisenhower suggested that Faubus keep the National Guard on the scene but that he change its orders to supporting the implementation of the court order. Eisenhower believed that the governor agreed to follow the orders of the federal judge reviewing the case, but the two could not agree on a joint statement following the meeting.

Faubus returned to Arkansas and did not change the National Guard's orders or his stance. Called to court to explain his actions, the governor sent his lawyers to question federal authority. The judge decided that desegregation would have occurred peacefully had Faubus not brought in the National Guard, and he enjoined the governor and National Guard from interfering with school desegregation in Little Rock. Faubus withdrew his troops three hours later but called on the black students not to enter the school until peace could be ensured.

On September 23 the black students again tried to enter the school and were again turned back by a mob. President Eisenhower then gave the Secretary of Defense the authority to enforce the orders of the judge and issued a Proclamation of Obstruction of Justice. The mayor of Little Rock sent a telegram to the President indicating that the mob was growing and armed, and that the police, now left in charge, could not control the situation.

Ten thousand members of the Arkansas National Guard were nationalized, and 1,000 combat-ready paratroopers of the 101st Airborne Division, veterans of the Korean War, arrived on the scene. The President then explained his actions on nationwide radio and television at 9 P.M. on September 24. The children successfully began their schooling at Central High School, but the President faced criticism from Governor Faubus that he was carrying out a military occupation to force integration.*

After Faubus again stated his intentions to let others obstruct the court order, and according to Duram (163) the administration released a set of four legal principles that had guided the President in this crisis:

1. The Executive Branch of the Federal Government does not participate in the formulation of plans effecting segregation. . . .

2. The period of time within which such plan should be put into effect likewise must be proposed by the local authorities and approved by the Courts. . . .

3. A final order of a Federal Court giving effect to a desegregation public school plan must be obeyed by State authorities and all citizens as the law of the land. . . .

4. Powers of a State Governor may not be used to defeat a valid order of a federal court.

Thus the statement made clear that the President's actions were in response to defiance of federal law, not to promulgate school desegregation. While Eisenhower then tried to keep a low profile on this situation, it drew much of his attention for two years. The federal troops were withdrawn after two weeks, but the National Guard remained for six months.

The school board returned to court in February 1958 to ask for a stay of two and one-half years. A different federal District Court judge agreed, the NAACP successfully appealed, and finally the U.S. Supreme Court, in *Cooper v. Aaron*, concluded that the students' constitutional rights should not be sacrificed because of violence and disorder. Clearly the Court decided that justice delayed is justice denied. To show unanimity, all nine Supreme Court justices individually signed the opinion, an unprecedented action.

Governor Faubus then closed all three Little Rock high schools rather than be forced to desegregate them. The violence, which included a number of Labor Day bombings, led to a retreat on the part of avid segregationists, and the schools were reopened on a desegregated basis. No one was ever prosecuted for an act of violence.

The decision set a precedent requiring the state to do what is necessary to protect citizens exercising their constitutional rights, even under the threat of violence. It also affirmed the supremacy of the decisions of the U.S. Supreme Court in upholding the U.S. Constitution over the actions of governors and state legislatures. Some viewed the entire incident and case as encouraging resistance to school desegregation, especially given President Eisenhower's reluctant enforcement of the school desegregation order.

References: Melba Beals, *Warriors Don't Cry: A Searing Memoir of the Battle to Integrate Little Rock's Central High* (New York: Pocket Books, 1994); Greenberg, *Crusaders in the Courts* (1994); Hall, *Oxford Companion* (1992); Duram, *A Moderate among Extremists* (1981); Elizabeth Huckaby, *Crisis at Central High, Little Rock, 1957–58* (Baton Rouge: Louisiana State University Press, 1980); Muse, *Ten Years of Prelude* (1964); Peltason, *Fifty-Eight Lonely Men* (1961).

COURTS OF APPEALS. The intermediate courts in the federal judicial system, standing between the U.S. District Courts* and the U.S. Supreme Court,* which hear appeals from District Court decisions. The U.S. Courts of Appeals may hear appeals from litigants who were parties to cases in the U.S. District Courts; their decisions may be reviewed by the U.S. Supreme Court. In 1996 there were a total of 12 circuit courts, divided geographically. Judges are nominated by the President and must be confirmed by the U.S. Senate.

While errors of procedure or law may be appealed, new evidence may not be introduced in the appeals process. Each side briefs the court after the appeal is filed. Often counsel for each side may deliver an oral argument before a three-judge panel. The court then considers the arguments and writes an opinion within several months. The decision of the court may be to dismiss, affirm, or reverse in whole or in part and with instructions to the District Court. As with the Supreme Court, judges may write the majority or minority opinion or author concurring opinions when they agree with the result but disagree with the logic of the majority. When decisions are highly controversial, the entire court may review the decision (*en banc*), rehear the appeal, and issue a fresh opinion.

U.S. Courts of Appeals were very active in the cases arising out of the U.S. Supreme Court's *Brown v. Board of Education** (1954) decision. Some of their decisions, such as *Briggs v. Elliott** (1955) by the Fourth Circuit and *United States v. Jefferson County Board of Education** (1966) by the Fifth Circuit, played a major role in the status of school desegregation* implementation in the South.* Decisions and opinions such as these also laid the groundwork for the reasoning of subsequent U.S. Supreme Court decisions. Grossman concludes that the formerly Atlanta-based "Fifth Circuit Court was, with the Supreme Court, the judicial bulwark against racial discrimination in the South'' (1993: 70), overturning segregationist laws in the areas of school segregation* and desegregation and public accommodations. When the U.S. Supreme Court does not grant certiorari, that is, review a case from the Court of Appeals, the lower court's decision stands. Thus the refusal of the U.S. Supreme Court to review the *Hopwood v. Texas** (1996) decision, in which the Fifth Circuit Court of Appeals ruled that any race-based criteria in admissions criteria were inappropriate and thus basically gutted the U.S. Supreme Court's 1978 ruling in *Bakke,** meant that the decision of the Court of Appeals stands. In 1996 the circuits included the following states:

First Circuit: Puerto Rico, Maine, New Hampshire, Massachusetts, Rhode Island

Second Circuit: New York, Vermont, Connecticut

Third Circuit: Pennsylvania, New Jersey, Delaware, Virgin Islands

Fourth Circuit: West Virginia, Maryland, Virginia, North Carolina, South Carolina

Fifth Circuit: Texas, Louisiana, Mississippi

Sixth Circuit: Ohio, Kentucky, Tennessee, Michigan

Seventh Circuit: Wisconsin, Indiana, Illinois

Eighth Circuit: North Dakota, South Dakota, Nebraska, Arkansas, Missouri, Iowa, Minnesota

Ninth Circuit: Alaska, Washington, Oregon, California, Hawaii, Arizona, Nevada, Idaho, Montana, Northern Mariana Islands, Guam

Tenth Circuit: Wyoming, Utah, Colorado, Kansas, Oklahoma, New Mexico

Eleventh Circuit: Alabama, Georgia, Florida

District of Columbia Circuit: Washington, D.C.

References: Mark Grossman, "Fifth Circuit Court of Appeals," in *The ABC-CLIO Companion to the Civil Rights Movement* (1993); Hall, *Oxford Companion* (1992); Jack Bass, *Unlikely Heroes: The Dramatic Story of the Southern Judges of the Fifth Circuit* (New York: Simon and Schuster, 1981); Frank T. Read, "The Bloodless Revolution: The Role of the Fifth Circuit in the Integration of the Deep South," *Mercer Law Review* 32 (Summer 1981): 1149–66.

CRAIN, ROBERT L. (born January 28, 1934, Louisville, Kentucky). A prominent sociological researcher supportive of school desegregation* who has been conducting significant research on school desegregation since 1964. Crain attended segregated schools in Louisville, Kentucky. He became a sociologist after careers as an engineer and a social worker. Crain received his B.A. in engineering and mathematics from the University of Louisville. He received his Ph.D. in sociology from the University of Chicago in 1964. Crain taught in the Department of Sociology at the University of Chicago (1963–1968) and at Johns Hopkins University in the Department of Social Relations (1968–1973). He worked for the Rand Corporation as a senior social scientist from 1973 to 1985, leading a team designing a national study of school desegregation for the U.S. Commission on Civil Rights.* The study was designed but never implemented. From 1978 to 1985 Crain served as the principal research scientist at the Center for Social Organization of Schools, Johns Hopkins University.

Crain has been an advocate for school desegregation for his entire career. His 1982 review of 93 studies of the effects of school desegregation on black achievement was the first formal meta-analysis in this field. The results indicated a positive effect, with the largest effect of school desegregation in kindergarten and first grade. This study has been cited many times in school desegregation court cases. Crain also led a 16-year follow-up study of minority students who had enrolled in Hartford's voluntary metropolitan busing* program, Project Concern.* As summarized by Armor* (1995), the study indicates that Project Concern participants were much more likely to stay in college, but the study is subject to methodological criticisms concerning the comparison group and self-selection biases of those participants who remained in Project Concern. Over the past 30 years Crain has testified in over ten cases, including Hartford and Seattle, usually on behalf of minority plaintiffs. He served as the court's expert in the Los Angeles case. Crain has served as professor of sociology and education at Teachers College, Columbia University, since 1985.

Works about: Armor, *Forced Justice* (1995).

Works by: with Amy Stuart Wells, *Stepping over the Color Line: African-American Students in White Suburban Schools* (New Haven: Yale University Press, 1997); with Rita Mahard, "The Effects of Research Methodology on Desegregation-Achievement Studies: A Meta-Analysis," *American Journal of Sociology* 88 (1983): 839–54; with Rita E. Mahard and Ruth E. Narot, *Making Desegregation Work: How Schools Create Social Climates* (Cambridge, MA: Ballinger, 1982); with Carol Sachs Weisman, *Discrimination, Personality, and Achievement: A Survey of Northern Blacks* (New York: Seminar Press, 1972); *The Politics of School Desegregation: Comparative Case Studies of Community Structure and Policy-making* (Chicago: Aldine, 1968).

CUMMING V. RICHMOND COUNTY BOARD OF EDUCATION, 175 U.S. 528 (1899).

U.S. Supreme Court* decision three years after the *Plessy v. Ferguson** opinion in which a unanimous Court, in a decision written by *Plessy* dissenter John Marshall Harlan,* did not enforce the equal part of the separate but equal* doctrine. Ware High School, the first high school for blacks in Georgia, was opened in Augusta in 1879. The school board had been pressured by blacks to open this school under a state law calling for separate but equal facilities. In 1897 the Augusta School Board closed the school, arguing that it needed the funds for primary schools for black students. The board, however, continued to operate a high school for white girls and one for white boys. A suit was brought by black parents who argued that the separate but equal principle demanded the maintenance of the black high school. The board claimed that it was not race that motivated its decision but limited funds. The Supreme Court allowed the board's decision. Justice Harlan concluded that the black parents would have had to prove that the school board's actions were entirely motivated by hostility to blacks; otherwise, federal interference with state programs of public education could not be justified.

References: Jones-Wilson et al., *Encyclopedia of African-American Education* (1996), 128–30; Hall, *Oxford Companion* (1992); Duram, *A Moderate among Extremists* (1981); Greenberg, *Judicial Process and Social Change: Constitutional Litigation Cases and Materials* (1977); Kluger, *Simple Justice* (1975).

D

DALEY, RICHARD JOSEPH (born May 15, 1902, Chicago–died December 20, 1976, Chicago). Mayor of Chicago for more than two decades whose political power led to the reversal of attempts to cut off federal funds to Chicago under the Civil Rights Act of 1964* in a major conflict of local versus federal power and authority. Daley directed the Cook County Democratic Central Committee while serving as mayor of Chicago and thus led America's strongest political machine. He began as a clerk in city hall, served in the state legislature, and was elected mayor in 1955. His father was a sheet-metal worker and supporter of the local Democratic party; his mother, a supporter of women's suffrage, often took him on her marches. He received his law degree at night from De Paul University.

Mayor's Daley's role in school desegregation* history was related to the Chicago School District and the Civil Rights Act of 1964. In the early 1960s, despite the high degree of school segregation* in Chicago and the mobilization of civil rights* groups in Chicago, Superintendent Benjamin Willis, a strong believer that the main business of schools was education and not social reform, refused to acknowledge segregation or make even modest efforts to limit it. For example, he would not permit black transfers to white schools with empty seats. Instead, he used expensive mobile classrooms—termed ''Willis wagons'' by civil rights advocates—to keep children in crowded segregated classrooms. Finally, a 1964 report documented segregation in the system, and a limited transfer program was enacted. Superintendent Willis, who had gained a national reputation for his strong efforts to eliminate double shifts in the city's schools, refused to enforce the program and threatened to resign, and the school board rescinded the policy.

On July 4, 1965, frustrated civil rights leaders in Chicago called on Washington to enforce Title VI of the 1964 Civil Rights Act, which prohibited discrimination* based on race, color, or national origin for activities funded by the federal government. They claimed that the Chicago schools were almost totally segregated, that this resulted from intentional discriminatory actions of the school board, and that officials even worked with the Chicago Real Estate Board and public housing officials to establish and maintain segregated schools.

Secretary of the Department of Health, Education, and Welfare* (HEW) John Gardner sent an investigative team to Chicago. Education Commissioner Francis Keppel, concerned that $32 million in new funds in the Elementary and Secondary Education Act of 1965* would go toward segregated schools, held up the disbursement of funds pending this investigation. There were a number of problems, however, with this step. Many of those who voted for the Civil Rights Act of 1964, including a key person in getting it passed, Senator Everett Dirksen of Illinois, did so in the belief that the act would not be applied in the North. The Office of Education* lacked clear criteria to apply to cases such as this, where there was no state statute segregating the schools. It was not clear what evidence was required to prove de jure segregation.* Nor did the Department of Health, Education, and Welfare and Office of Education officials work with President Lyndon B. Johnson* before acting.

Chicago mobilized its political power. On October 3, 1965, at the signing of the new immigration bill before the Statue of Liberty, Mayor Daley met with President Johnson to complain and demand that HEW's action be reversed. Johnson dispatched Under Secretary Wilbur Cohen to the Windy City to negotiate a settlement. According to Biles, Daley charged, "You're taking away the funds from me without ever having consulted me or asked me what my views are; you never tried to resolve it; all you do is you send a telegram and I read it in the newspapers" (1995:116). The settlement was negotiated in an hour; HEW released the funds, and the school board promised to look into its practices.

This incident had a number of consequences. Daley's perceived power was enhanced; in four days he reversed a $32-million federal government decision with his intervention. The Office of Education was embarrassed and its power limited; it had taken a major action without the President and Department of Justice's* support or a full analysis of the distinctive legal issues in the North. The incident certainly suggested that political resistance could overcome federal enforcement efforts. Francis Keppel was eased out of his job a few months later.

Works about: Biles, *Richard J. Daley* (1995); Orfield, *Must We Bus?* (1978); *Current Biography Yearbook 1976* (New York: H. W. Wilson Company, 1977), 103–9; Orfield, *The Reconstruction of Southern Education* (1969).

DAVIS, JOHN WILLIAM (born April 13, 1873, Clarksburg, West Virginia–died March 24, 1955, Charleston, South Carolina). A distinguished American lawyer, member of Congress, ambassador, Solicitor General, and presidential nominee who served as chief counsel for the defendants in *Brown v. Board of Education** (1954). Born to a proslavery, Calvinist lawyer, Davis was taught conservative values early in life—liberty and property were sacred, and government should not meddle. He attended Washington and Lee University, where this conservatism was reinforced. He served in the West Virginia House of Delegates and in the U.S. Congress for one term (1911–1913). President Woodrow Wilson then named him Solicitor General. He was victorious in 48 of 67 cases he argued before the U.S. Supreme Court.* He then served as ambassador to England. In 1924 he was nominated as the Democratic candidate for President on the 103d ballot. After his loss he served as a very highly paid corporate lawyer.

Thus at the time of the *Brown* U.S. Supreme Court hearing John Davis was a distinguished corporation and constitutional lawyer and a former ambassador to Great Britain. Pollack (1979:173) notes that Davis "had argued more cases before the U.S. Supreme Court than any man in the 20th century." He had turned down President Warren G. Harding's invitation to serve on the U.S. Supreme Court in 1922. Davis was 80 years old at the time of the *Brown* argument. Davis argued that precedent (*Plessy v. Ferguson** [1896] and seven subsequent cases) supported the continuation of school segregation,* that this was a matter of states' rights, and that segregation was compatible with the U.S. Constitution.*

Works about: Hall, *Oxford Companion* (1992); Pollack, *Earl Warren* (1979); Kluger, *Simple Justice* (1975).

DAVIS V. COUNTY SCHOOL BOARD, 103 F. Supp. 337 (1952). The Prince Edward County, Virginia, case consolidated under the landmark *Brown v. Board of Education** (1954) decision. The black Robert R. Moton High School in the district was dilapidated, and a series of promises to build a new high school for blacks had not been fulfilled. Students at the high school led a student protest in April 1951, and after the superintendent of schools refused to see them, they contacted the NAACP's* special counsel for the southeastern United States asking for assistance. They finally had an audience with the superintendent, but to no avail. After their strike had lasted for three days, they met with Oliver Hill and Spottswood Robinson of the NAACP, who urged them to support a suit against school segregation* rather than a new segregated high school. One hundred and seventeen students became the plaintiffs in the suit against Prince Edward County, with 14-year-old Dorothy E. Davis, a ninth grader at Moton, as the lead plaintiff. White leaders offered black leaders the opportunity for a new high school if they dropped the suit, and the school board appropriated funds to build one, but the suit was not withdrawn.

The suit was heard before a three-judge panel. The NAACP lawyers sought to have the Prince Edward schools judged unequal and the state's segregation laws declared in violation of the U.S. Constitution.* The case included testimony from Isidor Chein, former psychology professor at the City College of New York and director of research of the Commission on Community Interrelations of the American Jewish Congress, which summarized a survey he conducted of 517 social scientists about the effects of enforced segregation. Almost all of these respondents had indicated that segregation, even if the facilities provided were equal, caused a detrimental effect on the segregated group. Kenneth Clark* also reported the results of his interviews with 14 of Moton's students and concluded that the most detrimental consequence of segregation was that it led to a preoccupation of all involved with race. The defense argued that plans for a new high school for the black students were under way and that school segregation was not necessarily harmful to minority students. But Hill argued back that the district had had years to make the high schools equal and had not moved to do so. The decision concluded that district officials must move to make the schools equal, but that school segregation was a tradition, required by law, and "had begotten greater opportunities for the Negro."

The *Brown* decision reversed *Davis*. Virginia responded with massive resistance.* On June 2, 1959, Prince Edward County closed its public schools. It was not until September 1964, under pressure from the U.S. Supreme Court (*Griffin v. County School Board of Prince Edward County**), that the county reopened its schools.

References: Greenberg, *Crusaders in the Courts* (1994); Wolters, *The Burden of Brown* (1984); Kluger, *Simple Justice* (1975); Robert Collins Smith, *They Closed Their Schools: Prince Edward County, Virginia, 1951–1964* (Chapel Hill: University of North Carolina Press, 1965).

DAYTON BOARD OF EDUCATION V. BRINKMAN, 433 U.S. 406 (1977) (*Dayton I*); 443 U.S. 526 (1979) (*Dayton II*).

The Dayton, Ohio, case twice before the U.S. Supreme Court* that hinged on the discriminatory intent* and effect of official action in a northern school district. As a school district in the North, Dayton was not segregated by state law, although it had a number of schools serving predominantly whites and several predominantly educating blacks. The U.S. District Court* found that the city board was guilty of discrimination* through actions such as faculty assignments, use of optional attendance zones, and new school siting, but imposed a limited, rather than districtwide, remedy. The U.S. Court of Appeals* rejected this plan and required a school desegregation plan* encompassing the entire school district. In *Dayton I* the U.S. Supreme Court, however, overturned this decision in an 8–0 vote, with the opinion written by Justice William H. Rehnquist.* The court questioned two of the three actions previously judged to be discrimination and concluded that a systemwide remedy was not required. It ordered the District Court to hold new hearings to determine the extent of segregative impact that had resulted from the board's unconstitutional actions. The new hearings did not convince the District Court that a systemwide remedy was necessary, and again the Court of Appeals reversed. In this second decision the U.S. Supreme Court on a 5–4 vote agreed with the Court of Appeals. Justice White wrote the decision and was joined by Justices Brennan,* Marshall,* Blackmun, and Stevens. Justices Stewart, Powell,* and Rehnquist and Chief Justice Burger* dissented.

References: Armor, *Forced Justice* (1995); Nowak and Rotunda, *Constitutional Law* (1995); Kurland, *"Brown v. Board of Education* Was the Beginning'' (1994); Witt, *Congressional Quarterly's Guide to the U.S. Supreme Court* (1989).

DE FACTO SEGREGATION. *See* **Segregation, De Facto**.

DE JURE SEGREGATION. *See* **Segregation, De Jure**.

DEEP SOUTH. The states of South Carolina, Alabama, Mississippi, Louisiana, and Georgia. These states have in common that they contain a high percentage of black population, are former members of the Confederacy, were states where slavery flourished, and were involved in massive resistance* to school desegregation.* The Deep South is sometimes referred to as the Black Belt, once named because of the deep, rich black soil but later identified as the area with the greatest black population.

Southern states (the South*) generally include the states of the Deep South as well as the other states of the Confederacy: Arkansas, Tennessee, Texas, Virginia, North Carolina, and Florida. The border states are generally listed as Delaware, Kentucky, Maryland, West Virginia, Oklahoma, and Missouri (a state which is now considered to be in the Midwest by the Census Bureau).

References: Abraham and Perry, *Freedom and the Court* (1994); Earl Black and Merle Black, *Politics and Society in the South* (Cambridge, MA: Harvard University Press, 1987); W. D. Workman, "The Deep South," in *With All Deliberate Speed*, ed. Shoemaker (1957), 88–109.

DEFUNIS V. ODEGAARD, 416 U.S. 312 (1974). The first major affirmative action* case to reach the U.S. Supreme Court,* which was declared moot by a 5–4 vote. White law-school applicant Marco DeFunis, a Sephardic Jew, claimed that he would have been admitted to the University of Washington Law School if it did not have an affirmative action program, but while the case was in litigation he had been ordered admitted and was about to graduate. The case was therefore dismissed as moot by the U.S. Supreme Court.

DeFunis had graduated from the University of Washington with a 3.62 out of 4.0 undergraduate grade point average but had taken the Law Boards three times before receiving a high score of 668. While a number of law schools accepted him, he wanted to attend the University of Washington, near his home and near where he wanted to practice. Washington calculated a Predicted First Year Average (PFYA) for each applicant, derived from the applicant's last two years of college work and the Law School Admission Test (LSAT). DeFunis's score was in the middle group, too high for rejection but too low for acceptance. Blacks, Chicanos, American Indians, and Filipinos who applied were in a different process where the PFYA was given less weight, and their credentials were not compared with those of white applicants. DeFunis had a higher PFYA than all but one of the admitted minority candidates. The school did not establish quotas specifying the number of minorities to be admitted but did seek to admit a reasonable number of nonwhite applicants.

DeFunis sued in state court, won, and was admitted pending appeal, but on appeal the Washington Supreme Court reversed the ruling. DeFunis was allowed to stay in the law school pending the next appeal. The case took so long that DeFunis had started his last term at the law school by the time the U.S. Supreme Court heard the case. The Court then by a 5–4 vote declared the case moot, since he would graduate before it announced any decision.

References: Greenberg, *Crusaders in the Courts* (1994); Kaplin, *The Law of Higher Education* (1985); Wilkinson, *From Brown to Bakke* (1979).

DENTLER, ROBERT A. (born November 26, 1928, Chicago, Illinois). Sociologist and educator who was an advisor for 20 years to the federal court in the Boston case and to Judge W. Arthur Garrity* and who has written extensively on race relations* and school desegregation.* Dentler has served as an expert witness and/or planner in over 15 cases, including Yonkers, New York; Mobile, Alabama; Little Rock, Arkansas; Richmond, Virginia; Kansas City, Missouri; Los Angeles, California; Buffalo, New York; and New York City. Dentler received his B.S. from Northwestern University in 1949 and his M.A.'s from this school in 1950 and American University in 1954. He served as a reporter and then an intelligence officer. After three years as an instructor at Dickinson College (1954–1957), Dentler began his doctoral work at the University of Chicago, where he earned his Ph.D. in 1960. Following a one-year position at Dartmouth College, he served on the Teachers College (Columbia University) faculty (1962–1972). He became dean of the School of Education at Boston University in 1972, serving through 1979. Following several years (1979–1983) as a senior sociologist at the consulting firm of Abt Associates, Dentler was a professor at the University of Massachusetts at Boston (1983–1992) and was named emeritus professor of sociology in 1993. He served as a senior fellow at the McCormick Institute of Public Affairs during 1993–1994.

Works about: *Who's Who in America, 1997*, 1037.

Works by: with D. C. Baltzell and D. J. Sullivan, *University on Trial* (Cambridge, MA: Abt Books, 1983); with M. B. Scott, *Schools on Trial: An Inside Account of the Boston School Desegregation Case* (Cambridge, MA: Abt Books, 1981); with B. Mackler and M. E. Warshauer, *The Urban R's: Race Relations as the Problem in Urban Education* (New York: Praeger, 1967).

DEPARTMENT OF EDUCATION. The federal cabinet department created by merging the Office of Education* in the Department of Health, Education, and Welfare* (HEW), the National Center for Educational Statistics, the National Institute for Education, and other existing education-related offices. This department in the President's cabinet is responsible for the bulk of federal education programs, including those that previously had been administered outside the Office of Education, such as vocational rehabilitation. President Jimmy Carter* proposed that the Office of Education in the Department of HEW become a cabinet-level department; Congress passed legislation to do this, and the department came into existence on May 5, 1980, with U.S. Court of Appeals* Justice Shirley M. Hufstedler as the first Secretary of Education. Carter's proposal fulfilled his campaign promise to the National Education Association. President Ronald Reagan* tried unsuccessfully to dismantle the Department of Education.

The department has had responsibility for compensatory education* programs, aid to the handicapped, educational research through the National Institute of Education, and statistics through the Center for Educational Statistics. Some educational functions are located in other cabinet departments. For example, the Department of Justice* has responsibility for enforcement of most antidiscrimination laws relating to education.

After the passage of the Civil Rights Act of 1964* and the Elementary and Secondary Education Act of 1965,* the role of the Office of Education radically changed from a statistics-gathering agent of the status quo, in which local control was dominant, to a national force for major reform in American society. As Gary Orfield* documents, this was a difficult and controversial transformation. The office had administered programs whose control lay in state departments of education; the Office of Education merely ensured that the funds were properly distributed and collected information from the states. The office thus had a cooperative relationship with states, not a coercive one.

The funding programs of the Office of Education in the 1960s were part of the threat that the federal government held to force southern school districts to comply with school desegregation* orders. The Office of Education was responsible for establishing the school desegregation guidelines after the passage of the Civil Rights Act of 1964. The office had to consider whether to accept the plans that were found acceptable by the U.S. District Courts.* The first set of guidelines, issued in April 1965, included the acceptability of geographical zoning and freedom-of-choice plans.* In March 1966 the Office of Education, working with the Civil Rights Division* of the Justice Department, issued revised, tougher guidelines. These guidelines laid out very specific objectives, not vague statements of goals but the increase in the number of students in desegregated schools. That is, the emphasis changed from the prohibition of racial discrimination* to the insistence that schools become desegregated, even if that meant assigning students by race. But throughout the beginning of the enforcement process the office had to weigh the desire to get funds to school districts and students, many of whom were black, against the desire to force compliance with school desegregation guidelines.

The office's staff and funding grew along with its responsibilities. The staff in the 1960s was fivefold the 1950 staff, and the budget escalated from $40 million to $600 million in a little over a decade. In the 1990s the department had approximately 7,000 personnel and a $30-billion budget, but still represented less than half the funds spent on education by the federal government.

References: Milton Goldberg and Joseph C. Conaty, ''U.S. Department of Education,'' in *Encyclopedia of Educational Research*, ed. Alkin (1992), 1470–77; ''United States Department of Education,'' in *American Educators' Encyclopedia*, by Dejnozka and Kapel (1991), 587; Wilkinson, *From Brown to Bakke* (1979); Orfield, *The Reconstruction of Southern Education* (1969).

DEPARTMENT OF HEALTH, EDUCATION, AND WELFARE (HEW). Department in the President's cabinet that included the Office of Education.* On April 11, 1953, HEW grew from the Federal Security Agency into the nation's tenth cabinet department. At the time its major divisions included the Office of Education, the Public Health Service, Social Security, Welfare, and the Food and Drug Administration. On May 5, 1980, the Office of Education was merged into the new cabinet Department of Education,* and HEW became the Department of Health and Human Services. HEW had several purposes, including providing equal educational opportunity* to all Americans as well as protecting and advancing the health and welfare of all citizens. HEW played a major role in enforcing school desegregation* in the 1970s, primarily through the Office of Education and the Office for Civil Rights.* The desegregation guidelines issued by HEW after the passage of the Civil Rights Act of 1964* and the Elementary and Secondary Education Act of 1965* led to the desegregation of the South's* schools. In 1965 HEW's effort to withhold funds from the Chicago School District was reversed through the efforts of Chicago's powerful mayor, Richard J. Daley.*

References: Biles, *Richard J. Daley* (1995); ''United States Department of Health, Education, and Welfare (HEW),'' in *American Educators' Encyclopedia,* by Dejnozka and Kapel (1991), 587; Orfield, *The Reconstruction of Southern Education* (1969).

DEPARTMENT OF JUSTICE. Department in the President's cabinet responsible for the enforcement of the nation's laws, including civil rights* laws such as the Civil Rights Act of 1964.* The major enforcement agency for the department in civil rights, and therefore in school segregation* and school desegregation,* is the Civil Rights Division.* While the office of Attorney General was established in 1789, the department was not created until after the Civil War (1870). The office of Solicitor General was established at this time to represent the federal government in cases before the U.S. Supreme Court.* The department now includes not only the Civil Rights Division but also offices such as the Federal Bureau of Investigation and the Anti-Trust and Tax Divisions.

References: Civil Rights Division, Department of Justice, *Civil Rights Division* (1995); Yu and Taylor, eds., *New Challenges* (1995); Liss and Taylor, eds., *New Opportunities*

(1993); Detlefsen, *Civil Rights Under Reagan* (1991); Govan and Taylor, eds., *One Nation Indivisible* (1989); Charles C. Bullock III and Charles M. Lamb, *Implementation of Civil Rights Policy* (Monterey, CA: Brooks/Cole, 1984); Orfield, *The Reconstruction of Southern Education* (1969).

DESEGREGATION. The removal of systematic barriers such as laws, customs, or practices that separate, seclude, or isolate a group of persons from the general mass on the basis of race or other factors in public facilities, neighborhoods, organizations, or other arenas; in school desegregation,* the removal of barriers to the attendance of children of all racial-ethnic groups in the same schools. Desegregation can be attained by court orders, directives of administrative agencies, voluntary actions of governmental decision-making groups such as school boards, actions of individuals or interest groups, or some combination of these. Alternatively, desegregation means the bringing together of racial groups that have been separated. In school desegregation this has meant achieving racial balance,* fashioning schools with racial proportions reflecting the racial distribution in a school district or geographical area, or some standard, for example, half white and half black. Thus school desegregation has meant the removal of barriers maintaining segregation* as well as the affirmative action* of mixing those who have been separated.

Segregation in American society as established by the Jim Crow* laws in the South* has been challenged by the civil rights movement* that took hold in the 1960s. The legal segregation of public accommodations, facilities, employment, and other aspects of life has been challenged through changes in laws and customs. However, while the results on some dimensions are striking, such as the desegregation of public facilities, the results in other areas have been mixed, such as the desegregation of housing.

The meaning of desegregation has changed as the U.S. Supreme Court's* decisions have evolved. In *Brown** in 1954 the Court viewed school desegregation as the removal of barriers established by school segregation statutes requiring blacks to attend segregated schools, that is, the absence of explicit segregation by law. Thus freedom-of-choice* plans that allowed all students to select any school in a school district theoretically would be racially neutral. But in the 1968 *Green** decision the Court called for affirmative action to be taken because racially neutral plans such as freedom of choice were not racially neutral in practice or in their effects. Thus the Court moved from viewing desegregation as having laws neutral with respect to race to calling for affirmative steps to desegregate schools and achieve racial balance.

The Civil Rights Act of 1964* distinguished desegregation from racial balance: " 'Desegregation' means the assignment of students to public schools and within such schools without regard to their race, color, religion, or national origin, but 'desegregation' shall not mean the assignment of students to public schools in order to overcome racial imbalance." This definition was the result of Senator Hubert H. Humphrey's maneuver to overcome southern opposition to the bill; the clause was to allow for ending de jure segregation* but not forcing schools segregated by individual actions, that is, de facto segregation,* to have to achieve racial balance.

Integration* is generally viewed as achieving the next step in the process, bringing about the social interaction of the groups that have been brought together physically or the social assimilation of minority students into a school such that they are accepted as social equals and receive equal educational opportunity.* To some extent the federal courts have had integration as a goal in desegregation orders, for they have ordered ancillary programs* and examined the *Green* factors in their decisions, including the desegregation of staffs and extracurricular activities.

Most often today, desegregation refers to racial balance, that is, comparing school racial enrollments to systemwide balance. However, David Armor* has argued that the level of racial balance required by the courts has not been consistent across court cases. "The first challenge in designing a desegregation plan is to define desegregation . . . but even in federal case law no single standard defines a desegregated school" (1995:11). Nor does every school have to achieve a particular racial composition. Some schools, in fact, may remain predominantly black (or white) under certain circumstances.

The courts have referred to segregated school systems as dual systems* and desegregated systems as unitary systems.* The requirement of the landmark *Brown* decision was that the vestiges of dual school systems be eliminated "root and branch." In the last decade the requirements of a unitary system have been specified by U.S. Supreme Court decisions such as *Board of Education of Oklahoma City v. Dowell** (1991), *Freeman v. Pitts** (1992), and *Missouri v. Jenkins** (1995).

Some whites and blacks lament the Court's changing its requirements in school desegregation from a limited view of desegregation to a more expansive one. Derrick A. Bell* argues that desegregation should mean "the removal of all barriers based on race, but it should not mean the dismantling of autonomous Black institutions, like the Black press, Black political organizations, Black churches, and Black communal societies" (1980:45).

School desegregation plans* may be voluntary* or mandatory.* This refers to the degree of parental control over student assignment. The extent of desegregation may be measured by several indexes, including the index of dissimilarity,* the index of interracial exposure,* and the index of racial isolation.* The courts typically measure school desegregation with categorical racial balance standards (e.g., all or certain schools must be within 15 percentage points of the school district's racial composition) or absolute categorical standards (e.g., all or certain schools must be between 10 and 80 percent minority).

At the college and university level the definition of desegregation has also evolved over time, but the comprehensive federal decision was reached in 1992. In *United States v. Fordice** the U.S. Supreme Court concluded that simply removing the barriers that states had set to prevent blacks from attending state colleges and universities was not sufficient to achieve desegregation of higher education, that is, race-neutral policies were insufficient. States had the obligation to remove the vestiges of segregation. The Southern Education Foundation concluded in its 1995 report that the 12 southern states it studied had not achieved equal access for blacks in higher education. At most of the South's flagship universities whites constituted over 80 percent of the enrollment, while a majority of blacks attended historically black colleges and universities. In 1994 the states of Florida, Kentucky, Maryland, Pennsylvania, Texas, and Virginia were still under official scrutiny by the Office of Civil Rights,* and as a result of the *Fordice* decision the office was going to review the status of other states.

References: Armor, *Forced Justice* (1995); Panel on Educational Opportunity and Postsecondary Desegregation, *Redeeming the American Promise* (Atlanta, GA: Southern Education Foundation, 1995); Weinberg, *The Search for Quality Integrated Education* (1983); Bell, *Shades of Brown* (1980).

DESEGREGATION ASSISTANCE CENTERS. Authorized under the Civil Rights Act of 1964* (Section 403) to provide technical assistance and training services to local school districts faced with educational problems based on race, sex, and national origin. The centers initially assisted school districts in developing school desegregation plans,* training personnel, revising curricula and materials, altering, developing, or changing policies and procedures in areas such as discipline, and resolving conflict. The role of these centers in school desegregation* planning, which at first focused on helping local school districts write and implement school desegregation plans, was constrained in January 1972, and they have since focused on helping districts deal with educational, as opposed to logistical, issues focused on pupil assignment plans, and with overcoming problems related to sex and national origin as well as racial discrimination* matters. Such educational problems include discipline, testing, grouping for instruction, extracurricular activities, and other second-generation problems.* The centers must provide their assistance to school districts that request it.

The Florida School Desegregation Consulting Center at the University of Miami in Coral Gables received funding in the fall of 1965, for example. The Miami center, under the leadership of Gordon Foster,* assisted the Dade County (Miami) and Duval County (Jacksonville) districts in developing school desegregation plans. Desegregation assistance center personnel in a number of centers also helped to write plans in large metropolitan areas such as Birmingham, Raleigh, Tulsa, and Dayton as well as many smaller communities throughout the South.* In the 1970s the *Lau v. Nichols* * (1974) decision was a major spur toward broadening the role of the centers to include work related to national origin. Similarly, services related to gender discrimination were added about the same time.

In fiscal year 1996–1997 ten centers received awards. Each covers a defined geographical area and disseminates information about successful educational

practices and legal requirements to ensure nondiscriminatory educational programs. Specific information includes how to identify race bias in instructional
materials and selecting appropriate materials for limited-English-speaking students. Among the centers was the New England Desegregation Assistance Center at Brown University, which serves the New England states, and the Midwest
Desegregation Assistance Center at Kansas State University, which serves Iowa,
Kansas, Missouri, and Nebraska. State educational agencies also receive awards
under this program and must coordinate with the desegregation assistance centers. The awards are generally for three years. The centers are helpful because
they are separate from federal enforcement efforts and thus are less threatening
to local school districts, but they are also based on technical assistance and thus
have little or no use as a political force to overcome resistance and opposition
to change.

References: *Catalog of Federal Domestic Assistance, 1996*; Northwest Regional Educational Lab, coordinator, *Resegregation of Public Schools: The Third Generation* (Portland, OR: Northwest Regional Educational Lab, June 1989); Gordon Foster, *"Milliken
v. Bradley*: Implications for Desegregation Centers and Metropolitan Desegregation," in
*Milliken v. Bradley: The Implications for Metropolitan Desegregation; Conference before
the United States Commission on Civil Rights* (Washington, DC: U.S. Government Printing Office, November 9, 1974), 127–52.

DESEGREGATION PLANS. *See* **School Desegregation Plans**.

DISCRIMINATION. Action element of prejudice*; behavior denying members
of a particular racial or ethnic group access to societal rewards. This includes
the denial of access to major life goals such as schools, housing, jobs, and
justice. Discrimination may be individual, generally the implementation of prejudicial attitudes by a single individual or limited group of individuals, but may
also be based on perceptions of the norms or attitudes of others, for example,
a personnel director believing that her company does not want blacks hired for
certain jobs. It may also be the result of probabilistic estimates applied to individuals that are characteristics of the group, for example, not hiring blacks
because blacks as a group have a lower IQ than whites or not hiring women
because women are more likely to quit work after having a baby than are men.
Jencks (1985) calls this probabilistic discrimination, one of the forms of discrimination he calls "rational." Institutional discrimination is part of the legal
system or system of customs in a community; that is, it is legitimized. The most
significant example of this was the Jim Crow* laws, including school segregation.* These laws segregated facilities and services in the South* from theaters
to buses.

See also **Segregation, De Jure**.

References: Paul A. Winters, ed., *Race Relations: Opposing Viewpoints* (San Diego:
Greenhaven Press, 1996); Kujovich, "Equal Opportunity in Higher Education" (1992);

Marger, *Race and Ethnic Relations* (1991); Christopher Jencks, "Affirmative Action for Blacks," *American Behavioral Scientist* 28, no. 6 (July/August 1985): 731–60.

DISCRIMINATORY INTENT. The legal requirement that officials must have intended to discriminate as well as produce discriminatory impacts before the courts need to intervene to order a remedy. The issue is whether the equal protection clause* of the Fourteenth Amendment* in the U.S. Constitution* requires a finding simply of actions that affected some group negatively (disparate impact*) before the court can order a remedy, or whether the intent to discriminate is also required. In *Washington v. Davis** (1976) the U.S. Supreme Court* held that the equal protection clause required both disparate impact and discriminatory intent before the clause was violated. In this case the verbal-skills test required for applicants seeking to become police in the District of Columbia was judged to have a disparate impact, that is, a higher proportion of black than white applicants failed, but the Court ruled that the Constitution also required that the challengers prove that the test was intentionally aimed to racially discriminate. In school desegregation cases this requirement sets a difficult standard. Showing racially disparate impacts of school-board actions is an easier task than proving that a board's actions were intentionally aimed at harming blacks.

References: Armor, *Forced Justice* (1995); Hall, *Oxford Companion* (1992); Paul Brest, "Racial Discrimination," in *The Burger Court*, ed. Blasi (1983), 113–31; Gary Orfield, *Toward a Strategy for Urban Integration* (New York: Ford Foundation, 1981).

DISPARATE IMPACT. Actions that negatively affect individuals in particular groups as defined by race, color, religion, sex, or national origin; also referred to as disproportionate impact. In *Griggs v. Duke Power Company* (1971) the U.S. Supreme Court* held that actions that had an adverse effect on employees in protected classes, even if there was no intent to harm certain groups, was a violation of the Civil Rights Act of 1964.* But in 1976 the Court held in *Washington v. Davis** that in school desegregation* cases discriminatory intent* must also be proven for a constitutional violation. Thus minorities claiming that discriminatory action is unconstitutional must pass two tests; they must show that the action disproportionately harms them and that the discrimination is intentional.

References: Armor, *Forced Justice* (1995); Hall, *Oxford Companion* (1992); Paul Brest, "Racial Discrimination," in *The Burger Court*, ed. Blasi (1983), 113–31.

DISTRICT COURTS. Trial courts for federal cases in the federal judicial system. The U.S. District Courts were given the responsibility to determine the remedy or plan required to desegregate school districts that had been declared in violation of the 1954 *Brown v. Board of Education** decision. Decisions of the District Courts, with a few exceptions, may be appealed to the Court of

Appeals.* There are District Courts in all of the 50 states as well as in Puerto Rico.

Gary Orfield* stresses that the District Court judges who shouldered this responsibility were "born and trained in the South,* active in the community and political life of their states, and appointed to the bench with the endorsement of the state's leading politicians" (1969:16). They were thus part of the very system that had to be changed. In addition, the nature of this task was far different from their usual one. They were no longer dealing with specific violations by individuals but rather trying to remedy constitutional violations across a community with few standards or guidelines on what the remedies might look like and little support from the federal government.

References: C. K. Rowland and Robert A. Carp, *Politics and Judgment in Federal District Courts* (Lawrence: University Press of Kansas, 1996); Phillip J. Cooper, *Hard Judicial Choices: Federal District Court Judges and State and Local Officials* (New York: Oxford University Press, 1988); Orfield, *The Reconstruction of Southern Education* (1969); Peltason, *Fifty-Eight Lonely Men* (1961).

DUAL SYSTEM. A segregated school system where students are assigned to schools on the basis of race. Prior to the 1954 *Brown v. Board of Education** decision 17 southern states (Alabama, Arkansas, Delaware, Florida, Georgia, Kentucky, Louisiana, Maryland, Mississippi, Missouri, North Carolina, Oklahoma, South Carolina, Tennessee, Texas, Virginia, and West Virginia) and the District of Columbia operated dual educational systems by law (de jure), one system for whites and one for blacks, and four other states permitted school segregation (Arizona, Kansas, New Mexico, and Wyoming). The two systems had different buildings, students, teachers, and staff, although the school board and central administrative staff were often the same. Typically the black system was underfunded, and the schools were in far worse physical condition, despite the *Plessy v. Ferguson** (1896) U.S. Supreme Court* decision that permitted separate but equal* facilities to be operated by states.

The *Green** decision in 1968 was quite explicit on the need to dismantle dual systems. "The burden is on a school board to provide a plan that promises realistically to work *now*, and a plan that at this late date fails to provide meaningful assurance of prompt and effective disestablishment of a dual system is intolerable." In this case New Kent County had failed to dismantle its dual system with its freedom-of-choice* plan. The Court found that the district, even more than a decade after *Brown*, still had a "Negro" and a "white" school and that the racial identification of the schools involved not just the student bodies but "every facet of school operations—faculty, staff, transportation, extracurricular activities, and facilities. In short, the State, acting through the local school board and school officials, organized and operated a dual system, part 'white' and part 'Negro.' " The Supreme Court concluded that the school board had to create a new plan and "fashion steps which promise realistically to convert promptly to a system without a 'white' school and a 'Negro' school, but just schools.''

The antithesis of a dual system is a unitary system.* To achieve a unitary system, a school district that has previously been declared a dual or segregated system must meet the requirements of the court order to desegregate to the extent practicable, including pupil assignment components, and successfully address the *Green* factors of desegregating faculty, staff, transportation, extracurricular activities, and facilities.

References: Jones-Wilson et al., *Encyclopedia of African-American Education* (1996), 144–47; Orfield and Eaton, *Dismantling Desegregation* (1996); Armor, *Forced Justice* (1995); Kluger, *Simple Justice* (1975).

DU BOIS, WILLIAM EDWARD BURGHARDT (born February 23, 1868, Great Barrington, Massachusetts–died August 27, 1963, Accra, Ghana). America's most important black protest leader in the first half of the twentieth century who helped to found the NAACP,* was editor of its magazine, *Crisis*, from 1910 to 1934, and challenged Booker T. Washington's* advocacy for industrial education for blacks. Du Bois was a college professor, historian, sociologist, and advocate for black equality for several decades.

W.E.B. Du Bois was born to free parents of African, French, and Dutch ancestry in Great Barrington, Massachusetts, a small, mostly white western Massachusetts town, in 1868. He completed his undergraduate work at Fisk University in Nashville in 1888 and received a doctorate in history from Harvard University in 1895. In 1896 his Harvard dissertation was published as *The Suppression of the African Slave-Trade to the United States, 1638–1870*. This work highlighted the role of the slave trade in the development of capitalism and the economy of the nation. After marrying Nina Gomer in 1886, Du Bois moved to Philadelphia and taught at the University of Pennsylvania. He served as chair of the sociology program at Atlanta University (now Clark Atlanta University) from 1897 to 1910.

Du Bois was a well-received sociologist and historian, publishing books such as *The Philadelphia Negro: A Social Study* (1899), the first case study of a black community in the United States, and *Black Reconstruction: An Essay toward a History of the Part Which Black Folk Played in the Attempt to Reconstruct Democracy in America, 1860–1880* (1935). In the latter he argued that Reconstruction was a period of democracy, reform, and wealth redistribution rather than one of misrule, scandal, and corruption.

Du Bois's *The Souls of Black Folk* (1903) is a study of the psychology of African Americans. The book was first published in April 1903 and was reprinted 24 times by its first publisher. Many of the essays in this collection had been published elsewhere. Among the essays in the volume was one criticizing Booker T. Washington's advocacy of industrial education, not only because of Du Bois's questions about limiting black education to mechanical arts, but also because he asked whether it was successful on its own terms, for example, teaching blacks smithing during the revolutionary development of the automobile. *The Souls of Black Folk* emphasized the liberally educated person. The book also included essays on the Freedmen's Bureau,* which established schools for blacks in the Reconstruction South.*

Du Bois believed that education must not only teach students how to do a job, it must also teach how to deal with life. Du Bois viewed education as having three functions: strengthening character, increasing knowledge, and teaching one how to earn a living.

Du Bois came to political prominence because of his disagreement with Booker T. Washington's accommodation to segregation.* Du Bois sought to challenge rather than to accommodate Jim Crow* and segregation. This led him to help establish the Niagara Movement* in 1905, which developed into the NAACP. While early in his career Du Bois believed that social science could be the salvation of blacks in the United States, over time he came to see virulent racism* as the major obstacle to social change. He believed that agitation and protest would be necessary to improve the status of blacks in the nation.

Du Bois and Washington debated in writing and face-to-face over the merits of industrial versus higher education for blacks. While Washington favored education that centered on practical and vocational training, Du Bois viewed the liberal arts as the basis for education and success in society. Du Bois looked cynically at Washington's policy of accommodation, which in his mind had led to the disenfranchisement of blacks, the legal separation of blacks, and a steady withdrawal of aid for the higher education of blacks. He even brought his message to historically black colleges and universities* that followed Washington's philosophy, for example, Hampton Institute.

Du Bois played a key role in the NAACP. He became the organization's director of research and editor of the NAACP's journal, *Crisis. Crisis* became the leading organ of black opinion and included commentary on domestic and international issues of concern to blacks. Du Bois was a major spokesperson for black protest from 1910 to 1934.

In 1934 Du Bois came into conflict with the NAACP leadership over his advocacy of promoting black solidarity through the formation of producer and consumer cooperatives, which was viewed by some as a form of self-segregation. While Du Bois was primarily an integrationist, his thinking also included separatist-nationalist tendencies. Du Bois was a believer in black leadership and black power.* His advocacy of pan-Africanism, "the belief that all people of African descent had common interests and should work together in the struggle for their freedom" (*Britannica Online*), and nationalism, leading to his view that blacks should develop a separate "group economy," led to his battles with others in the NAACP. The latter view in part reflected Du Bois's sympathy toward Marxist ideas and socialistic doctrines, as well as his holding of the value of education over desegregation* and integration.*

In 1935 Du Bois published an article entitled "Does the Negro Need Separate Schools?" in the *Journal of Negro Education* in which he argued, "I know that race prejudice* in the United States today is such that most Negroes cannot receive proper education in white institutions.'' He argued that separate but equal* was not equal because black institutions were shortchanged by white-dominated decision makers. But Du Bois noted that he was not calling for desegregated schools. Rather, ''It is saying in plain English: that a separate Negro school, where children are treated like human beings, trained by teachers of their own race, who know what it means to be black in the year of salvation 1935, is infinitely better than making our boys and girls doormats to be spit and trampled upon and lied to by ignorant social climbers.'' Du Bois concluded that ''the Negro needs neither segregated schools nor mixed schools. What he needs is Education.''

Upon leaving the NAACP in 1934, Du Bois returned to Atlanta University. He continued his writing and research in history and economics at Atlanta until he was asked to retire, at age 76, in 1944. At this point he returned to the NAACP to work on international issues, focusing on the decolonialization of Africa. Du Bois, who had joined the Socialist party years earlier, found himself isolated at the NAACP when he became an avid supporter of Henry Wallace's third-party campaign for President on the Progressive party ticket over Democratic candidate Harry Truman.* This conflict, personal conflicts with NAACP leaders Roy Wilkins and Walter White, and disagreement over how to deal with human rights violations in Africa led to a second bitter argument and his being fired in 1948.

Du Bois then founded the Peace Information Center, which campaigned against nuclear arms and the Korean War. He was indicted as an agent of an unnamed foreign power, but was acquitted. In 1961 he joined the Communist party and moved to Ghana. He died in Ghana after renouncing his American citizenship.

Works about: *Britannica Online* (1996); Michael W. Williams, *The African American Encyclopedia* (1993), vol. 2, 483–86; Marcus and Stickney, *Race and Education* (1981); Willie, *The Ivory and Ebony Towers* (1981); Metcalf, *Black Profiles* (1968).

Works by: Eric Sundquist, ed., *The Oxford W.E.B. Du Bois Reader* (New York: Oxford University Press, 1996); *The Autobiography of W.E.B. Du Bois: A Soliloquy on Viewing My Life from the Last Decade of the First Century* (New York: International Publishers, 1968); *The Souls of Black Folk: Essays and Sketches* (New York: Blue Heron Press, 1953, originally published by A. C. McClurg and Company of Chicago in April 1903).

E

EAGLETON-BIDEN AMENDMENT. Passed on December 9, 1977, by a 51–42 vote to plug a loophole in the Byrd Amendment* to ensure the prohibition of the use of federal funds to require busing* to implement school desegregation plans* where grade structures were altered. The Department of Health, Education, and Welfare* (HEW) had continued to require busing even after the Byrd Amendment was passed, so Congress passed the Eagleton-Biden Amendment to the Labor-HEW Appropriations Act of 1978. This amendment prohibited the federal government from using federal funds to require busing beyond the nearest school to implement desegregation plans based on pairing* or clustering* schools or building new school facilities. This amendment thus was aimed at restricting HEW's administrative authority by plugging the loophole that the Carter* administration had used to continue to press local districts for plans with busing. The Office for Civil Rights* may still refer cases to the Department of Justice* to bring to the federal courts to attempt to get a court order to require busing, if that is the remedy that is viewed as necessary. The effect of this amendment is to stop the federal executive branch from requiring busing, but the power of the federal courts was not affected.

References: Amaker, *Civil Rights and the Reagan Administration* (1988); Yudof et al., *Kirp and Yudof's Educational Policy and the Law* (1987); Metcalf, *From Little Rock to Boston* (1983).

EDUCATION AMENDMENTS OF 1972. These amendments included a busing* moratorium restricting the federal courts that had no real impact on federal court orders. The amendment read as follows: ''No provision of this act shall be construed to require the transportation of students or teachers in order to overcome racial imbalance.*'' Nor can any federal funds through this act be used for such a purpose. While a U.S. Court of Appeals* justice, Lewis Powell* provided a narrow interpretation of this restriction, deciding that the restriction was for cases when the court might order transportation for racial balance* purposes as opposed to orders based on constitutional violations because of de jure segregation,* but he made it clear that this restriction would apply to judges who ''have misused their remedial powers.''

References: Keynes and Miller, *The Court vs. Congress* (1989); Yudof et al., *Kirp and Yudof's Educational Policy and the Law* (1987); Bolner and Shanley, *Busing* (1974).

EDUCATIONAL PARK. Large enrollment center or consolidated campus, for example, one serving 20,000 students, located between cities and suburbs and proposed to desegregate metropolitan areas across city/suburban lines. Educational parks were proposed by Commissioner of Education Harold Howe II* in a May 1966 speech. The parks were envisioned to be a solution to school desegregation* problems because they would be on ''neutral'' territory and be new and educationally exciting, given their scale. Although this proposal received much consideration in *Racial Isolation in the Public Schools,** the feasibility of building new schools and locating and purchasing large tracts of land in an urban area, the increased busing,* the convergence of a wide range of children at a single site, and the need for city-suburban cooperation inhibited the use of educational parks. An appropriation of over $5 billion for such parks was included in a draft bill, the ''Equal Educational Act of 1967,'' prepared by an Office of Education* task force, but the bill was not enacted.

References: ''Educational Park,'' in *American Educators' Encyclopedia*, by Dejnozka and Kapel (1991), 192; Gary Orfield, *Toward a Strategy for Urban Integration* (New York: Ford Foundation, 1981); Hughes, Gordon, and Hillman, *Desegregating America's Schools* (1980); Orfield, *Must We Bus?* (1978); U.S. Commission on Civil Rights, *Racial Isolation in the Public Schools* (Washington, DC: U.S. Government Printing Office, 1967).

EISENHOWER, DWIGHT DAVID (born October 14, 1890, Denison, Texas– died March 28, 1969, Washington, D.C.). Thirty-fourth President of the United States (1953–1961), whose administration supported the ending of school segregation* in court in the 1954 *Brown* case and was forced to send troops to implement the court's decision in Little Rock in 1957. President Eisenhower was a reluctant supporter of school desegregation.*

Dwight D. Eisenhower graduated from West Point in 1915. He was appointed Supreme Commander of the Allied forces in Western Europe and organized the D-day invasion during World War II. Eisenhower served as president of Columbia University from 1948 to 1950.

In June 1952 Eisenhower retired from his army post and began to campaign for the presidency under the Republican label. He won the party's nomination on the first ballot, defeating conservative Senator Robert A. Taft of Ohio. Eisenhower named Senator Richard M. Nixon* of California as his running mate. The Eisenhower-Nixon ticket easily defeated Governor Adlai E. Stevenson of Illinois and Senator John Sparkman of Alabama, winning 39 states.

President Eisenhower was generally conservative on domestic affairs. His administration called for reduced taxes, a balanced budget, and a decrease in governmental control over the economy. However, Eisenhower did preside over the creation of the Department of Health, Education, and Welfare* (HEW) in 1953.

Eisenhower's administration submitted a brief to the U.S. Supreme Court* supporting the plaintiffs in the implementation of the *Brown* decision. President Eisenhower sent a telegram to the NAACP's* 1954 annual meeting calling the decision a "milestone of social advance" while calling for patience, calm, and understanding. Throughout, Eisenhower made it clear that the Court's decision must be upheld, although he had misgivings about the original *Brown* decision.

In the 1956 election Eisenhower was again victorious over Adlai Stevenson. In 1957 Eisenhower was forced to send 1,200 army paratroopers to Little Rock to deal with the defiance of Arkansas Governor Orval E. Faubus* during the attempt to desegregate Central High School in Little Rock, Arkansas. Eisenhower has been criticized both for acting too strongly and for not intervening early enough in the crisis. He viewed the crisis as a constitutional one where he was forced to uphold the law, not as a struggle for integration.* He was concerned about the depth of feeling in the South* over the race issue and misjudged Governor Faubus's intentions. He saw school desegregation as a difficult and complex issue, as opposed to a moral crusade or a threat to his society. Thus in his September 24, 1957, speech on the Little Rock crisis he acknowledged that the Supreme Court had decided that "separate public educational facilities for the races are inherently unequal and therefore compulsory school segregation laws are unconstitutional," but he did not state that he agreed that segregation was wrong. Eisenhower signed the Civil Rights Act of 1957,* which strengthened the Civil Rights Division* of the Department of Justice.*

President Eisenhower was generally considered at most a moderate on school desegregation. He counseled a go-slow approach on implementing the *Brown* decision and had the Justice Department involved only upon court request for help in dealing with defiance of school desegregation orders. While he believed in racial equality, he did not support the federal government intervening in state and local government to deal with racial issues.

J. W. Peltason provides a critical view of President Eisenhower in his analysis of the early years of the implementation of the *Brown** decision: "President Eisenhower refused to provide moral leadership or to use his powers as Chief Executive in support of the Supreme Court decision. Except for his momentary intervention in Little Rock, which he did not follow up, he refused to take any part in this, the most important domestic crisis of postwar America" (1961:46). By criticizing "extremists" on both sides, he equated white citizens councils,* working to defy the Constitution,* with the NAACP, working to ensure compliance. He thought that only moral suasion could lead to compliance and did not focus on law enforcement as another weapon. He did not answer segregationists and did not support the content and reasoning of the *Brown* decision. Eisenhower's support of going slow undercut southern moderates, according to Peltason, who could not be more aggressive than the President. Eisenhower refused to use the power of his office to support those working for integration. Similarly, U.S. District Court* Judge Constance Baker Motley (1996) is critical of Eisenhower for not flying back to Washington during the Little Rock crisis. It was Attorney General William Rogers who flew to the President and joined him on the golf course in Rhode Island to deal with what he considered a constitutional crisis. In President Eisenhower's defense, he did follow through on the desegregation of the armed forces begun under President Harry Truman,* he did oversee the desegregation of the Washington, D.C., school district, he sent troops to Little Rock when he had to, and he never said that the *Brown* decision was not correct despite massive resistance* in the South to school desegregation.

See also **Cooper v. Aaron**.

Works about: Constance Baker Motley, "The Legacy of *Brown v. Board of Education*," in *Brown v. Board of Education*, ed. Lagemann and Miller (1996), 37–43; *Britannica Online* (1996); O'Reilly, *Nixon's Piano* (1995); Stern, "Eisenhower and Kennedy" (1993); Robert F. Burk, *The Eisenhower Administration and Black Civil Rights* (Knoxville: University of Tennessee Press, 1984); Duram, *A Moderate among Extremists* (1981); Peltason, *Fifty-Eight Lonely Men* (1961).

Works by: *The White House Years* (Garden City, NY: Doubleday, 1963–65), 2 vols.

ELEMENTARY AND SECONDARY EDUCATION ACT OF 1965 (ESEA). This act provided school districts throughout the nation with significant federal aid to improve the quality of education and, in tandem with the Civil Rights Act of 1964,* which prohibited federal funds going to school districts that discriminated, became the major foundation for the desegregation* of the South's* schools. This legislation, aimed at providing financial and programmatic help to meet the educational needs of disadvantaged children, passed Congress on April 11, 1965. Because of the significant amount of new federal funds available through this legislation, this act raised the stakes for those school districts that did not desegregate. The act had the following provisions:

Title I granted over $1.5 billion for local school-district educational expenditures on children of low-income families. Funds were provided based on the number of low-income children residing in the local school district. Over five million students were estimated to have received help through this provision of the bill.

Title II provided millions of dollars to states for the acquisition of library resources, texts, and audiovisual materials.

Title III allocated funds to local school districts to establish supplementary educational programs.

Title IV provided funding for education research and training facilities.

Title V provided $25 million to state departments of education for improvement of services to local districts.

Title VI provided funds to establish a federal bureau to serve handicapped students.

Title VII established the general provisions of the legislation.

The 1981 Education Consolidation Improvement Act superseded the ESEA, and the functions of Title I were then contained under Chapter 1 of Title V of the new law. A decade later federal legislation changed the program's name to Title I again.

References: Milbrey W. McLaughlin, "Implementation of ESEA Title I: A Problem of Compliance," in *Making Change Happen?* ed. Dale Mann (New York: Teachers College Press, 1978); Orfield, *The Reconstruction of Southern Education* (1969); Stephen K. Bailey and Edith K. Mosher, *ESEA: The Office of Education Administers a Law* (Syracuse, NY: Syracuse University Press, 1968).

EMERGENCY SCHOOL AID ACT OF 1972 (ESAA). This act provided financial assistance to school districts undergoing school desegregation.* The objectives of the legislation were to "(1) meet the special needs incident to the elimination of minority-group segregation among students and faculty in elementary and secondary schools, (2) encourage the voluntary elimination, reduction, or prevention of minority-group isolation, and (3) aid school children in overcoming the educational disadvantages of minority-group isolation," according to Judith A. Winston (1996:158). Four years later the scope of the legislation was expanded to include funds for planning and implementing magnet schools.* The funds could not be used for busing.*

In 1970 President Richard M. Nixon* proposed a $1.5-billion grant program for helping the rural South* to desegregate (see his "School Desegregation: 'A Free and Open Society.' ") Districts ordered to immediately desegregate faced large expenses for buses. But after the Department of Health, Education, and Welfare (HEW) drafted the bill, Nixon added a provision to ban the use of these funds for busing. Congress passed a 1970 interim appropriation of $75 million while the battle over the bill took place. After some early abuses were noted, Congress passed a bill with a more national than southern orientation, a stronger oversight provision, and some incentives for school desegregation. The temporary two-year program was extended twice by Congress. In 1974 there was over $250 million available, with about 570 districts receiving funds. Between 1973 and 1976 resources for the program declined, but the funding did reach a maximum of $300.5 million in 1978.

In 1976 an amendment to this act authorized the funding of magnet-school programs to encourage voluntary plans* in the desegregation of schools. The 1977 allocation was $7.5 million, but by 1980, after an extensive evaluation and revision by the Carter* administration, the amount had been increased to $36.3 million. The program was folded into the Chapter 2 block grant program in 1981 during the beginning of the Reagan* administration. This ended the federal financial commitment to desegregating most school districts.

To replace this program, Congress enacted the Magnet Schools Assistance Program* in 1984, a section under the Elementary and Secondary Education Act* that consolidated all magnet-school support, and the allocation was set at about $75 million for 1985, 1986, and 1987. The 1995 authorization was $120 million, but no aid has been available for nonmagnet desegregation costs.

References: Judith A. Winston, "Fulfilling the Promise of *Brown*," in *Brown v. Board of Education*, ed. Lagemann and Miller (1996), 157–66; Richard M. Nixon, "School Desegregation: 'A Free and Open Society,' " in Douglas, *School Busing* (1994), 121–50; Orfield, *Must We Bus?* (1978); Orfield, *Congressional Power* (1975).

EPPS, EDGAR G. (born August 30, 1929, Little Rock, Arkansas). Educator, researcher, and leader in the education of black Americans, especially at the higher-education level. Epps graduated from Talladega College in Alabama in 1951 and received his M.A. from Atlanta University in 1955 and his Ph.D. in sociology from Washington State University in 1959. He served on the faculties of Tennessee State University (1958–1961), Florida A and M University (1961–1964), the University of Michigan (1964–1967), and Tuskegee University (1967–1970). Since 1970 Epps has served as the Marshall Field IV Professor of Urban Education at the University of Chicago. He has also served as visiting professor at several nationally renowned universities, including Harvard University. His books have focused on the role of black students in white schools, black consciousness, and race relations.* From 1974 to 1980 Epps was a member of the Chicago Board of Education and was on the board of directors of the Southern Education Foundation from 1976 to 1986. He has worked with the Department of Education* on technical review panels dealing with the education of minority children. Epps was an expert witness in the Alabama higher-education desegregation case (*Knight v. Alabama*).

Works about: Jones-Wilson et al., *Encyclopedia of African-American Education* (1996), 158; Shirelle Phelps, ed., *Who's Who among Black Americans, 1994–95* (Detroit: Gale Research, 1994), 448.

Works by: edited with Walter Allen and Nesha Haniff, *College in Black and White: African American Students in Predominantly White and in Historically Black Public Universities* (Albany: State University of New York Press, 1991); *Race Relations: Current Perspectives* (Cambridge, MA: Winthrop, 1973).

EQUAL EDUCATIONAL OPPORTUNITIES ACT OF 1974. *See* Esch Amendment.

EQUAL EDUCATIONAL OPPORTUNITY. The goal that all children should

have equivalent chances to succeed in school regardless of their background;

equal access to a high-quality basic education. The traditional view of equal educational opportunity emphasizes a fair process and equal resources and opportunities for each student, regardless of race or other social factors. Each student is judged and receives resources on an individual basis unaffected by his or her racial or other background characteristics. This view demands the absence or the elimination of discrimination* boundaries, for example, school segregation* required by statute. From this view developed a second definition of equal educational opportunity that took into account the need for additional and special efforts to overcome past discrimination. These additional efforts have included special efforts to bring more of these discriminated-against groups into the pool of qualified candidates for courses or admissions and additional support for those less able to compete, for example, remedial programs. This approach to equality of educational opportunity is tied, in some people's minds, to equality of results, that is, the notion that equal educational opportunity only exists where roughly the same proportion of minority groups or groups that have been discriminated against achieve roughly the same as majority or nondiscriminated-against groups. Where results are disproportionate, there is a presumption of unequal educational opportunities and the need to guarantee equal results, even if this requires quotas.

Definitions may be differentiated even more. Gordon (1974) points out that our conception of equal educational opportunity has changed as the needs of society have changed over time, leading to changes in job requirements and the meaning of education. Gordon has thus identified several definitions of equal educational opportunity and criteria to measure it. One set of definitions ties equal educational opportunity to the intelligence and intellectual abilities of the students. Under this view the educational experience should be a function of the student's capabilities. For example, schools should make the most use of the distinctive abilities each child possesses. This view may lead to racial and ethnic stereotyping, however. A second view, as expressed by Kenneth Clark,* holds that we should define the essential features of a good education, and all children should have access to this education. This view falls victim to the criticisms that it is too tied to the status quo (the best practice is not necessarily the best potential practice) and ignores results. Gordon offers a third view, that educational opportunity requires the achievement of a basic set of core competencies that all children except the "truly mentally defective" (26) would achieve. The school would have to utilize whatever methods are needed to help students achieve such competencies in basic communication skills and problem solving. "Equal educational opportunity demands that, where what children bring to the school is unequal, what the school puts in must be unequal and individualized to insure that what the school produces is at least equal at the basic levels of achievement" (26).

Meier, Stewart, and England view equal educational opportunity as integrated education with "students treated equally regardless of race, and learning takes place in a multiracial situation'' (1989:21). Desegregation, in this view, is defined as the mechanical process of mixing students.

Farrell (1994) makes a distinction among the following facets of educational equality, with the examples altered somewhat for the American context:

A. Equality of access: the probabilities that children from different social groupings will attend schools with different resources

B. Equality of survival: the probabilities that children from various social groupings will graduate from high school or college

C. Equality of output: the probabilities that children from various social groupings will learn the same amount by specific points in their schooling, for example, high-school graduation

D. Equality of outcome: the probabilities that children from various social groupings will have similar living standards as a result of schooling, for example, equal incomes or job status

The landmark 1966 Coleman Report* was formally entitled *Equal Educational Opportunity* and was an attempt to measure the extent to which students in the United States had equal school resources such as language labs, experienced teachers, and expenditures. Alternatively, as Farrell's definitions point out, equal educational opportunity should be contrasted with equal educational results, which refers to the outcomes of education, that is, comparisons among types of students in their actual school achievement as measured on standardized tests, graduation rates, and dropout rates.

The *Plessy v. Ferguson** (1896) decision allowed a definition of equal opportunity to include separate but equal* schools, that is, schools equal in tangible ways. One question has been whether there can be equality of educational opportunity if resources are equal but students are segregated. This question faced the NAACP Legal Defense Fund* (LDF) in its struggles before the *Brown** victory. Should it seek separate but truly equal schools, or could separate schools never be truly equal? The LDF ultimately decided on the latter answer. Feldman, Kirby, and Eaton's 1994 study of schools that were not involved in desegregation plans and remained black while receiving extra resources concludes that separate but equal, or even more than equal, is still not an effective strategy. The resegregation* of school districts, as lamented by Orfield* and Eaton in *Dismantling Desegregation*, again raises the question of whether separate schools can be equal.

References: Kenneth R. Howe, *Understanding Equal Educational Opportunity: Social Justice, Democracy, and Schooling* (New York: Teachers College Press, 1997); Orfield and Eaton, *Dismantling Desegregation* (1996); J. B. Farrell, ''Social Equality and Educational Expansion in Developing Nations,'' in *The International Encyclopedia of Education*, ed. Husén and Postlethwaite, vol. 9 (1994), 5532–39; Joseph Feldman, Edward Kirby, and Susan E. Eaton, *Still Separate, Still Unequal: The Limits of Milliken II's Educational Compensation Remedies* (Cambridge, MA: Harvard Project on School Desegregation, April 1994); K. R. Howe, "Equality of Educational Opportunity: Philosophical Issues," in *The International Encyclopedia of Education*, ed. Husén and Postlethwaite, vol. 4 (1994), 2001–4; Jonathan Kozol, *Savage Inequalities* (New York: Crown, 1991); Meier, Stewart, and England, *Race, Class and Education* (1989); Sindler, *Bakke, DeFunis, and Minority Admissions* (1978); Edmund W. Gordon, "Toward Defining Equality of Educational Opportunity," in *Equality of Educational Opportunity: A Handbook for Research*, ed. Lamar P. Miller and Edmund W. Gordon (New York: AMS Press, 1974); Coleman et al., *Equality of Educational Opportunity* (1966).

EQUAL PROTECTION CLAUSE. Key clause of the Fourteenth Amendment* prohibiting states from denying persons within their jurisdiction the equal protection of the law; this clause over time became the basis of decisions overturning school segregation* by the U.S. Supreme Court.* The Fourteenth Amendment was passed by Congress and ratified by the states in 1868 after the Civil War to achieve full citizenship and equality for black Americans. The clause states:

All persons born or naturalized in the United States, and subject to the Jurisdiction thereof, are citizens of the United States and of the state wherein they reside. No State shall make or enforce any law which shall abridge the privileges or immunities of citizens of the United States; nor shall any State deprive any person of life, liberty, or property, without due process of law; nor deny to any person within its jurisdiction the equal protection of the laws.

The Supreme Court greatly weakened the force of this clause in three sets of decisions. In the *Slaughterhouse Cases** the Court ruled that the privileges and immunities of U.S. citizens were distinct from those of state citizens, thus narrowing the scope of the equal protection clause in cases based on state violations of the clause. In the *Civil Rights Cases** the Court limited the scope of this clause to put private actions beyond its reach. Finally, in *Plessy v. Ferguson** (1896) the Court accepted the notion that separate but equal* facilities were constitutionally acceptable, even under the equal protection clause. The Court found that separating the races was not necessarily harmful to blacks; such harm was in the eyes of the perceivers since both races were treated equally. Decades of segregation could not be broken after these three verdicts.

Beginning in the 1930s NAACP* lawyers built their attack on school segregation on the separate but equal ruling that had been derived from the cases built upon the equal protection clause. Chipping away at the notion of separate but equal, the NAACP questioned whether separate black professional and graduate education was indeed equal to that received by whites in cases such as *Missouri ex rel. Gaines** (1938), *Sipuel** (1950), and *Sweatt** (1950). With the landmark *Brown v. Board of Education** decision in 1954 the Supreme Court accepted the argument that separate education could not be equal education, at least at the elementary and secondary level.

In the four decades that followed *Brown* the Court has had to define when the equal protection clause was violated. Cases of clear de jure segregation,* where the state had laws separating black from white students, were followed by Court decisions requiring plaintiffs to prove that governmental actions had a disparate impact* and were intentionally meant to harm blacks (discriminatory intent*). The Court has also had to cope with defining the remedies necessary to restore the equal protection of the laws. Is it sufficient to eliminate race-based school attendance policies, or must schools achieve racial balance* to restore equality? In short, the history of school segregation and desegregation* is intertwined with the development and interpretation of the equal protection clause.

References: Abraham and Perry, *Freedom and the Court* (1994); Bernard Schwartz, *A History of the Supreme Court* (1993); Hall, *Oxford Companion* (1992); Elder Witt, "Equal Rights," in *Congressional Quarterly's Guide to the U.S. Supreme Court* (1989), 575–617; Yudof et al., *Kirp and Yudof's Educational Policy and the Law* (1987).

EQUAL-STATUS CONTACT. *See* **Contact Theory**.

EQUITY AND EXCELLENCE. See Integrated Education.

ESCH AMENDMENT. An amendment proposed by Republican Michigan Congressman Marvin Esch to the education aid bill in 1974 (Equal Educational Opportunities Act of 1974) that placed limits on the authority of the Department of Justice* and the courts to seek busing* as a remedy. Esch's original amendment was altered in the Senate to allow the federal courts to order busing if districts were in violation of the Fifth or Fourteenth Amendments.* Yudof et al. specify the priority of remedies in the resulting amendment to the education aid act: "assignment to neighborhood schools,* taking into account school capacity and natural barriers; the assignment to neighborhood schools but considering school capacity only; the transfer of students from schools where their racial group is a majority to schools where their group is a minority; the creation or revision of attendance zones with minimum transportation; the building of new schools or the closing of old ones; the creation of magnet schools; and finally, any other plan" (1987:590–91). Section 1755 states that "no court of the United States shall order the implementation of any plan to remedy a finding of de jure segregation* which involves the transportation of students, unless the court first finds that all alternative remedies are inadequate." If busing is ordered, students cannot be transported to a school beyond the one next closest to their home unless the court determines that such busing is necessary to ensure the protection of constitutional rights. A 1974 First Circuit Court of Appeals* decision found that the 1974 amendment had the purpose "not to limit judicial purpose but to guide and channel its exercise." Thus the effect of the Esch Amendment was greatly limited by the action of the Senate.

References: Keynes and Miller, *The Court vs. Congress* (1989); Yudof et al., *Kirp and Yudof's Educational Policy and the Law* (1987); Metcalf, *From Little Rock to Boston* (1983).

EVANS V. BUCHANAN, 393 F. Supp. 428 (1975); 447 U.S. 916 (1980). Interdistrict metropolitan school desegregation* case in which the Wilmington
School District (Delaware) was ordered merged with ten surrounding suburban
school districts; the decision was affirmed by the Court of Appeals.* The U.S.
Supreme Court* refused to hear the case, thus allowing the decision.

Delaware was one of the states with litigation constituting the *Brown v. Board
of Education** (1954) cases. The original Delaware case had two components,
*Belton v. Gebhart** (1953) and *Bulah v. Gebhart** (1953). In the first suit seven
black students at Howard High School who lived outside Wilmington in Claymont sought to enter the superior high school near them, Claymont High School.
In the second suit Sarah Bulah first sought to have her daughter ride the white-
only bus to her black school, but when the bus driver refused, she became the
lead plaintiff in a suit that sought to have her daughter attend the white school
because the black school was inferior.

These two suits were considered in the Delaware Court of Chancery by Judge
Collins J. Seitz, who focused on the extent to which black students were in
reality treated equally with white students. He visited the schools involved and
ruled that the black schools were not equal to the white schools. As Vice-
Chancellor, Seitz in 1950 had ruled that the state of Delaware, through the white
University of Delaware and black Delaware State College, was not providing
an equal education to black college students, and had therefore ordered a black
student admitted to the university. The University of Delaware thus became the
first southern coeducational institution to be desegregated at the undergraduate
level. Seitz stated that the U.S. Supreme Court precedents limited his authority
to deal with the principle of separate but equal,* implying that he would overrule
the principle if he could.

The Delaware case was consolidated with cases from Kansas, Virginia, and
South Carolina in the *Brown v. Board of Education* case before the U.S. Supreme Court. The Delaware case was the only one where the judge had ruled
in favor of the plaintiffs and ordered school desegregation.* The Delaware case
is also noteworthy because of the problems with implementation of the *Brown*
decision in one small southern Delaware community. In Milford, Delaware, the
local school board decided to comply with the *Brown* decision and accepted the
requests of 11 black students to attend Milford High School quickly and without
any publicity. When some local community people found out, emotions ran high
and 1,500 people met at the American Legion Hall. After the superintendent
closed the schools, the state board ordered them opened with the black children
in attendance. The local board resigned, and the state board was forced to take
over the schools. Soon an outside rabble-rouser, Bryant Bowles, came into town,
representing the National Association for the Advancement of White People,
and led protests, including a rally of 4,000 people at the local airport, and a
school boycott. The situation became quite tense, and the Delaware Supreme
Court delayed desegregation, bowing to the pressure.

In 1957 black parents started a new suit over the lack of implementation of the *Brown* decision. The suit was called *Evans v. Buchanan*. The state fought the suit but lost in federal District Court.* The southern Delaware school districts desegregated primarily by eliminating separate black and white school districts. In practice this meant closing black schools. In the city of Wilmington racially neutral geographical attendance zones had been created, but a pupil transfer plan had also been in place and little desegregation had occurred. While desegregation was peaceful, it was not extensive.

In 1971 the Delaware school desegregation case was reopened as *Evans v. Buchanan*. The black Wilmington plaintiffs claimed that the state, despite its affirmative obligation under *Brown*, had never desegregated several of the formerly black schools in the city, which had remained over 90 percent white. The plaintiffs argued that the major obstacle to school desegregation in the city was the 1968 Educational Advancement Act, which allowed the Delaware Board of Education to consolidate and reorganize school districts throughout the state except for the Wilmington School District. This had the effect of keeping blacks in the city district while the suburbs remained almost entirely white. The plaintiffs also argued that the state's busing* of parochial students from the city to nonpublic schools, including schools outside the city, was further state action that maintained or heightened school segregation.* The case was heard by a three-judge panel that in 1974 declared the Wilmington schools segregated and in 1975 declared the Educational Advancement Act unconstitutional and ordered the state to design an interdistrict metropolitan school desegregation plan.*

After the *Milliken v. Bradley** (1974) case seemed to put rigid boundaries around metropolitan school desegregation cases, the plaintiffs argued that the Wilmington case was distinct from the Detroit case. Wilmington was in a state that had a de jure segregated school system, the practical aspects of any Wilmington metropolitan school desegregation plan would be much more feasible given its more limited area and number of school districts (under a dozen compared to over 50), and the Educational Advancement Act made it clear that the state had played a role in limiting school desegregation and thus the state could be part of the remedy. The three-judge panel accepted this argument.

The school desegregation plan ordered in the Wilmington area for the start of the 1978 school year was based on the combining of the city school district with the ten surrounding suburban school districts comprising almost all the school districts in the county. Suburban students were assigned to schools in the city for 3 consecutive years, depending on where they resided, and city students were assigned to suburban schools for 9 of the 12 postkindergarten years. Over 20,000 students were reassigned and bused in September 1978 to meet the court order. Ancillary program* components, such as the hiring of human-relations specialists, were also included in the order.

In 1981 the state's General Assembly bowed to public pressure and finally helped to reshape the remedy by dividing the county-sized school district into four ''pie-shaped'' districts, each including a section of Wilmington with a larger piece of the suburban part of the county (the districts were named Bran-

dywine, Colonial, Christina, and Red Clay Consolidated after four local rivers).
The public had objected to the large bureaucracy that the court order had created.

In 1993 the state requested that the four school districts be declared unitary.*
The plaintiffs, now represented by the Coalition to Save Our Children, argued
that the large disparities in student test scores and disciplinary action and special
education assignments by race indicated that unitary status had not been
achieved. In August 1995 federal District Court Judge Sue L. Robinson accepted
the defendant's arguments and declared the four districts of New Castle County
unitary school systems. She concluded that the state and districts had followed
the requirements of the court order and that the schools had assigned pupils to
achieve desegregated schools, and she did not accept the plaintiffs' argument
that achievement-test-score discrepancies between whites and blacks could be
traced to discrimination* in the public schools. The U.S. Court of Appeals supported her decision, which was not appealed further.

References: Varady and Raffel, *Selling Cities* (1995); Raymond Wolters, "The Consent
Order as Sweetheart Deal: The Case of School Desegregation in New Castle County,
Delaware," *Temple Political and Civil Rights Law Review* 4, no. 2 (Spring 1995): 271–
99; Julie Schmidt, "School Desegregation in New Castle County, Delaware: Historical
Background," in *Metropolitan Desegregation*, ed. Green (1985), 37–60; *Wolters, The
Burden of Brown* (1984); Jeffrey A. Raffel, *The Politics of School Desegregation: The
Metropolitan Remedy in Delaware* (Philadelphia: Temple University Press, 1980);
Kluger, *Simple Justice* (1975).

"THE EVIDENCE ON BUSING." Article by David Armor* in the journal
Public Interest published in 1972 that caused a social science and public debate
over the effects of school busing* on white enrollment and black student
achievement,* aspirations, self-esteem,* race relations,* and opportunities for
higher education. According to the editors of the journal, "Rarely can an unpublished academic article have attracted as much attention and publicity as has
this analysis of busing." Before the article was even published, reports of its
contents were appearing in national newspapers such as the *New York Times*
and *Washington Post*, and critics were already denouncing Armor's results. The
foundation of the article was his analysis of METCO,* a voluntary metropolitan
school desegregation* program that bused black students from Boston into
white, middle-class suburban schools. The METCO study was based upon a
longitudinal design covering October 1968 through May 1970. Armor did not
find that METCO had a positive impact on academic achievement of the bused
students or on educational or occupational aspirations. In fact, there was evidence that aspirations and self-concept declined as a result of attendance in
suburban schools. Racial attitudes also were not changed positively; racial identity and consciousness were heightened, support for racial isolation increased,
and interracial contact declined over time. The one positive finding was that the
METCO students were more likely to start college than the comparison group
of siblings of METCO enrollees, but this attendance gap disappeared by the
second year of college.

Public Interest published a critique of Armor's article in 1973 by four authors led by Thomas F. Pettigrew,* a professor of social psychology at Harvard University and a leading proponent of school desegregation. The critics argued that Armor had "presented a distorted and incomplete review of this politically charged topic." They had four specific criticisms. First, Armor was setting too high a standard to judge the success of busing; positive effects would take longer than a year or two and would only occur in genuinely integrated schools. Second, only selected studies had been included in his review; several more positive studies had been ignored. Third, the METCO study had several major methodological flaws, including an inadequate control group and a high nonresponse rate. Fourth, Armor's article was criticized for being based too much on social scientific and technical arguments and not enough on constitutional rights. Armor's retort was printed in the same issue.

References: David J. Armor, "The Double Double Standard: A Reply," *Public Interest*, no. 30 (Winter 1973): 119–131, reprinted in *The Great School Bus Controversy*, ed. Mills (1973); Thomas F. Pettigrew, Elizabeth L. Useem, Clarence Normand, and Marshall S. Smith, "Busing: A Review of 'The Evidence,' " *Public Interest*, no. 30 (Winter 1973): 88–118, reprinted in *The Great School Bus Controversy*, ed. Mills (1973); David J. Armor, "The Evidence on Busing," *Public Interest*, no. 28 (1972): 90–126, reprinted in *The Great School Bus Controversy*, ed. Mills (1973) and Douglas, *School Busing* (1994).

F

FAUBUS, ORVAL EUGENE (born January 7, 1910, Greasy Creek, Arkansas–died December 14, 1994, Conway, Arkansas). Governor of Arkansas from 1954 to 1967 who precipitated a constitutional crisis by blocking the token school desegregation* of Central High School in Little Rock, Arkansas, in 1957 by calling out the Arkansas National Guard to "prevent violence."

Orval Faubus was a rural schoolteacher from 1928 to 1938. He then served as county recorder (1939–1942) and acting postmaster (1946–1947) and later postmaster (1953–1954) for Huntsville, Arkansas, while owning and running a newspaper. From 1949 to 1953 he served as assistant to the governor and director of highways. He was elected governor and served from 1954 to 1967.

Faubus was generally considered a southern populist who supported New Deal policies. After he was elected governor, he named six black men to the Democratic State Committee. This led to a 1956 campaign charge that he was "soft" on racism* by his opponent, former state Senator Jim Johnson. Faubus had boasted that he had put Negroes on the Democratic State Committee and that his son was attending an integrated school.

According to Wilkinson (1979:88), Arkansas, "though opposed to integration, was not the Deep South.*" Blacks had attended the University of Arkansas, and by 1955 ten school districts had school desegregation plans.* Little Rock had not had racial troubles and had a progressive mayor, congressman, and newspaper.

By 1957 Faubus, known as urbane and a personable governor rather than as a "redneck," saw his political future, which included a third gubernatorial term, tied to stopping school desegregation. He received much publicity for his anti-desegregation efforts, including great national television exposure.

In the name of stopping violence, in 1957 Governor Faubus called on the National Guard to come to Central High School in Little Rock, effectively aiding and abetting those blocking the entrance of the nine black students poised to desegregate the school. President Dwight D. Eisenhower* was forced to send in federal troops, and federalized National Guardsmen protected the nine black students for the school year from repeated violent acts. After leaving office in 1967, Faubus worked as a bank clerk and ran three more times, unsuccessfully, for the governorship.

See also **Cooper v. Aaron**.

Works about: *Britannica Online* (1996); *Who's Who in America* (Chicago: Reed Reference Publishing, 1994), 961; Duram, *A Moderate among Extremists* (1981); Wilkinson, *From Brown to Bakke* (1979).

FLORIDA EX REL. HAWKINS V. BOARD OF CONTROL, 350 U.S. 413 (1956). U.S. Supreme Court* decision that held that the *Brown* (1954) decision also applied to higher education and that the higher-education system of Florida should be desegregated immediately.

In 1949 Virgil Hawkins and three other Negroes were denied admission to law school at the University of Florida. The state court found that a suitable remedy would be for the black applicants to attend separate facilities provided by the state for blacks. Hawkins then argued that the state's law school for blacks was inadequate and unequal. The state, however, was spending a good deal of money developing the law school at historically black Florida A and M. The Florida court found for the defendants. This decision was pending before the U.S. Supreme Court when it decided *Brown*. One week after *Brown* the U.S. Supreme Court sent the case back to Florida for reconsideration based on its landmark school desegregation* decision.

In the new conflict the NAACP* argued that *Brown* called for Hawkins to be admitted to the University of Florida Law School, but the state raised questions about the practicalities of implementation of the admission of blacks to this school. The Supreme Court ruled that not only did Hawkins have to be admitted, he must be admitted immediately. The Court decided that the practical obstacles to desegregating elementary and secondary schools did not apply to higher education and that there was ''no reason for delay.'' Ultimately Hawkins was denied admission because the state changed admission standards and Hawkins's scores on the school's admissions test were too low. In 1964 Hawkins earned a law degree from the New England School of Law and was admitted to the Florida bar after the state's legislature passed a special statute.

References: Greenberg, *Crusaders in the Courts* (1994); Kujovich, ''Equal Opportunity in Higher Education'' (1992); Preer, *Lawyers v. Educators* (1982).

FOOTNOTE 11. Citation of the U.S. Supreme Court* in the 1954 *Brown v. Board of Education** opinion (1954) referencing a number of social science sources, including work by Kenneth Clark* and other prominent psychiatrists, psychologists, sociologists, and anthropologists, that supported the Court's conclusion that racial segregation* caused a feeling of inferiority that harmed the psychological and educational state of black schoolchildren. The Court was criticized by some for relying on inexact social science instead of constitutional analysis in reaching its decision. Others defended the Court, noting that the social science argument was only part of the Court's reasoning. The footnote read as follows:

11. K. B. Clark, *Effect of Prejudice and Discrimination on Personality Development* (Mid-century White House Conference on Children and Youth, 1950); Witmer and Kotinsky, *Personality in the Making*, c. 6 (1952); Deutscher and Chein, "The Psychological Effects of Enforced Segregation: A Survey of Social Science Opinion," 26 *J. Pschol.* 259 (1948); Chein, "What Are the Psychological Effects of Segregation under Conditions of Equal Facilities?" 3 *Int. J. Opinion and Attitude Res.* 229 (1949); Brameld, "Educational Costs," in *Discrimination and National Welfare*, 44–48 (MacIver, 1949); Frazier, *The Negro in the United States*, 674–81 (1949). And see Myrdal, *An American Dilemma** (1944).

References: Hall, *Oxford Companion* (1992); Wasby, D'Amato, and Metrailer, *Desegregation from Brown to Alexander* (1977); Kluger, *Simple Justice* (1975); *Brown v. Board of Education* 347 U.S. 483 (1954).

FORCED BUSING. *See* **Busing**.

FORDICE. See **United States v. Fordice**.

FOSTER, GORDON (born May 17, 1919, Cincinnati, Ohio). Director of a desegregation assistance center* since 1966, first at the University of Miami, Coral Gables, Florida (1966–1990), then at the Southern Education Foundation (1990–1993), and then at Miami Equity Associates (1993–   ). In this capacity Foster has helped to develop school desegregation plans* for many school districts, including Dade County, Duval County (Jacksonville), and Fort Lauderdale. Foster has been an expert witness for the plaintiffs in many court cases, including those in Boston, Richmond, Memphis, Detroit, Dayton, and Wilmington, Delaware. Foster has served as a professional consultant to approximately 50 school boards, 8 state boards, and 30 assorted agencies. He has helped to develop school desegregation plans in about 30 school districts in Florida and in a majority of the remaining states. He has remained a staunch advocate of busing* to achieve school desegregation.*

Foster received his B.A. in political science and economics from Oberlin College in 1940. As a seventh-generation Quaker, in lieu of military service, he patrolled the Blue Ridge Parkway as a member of the Civilian Public Service. He lived in a commune and worked for the American Friends Service Committee. From 1956 to 1961 he worked in Ohio as a teacher and school administrator. In 1960 he earned a master's in education (educational administration) from Miami University and served on the Miami University faculty. In 1965 he received a Ph.D. from Ohio State University in educational administration and in 1966 joined the faculty of the University of Miami, Florida, and began his long term as director of the desegregation assistance center. Foster was named professor of education in 1973. In 1994, on the fortieth anniversary of the *Brown* decision, Foster was honored with the naming of a chair in his honor at Miami-Dade Community College.

Works about: Jodi Mailander, "Calm in the Center of the Storm: Chair Honors Key Figure in Desegregation," *Miami Herald*, October 16, 1994, B1, B4.

Works by: "*Milliken v. Bradley*: Implications for Desegregation Centers and Metropolitan Desegregation," in *Milliken v. Bradley: Implications for Metropolitan Desegregation: Conference before the United States Commission on Civil Rights* (Washington, DC: U.S. Government Printing Office, November 9, 1974), 127–37; "Desegregating Urban Schools: A Review of Techniques," *Harvard Educational Review* 43, no. 1 (February 1973): 5–36.

FOURTEENTH AMENDMENT. Passed by Congress and ratified by the states in 1868 after the Civil War to achieve full citizenship and equality for black Americans, this amendment to the U.S. Constitution* has been the centerpiece of legal challenges to school segregation.* The amendment includes the Equal Protection Clause.*

The Fourteenth Amendment had been offered by Republicans after the Civil War to ensure that the admission of Confederate states back to the Union would be accompanied by a guarantee of equal rights for blacks. This amendment reversed the *Dred Scott* (1857) decision, which had held that blacks, even free blacks, were not citizens and therefore not entitled to constitutional guarantees. The effect of this amendment was greatly limited by the U.S. Supreme Court* in the *Slaughterhouse Cases** (1873), which held a very narrow interpretation of such federal guarantees of rights. State laws were seen as paramount over federal protections for rights and liberties. In the landmark *Plessy v. Ferguson** decision in 1896 the Court held that the equal protection clause of the Fourteenth Amendment was not violated by state laws requiring separate but equal* railroad accommodations, and, by extension, such laws could apply to many areas of southern life, including public schools.

In 1953, after extensive discussions of the *Brown** cases, the U.S. Supreme Court asked for a reargument focused on the Fourteenth Amendment. The Court wanted to know if Congress and the states that ratified the amendment thought that it would abolish segregation in the public schools. Thurgood Marshall,* representing the NAACP Legal Defense Fund,* argued that the amendment was intended to eliminate all segregation* in the nation. He argued that the abolitionist framers of this amendment sought that goal. He also cited the debates over the Civil Rights Act of 1866.* Lawyers for the school boards disagreed, arguing that 23 states did not have that understanding at the time of ratification and 14 never even discussed the question. The intent of the framers was not clear. In *Brown v. Board of Education* (1954) the U.S. Supreme Court concluded that state-ordered racial segregation in public schools did violate the Fourteenth Amendment, but it did not base its decision on the framers' intent; the Court decided that the intent was ambiguous.

See also **Bickel, Alexander M.; Jim Crow**.

References: *1996 Deskbook Encyclopedia of School Law* (Rosemount, MN: Data Research, 1996); Nowak and Rotunda, *Constitutional Law* (1995); Hall, *Oxford Companion* (1992); Kluger, *Simple Justice* (1975).

FREEDMEN'S BUREAU. The federal agency (with the official title Bureau of Refugees, Freedmen, and Abandoned Lands) within the War Department given general supervision over the education of freed slaves after its creation in 1865 by the reconstructionist Congress trying to help former slaves, provide relief to Civil War refugees, and dispose of confiscated Confederate property. The bureau was not given authority to fund and run schools but accepted leadership for this function. Funds for its programs were obtained by selling Confederate lands. The bureau initiated 4,239 schools, hired 9,307 teachers, and provided instruction for almost one-quarter of a million children. The bureau supplied buildings and some equipment, while private associations (e.g., the American Missionary Association,* once prominent in the abolitionist movement) provided teachers. The bureau advocated normal schools to train black teachers to educate former slaves in elementary schools as early as 1866. The philosophy of the bureau stressed the values of obedience to the law, respect for property rights, racial harmony, patience, and moderation. The bureau also protected black schools and their personnel from white violence and intimidation. It encouraged the establishment of teacher-training institutions to train black teachers, and by 1869 a majority of teachers in the bureau's schools were black. The bureau also provided food to southern blacks, helped locate jobs, supervised labor contracts to ensure fairness, established hospitals, and worked to protect the civil liberties of blacks in hostile towns.

References: Kujovich, "Equal Opportunity in Higher Education," (1992); Weinberg, *The Search for Quality Integrated Education* (1983); Marcus and Stickney, *Race and Education* (1981); W.E.B. Du Bois, *Black Reconstruction* (Millwood, NY: Kraus-Thomson Organization, 1976; originally written in 1935).

FREEDOM OF CHOICE. A type of voluntary school desegregation plan,* used in the South* in the 1960s, providing students with the freedom to choose from among at least two public schools after having been assigned to the school for their race. After 1968 such plans were generally disallowed by the federal courts on the premise that they did not work, that is, did not desegregate formerly black schools. Generally, freedom-of-choice plans were constructed by blending or merging attendance zones of individual white and black schools to include both schools and provide students with a choice of schools. A subset of freedom-of-choice plans, majority-to-minority transfer programs* (M-to-M), limited choice to schools where the student was transferring from being in the majority to being in the minority race.

Freedom-of-choice plans are based on the premise that since school segregation* limits where a minority student can attend school, the appropriate remedy is to allow minority students to choose among schools that include "white" schools. These plans were popular after the 1954 *Brown v. Board of Education** decision. Freedom-of-choice plans provided minority students and their parents with the formal right to select a school other than their formerly assigned "black" school. The implementation of such plans left much to be desired. Few blacks chose to attend a white school. The reasons included lack of information, intimidation, lack of space or seats at the alternative school, and a lack of free busing* or transportation.

Freedom-of-choice plans may be viewed positively by those seeking to provide black parents with a choice of a desegregated school. However, since they leave schools all black, those seeking to eliminate segregated schools, that is, black schools, oppose such plans. In the *Green** (1968) case the U.S. Supreme Court* ruled that freedom-of-choice plans were only acceptable if they "worked," that is, if they were effective at desegregating the schools in the sense of causing racial balance.*

See also **Open Enrollment; Voluntary Plan**.

References: Gordon, "The Implementation of Desegregation Plans since *Brown*" (1994); Wilkinson, *From Brown to Bakke* (1979); Christopher Jencks, "Busing: The Supreme Court Goes North," in *The Great School Bus Controversy*, ed. Mills (1973), 14–26.

FREEMAN V. PITTS, 503 U.S. 467 (1992). U.S. Supreme Court* decision that established the possibility that court control could be eliminated from school districts in stages as compliance was achieved in particular areas of school-district compliance, for example, pupil assignment or faculty assignments. The decision also reinforced the *Board of Education of Oklahoma City v. Dowell** (1991) decision that there are practicable limits to what school districts can do to remedy school segregation* and that judicial intervention is a temporary necessity.

In 1969 DeKalb County, Georgia, a large suburban school district near Atlanta, adopted a mandatory* court-ordered school desegregation plan* using neighborhood zones. At the time the student enrollment was only 5 percent black. After years of heavy black immigration, by the mid-1980s the district was about half black, and most of the black students were concentrated in the schools in the southern end of the county.

The U.S. District Court* decided in 1986 that the DeKalb County School

District had achieved a unitary system on four *Green** (1968) factors—student assignments (although demographic changes that increased the percentage of black students from 6 to 47 percent restricted what the district could do), transportation, physical facilities, and extracurricular activities—but had not accomplished what was necessary on faculty assignments and resource allocation. In these areas vestiges of school segregation remained. The Eleventh Circuit U.S. Court of Appeals* then reversed this decision, concluding that the District Court should maintain full remedial authority over the district until all the *Green* factors were satisfactory and that the district could not shirk its constitutional obligations by blaming demographic changes.

The Supreme Court ruled that the court could relinquish its oversight in stages. In doing so it should examine whether the district complied with the original court order, whether continued control was necessary to ensure compliance in other areas, and whether the district had demonstrated good faith in its actions. (Justice Anthony Kennedy delivered the opinion and was joined by the other judges directly or in concurring opinions except for Justice Clarence Thomas, who took no part in the case.) The Supreme Court also stated that "racial balance* is not to be achieved for its own sake. It is to be pursued when racial imbalance* has been caused by a constitutional violation." Thus if the original violation is remedied, the district does not need to continue to redesign its pupil assignment plan to adjust to demographic changes. The school district must show that racial imbalance is not now due to the constitutional violation. The Court stated, "Where resegregation* is a product not of state action but of private choices, it does not have constitutional implications." This decision thus made it less onerous for school districts under school desegregation* orders to move to unitary status* and be relieved from judicial supervision. The decision also helps to specify what criteria districts seeking unitary status must meet.

References: Orfield and Eaton, *Dismantling Desegregation* (1996); Armor, *Forced Justice* (1995); Zirkel, Richardson, and Goldberg, *A Digest of Supreme Court Decisions Affecting Education* (1995).

G

GARRITY, W. ARTHUR, JR. (born June 20, 1920, Worcester, Massachusetts). W. Arthur Garrity served as a federal District Court* judge from 1966 in the Boston district and was responsible for the remedy in the Boston school desegregation* case. Garrity graduated from Holy Cross College in 1941 and received his law degree from Harvard University in 1946. He served as a U.S. Attorney from 1961 to 1966. Judge Garrity became the symbol of overzealous federal judges to the opponents of busing* in Boston. He found that the Boston public schools were unconstitutionally segregated in 1974 in the *Morgan v. Hennigan* case. The Boston School Committee refused to be part of the remedy phase* of the desegregation* process, and Garrity "took over" the Boston School District, appointed an administration of his choosing, and played a strong role in directing its policies.

Works about: *Who's Who in America, 1997*; D. Garth Taylor, *Public Opinion and Collective Action: The Boston School Desegregation Conflict* (Chicago: University of Chicago Press, 1986); Orfield, *Must We Bus?* (1978).

GEBHART V. BELTON. See Belton v. Gebhart.

GEIER V. UNIVERSITY OF TENNESSEE, 597 F.2d 1056 (6th Cir. 1979). Decision of the U.S. Court of Appeals* for the Sixth Circuit that ordered the merger of two postsecondary institutions of the state of Tennessee, concluding that the open-admissions* policy of the state was not sufficient to dismantle the state's dual system* of higher education. In 1968 the expansion of the University of Tennessee at Nashville (UT-N), a traditionally all-white university planning to construct a new building downtown, was challenged by Rita Sanders (later Rita Geier) as impeding the desegregation* of Tennessee State University (TSU), an all-black institution. The U.S. District Court* did not stop this expansion but did order the state to develop a long-range school desegregation plan* to desegregate institutions once segregated by law (de jure segregation*). Over almost a decade the state and the University of Tennessee submitted plans that the court found unacceptable. When the plans failed to accomplish desegregation at Tennessee State University, the District Court finally ordered the two institutions merged within three years from July 1, 1977.

The Court of Appeals affirmed this decision, noting that the state had an affirmative obligation to desegregate its segregated institutions at the higher as well as the elementary and secondary levels because freedom of choice* had not produced desegregation. The Court of Appeals thus referred to the 1968 *Green** decision and applied it to higher education. The court judged that "the Constitution may be violated by inaction as well as deeds." While the University of Tennessee doubled its enrollment during the course of the litigation (almost a decade), the black TSU enrollment remained static. The state's action of converting the UT-N from a non-degree-granting center to a university with four-year degree programs made it impossible for TSU to attract white students in order to desegregate. The court therefore concluded that the District Court had the authority to order the merger of the institutions. *Richardson v. Blandon*, 597 F.2d 1078 (6th Cir. 1979), was the companion decision that upheld the state's plan for desegregating its higher-education system. The comprehensive plan for the merger is described in Matlock and Humphries (1981).

References: Amaker, *Civil Rights and the Reagan Administration* (1988); Kaplin, *The Law of Higher Education* (1985); John Matlock and Frederick Humphries, "A Blueprint for Merging Higher Education Institutions: A Case Study of the Planning of the Merger of Tennessee State University and the University of Tennessee at Nashville," in *The Impact of Desegregation on Higher Education*, ed. Smith (1979), 155–80.

GONG LUM V. RICE, 275 U.S. 78 (1927). U.S. Supreme Court* ruling that the state of Mississippi regulated public education and therefore had the authority to classify a Chinese student as "colored" and operate separate schools for whites and nonwhites. Martha Lum, a nine-year-old Chinese student in Bolivar County, Mississippi, had been excluded from a white school by the superintendent of education because she was not a member of the white race. The state's constitution called for separate schools for white and colored races. U.S. Supreme Court Justice William Howard Taft concluded that this question had been settled before, citing 15 state court cases, including *Roberts v. City of Boston** (1849), and the case of *Cumming v. Richmond County Board of Education** (1899).

References: Finch, *The NAACP* (1981); Greenberg, *Judicial Process and Social Change: Constitutional Litigation Cases and Materials* (1977); Kluger, *Simple Justice* (1975).

GREEN V. COUNTY SCHOOL BOARD OF NEW KENT COUNTY, 391 U.S. 430 (1968). The most significant post-*Brown** decision by the U.S. Supreme Court* that helped to define the standards by which the Court judged whether a violation of the U.S. Constitution* had been remedied in school segregation* cases. Freedom-of-choice* plans were questioned, although not totally dismissed, in this decision. This opinion, written by Justice William J. Brennan* after a 9–0 vote, is viewed as the major turning point or watershed in school desegregation plans* since the objective of the remedy changed from eliminating race-based pupil assignments to creating schools that were to the maximum feasible extent racially balanced,* and the subject of public argument changed from debate over the principle of school desegregation* to the means.

New Kent County is a small, rural school district in eastern Virginia that had only two schools, one serving whites from elementary to high school (New Kent School) and the other serving blacks across the full grade span (Watkins School). The county was not residentially segregated. The county school board had maintained segregated schools, supported by Virginia law, up to the time of the *Brown* (1954) decision and had failed to desegregate these schools for ten years after *Brown.* Under the threat of losing federal funds posed by the 1964 Civil Rights Act,* in 1965 the school board adopted a ''freedom-of-choice plan.'' Under this plan each student, except those entering first or eighth grade, selected which of the two schools to attend. If no choice was made, the student was assigned to the school attended previously. In first and eighth grades students had to select one of the two schools. This plan was challenged, and the case reached the U.S. Supreme Court.

In a unanimous decision written by Justice Brennan the Court concluded that New Kent County had been operating a dual system* of public schools as ruled unconstitutional in *Brown.* Not only were the student bodies of the two schools segregated, but ''every facet of school operations—faculty, staff, transportation, extracurricular activities and facilities'' was also racially identifiable. (These later became known as the ''*Green*'' factors.)

The Court decided that the board had not acted in good faith. The board had waited ten years after *Brown II** (1955) to begin to undo the dual system. Moreover, the freedom-of-choice plan adopted by the board had not resulted in any whites applying to attend the black school, and only 115 black children chose to attend the white school. While the Court did not outlaw freedom-of-choice plans in every case, it declared that in this case the plan held no promise to desegregate the schools, and procedures that would work, such as neighborhood-based attendance zones, must be adopted by the board of education. The Court required a plan that ''promise[d] realistically to convert promptly to a system without a 'white' school and a 'Negro' school, but just schools.''

In essence the Court's decision indicated that neutrality was insufficient in cases of residual de jure segregation.* Fear of hostility, undue influence by school officials, and unequal facilities across the schools as well as other factors might well work against students changing schools. Thus the school board had the "affirmative duty to take whatever steps that might be necessary to convert to a unitary system in which racial discrimination would be eliminated root and branch." This decision thus confirmed the decision of Judge John Minor Wisdom* in the Fifth Circuit of the Court of Appeals,* *United States v. Jefferson County Board of Education** (1966). According to Wilkinson, "*Green* was a watershed case not because of what was said but because the Supreme Court said it" (1979: 117). The U.S. Supreme Court had accepted Judge Wisdom's skepticism toward freedom-of-choice plans, his support of statistical objectives, and his insistence on the affirmative duty of school boards.

References: Armor, *Forced Justice* (1995); Hall, *Oxford Companion* (1992); Yudof et al., *Kirp and Yudof's Educational Policy and the Law* (1987); Wolters, *The Burden of Brown* (1984); Wilkinson, *From Brown to Bakke* (1979).

GREENBERG, JACK (born December 12, 1924, Brooklyn, New York). Lawyer who worked for the NAACP Legal Defense Fund* (LDF) for 35 years and was director-counsel for over two decades. Greenberg grew up in the Bensonhurst section of Brooklyn, the son of a certified public accountant. He witnessed his first racial injustice as a lieutenant junior grade on a ship in the Pacific, and this inspired him to work against racial bigotry. He attended Columbia Law School, where he spent much extracurricular time working with the American Civil Liberties Union.* Greenberg joined the LDF as staff counsel in 1949 and worked on the Delaware challenges to *Plessy v. Ferguson** (1896). He became director-counsel in 1961 upon the appointment of Thurgood Marshall* to the U.S. Court of Appeals* for the Second Circuit. Greenberg directed the LDF staff during the period of implementation of the 1954 *Brown** decision in the South.* In 1981 Greenberg retired from the LDF. He became a law professor at Columbia Law School and subsequently dean.

    See also **Belton v. Gebhart; Bulah v. Gebhart**.

Works about: Hall, *Oxford Companion* (1992).

Works by: *Crusaders in the Courts* (New York: Basic Books, 1994); *Judicial Process and Social Change: Constitutional Litigation Cases and Materials* (St. Paul: West Publishing, 1977); *Race Relations and American Law* (New York: Columbia University Press, 1959).

GRIFFIN V. COUNTY SCHOOL BOARD OF PRINCE EDWARD COUNTY, 377 U.S. 218 (1964). U.S. Supreme Court* decision that forced Prince Edward County, Virginia, to reopen its public schools, closed to avoid school desegregation,* and in which the Court ruled that "the time for mere 'deliberate speed' had run out."

    Prince Edward County, in rural Virginia, resisted school desegregation after the 1954 decision in *Brown v. Board of Education,** with which the Prince Edward County case *Davis v. County School Board** (1952) had been consolidated. In 1959 the county ceased to finance its public schools, which were closed from 1959 through 1964. During this time period white students attended a private academy (Prince Edward Academy, which included several schools). Black students lacked public or private school until the Prince Edward Free School Association opened in 1963. The county did offer tuition grants and tax credits for those whites sending their children to private schools, thus subsidizing racially segregated ''private'' schools.

The NAACP* argued that the 13-year-old son of Reverend L. Francis Griffin had been denied an equal education by the effort of the Prince George's Board of Supervisors to circumvent the *Brown* decision. The county was collecting tax money and providing it to parents to send their children to segregated ''private'' schools. The county argued that *Brown* did not require a district to operate public schools, only to desegregate them if they existed.

A decade after the first *Brown* decision, in May 1964, the U.S. Supreme Court in a 9–0 vote sided with the NAACP. Justice Hugo Black wrote the decision. The Court found that all other children in the state could attend public schools, but children in Prince Edward County could not. The decision was unanimous: the county, by failing to fund its public schools, had denied children equal protection. But when the county opened the public schools in June 1964, only 7 white children joined the 1,400 blacks in classes. This percentage had increased to 23 percent by 1980. By 1989 the county's public schools were 62 percent black and 38 percent white. The white private school, with 630 white students and 6 black students, still was operating.

By this decision the Court thus rejected extreme tactics used to limit the implementation of the *Brown* decision. The Court also indicated that the period to accomplish school desegregation with all deliberate speed* had run out.

References: Zirkel, Richardson, and Goldberg, *A Digest of Supreme Court Decisions Affecting Education* (1995); Wolters, *The Burden of Brown* (1984); Robert Collins Smith, *They Closed Their Schools: Prince Edward County, Virginia, 1951–1964* (Chapel Hill: University of North Carolina Press, 1965).

H

HARLAN, JOHN MARSHALL (born June 1, 1833, Boyle County, Kentucky–died October 14, 1911, Washington, D.C.). Associate justice of the U.S. Supreme Court* (1877–1911) who was the lone dissenter objecting to relegating blacks to legal inferiority in the 1896 *Plessy v. Ferguson** case. Harlan grew up in a slaveholding family and was a slaveholder for a short time. He also joined the Know-Nothings and was an advocate for racist and states' rights in numerous speeches. But with secession, Harlan joined the Union army.

Harlan served on the U.S. Supreme Court from his appointment by President Rutherford B. Hayes on November 29, 1877, until his death in 1911. Justice Harlan is known for his dissents favoring the rights of blacks. As the lone dissenter in the *Plessy v. Ferguson* decision, he argued that "our Constitution is color-blind, and neither knows nor tolerates classes among citizens." Harlan asserted that "every one knows" why such laws that, on the surface, allow members of each group to keep to themselves were really a way to segregate blacks. Harlan's dissents foreshadowed mid-twentieth-century opinions by the Court. Harlan's grandson, also John Marshall Harlan, was on the U.S. Supreme Court six decades later when it decided the *Brown** case.

Works about: *Britannica Online* (1996); Hall, *Oxford Companion* (1992); Leon Friedman and Fred L. Israel, eds., *The Justices of the United States Supreme Court, 1789–1969: Their Lives and Major Opinions*, vol. 2 (New York: Chelsea House, 1969), 1281–95.

HAWLEY, WILLIS D. (born December 16, 1938, San Francisco). Education-school dean and policy analyst whose research and writing have focused on improving the implementation of school desegregation.* Hawley received his B.A. (1960), M.A. (1963), and Ph.D. (1970) in political science from the University of California at Berkeley. After a stint as an assistant city manager in Daly City, California, and a college instructor and analyst for the University of California system of higher education, Hawley became an assistant professor at Yale University in 1969. He moved to Duke University in 1972 and served there as an associate professor of policy sciences and political science until 1980, when he was hired by Vanderbilt University. During the last part of his time at Duke Hawley served as director of the Center for Educational Policy from 1978 to 1980. In 1983 Hawley became the dean of Peabody College, Vanderbilt University's School of Education and Human Development. In 1989 Hawley became director of the Center for Education and Human Development in Vanderbilt University's Institute for Public Policy Studies. In 1993 he began serving as professor of education and public affairs and dean of the College of Education at the University of Maryland at College Park. Hawley has worked in government and with policy makers in a variety of capacities. From 1977 to 1978 he was director of the education component of the President's Reorganization Project, U.S. Office of Management and Budget. From 1979 to 1981 he was director of the U.S. Department of Education's* Education Policy Development Center for Desegregation. Since 1991 he has served on the advisory commission on education to the NAACP.* Hawley has written numerous reports on achieving effective school desegregation for federal agencies such as the National Institute of Education and the U.S. Department of Education.

Works about: *Who's Who in the East, 1995–1996*, 500.

Works by: coeditor with Anthony W. Jackson, *Toward a Common Destiny: Improving Race and Ethnic Relations in America* (San Francisco: Jossey-Bass, 1995); coeditor, with Robert L. Crain, Christine H. Rossell, et al., *Strategies for Effective Desegregation: Lessons for Research* (Lexington, MA: Lexington Books, 1983); coeditor with Christine H. Rossell, *The Consequences of School Desegregation* (Philadelphia: Temple University Press, 1983); editor, *Effective School Desegregation: Equity, Quality, and Feasibility* (Beverly Hills, CA: Sage, 1981).

HICKS, LOUISE DAY (born October 16, 1919, or 1923 according to some sources, Boston, Massachusetts). Louise Day Hicks reached prominence (or notoriety) in the 1960s when she led the fight against busing* in Boston as an advocate for neighborhood schools.* She ran for School Committee, the Boston City Council, and the U.S. House of Representatives and won. Her two bids to become mayor of Boston, however, were not successful.

Louise Day Hicks was raised in a three-story South Boston frame house in a tightly knit Irish Catholic community. She graduated from parochial schools and then attended Wheelock College, ultimately receiving a B.S. in education from Boston University in 1952. She taught first grade in Brookline and clerked in her father's law office in Boston. In 1955 she received her law degree from Boston University. She and her brother John founded Hicks and Day, a law firm specializing in property transfers. She also served as counsel to the Boston Juvenile Court, providing free legal help to poor children.

In the spring of 1961 she became a candidate for the five-member Boston School Committee. Running as a moderate, Hicks received 38 percent of the vote. She began her term as a noncontroversial board member who asked the black community for advice and support in the development of compensatory education* programs, but on June 11, 1963, she had a confrontation with representatives of Boston's NAACP* over de facto segregation.* In November 1963, after she had her confrontation with black civil rights* leaders, Hicks's proportion of the school committee vote jumped to almost three in four. Her 1964 bid for the Democratic nomination for the office of state treasurer, however, proved unsuccessful.

In 1965 the passage of the Massachusetts Racial Imbalance Act* and a state report on racial imbalance* in Boston led Hicks to denounce the state board of education. The failure to pass a busing proposal led to the loss of $6,300,000 in state aid for the Boston school district. Assisted by Mothers for Neighborhood Schools, which she helped to organize, Hicks ran for her third school committee term, receiving 64 percent of the vote and defeating five anti-Hicks candidates.

On May 1, 1967, Hicks entered the Boston mayoral race with the slogan "You Know Where I Stand." In the September 26, 1967, nonpartisan primary contest she received almost 30 percent of the votes. Kevin H. White, the state's Secretary of State, was her opponent in the general election. A liberal, he defeated her by 10,000 votes. In June 1967 Hicks began her run for Boston City Council on a more moderate platform. She garnered 28,000 more votes than the second-place finisher. She ran for the seat of Speaker of the U.S. House of Representatives John W. McCormack when he retired in 1970 and won. In June 1971 she ran for mayor for a second time, but Kevin White beat her again by 40,000 votes. In November 1972 she lost a three-way battle for her House seat to John J. Moakley. In November 1973 she was reelected to the Boston City Council.

Louise Day Hicks became the focal point for criticism of busing, for the white alienated voter, and for class conflict over school desegregation* in the North. To many she symbolized the white bigot, but to others she was the expression of the concerned mother fighting for her children and their neighborhood.

Works about: D. Garth Taylor, *Public Opinion and Collective Action: The Boston School Desegregation Conflict* (Chicago: University of Chicago Press, 1986); *Current Biography Yearbook 1974* (New York: H. W. Wilson Company, 1974), 174–76.

Works by: Statement before the House of Representatives Subcommittee No. 5 of the Committee on the Judiciary, Washington, D.C., May 24, 1972, in Douglas, *School Busing* (1994), 215–20.

HIGHER EDUCATION ACT OF 1965. Under this legislation basic education opportunity grants and other financial aid were made available to disadvantaged students, increasing minority enrollment at postsecondary institutions. Title III, Strengthening Developing Institutions, helped historically black colleges and universities* (HBCUs). Originally this title did not mention HBCUs by name but described institutions facing problems threatening their survival, isolated from the mainstream of academic life, and hoping to increase their academic standing. This program now provides funds to both graduate and undergraduate HBCUs for scientific equipment, classroom, library, or other instructional facilities, support of faculty exchanges and fellowships, library books and periodicals, student services, and even endowments for graduate study. The use of funds has to be consistent with any state plan of higher education or desegregation* plan. This program was expanded in 1972, and in fiscal year 1995 $129 million was available for strengthening HBCUs.

References: *Catalog of Federal Domestic Assistance, 1996*; Roebuck and Murty, *Historically Black Colleges and Universities* (1993); Myers, *Desegregation in Higher Education* (1989); Marcus and Stickney, *Race and Education* (1981).

HISTORICALLY BLACK COLLEGES AND UNIVERSITIES (HBCUs).

Black academic institutions that have the principal mission of educating black Americans. In 1993 there were 109 HBCUs (according to Roebuck and Murty), including 50 public and 59 private institutions. Four-fifths were four-year institutions, almost all National Association for Equal Opportunity in Higher Education* (NAFEO) members. In 1994 HBCUs enrolled about 16 percent of the total number of black college and university students in the nation, a percentage that had increased over the last decade. In states with HBCUs the percentage of black undergraduate students enrolled in HBCUs increased from 28.3 percent to 37.8 percent from 1982 to 1992. A number of reasons have been offered for this increase, including the failure of many black students to graduate from historically white colleges in four years, an increasing number of racial incidents on white campuses, and increasing segregation* in society that makes attending a desegregated campus a bigger step for many blacks.

The first black colleges were Cheyney College, founded by Quakers in 1837 in Pennsylvania, originally as an elementary and high school for runaway blacks, Lincoln College, founded as Ashmun Institute in 1854 by the Presbyterian church, also in Pennsylvania, and Wilberforce College, founded in 1856 in Ohio by the Methodist Episcopal church. Almost all black public and private institutions were established after the Civil War by the 17 southern and border states to provide emancipated slaves with a basic education. The first public black college was created through the financial efforts of soldiers who had served in the colored infantries during the Civil War. The Lincoln Institute in Jefferson City, Missouri, was established as a normal school in 1866. The emphasis on teacher training remained in black colleges for decades. Other schools established included Atlanta University (1865), Fisk University (1866), Howard University (1867), and Hampton Institute (1868). These schools were established and funded with the help of the Freedmen's Bureau,* philanthropic organizations, religious bodies (e.g., the African Methodist Episcopal church), and state governments.

In 1890 Congress passed the Morrill Act of 1890* or the Second Morrill Act, which provided grants to states that chose to establish separate but equal* public institutions for blacks. While the law required that funds be "equitably divided" between the black and white institutions, the black schools never received a fair share. This lack of state funding was exacerbated by the small percentage of funding that HBCUs received from private sources.

The public historically black colleges were the only institutions serving blacks in the 17 segregated states until the challenge to separate but equal in the 1940s at the postsecondary level. According to Kujovich's careful study, "Public higher education for black students was always racially separate but never equal" (1992:233). The amount of federal and state funds available to black institutions in the 17 states was nowhere near the funds made available to white institutions of higher learning, even in land grant colleges under the Second Morrill Act.

Kujovich has argued that these schools "seldom sought to develop the intellectual potential of the black community or to use black colleges to achieve either cultural assimilation or social advancement" (265). Graduate education did not exist before the 1930s at these schools.

HBCUs produced the vast majority of black college graduates for years. From the Civil War to 1895 HBCUs in the southern and border states graduated over 1,100 students, while fewer than 200 blacks graduated from white colleges in the North. This pattern extended into the 1960s, but by 1972 the number of blacks attending HBCUs had dropped to the number attending historically white schools. Thus the majority of black professionals received their undergraduate degrees from HBCUs. HBCUs have educated almost 70 percent of the nation's black college graduates over the years, including three-quarters of the Ph.D.'s, half of the black engineers, 80 percent of black federal judges, and 85 percent of black doctors. In the 1990s they enrolled less than 20 percent of the nation's black students but graduated about one-third of the nation's black graduates. HBCU enrollment rose from 70,000 in 1954 to 257,804 in 1990 (13.1 percent of the students were white).

A number of threats to HBCUs have arisen in recent years. Several states have opened branches of their prestigious state university near an HBCU. For example, branches of Auburn University and the University of Maryland were opened, respectively, in Montgomery near Alabama State and in Baltimore near Coppin State and Morgan State. In addition, whites are enrolling in HBCUs. By the early 1970s West Virginia State and Bluefield State, both HBCUs in West Virginia, were majority white. The HBCUs have been losing enrollments as historically white institutions have opened their doors to minorities, and many of the potential students have been the more academically qualified. Finally, court decisions that do not recognize the unique role of HBCUs threaten their existence.

HBCUs have been criticized as anachronisms since historically white institutions now readily admit minority students. As vestiges of racial segregation they have been viewed as counterproductive to an integrated society. They are also criticized for accepting students who do not have the academic backgrounds to attend college. HBCUs have a vested interest in maintaining mediocrity and segregation, according to some critics.

Advocates of HBCUs have responded to their critics by arguing that a number of HBCUs are of very high academic quality, including the so-called Black Ivy League schools of Fisk University, Morehouse College, Spelman College, Dillard University, Howard University, Hampton University, and Tuskegee University. HBCUs provide black students with an emotionally supportive atmosphere and are centers of black heritage, fostering ethnic pride and self-esteem.* They foster leadership and service roles for black students. Moreover, they educate students with learning problems who otherwise would probably not attend a four-year college. According to Walters as quoted by Roebuck and Murty (1993), the functions of HBCUs include maintaining the black historical and cultural tradition, providing leadership in the black community, providing black role models, providing graduates able to deal with interracial problems, providing graduates capable of addressing black concerns, and playing a major economic role in the black community.

The role of black colleges in the desegregation of higher education presents a dilemma. In the *Brown** decision in 1954 the U.S. Supreme Court* called for the disestablishment of schools for blacks and for eliminating such segregation root and branch. In higher education, however, black colleges are viewed as necessary for the preservation of black traditions and culture and the education of many black students, especially those with modest social backgrounds. Kujovich therefore concludes that "perhaps most importantly, the survival of colleges having the primary purpose of educating America's black minority ensures a continuing commitment to black higher education, particularly for those black students suffering from educational disadvantages that would bar their admission to formerly white public colleges or make their success unlikely" (221).

References: President's Board of Advisors on Historically Black Colleges and Universities, *A Century of Success: Historically Black Colleges and Universities, America's National Treasure* (Washington, DC: Author, September 1996); Bennett, "Research on Racial Issues in American Higher Education" (1995); "The Historically Black Colleges and Universities: A Future in the Balance," *Academe* 81, no. 1 (Washington, DC: American Association of University Professors, January/February 1995), 51–57, Roebuck and Murty, *Historically Black Colleges and Universities* (1993); Kujovich, "Equal Opportunity in Higher Education" (1992); Marcus and Stickney, *Race and Education* (1981).

HOBSON V. HANSEN, 269 F. Supp. 401 (D.D.C.) (1967). Significant decision concerning abuses in the tracking system in the Washington, D.C., school system. The court (Judge Skelly Wright) found that the tracking system as implemented in Washington, D.C., schools was a form of ability grouping* and denied equal educational opportunity* to blacks and poor students in the school system. That is, the court found that the tracking system violated the Fourteenth Amendment* of the U.S. Constitution* by resegregating black students within individual schools. In the appeal process the court ruled that the implementation of the tracking system was invalid, but not the system itself as long as the abuses were eliminated.

Carl Hansen, the system's superintendent of schools, believed that students with different needs should be treated differently and separately. That is, the schools should be structured so that different levels of education were offered to students with different levels of academic ability. The school system thus had three tracks for elementary and junior-high-school students, Basic or Special Academic (for retarded students), General (average and above-average students), and Honors (gifted). In the senior high schools a Regular Track for students planning to attend college was also offered.

The court concluded that the tracking system was based on three fundamental assumptions: "First, a child's maximum educational potential can and will be accurately attained. Second, tracking will enhance the prospects for correcting a child's remedial educational deficiencies. Third, tracking must be flexible so as to provide an individually tailored education for students who cannot be pigeonholed in a single curriculum." The court found, however, that those assigned to the lowest track hardly ever moved to a higher track, that those on the lower track received a "lesser education," and that the sorting process was greatly flawed. In addition, the very assignment of a student to a lower track stigmatized the student, reducing the student's self-worth and worth in the eyes of others. The court ruled that the track system "simply must be abolished." Oakes has called this case "the best known and probably still the most important ruling on tracking" (1985:184).

References: Yudof et al., *Kirp and Yudof's Educational Policy and the Law* (1987); Oakes, *Keeping Track* (1985); Wolters, *The Burden of Brown* (1984).

HOPWOOD V. STATE OF TEXAS, 116 S. Ct. 2581 (mem.) (1996). Fifth Circuit Court of Appeals* (Texas, Mississippi, Louisiana) decision that runs counter to the U.S. Supreme Court's* *Bakke** decision by ruling that the law-school admissions process for the University of Texas was unconstitutional because it took the applicant's race into account. Two members of the three-judge panel agreed with white applicants denied admission to the 1992 law-school class who challenged the admissions process because of the preferences given to minorities. The panel concluded that the 1978 *Bakke* decision was no longer valid, given more recent Supreme Court decisions on affirmative action.* It decided that race was not an appropriate factor to consider in college admissions. The state of Texas appealed the decision, and the U.S. government sided with it as *amicus curiae** (friend of the court). In July 1996 the U.S. Supreme Court decided not to hear an appeal of this case because, as Justice Ruth Bader Ginsburg (joined by Justice David Souter) explained in a one-paragraph opinion, the case was now moot, given Texas's change in its law-school admissions procedures.

Four white applicants to the University of Texas's 1992 law-school class claimed that they had been denied admission because of their race. The law school computed a Texas Index (TI) for all applicants, a weighted combination of the applicant's score on the Law School Admissions Test and his or her grade point average. The law school followed a procedure to admit about a 5 percent black and 10 percent Mexican-American enrollment. This resulted in lower scores for the successful minority applicants. All the white applicants who brought suit would have had TIs high enough for admission had they been minority applicants. The university claimed that these four applicants were mediocre students and were using affirmative action as a scapegoat.

In August 1994 U.S. District Court* Judge Sam Sparks found that the law school's admissions practice of having two separate committees to judge applicants was unconstitutional. He also suggested that the use of two cutoff scores, one for majority and one for minority applicants, was also unconstitutional. He did sanction the use of racial goals and preferences in the admissions process.

A majority of the Fifth Circuit's three-judge panel rejected Judge Lewis Powell's* analysis in the *Bakke* decision with the reasoning that his opinion was not adopted by the other judges and therefore did not represent the majority opinion in that case. The panel concluded that remedying past discrimination* was the only way to justify racial preferences. It reasoned, however, that the discrimination had to be that conducted by the specific institution in question, that is, the law school and not the state. It concluded that admissions committees may use a variety of criteria for judging applicants such as diversity of viewpoints and economic and social background, but they may not use race if no discrimination by that particular institution has been declared unconstitutional.

Technically, only the three states under the Fifth Circuit are now compelled to abide by this decision, but the decision has worried many advocates of affirmative action. The University of Texas Law School, for example, began the 1997–1998 academic year with only 4 black and 26 Mexican-American students, down from 31 blacks and 42 Mexican Americans the previous year. The school had been the leader in the nation in the previous decade in graduating students from these two minority groups.

References: Douglas Lederman and Stephen Burd, "High Court Refuses to Hear Appeal of Ruling That Barred Considering Race in Admissions," *Chronicle of Higher Education*, July 12, 1996, A25, A29; Michael S. Greve, "Ruling Out Race: A Bold Step to Make Colleges Colorblind," *Chronicle of Higher Education*, special section on "The Affirmative Action Decision," March 29, 1996, B2; Michael A. Olivas, "The Decision Is Flatly, Unequivocally Wrong," *Chronicle of Higher Education*, special section on "The Affirmative Action Decision," March 29, 1996, B3.

HOSTAGE THEORY. The hostage theory proposes that school desegregation* helps black children because white officials will avoid harming white children who are reassigned to schools with black children. The theory therefore is given as a reason to seek desegregated schools by those advocating enhanced resources and education for minority students. However, to the extent that white school-board members remain in office while sending their children to private schools and then have no qualms about harming the public schools, for example, by lowering tax rates and expenditures, this theory loses some force.

In a broader context the argument is made that segregation* isolates a minority group, thus permitting its inferior treatment. When minorities and majorities are integrated, policies to provide less benefits to blacks are more difficult to implement. Thus the 1896 *Plessy** decision, despite the U.S. Supreme Court's* conclusion that the stigma of segregation was only in the eye of the beholder, permitted the inferior treatment of blacks in the provision of services. Orfield and Eaton (1996) argue that given the relation of poverty status to race, the segregation of the races in schools reinforces the separation of resources from need. Thus desegregation, in their view, is necessary for reasons beyond "race-mixing"; desegregation may be the only way to tie the resources of a metropolitan area to minorities in areas of isolated poverty.

References: Orfield and Eaton, *Dismantling Desegregation* (1996); Meyer Weinberg, "Improving Education in Desegregated Schools," in *Metropolitan Desegregation*, ed. Green (1985), 143–160.

HOUSTON, CHARLES HAMILTON (born September 3, 1895, Washington, D.C.–died April 22, 1950, Washington, D.C.). Lawyer and educator who transformed Howard Law School* into a generator of civil rights* advocates that produced many of the key attorneys in the civil rights movement* and the special counsel for the NAACP,* Thurgood Marshall.* Charles Hamilton Houston led the fight for civil rights from 1929 until 1950. The grandson of slaves, Houston was the only son of a prominent Washington couple, William and Mary Houston. His father earned his law degree at Howard's night law school while serving as a clerk in the Record and Pension Office of the War Department. After attending segregated schools in Washington, D.C., Charles Houston graduated from Amherst College, earning his Phi Beta Kappa pin and serving as one of his class's valedictorians in 1915. He served as an officer in the segregated army in World War I. He graduated in the top 5 percent of his class in 1922 at the Harvard Law School and was the first black elected to the *Harvard Law Review*. He continued his education with Felix Frankfurter at Harvard, who served as his mentor while he was the leading counsel of the American Civil Liberties Union* and on the NAACP's legal advisory board and was at the time the only Jew on the law-school faculty. Houston earned a doctorate in juridical science after earning his law degree.

In 1924 Houston went into practice with his father in Washington, D.C., and taught part-time at Howard Law School. He was named dean of the Howard Law School in 1929 and, according to Jack Greenberg,* turned the part-time faculty and student body "into an accredited institution that became a West Point of Civil Rights, producing an annual crop of lawyers rigorously trained to do battle for equal justice'' (1994: 5). Houston calculated that in a city having seven white law schools Howard University needed to differentiate itself. He raised admission standards, improved the library, and removed some faculty while bringing in excellent young black scholars such as James Nabrit, Jr.* The number of students was kept small, no more than 60 students at a time. Within two years Houston had gained American Bar Association full accreditation for the school, and Howard became a member of the Association of American Law Schools. Thurgood Marshall was Houston's student; Houston was Marshall's mentor. They joined forces to win the first admission of a black student to a white southern law school (*Pearson v. Murray** [1936]).

Houston was named by the NAACP's Executive Board in 1934 to replace Nathan R. Margold to direct the NAACP's legal attack on segregation.* (He was officially part-time counsel and then named the first full-time, salaried, special counsel in 1935.) Houston was vice dean of the Howard Law School at the time. He had been in the forefront of training lawyers to defend civil rights. He recruited a dedicated core of brilliant lawyers for the NAACP legal department, including Marshall in 1936 from the Howard campus. In 1938, due to illness and family obligations, he returned to Washington, leaving the NAACP with Marshall in command. Houston died unexpectedly at the age of 54 of a heart attack after making his mark as a civil rights strategist, advocate, and litigator of the first order and a successful educator and dean.

Houston cleverly strategized and began the attack on segregated graduate-professional schools. Houston's strategy was based on the premise that inequality at this level could be easily proven. The duplication of dual facilities at this level would be prohibitively costly, and this would provide pressure for desegregation.* Judges, he reasoned, would be more sympathetic at this level because of the low threat of violence. Furthermore, the result, even if based on the separate but equal* thesis, would increase the black leadership class, and, of course, judges might also be sympathetic to young people seeking to become lawyers.

See also **Margold Report; NAACP Legal Defense and Educational Fund, Inc. (LDF).**

Works about: Jones-Wilson et al., *Encyclopedia of African-American Education* (1996), 216–17; Greenberg, *Crusaders in the Courts* (1994); Genna Rae McNeil, *Groundwork: Charles Hamilton Houston and the Struggle for Civil Rights* (Philadelphia: University of Pennsylvania Press, 1983); Marcus and Stickney, *Race and Education* (1981); Kluger, *Simple Justice* (1975).

HOWARD LAW SCHOOL. Howard Law School in Washington, D.C., was the major producer of black civil rights* attorneys in the decades of the development of civil rights and school desegregation* law. It was transformed by Charles Hamilton Houston* in the 1930s into a first-class law school for those studying civil rights law. Howard Law School graduates included Thurgood Marshall* and other legal leaders of the civil rights movement* such as James M. Nabrit,* Spottswood Robinson III, and William Henry Hastie. Howard University was the university for America's blacks at the time, for no university in the South* would accept black applicants at the graduate or professional level, and few blacks in the North had the funds for desegregated schools. Howard had begun in a former beer-and-dance hall through efforts of the Freedmen's Bureau.* At the time there were over 12 million blacks in the United States, but only about 1,100 black lawyers. Mordecai Johnson, president of Howard University, had been stung by a comment made by U.S. Supreme Court* Justice Louis Brandeis that the legal education of blacks was inferior. Greenberg relates Brandeis's claim that he could "tell most of the time when I'm reading a brief by a Negro attorney" (1994:5). Johnson hired Houston in 1929 to overhaul the law school, and in six years Houston turned the law school with part-time faculty and student body into one that received accreditation from the American Bar Association in 1931 and became, according to Greenberg, "a West Point of civil rights" (5).

In 1932 Howard University began publishing the *Journal of Negro Education.** In 1952 the university became the center of a group of scholars, lawyers, and others brought together by this journal for a summit on strategy to attack school segregation.*

Howard University was founded shortly after the Civil War and chartered by Congress in 1867. The law department was organized two years later. The university is named after General Otis H. Howard, the founder of the Freedmen's Bureau, which provided the early financial support for this private institution. The university continues to receive federal financial support. The student body, approximately 10,000 in total, is primarily black. In addition to the law school, Howard has programs in medicine, theology, education, nursing, engineering, and business.

In the 1990s the law school conferred an average of 185 degrees annually. Its faculty has 35 full-time and 12 adjunct instructors. The main campus has almost 90 acres; the School of Law is situated on the 22-acre West Campus.

References: Greenberg, *Crusaders in the Courts* (1994); "Howard University," in *American Educators' Encyclopedia*, by Dejnozka and Kapel (1991), 269; Kluger, *Simple Justice* (1975).

HOWE, HAROLD, II (born August 17, 1918, Hartford, Connecticut). Strong advocate of school desegregation* who served as U.S. Commissioner of Education during the period of strong enforcement of the Civil Rights Act of 1964* and who received vitriolic criticism by a number of southern politicians, who called him everything from the "U.S. Commissioner of Integration" to the "Commissar of Education." Howe is the grandson of Samuel Chapman Armstrong, founder of the Hampton Institute (now Hampton University) and Union army general and commander of a black regiment. His grandmother was an abolitionist who left her native New England to teach blacks in the South* after the end of the Civil War. He is the son of the Reverend Arthur Howe, former president of the Hampton Institute and college professor at Dartmouth. He received his B.A. degree from Yale University in 1940 and his M.A. in history from Columbia University in 1947.

Howe worked as a history teacher at the Darrow School in upstate New York. He was the captain of a minesweeper during World War II. After the war he taught history at the Phillips Academy in Andover, Massachusetts. In Andover he later served as a junior- and senior-high-school principal and then became principal of the prestigious Walnut Hills High School in Cincinnati, Ohio, in 1953. Howe then became the principal of another nationally known high school, Newton High School in Massachusetts, in 1957, where the Oxford-type house system he devised became nationally recognized. In 1960 he became the superintendent of schools in Scarsdale, New York. In 1964 he served as an aide to Governor Terry Sanford in North Carolina, directing the Learning Institute of North Carolina, a private nonprofit experimental educational organization. He was named Commissioner of Education in 1965 and served until 1968.

Howe believed that schools should be the instrument for social change, and he was an advocate for strong federal involvement in desegregating urban schools while he served as Commissioner of Education. In March 1966 Howe announced a set of strict guidelines for southern school districts to meet to qualify for federal aid under the Elementary and Secondary Education Act of 1965,* thus earning the enmity of southern congressmen. In June 1966 in Chicago he called for ways to eliminate the "inferior ghetto school," and he asked local officials to consider city-suburban school-district mergers and the construction of educational parks* to desegregate urban schools. As Office of Education* officials checked whether freedom-of-choice* plans had led to school desegregation across the South, Howe became the object of personal attacks, and demands for his resignation increased. He was charged with calling for the destruction of neighborhood schools* and planning to force busing* upon America's cities. In September 1968 Howe appeared before the House Rules Committee, where members of the committee attacked not only the guidelines he established but Howe himself. While Howe survived, in October the Senate Appropriations Committee cut funding for the Office of Education by $3.1 million and Congress passed legislation prohibiting him from deferring funds to be provided to local school districts for more than 90 days without a hearing on their school desegregation compliance, thus limiting his authority and discretion. Howe held on to his job as support for civil rights* waned during this time.

Howe later chaired the William T. Grant Foundation Commission on Work, Family, and Citizenship, which issued a report called *The Forgotten Half.* Before retiring, Howe was a senior lecturer at the Harvard Graduate School of Education. Howe has received many honors throughout his career, including several honorary degrees.

Works about: *Who's Who in America,* 1997, 2030; Orfield, *The Reconstruction of Southern Education* (1969); *Current Biography Yearbook* (New York: H. W. Wilson Company, 1967), 185–88.

Works by: *Thinking about Our Kids* (New York: Free Press, 1993).

I

INDEX OF DISSIMILARITY. Also called the Taeuber Index after Karl and Alma Taeuber, who popularized its use (although it was developed by Otis and Beverly Duncan); a measure of racial balance,* originally used to measure housing desegregation,* indicating the proportion of either white or black students who would have to change schools in order to achieve the exact same percentage in each subarea as in the whole area. If all schools were perfectly racially balanced, the index would be 0. If all whites attended schools enrolling only whites and blacks only schools enrolling blacks, the index would be 100. The index uses as the standard the overall racial composition of an area and then compares the racial composition of subareas to the racial composition of the entire area. Specifically, if in each subarea I there are $w(I)$ whites and $b(I)$ blacks and the entire area contains W whites and B blacks, the index would be

$$D = [\tfrac{1}{2} \ \Sigma \mid b(I)/B - w(I)/W \mid] \times 100$$

"D is equal to one-half the sum of the absolute value of the number of blacks in each school divided by the total number of blacks in the district minus the number of whites in each school divided by the total number of whites in the district, multiplied by 100. The index represents the percentage of black students who would have to be reassigned to white schools, if no whites are reassigned, in order to have the same proportion of blacks in each school in the entire district'' (Fife, 1992:17). This is a measure of racial imbalance* and thus is used in conjunction with the racial balance definition of school desegregation.*

A major limitation of this index is that it adjusts to the percentage of major-ities/minorities in the unit being analyzed. It cannot measure the degree of in-terracial contact, that is, tell what the absolute white or minority percentage is in the schools. For example, the index of dissimilarity may indicate that schools reflect the overall district population, but it will not indicate that there are few whites left in the district. Thus a school district that is 90 percent black can have a low, that is, good, index of dissimilarity because all the schools are 90 percent black, but this is certainly not a "desegregated district." A school de-segregation plan* that has produced racial balance in all the schools but also a loss of white enrollment may have an impressive index of dissimilarity but very little interracial contact across racial groups. Thus the index of interracial ex-posure* has been used as an alternative or additional measure of the demo-graphic effects of school desegregation.

References: Armor, *Forced Justice* (1995); Fife, *Desegregation in American Schools* (1992); Rossell, *The Carrot or the Stick for School Desegregation Policy* (1990); Reyn-olds Farley, "Residential Segregation and Its Implications for School Integration," in *The Courts, Social Science, and School Desegregation*, Part 1, ed. Betsy Levin and Willis D. Hawley, School of Law, Duke University, 39 (Winter 1975): 164–93; Otis D. Duncan and Beverly Duncan, "A Methodological Analysis of Segregation Indexes," *American Sociological Review* 20 (March 1955): 210–17.

INDEX OF INTERRACIAL EXPOSURE. An alternative to the index of dis-similarity,* created by Christine Rossell,* which in its current use measures the degree of interracial exposure across all schools in a district. According to David Armor,* "For a given minority group, the index is the average percent white in schools attended by the typical black or Hispanic student" (1995:164):

$$Smw = \Sigma \; kN_{km}P_{kw} \; / \; \Sigma \; kN_{km},$$

where

k = each individual school,

N_{km} = number (n) of minorities (m) in a particular school (k), and

P_{kw} = proportion (P) white (w) in the same school (k).

"*Smw* is equal to the proportion of white students in the average minority child's school. The number of minority students in each school is multiplied by the proportion of white students in the same school. This number is summed for all schools and divided by the number of minority students in the school system to produce a weighted average—the proportion white in the average minority child's school" (Fife, 1992:18). Thus the index ranges from 0, that is, no white students in classes attended by minorities, to its maximum possible value, which is the percentage white in the system. This index is useful in tracking school desegregation* in a school district over time because it takes into account the loss of white students and measures the extent of school desegregation. For example, Rossell and Armor's (1996) national survey of desegregation in larger school districts indicated that using the index of dissimilarity as a measure of racial balance, racial balance has improved over time. When the interracial exposure index is used to measure racial balance, however, it is apparent that after an initial increase in black exposure to whites in the early 1970s (after *Swann**), black exposure has declined over time because fewer whites are attending schools in large school districts with blacks.

References: Rossell and Armor, "The Effectiveness of School Desegregation Plans, 1968–1991'' (July 1996); Armor, *Forced Justice* (1995); Fife, *Desegregation in American Schools* (1992); Rossell, *The Carrot or the Stick for School Desegregation Policy* (1990).

INDEX OF RACIAL ISOLATION. A measure of the degree of school segregation* that indicates the percentage of a racial group that attend schools with a particular racial composition. For example, one can define a segregated school as one with 80 percent or more minority students or 90 percent or more. The index would then measure the percentage of students by race in each school and/or across the schools with this degree of racial isolation, for example, 42 percent of black students in this district attend schools that are at least 80 percent black. Gary Orfield's* 1993 analysis of school segregation, for example, found that in 1968–1969, 64.3 percent of blacks attended schools that were 90–100 percent minority. In 1991–1992 this percentage had dropped to 33.9 percent.

References: Armor, *Forced Justice* (1995); Gary Orfield, *The Growth of Segregation in American Schools: Changing Patterns of Separation and Poverty since 1968*, Report of the Harvard Project on School Desegregation to the National School Boards Association (Alexandria, VA: NSBA, December 1993); U.S. Commission on Civil Rights, *Racial Isolation in the Public Schools* (Washington, DC: U.S. Government Printing Office, 1967).

INTEGRATED EDUCATION. Journal founded and edited by Meyer Weinberg* devoted to the subject of school desegregation* and related issues founded in 1963; now *Equity and Excellence in Education.* Weinberg, working in the City Colleges of Chicago, began *Integrated Education* (also titled *Integrateducation*) as a magazine to further the idea of desegregating the Chicago public schools. At the time there were few articles on school desegregation in academic journals. The journal focused on educational equality issues and included articles on the status of school desegregation in various locations throughout the nation and the status of education for minority groups, including not only blacks but also American Indians and Asian Americans. The journal was formally published by Weinberg's Integrated Education Associates (School of Education, Northwestern University) until 1986, when he dissolved this organization and transferred the authority to publish the journal to the University of Massachusetts at Amherst. At that time the name was also changed to *Equity and Excellence* (later *Equity and Excellence in Education*) to signal a broadening of the scope of its content and to avoid the confusion with integrating subject-area curriculum that *Integrateducation* had engendered.

References: *Equity and Excellence* 22, nos. 4–6, Special Transition Issue (Amherst: University of Massachusetts School of Education, Summer 1986).

INTEGRATION, RACIAL. Qualitative concept based on the goal of social integration as opposed to a quantitative concept of physical inclusion. In an integrated school or school district the social situation reflects mutual respect and equal dignity across the races in attendance. The school atmosphere is one of acceptance and encouragement of distinctive cultural patterns. An integrated school provides equal educational opportunity* and results, educating all children effectively, regardless of race or class. Thus all integrated schools are desegregated, but not all desegregated schools are integrated. A secondary meaning of racial integration refers to attempts to attain schools that are in racial balance.* Thus conservative critics accuse the federal courts of moving beyond race-neutral school assignments to working toward specific ratios of black and white students in each school.

How to achieve racial integration in its first meaning has been the subject of much research, especially with respect to achieving school integration.* The appropriateness of integration as a goal has been questioned by advocates of black nationalism* and black power.* To the extent that integration means assimilation, black leaders have argued that it is wrong and unwise for blacks to accept or be forced to accept the dominant white culture. While the definition of racial integration includes respect for all minority cultures, the reality of efforts to achieve this goal may not be free from efforts to move toward the school's dominant culture. Indeed, one of the presumed positive forces of school desegregation and integration is the higher educational standards likely in a school dominated by middle-class students, as indicated in the Coleman Report* in 1966.

In its ideal sense integration can thus be viewed as the last stage of school desegregation,* in which the cultural and structural integration of all students, staff, and families has been achieved. Such schools achieve equal educational opportunity*; they ensure that all children acquire the knowledge, skills, and abilities to participate in mainstream American society. Students receive a multicultural education* that recognizes the contributions of all ethnic and racial groups. Students respect their differences and different heritages. Students, staff, and parents hold equal-status roles across all racial backgrounds.

At the postsecondary level the conflict between maintaining historically black colleges and universities* and desegregating historically white institutions has been the subject of concern and debate. Current federal court decisions, such as *United States v. Fordice** (1992), favor maintaining and upgrading HBCUs while increasing the number of minorities and improving their treatment at historically white institutions.

References: Kunen, "The End of Integration" (April 29, 1996); Lagemann and Miller, *Brown v. Board of Education* (1996); Thomas G. Greene and John F. Heflin, "State Governments and Multicultural Education Policy," *Equity and Excellence* 25, nos. 2–4 (Winter 1992): 145–50; Hawley et al., *Strategies for Effective Desegregation* (1983); Gary Orfield, *Toward a Strategy for Urban Integration* (New York: Ford Foundation, 1981).

INTERPOSITION. The theory that states should "interpose" their own authority between usurping federal courts and "the people" in order to protect their citizens from unconstitutional actions of the federal government. Advocated by *Richmond News Leader* editor James Kirkpatrick in November 1955 to fight school desegregation,* interposition became the battle cry of massive resistance.* The idea caught hold among southern politicians, and within 18 months all of the Deep South* states had passed interposition resolutions and a number of laws to maintain segregation.* These laws, interposed between the federal courts and the local schools, included pupil placement laws,* aid to students attending private schools, and laws weakening compulsory attendance. Despite the questionable basis of interposition in constitutional law, its advocates rallied behind state action to resist the 1954 *Brown** decision. The motivation was based on support for racial segregation* and states' rights.

Interposition was first advocated before the Civil War period. Virginia proposed it in reaction to the Sedition Act in the Virginia Resolution of 1798. South Carolina did the same over a federal tariff in the 1830s, but President Andrew Jackson threatened military force, and the state backed down. Senator John C. Calhoun called for interposition to stop the delivery of abolitionist mail in the South.* In the 1850s many Northerners called for interposition to protest the Fugitive Slave Act of 1850. In *Abelman v. Booth* (1859) Chief Justice Roger B. Taney spoke for the U.S. Supreme Court,* holding that interposition was unconstitutional and that the action taken by the Wisconsin Supreme Court, which held that the federal Free Slave Act was unconstitutional, was incorrect; the U.S. Supreme Court had the final authority to interpret the U.S. Constitution.* Thus interposition was found to have no legal standing and was judged to be an illegal defiance of constitutional authority.

The South split over whether to adopt interposition or to accept the doctrine of nullification.* Both doctrines denied the validity of the Supreme Court decision, but not all southern leaders were willing to advocate nullifying the federal court's ruling. States of the upper South generally accepted the validity of the *Brown* decision but worked to limit its effect, while states of the Deep South* challenged the legitimacy of the decision. *Abelman v. Booth* was cited by the federal courts in the 1958 *Cooper v. Aaron** decision concerning resistance to school desegregation in Little Rock, Arkansas, as the Supreme Court reaffirmed that it had the final say on the meaning of the Constitution.

References: Forrest R. White, "*Brown* Revisited" (September 1994); Hall, *Oxford Companion* (1992); Bartley, *The Rise of Massive Resistance* (1969).

J

JIM CROW. The segregation* of whites and blacks required or permitted by state and local authorities in restaurants, theaters, hotels, drinking fountains, neighborhoods and housing, beaches and swimming pools, churches, buses, streetcars, taxicabs, trains, waiting rooms, comfort stations, barbershops, ticket windows, baseball teams, libraries, state colleges and universities, and other facilities. Such segregation was given legal sanction by the U.S. Supreme Court* in the *Plessy v. Ferguson** decision in 1896. The segregation was imposed by authorities or permitted private individuals and groups to segregate facilities by race. This era began after the decade of Reconstruction from 1865 to 1877 with the resolution of the Tilden-Hayes election conflict and the pullout of federal troops from the South* agreed to in the Compromise of 1877.* Despite the legal requirement of separate but equal,* facilities were separate but rarely equal. Laws prohibiting interracial marriage were also passed during this period. By 1885 all the former Confederate states had passed laws to segregate blacks from whites. Segregation was enforced legally and through other means such as the Ku Klux Klan's* violent actions.

The slang term "Jim Crow" comes from a minstrel song by Thomas Dartmouth "Daddy" Rice, "Wheel About and Turn About and Jump, Jim Crow." The song was popular about 1835 and was related to the black color of a crow. A dance or jig was associated with this term. Rice, later billed as Jim Crow, appeared in blackface and danced around the stage ("jumped Jim Crow") in a manner denigrating blacks, like the laws named after the song. Around 1840 the segregated car on the Boston Railroad was known as the "Jim Crow."

Black seamstress Rosa Parks challenged Jim Crow by refusing to give up her seat on a Montgomery, Alabama, bus in 1955. Her arrest provoked a yearlong boycott of the city's buses led by Dr. Martin Luther King, Jr.* The U.S. Supreme Court* struck down the city ordinance that required bus segregation in 1956. The black freedom riders challenged the Jim Crow laws in the South in 1961 on buses and in restaurants. A chant during the civil rights movement* was "Jim Crow—Must Go!"

References: Henry J. Abraham and Barbara A. Perry, *Freedom and the Court: Civil Rights and Civil Liberties in the United States*, 6th ed. (New York: Oxford University Press, 1994); Safire, *Safire's New Political Dictionary* (1993); Marger, *Race and Ethnic Relations* (1991); Wilkinson, *From Brown to Bakke* (1979); C. Vann Woodward, *The Strange Career of Jim Crow*, 3rd rev. ed. (New York: Oxford University Press, 1974); Newby, *The Development of Segregationist Thought* (1968); Stetson Kennedy, *Jim Crow Guide to the U.S.A.: The Laws, Customs, and Etiquette Governing the Conduct of Nonwhites and Other Minorities as Second-Class Citizens* (London: Lawrence and Wishart, 1959).

JOHNSON, LYNDON BAINES (born August 27, 1908, Gillespie County, Texas–died January 22, 1973, San Antonio, Texas). Thirty-sixth President of the United States (1963–1969) who was a strong advocate of civil rights* and whose Great Society instituted more social legislation than any other President, including the Civil Rights Act of 1964.* Johnson grew up in a poor family in the hills of southwest Texas. Johnson's father and grandfather had both served in the Texas state legislature. Lyndon Johnson completed his teaching degree at Southwest Texas State Teachers College at San Marcos in three years. While beginning work as a teacher in Sam Houston High School in Houston, Texas, by the time he was 30 years old Johnson was the secretary to Richard M. Kleberg, Sr., one of the owners of the King Ranch and a Texas congressman, and was the protégé of old family friend Sam Rayburn. From 1935 to 1937 Johnson, still not yet 30, served as Texas state director of the National Youth Administration program. Johnson had learned about the problems of Mexican Americans during his teaching years and became an advocate of Mexican Americans.

Johnson ran for Congress when Congressman James P. Buchanan died, and he served from 1937 to 1949. In his first term he defended the New Deal from conservative attack and became a political protégé of President Franklin Roosevelt. While he was a strong New Deal supporter on economic legislation that helped poor minorities, Johnson held to the southern position on civil rights. He voted against every piece of civil rights legislation, including antilynching proposals and laws against the poll tax. In his 1948 U.S. Senate campaign Johnson, in a close battle with conservative, antiblack segregationist Coke Stevenson, ran as a strong segregationist. His record, however, encouraged black support, and he won the runoff election by 87 votes, gaining the nickname "Landslide Lyndon." He served as Democratic whip (1951–1953), minority leader (1953–1954), and majority leader (1954–1961). Johnson was the youngest majority leader ever to hold the position and was so successful at the wheeling and dealing that he became known as "the Great Persuader."

The *Brown** decision was announced in 1954 when Johnson was Senate majority leader, and he reacted as a national, not a southern, politician. He declared that the decision had now been made and thus had to be implemented. When the Southern Manifesto* reached the Senate floor on March 12, 1956, Johnson publicly declared that he, as majority leader, could not sign it and place himself as opposed to the law of the land. Johnson helped to pass the Civil Rights Act of 1957,* arguing to his constituents that it was a voting rights, not a civil rights, law, and that the most onerous provisions had been eliminated or fended off.

Failing in a bid to be nominated for president in 1960, Johnson was selected by nominee John F. Kennedy* to be his vice-presidential running mate, thus balancing the ticket in terms of geography and age. Stern (1992:155) observes that Johnson, as Vice President, "became a vocal and articulate administration spokesman for civil rights." When Kennedy was assassinated in Dallas, Texas, in November 1963, Johnson was sworn in as President. Five days after the assassination President Johnson called for the enactment of civil rights legislation before a joint session of Congress and national television cameras. "No memorial or eulogy could more eloquently honor President Kennedy's memory than the earliest possible passage of the civil rights bill for which he fought so long."

Johnson's landslide victory over Barry Goldwater in 1964 was followed by a period of incredible activity in social legislation. Johnson interpreted his huge election victory as a mandate for his social reform legislation. In a few months after winning office his Great Society program was enacted into law. The program included the Civil Rights Act of 1964, for which Johnson worked very hard, the Voting Rights Act of 1965, and the Medicare bill of 1965.

The Vietnam War proved Johnson's downfall, and on March 31, 1968, he made a television speech concluding that he would not be a candidate for another term. Less than one week after the United States signed the peace agreement to end the war in Vietnam, Lyndon Johnson suffered a heart attack and died.

Johnson was a supporter of the civil rights movement* even before his presidency. When he refused to sign the Southern Manifesto, he was one of only three southern Senators to do so. He appointed the first black, Thurgood Marshall,* to the U.S. Supreme Court* and pushed the Civil Rights Act of 1964 through Congress as well as the Voting Rights Act of 1965 and the Fair Housing Act of 1968.

Works about: *Britannica Online* (1996); O'Reilly, *Nixon's Piano* (1995); Stern, *Calculating Visions* (1992); Cashman, *African-Americans and the Quest for Civil Rights, 1900–1990* (1991); Dan Morris and Inez Morris, *Who Was Who in American Politics* (New York: Hawthorn Books, 1974), 343–44; Ruth P. Morgan, *The President and Civil Rights* (New York: St. Martin's Press, 1970, and Lanham, MD: University Press of America, 1987).

Works by: *To Heal and to Build: The Programs of Lyndon B. Johnson* (New York: McGraw-Hill, 1968).

JOURNAL OF NEGRO EDUCATION. Refereed scholarly periodical published by Howard University focusing on the education of blacks. When it was launched in 1932, the journal filled a void with its mission, described in Jones-Wilson et al. (1996) as "first, to stimulate the collection and facilitate the dissemination of facts about the education of black people; second, to present discussions involving critical appraisals of the proposals and practices relating to the education of black people; and third, to stimulate and sponsor investigations of issues incident to the education of black people." The journal documented the status of black, segregated schools and analyzed the impact of school segregation.* Some of the journal's published articles were used in arguing the successful *Brown v. Board of Education** (1954) case. The journal is edited and published by the faculty of the Department (now School) of Education at Howard University.

References: "*Journal of Negro Education*: A Howard University Quarterly of Issues Incident to the Education of Black People," in *The Encyclopedia of African-American Education*, ed. Jones-Wilson et al. (1996), 240–41; Aaron B. Stills and Fay Flanagan, "Charles H. Thompson's Journal: To Protect and Serve," *Journal of Teacher Education* 3, no. 1 (1952): 65–69; Charles H. Thompson, "Editorial Comments: Why a Journal of Negro Education?" *Journal of Negro Education* 1, no. 1 (1932): 1–4.

JUSTICE DEPARTMENT. *See* **Department of Justice**.

K

KENNEDY, JOHN FITZGERALD (born May 29, 1917, Brookline, Massachusetts–died November 22, 1963, Dallas, Texas). Thirty-fifth President of the United States (1961–1963) whose low profile on civil rights* was overtaken by events when he was forced to send troops to help James Meredith* enroll at the University of Mississippi and had to confront Alabama Governor George C. Wallace* over the entrance of two black students to the University of Alabama. His administration authored what was to become the Civil Rights Act of 1964* after his assassination.

The second of nine children of Joseph Patrick and Rose Fitzgerald Kennedy, John Fitzgerald Kennedy was a war hero and Harvard University graduate (B.S., 1940). His senior thesis was expanded into a best-selling book, *Why England Slept* (1940). Kennedy ran for Congress in 1946 in the Massachusetts 11th District at age 29. He won overwhelmingly. He served in the House of Representatives from 1947 to 1953 and advocated liberal policies such as more Social Security and public housing. His parents remained a major force in his life. His father was a multimillionaire businessman who was appointed head of the Securities and Exchange Commission and ambassador to Great Britain.

In 1952 Kennedy ran for the U.S. Senate against Henry Cabot Lodge, Jr., the popular incumbent. Despite Dwight D. Eisenhower's* victory in the presidential race in the state, Kennedy won by a substantial margin. In 1956 Kennedy wrote the Pulitzer Prize–winning *Profiles in Courage*, a study of eight great American political leaders who defied public opinion to act out their conscience. In the same year Kennedy reached national prominence during his losing battle at the Democratic convention to become Adlai Stevenson's running mate.

Kennedy, while generally having a positive civil rights record, did get in trouble with civil rights activists for going along with southern senators in the battle over the Civil Rights Act of 1957.* He voted to send the proposed bill to the Senate Judiciary Committee headed by Senator James Eastland of Mississippi, a certain death for the bill, and he also supported a jury-trials amendment that would have made enforcement of voting rights more difficult. Kennedy, like President Harry S. Truman* before him, was trying to balance the demands of the black and liberal wing of the Democratic party with the white southern faction.

In 1958 he won reelection to the Senate by the largest margin of votes in the history of the state. He was helped in this effort by the support of a letter from NAACP* leader Roy Wilkins positively evaluating his civil rights record.

In 1960 Kennedy and running mate Lyndon B. Johnson* narrowly won the presidential election, defeating Richard M. Nixon.* Kennedy became the youngest man (aged 43) and first Roman Catholic to be elected President of the United States. While he was a very popular President, Kennedy's thin margin of victory did not give him much sway over Congress. His appointment of his brother, Robert, as Attorney General provided his administration with a strong civil rights advocate. John F. Kennedy, however, did not come to his presidency with a knowledge of civil rights issues. His only activity in this issue had been his telephone call in October 1960, during the election campaign, to Coretta Scott King to express his concern and voice his support for her husband, Martin Luther King,* when he was jailed on a technicality when picketing a department store in Atlanta. His call of sympathy was followed by a call of his brother, as his confidant and voice on civil rights matters, to the Alabama judge, and King was freed.

As President, Kennedy put civil rights on the back burner. Stern (1992) calls Kennedy ''an intimidated president,'' concerned that he needed to develop his relationship with Congress before putting forward any decisive legislation. He did not want to split the Democratic party. Trying to balance the factions in the party, Kennedy appointed five black judges while also appointing five segregationist judges in the South,* including William Howard Cox, a lifelong friend of segregationist Mississippi Senator James Eastland. While a major advisor to him on civil rights had been attorney Harris Wofford, Kennedy skipped over him to appoint Burke Marshall to head the Civil Rights Division* of the Department of Justice.*

Making clear that segregation was wrong, Kennedy did publicly endorse the substance of the 1954 *Brown** decision. His administration did enforce the law through the judicial process but was also open to negotiations on school desegregation plans* with local school districts. He did propose major civil rights legislation that, after his death, Lyndon B. Johnson got through Congress as the Civil Rights Act of 1964.

Kennedy, like President Dwight D. Eisenhower before him, used federal troops as necessary to enforce the implementation of a school desegregation court order over a defiant governor. In this case it was to ensure that James Meredith could enter the University of Mississippi in 1962.

Kennedy also had a confrontation with Governor George Wallace of Alabama over the admission of two students to the University of Alabama. Vivian Malone and Jimmy Hood sought to enter the University of Alabama in May 1963. At that point, only Alabama lacked a black student in its white state university system. The NAACP Legal Defense Fund* added its request to the still-pending 1955 *Lucy* case. When the judge ordered the students admitted for the June 10 session, Governor Wallace announced that he would keep them out. He then filed a U.S. Supreme Court* case to stop the President from ordering federal troops to enforce their admission. President Kennedy issued a proclamation on June 11, 1963, commanding the Governor and others not to obstruct justice.

Wallace stood in the schoolhouse door, and Deputy Attorney General Nicholas Katzenbach ordered the students admitted. According to Jack Greenberg,* "Wallace's opposition was real, but the incident in the schoolhouse door was strictly for public consumption" (1994:340). On June 11 President Kennedy spoke to the nation, asking eloquently, "If an American, because his skin is dark, cannot eat in a restaurant open to the public, if he cannot send his children to the best public school available, if he cannot vote for the public officials who represent him, if, in short, he cannot enjoy the full and free life which all of us want, then who among us would be content to have the color of his skin changed and stand in his place?" Kennedy said that "we are confronted primarily with a moral issue. . . . I hope that every American, regardless of where he lives, will stop and examine his conscience about this and other related incidents." Kennedy called for a stronger federal commitment to civil rights and submitted a comprehensive civil rights bill, the foundation of the Civil Rights Act of 1964, a week later. It was Lyndon Johnson who saw that the bill was passed, however, after Kennedy's assassination on November 22, 1963, in Dallas, Texas.

Works about: *Britannica Online* (1996); O'Reilly, *Nixon's Piano* (1995); Greenberg, *Crusaders in the Courts* (1994); Stern, *Calculating Visions* (1992); Carl M. Brauer, *John F. Kennedy and the Second Reconstruction* (New York: Columbia University Press, 1977).

KEYES V. DENVER SCHOOL DISTRICT NO. 1, 413 U.S. 189 (1973). Decision in which the U.S. Supreme Court* by a 7–1 vote, with the majority opinion written by Justice William Brennan,* ruled that de jure segregation* in one geographical area of the Denver School District required a school desegregation* remedy for the entire district. This was the first nonsouthern school desegregation case before the Supreme Court after *Brown** (1954) and widened the scope of implementation remedies to include northern and western cities, not just the South,* because it allowed for discrimination* based on actions other than just a statute calling for segregated schools to prove de jure segregation. In this decision the Court opened the door for systemwide desegregation of northern school districts, which had no statutes or constitutional provisions to segregate the schools by race but may well have taken actions, such as student assignment plans and school location decisions, to segregate.

In 1969 the school board of Denver, Colorado, adopted three resolutions aimed at desegregating the schools of the Park Hill area. At the next school-board election a new board majority was elected and promptly voted to rescind the resolutions and establish a voluntary student transfer program. The U.S. District Court* agreed with the plaintiffs that given the board's actions, which included building a new small elementary school in the middle of a black area, gerrymandering of student attendance zones, and the extensive use of mobile classrooms, the Denver School Board had engaged in unlawful school segregation* for almost a decade in the Park Hill area. The District Court, however, did not accept the plaintiffs' argument that all segregated schools in Denver, not just those in the Park Hill area, should be ordered to be desegregated. The District Court ruled that the plaintiffs would have to prove unlawful de jure segregation in each area of the city where they sought to have the court order desegregation. The District Court assumed that segregation was a result of de facto segregation* where de jure segregation had not been proved.

The question before the U.S. Supreme Court was therefore whether the finding of de jure segregation in one portion of a school district not already part of a statutory dual system* warranted a court order of desegregation in the entire school system. The Court concluded that "where plaintiffs prove that the school authorities have carried out a systematic program of segregation affecting a substantial portion of the students, schools, teachers, and facilities within the school system, it is only common sense to conclude that there exists a prejudice for a finding of the existence of a dual system." The segregatory actions of the school board in one area of the district, for example, building a school to serve only black students, affected the schools in other areas of the district, for example, by reducing the number of black students available to desegregate other schools. The Court thus concluded that the presumption of segregatory or discriminatory intent* had shifted once segregatory intent was proved in one area of the district. The burden of proof* then shifted to the school board to prove that the schools outside of the Park Hill area were not segregated by intent (de jure) as opposed to being segregated by de facto reasons.

In a dissenting opinion Justice Lewis Powell,* who had served as a member of the Richmond School Board, argued that the distinction between de jure and de facto school segregation had "outlived its time." He argued that where school segregation was found to a substantial degree, school authorities were responsible for demonstrating that they were operating a "genuinely integrated school system." Powell objected to the courts being concerned with "effect" in southern school districts, that is, fulfilling the affirmative duty to desegregate in de jure districts, versus discriminatory "intent" in northern districts, that is, proving whether districts purposefully segregated the schools. He called for the same standard throughout the nation.

Justice William Rehnquist* also dissented, objecting to applying the evidentiary standards of *Green** (1968) to northern school districts as well as continuing to move from racial neutrality to racial balance* goals. The disagreements in the Court over school desegregation became more apparent with this opinion.

This case is significant because it helped to establish the operational distinction between de jure and de facto school segregation. The Supreme Court chose a middle ground between requiring that the plaintiffs show that all segregation in a district was caused by government action as opposed to asserting that all segregation had violated the equal protection clause* of the Constitution.* The middle ground established by the Court was that once some intention was shown, it would rely more on the pattern of segregatory results and not require more proof of intentional segregation. To further ease the standard of proof of de jure segregation, the Court accepted the notion that when school authorities took action that would obviously increase segregation instead of action that would decrease segregation, this was sufficient proof of unlawful segregation. This decision removed the potential onerous burden to those bringing suits to prove intentional segregation at each school, an approach suggested by the Department of Justice* under President Richard Nixon.*

This case also decided the status of Hispanics in school desegregation cases. The Court concluded that Hispanics had been discriminated against like blacks and were therefore entitled to a similar remedy. Denver's Hispanic enrollment was twice its black enrollment. In September 1995 U.S. District Court Judge Richard P. Matsch declared the Denver school system desegregated, releasing the district from 21 years of federal court oversight.

References: Armor, *Forced Justice* (1995); James J. Fishman and Lawrence Strauss, ''Endless Journey: Integration and the Provision of Equal Opportunity in Denver's Public Schools: A Study of *Keyes v. School District No. 1*,'' in *Justice and School Systems*, ed. Flicker (1990), 185–231; Yudof et al., *Kirp and Yudof's Educational Policy and the Law* (1987); Orfield, *Must We Bus?* (1978).

KING, MARTIN LUTHER, JR. (born January 15, 1929, Atlanta, Georgia–died April 4, 1968, Memphis, Tennessee). An eloquent Baptist minister who was the leader of the civil rights movement* from the mid-1950s until his assassination in 1968 and helped set the stage for the passage of the Civil Rights Act of 1964.*

King received his bachelor's degree in sociology from Morehouse College (1948), a B.D. from Crozer Theological Seminary (1951), and a Ph.D. from Boston University in 1955. King was a pastor of the Dexter Avenue Baptist Church in Montgomery, Alabama, when Rosa Parks refused to give up her bus seat to a white passenger, was arrested for violating the city's segregation law, and began a boycott of the transit system. King was elected as the leader of the Montgomery Improvement Association and reached national visibility and prominence.

In 1960 King moved to Atlanta to become copastor, with his father, of the Ebenezer Baptist Church. He worked with black students organizing sit-in demonstrations at segregated lunch counters. King was a student of Mahatma Gandhi's work and further developed his ideas of nonviolent civil disobedience. In October 1960 he was arrested at a lunch counter at an Atlanta department store. Although these charges were dropped, King was arrested for violating his probation on a minor traffic offense and sentenced to a state prison farm. King was released when presidential candidate John F. Kennedy* intervened, an act that was thought to have helped push the candidate into the White House eight days later.

In 1963 King joined other black leaders to organize the March on Washington, an interracial gathering of 200,000 by the Lincoln Memorial, to demand equal justice for all citizens. It was at this event that King gave his eloquent "I have a dream" speech. King's actions and words helped set the stage for the passage of the Civil Rights Act of 1964. He was awarded the Nobel Prize for peace in Oslo in December of that year and was named *Time* magazine's first black Man of the Year.

In 1965 King's call for nonviolence came increasingly under attack. The riots in Los Angeles's Watts district in August 1965 showed the deep racial divide and pent-up anger in urban black ghettos. On April 4, 1968, King was assassinated in Memphis, Tennessee, while working in support of the city's striking sanitation workers.

King was an advocate of integration* and nonviolence. He was the founder of the Southern Christian Leadership Conference and promoter of the March on Washington (August 28, 1963) to achieve civil rights.* Congress voted to observe a national holiday in his honor in 1986 (the third Monday in January). Martin Luther King will be remembered as an eloquent spokesman for nonviolent change and equal justice as well as integration. His words and actions moved both blacks and whites to reexamine their thoughts and actions toward race and equality, and his efforts helped to set the stage for school desegregation.*

Works about: *Britannica Online* (1996); Richard Lischer, *The Preacher King: Martin Luther King, Jr., and the Word That Moved America* (New York: Oxford University Press, 1995); Metcalf, *Black Profiles* (1968).

Works by: *Why We Can't Wait* (New York: Harper and Row, 1964).

KU KLUX KLAN (KKK). "The Invisible Empire of the South," an organization aimed at keeping the Negro in his place during Reconstruction by using violence, for example, lynchings, and the threat of violence, such as cross burnings, to stop black action toward equal rights; formed again in 1915. There was not a single klan but numerous klaverns throughout the South.* Their tactics included intimidation of those blacks willing to fight for school desegregation,* even the NAACP Legal Defense Fund's* top lawyers.

The original KKK was organized by veterans of the Confederacy in Pulaski, Tennessee, in 1866 to maintain white supremacy during the Reconstruction period following the Civil War. The Klan's characteristic use of white sheets, robes, and pillowcases to cover bodies and heads became its symbol, and these objects were worn to hide their identities and to scare blacks into submission. In 1867 the individual groups were organized into a regional organization at a Nashville, Tennessee, convention. They were formally disbanded in 1869, after they had helped to institutionalize white supremacy, but the Force Act of 1870 and the Ku Klux Act of 1871 (declared unconstitutional in 1882) were not successful in leading to the conviction of members.

In 1915 in Georgia the Klan was reborn and spread beyond the South. Burning crosses became the Klan's symbol, and in the 1920s the KKK claimed 4 million members, primarily throughout the South and Midwest. The roots of the second coming of the KKK were in American nativist tradition, an aversion not only to blacks but also to immigrants, Roman Catholics, Jews, and organized labor. The membership declined greatly during the depression, and the Klan temporarily disbanded in 1944, but rose again, albeit on a much smaller scale, in the 1960s. The membership dropped to 10,000–40,000 as bombings, whippings, and shootings were used to fight the civil rights movement* and federal civil rights* actions in the South. Increased racial tolerance and antiviolence have diminished the organization to a few right-wing extremists.

References: *Britannica Online* (1996); Arnold S. Rice, *The Ku Klux Klan in American Politics* (New York: Haskell House, 1972); Thomas H. Johnson, *The Oxford Companion to American History* (New York: Oxford University Press, 1966), 453.

L

LARRY P. V. RILES, 793 F.2d 969 (9th Cir. 1984). Critical case on student testing and disproportionate placement of minority students in special education. This case had two phases separated by seven years: the granting of the preliminary injunction in 1972, affirmed by the Ninth Circuit Court of Appeals* in 1974, followed by a decision on the merits of the case in 1979, affirmed in 1980. In 1984 the Ninth Circuit upheld the district court's order to eliminate disproportionate placement of minority students in special education.

In 1971 the plaintiffs, black children attending the San Francisco public schools, charged that their placement in educable mentally retarded (EMR) classes was discriminatory because the IQ tests used in their placement were culturally biased. (Students with scores lower than 75 were considered EMR on the state test.) The plaintiffs had the children retested by black psychologists who made attempts to establish rapport with the students before testing, reduce distractions, and give credit for answers in the language and culture of these students. All then received scores above 75. The court accepted the argument that irreparable harm would come from EMR placement because the placement remained on a student's permanent record, the educational program was limited, and the student would be stigmatized.

The plaintiffs argued that the testing procedure in the San Francisco schools violated the equal protection clause* of the Fourteenth Amendment* because black children were disproportionately harmed by the process. They did not argue that the fact that black students were more than twice as likely to be placed in EMR classes in the city was based on explicit racial discrimination,* only that the effect of the procedure was to harm black children. The plaintiffs

sought to shift the burden of proof* from their having to prove that the classification process was irrational and arbitrary to the school system having to prove
the appropriateness of its procedures. The court accepted the argument and
granted a preliminary injunction, stopping the school system from continuing to
use the test as the primary means to assign students, but did not reassign students
already in EMR classes. The trial on the merits of the case was held five years
later and lasted six months.

In October 1979 U.S. District Court* Judge Robert F. Peckham of San Francisco concluded that the state education department violated the rights of black
children because students were mislabeled as EMR, and they were over-
represented in classes for the mentally retarded. The court held that the state
had to prove that the tests used to place minority children were valid in isolating
children who could not profit from regular schooling, not just those who would
perform poorly. The court had judged EMR classes as being for those incapable
of learning in regular classes. The court concluded that the state was guilty of
discriminatory intent* because it had permitted the placement of a disproportionate number of minority children in EMR classes without carefully monitoring the testing and placement process. The court then required an end to the
use of standardized intelligence tests to place black children in EMR classes,
except where the court gave permission. In addition, the court required school-
district plans to correct significant imbalances in EMR placements. Finally, the
state needed to ensure that all misidentified students would have individual education plans readied. The 1984 decision by the Ninth Circuit Court of Appeals
upheld the court's remedy.

See also **Second-Generation Problems**.

References: Mark G. Yudof, David L. Kirp, and Betsy Levin, *Educational Policy and
the Law*, 3rd ed. (St. Paul, MN: West Publishing, 1992); Yudof et al., *Kirp and Yudof's
Educational Policy and the Law* (1987); Weinberg, *The Search for Quality Integrated
Education* (1983); Mark Yudof, "Suspension and Expulsion of Black Students from the
Public Schools: Academic Capital Punishment and the Constitution," *Law and Contem-
porary Problems* 39, no. 1 (1975): 374–411.

LAU V. NICHOLS, 414 U.S. 563 (1974). Unanimous U.S. Supreme Court*
decision holding that the San Francisco schools must provide special training
for Chinese-speaking children. The Court sustained the 1970 Department of
Health, Education, and Welfare* (HEW) guidelines that required the district to
rectify the language deficiency of such students.

After desegregating in 1971, the San Francisco School District had not established remedial English-language instruction or special compensatory programs* for about 1,800 Chinese-speaking students. The plaintiffs argued that
this violated Title VI of the Civil Rights Act of 1964* as stated in an HEW
guideline that where language excludes minority children from effective participation in school, the school district must take steps to meet the students' needs.
The U.S. District Court* and U.S. Court of Appeals* had denied relief, but the

U.S. Supreme Court, while not requiring bilingual education* per se, did require some remedial action on the part of the school district.

This decision was important for Hispanics, who, like Chinese, rely on their native language. But the decision also raised issues about the conflict between the bilingualism strategy, which called for the concentration of language/cultural students in special language classes where their unique culture would also be emphasized, versus desegregation,* which required dispersion of such students. The decision gives great discretion to school districts on how to help students make the transition to English but does indicate that help is required.

References: Zirkel, Richardson, and Goldberg, *A Digest of Supreme Court Decisions Affecting Education* (1995); *U.S. Supreme Court Education Cases*, 3d ed. (Rosemount, MN: Data Research, 1993); Abernathy, *Civil Rights and Constitutional Litigation* (1992); Yudof et al., *Kirp and Yudof's Educational Policy and the Law* (1987); Christine H. Rossell and J. Michael Ross, "The Social Science Evidence on Bilingual Education," *Journal of Law and Education* 15, no. 4 (Fall 1986): 385–419.

LDF. *See* **NAACP Legal Defense and Educational Fund, Inc. (LDF).**

LEADERSHIP CONFERENCE ON CIVIL RIGHTS. Organization consisting of approximately 185 member organizations that coordinates lobbying in Washington, D.C., for integration,* "equal rights, equal opportunities, and equal justice without regard to race, sex, religion, ethnic origin, handicap or age." The conference was founded in 1950 by three civil rights* activists, including Roy Wilkins of the NAACP,* to implement President Harry S. Truman's* Committee on Civil Rights report *To Secure These Rights.* It coordinated campaigns for civil rights laws from 1957 on and spearheaded the fight that led to the defeat of Clement Haynsworth, G. Harrold Carswell, and Robert Bork to the U.S. Supreme Court by Presidents Richard Nixon* and Ronald Reagan.* Member organizations include the American Civil Liberties Union,* Mexican American Legal Defense and Educational Fund,* the NAACP Legal Defense Fund,* the NAACP, several unions, and good-government groups such as the League of Women Voters. The primary purpose of the conference is to push for the enactment of legislation supportive of its goals.

References: Jaszczak, *Encyclopedia of Associations* (1996), 2066–67; *Leadership Conference on Civil Rights 45th Anniversary Commemorative Journal*, May 3, 1995; Jost, "Rethinking Affirmative Action" (April 28, 1995).

LEGAL DEFENSE FUND. *See* **NAACP Legal Defense and Educational Fund, Inc. (LDF).**

LIABILITY PHASE. Stage of a school segregation* case in which the court determines the nature of the constitutional violation and the boundaries of any remedy needed. The responsibility for any constitutional violation is decided by the U.S. District Court* in this phase. The next phase of the court's deliberations is called the remedy phase.* In school desegregation* cases the liability phase is generally centered on whether the equal protection clause* of the Fourteenth Amendment* of the U.S. Constitution* has been violated. The Fourteenth Amendment is violated when a school policy or action leads to segregation and is intended to lead to segregation rather than to serve a legitimate educational purpose. It is far easier to prove segregative effect or disparate impact* of governmental actions, for example, racial imbalance* in school enrollments or unequal resources at schools serving different races, than intentional purpose or discriminatory intent.*

References: Armor, *Forced Justice* (1995); Joseph R. Nolan and Jacqueline M. Nolan-Haley, "Liability," in *Black's Law Dictionary* (St. Paul: West Publishing, 1990), 91.

LIDDELL V. MISSOURI, 731 F.2d 1294 (8th Cir. 1984), cert. denied, 469 U.S. 816 (1984). St. Louis school desegregation* case that resulted in a voluntary metropolitan plan* including the city and 23 suburban school districts. The Missouri constitution before the 1954 *Brown** decision required that the state's schools be segregated. Following *Brown*, the city schools had adopted a neighborhood school plan* so that black as well as white students attended their local schools. St. Louis, however, like many American cities after World War II, experienced a decline in white population, and by 1977 three-quarters of the city's students were black. The city plaintiffs filed a class-action suit in 1972, and after Judge James H. Meredith of the U.S. District Court* denied a motion to include the state and suburban districts, a consent decree* to increase the number of minority teachers and achieve racial balance* was accepted by the court. The case was reopened in 1977, and this time the court added the state of Missouri, the state board of education, and the state's commissioner of education to the city school board as defendants. After a trial to determine if the city schools were still unconstitutionally segregated, the U.S. District Court ruled that the district's neighborhood school* policy was constitutional and the district was a unitary system.* But the Eighth Circuit Court of Appeals* reversed this decision in *Adams v. United States* (1980) and found the city and the state both liable for the city's segregated schools because they had failed to take affirmative action* to remedy the segregation that had resulted from the state's constitutional requirement of segregated schools.

With the threat of a court-imposed mandatory interdistrict school desegregation plan* before it, the city and suburban school districts agreed to a voluntary plan* requiring each suburban district to accept black students from the city and the city to establish magnet schools* to attract white suburban students. The state challenged this decision, arguing that it should not have to pay the costs of the magnet schools and the interdistrict plan, but the Court of Appeals upheld the decision and the U.S. Supreme Court refused to hear the case. By 1988 about 12,000 black students were attending suburban schools, but only 650 whites from the suburbs were traveling into the city for their schooling. The number of city students attending all-black schools dropped from 30,000 to 19,000 under the plan.

References: *"Liddell v. Missouri,"* in *Encyclopedia of African-American Education*, ed. Jones-Wilson et al. (1996), 262–65; Wolters, *Right Turn* (1996); Daniel J. Monti, *A Semblance of Justice: St. Louis School Desegregation and Order in Urban America* (Columbia: University of Missouri Press, 1985).

M

MAGNET SCHOOL. A school, or program within a school, with the following characteristics: (1) a special curricular theme or method of instruction, for example, a science and technology high school or a Montessori program, (2) a role in a voluntary plan* to desegregate the schools in a school district, (3) some choice of school by student and parent, and (4) access by students beyond the neighborhood attendance zone. Magnet schools are developed to attract students to a school that they would otherwise not attend. Generally they are established to attract white students to formerly black schools.

Magnet schools have spread rapidly in central-city school districts since the early 1970s because they offer a voluntary approach to school desegregation, provide a variety of educational and curricular options to students, often focus on outcomes and careers, and indicate a renewed concern about educational quality. Magnet schools have been viewed as an important means to retain and attract middle-class students to city schools. Since middle-class families living in cities and dissatisfied with city schools generally can move to the suburbs or send their children to nonpublic schools, cities have tried to provide alternative schools within their own borders to keep their middle-class students or even attract new ones.

Magnet schools are primarily found in city school systems. Magnet schools exist across the nation from Cambridge, Massachusetts, to Houston, Texas, to San Diego, California. Some suburban school districts, for example, Prince George's County, Maryland, have also adopted magnet-school plans. Montgomery Blair High School in adjoining Montgomery County, with an enriched math, science, and computer program, was designed to attract whites and Asians into the predominantly black and Hispanic school. Not only has the school attracted white and Asian students, but three of its students were named as Westinghouse finalists in 1993, the most of any high school in the county.

In a whole-school magnet all students in the school are included in the magnet programs. In a program-within-a-school magnet, only some of the school's students participate in the school's magnet program.

The first desegregation remedies involving magnet plans approved by federal courts were in Houston (1975), Milwaukee (1976), and Buffalo (1976). In 1991–1992 there were 2,433 magnet schools in the nation, over twice as many as in 1983, according to the American Institutes for Research. Three times as many students (approximately 1.2 million) were in magnet schools in 1991–1992 as in 1983.

While magnet schools are now common in city school districts, their impact on retention and attraction is not well established. Much of the support for the contention that magnet schools hold, or even attract, middle-class students is anecdotal. The most extensive, systematic, and quantitative study of the effect of magnet schools on student enrollment has been conducted by Christine Rossell.* Rossell found that districts with magnet schools as the basis of voluntary desegregation plans had less white flight* from schools and more interracial contact of minority and white students over time than mandatory plans.*

The educational effects of magnet schools are uncertain. While the argument that students learn more in magnet schools has been offered, this claim is not based on solid social science research. The better test scores of students in magnet schools could well reflect a ''creaming'' effect that is, more motivated and higher-achieving students seek to attend and do attend magnet schools. Without a comparison group of nonmagnet students and a statistical control for premagnet achievement, one cannot determine if magnets are causing the higher achievement of magnet students. In addition, to the extent that magnet schools are successful, the positive effects may be the result not of the curriculum or other aspects of magnet schools but of the desegregation of the student body.

Critics of magnet schools are concerned that magnet schools siphon the better students from a school district, leaving the problem of educationally at-risk students in the nonmagnet, neighborhood schools.* They worry that magnet schools are aimed at an already-well-served middle-class clientele, thus removing resources from those students most in need. The argument is that certain groups, for example, blacks, the poor, and low attendees, are more likely to wind up in nonselective neighborhood schools. The causes of this segregation* can be attributed to the recruitment and selection processes, for example, including junior-high counselors who work more with students likely to succeed in option programs, selective recruitment of better students, unclear and questionable admission standards, and, in general, political pressure from middle-income parents.

The second major criticism and limitation of implementing magnet plans is financial: magnet schools cost more than traditional schools and may take resources from regular schools. It is difficult, however, to determine the cost of magnet schools above and beyond the normal operating costs of a school system. Magnets usually involve construction or renovation costs, one-time teacher-training costs, transportation costs beyond those normally associated with a neighborhood-based desegregation plan, equipment costs, and, depending on the plan, added personnel costs, such as funds for specialists. It is difficult, however, to separate such expenditures needed for magnets from those for traditional programs. Furthermore, the costs of magnets relate to the ambitiousness of the plan. The Yonkers School District implemented 12 magnets for a start-up cost of $843,000 and operating costs of $633,000. These estimates exclude new-school-construction and transportation costs. The magnet and theme schools established in Kansas City, Missouri, the heart of perhaps the most ambitious school desegregation plan* ever attempted, involved an expenditure of almost $1 billion.

In a broader sense magnet schools are a form of school choice, a system where student enrollment in a state or school district is based on parental selection. Under school choice plans there are generally fewer restrictions on the choice of parents because there is no need to racially balance schools. Voluntary plans may include magnet schools as a key component, but mandatory plans may also include some magnet schools.

References: Steel and Levine, *Educational Innovation in Multiracial Contexts* (1994); William Lowe Boyd and Herbert J. Walberg, eds., *Choice in Education: Potential and Problems* (Berkeley, CA: McCutchan, 1990); William H. Clune and John F. Witte, eds., *Choice and Control in American Education,* vols. 1–2 (London: Falmer Press, 1990); Rossell, *The Carrot or the Stick for School Desegregation Policy* (1990).

MAGNET SCHOOLS ASSISTANCE PROGRAM. A program developed to replace the Emergency School Aid Act,* which had been folded into the Chapter 2 block grant program in 1981. Congress enacted the Magnet Schools Assistance Program in 1984, a section under the Elementary and Secondary Education Act,* and consolidated all magnet-school* support. The allocation was set at about $75 million for 1985, 1986, and 1987. The legislation provides grants for local school districts for use in planning and implementing magnet schools as part of approved school desegregation plans.* Funds may be used for a variety of activities, including the development, expansion, continuation, and enhancement of academic programs at magnet schools. Book purchases and the enhancement of teacher salaries, but not transportation expenses, may be funded. This program requires that recipients be operating under a court order or federally approved school desegregation plan.

From 1985 to 1991 over $739 million was provided to 117 school districts through this act to help with the development and implementation of new magnet programs as well as expanding existing programs. This program was reauthorized in the fall of 1994 as Title V, Part A, of the Elementary and Secondary

Education Act.* For fiscal year 1995 President Clinton proposed $120 million, Congress authorized $111.5 million, and 64 awards were made.

Two studies have raised questions about the effectiveness of magnet schools subsidized through this program in meeting their desegregation* goals. In almost half the schools receiving aid, no specific desegregation goals were set; in the schools with goals, fewer than half had reached them.

References: *Catalog of Federal Domestic Assistance, 1996*; Caroline Hendrie, ''Magnets' Value in Desegregating Schools Is Found to Be Limited,'' *Education Week* 16, no. 11 (November 13, 1996): 1, 27; Peter Schmidt, ''New Magnet Law Emphasizes Desegregation,'' *Education Week* 14, no. 13 (November 30, 1994): 20; Steel and Levine, *Educational Innovation in Multiracial Contexts* (1994).

MAJORITY-TO-MINORITY TRANSFER PROGRAM (M-TO-M). Technique in a school desegregation plan* whereby students in the majority race in a school are allowed to transfer to a school where they are in the minority race, thus increasing desegregation* at both schools. This is a technique used in voluntary plans.* Transportation to the new school is generally provided. Few whites have ever used such a plan; some blacks have transferred to schools that have been predominantly white.

References: Armor, *Forced Justice* (1995); Rossell, ''The Convergence of Black and White Attitudes on School Desegregation Issues during the Four Decade Evolution of the Plans'' (January 1995); Gordon Foster, ''Desegregating Urban Schools: A Review of Techniques,'' *Harvard Educational Review* 43, no. 1 (February 1973): 5–36.

MALCOLM X (original name, Malcolm Little; Muslim name, El-Hajj Malik El-Shabazz) (born May 19, 1925, Omaha, Nebraska–died February 21, 1965, New York City). A militant black leader who was an advocate of black nationalism,* racial pride, and racial separation (a precursor of the black power* movement) for much of his public life during the 1960s. While Malcolm was a child in Lansing, Michigan, his house was burned down by members of the Ku Klux Klan,* his father was murdered two years later (the family thought that his advocacy of views of Marcus Garvey led to his murder), and his mother was later sent to a mental institution. Malcolm had a troubled youth, spending much of it in detention homes. In his early teenage years he moved to join his sister in Boston. He drifted to New York City and became a figure in the city's underworld of drugs, prostitution, and confidence games. He converted to the Black Muslim faith after reading extensively in the teachings of Elijah Muhammad while serving time in prison for burglary (1946–1952). When he was released from prison in 1952, Malcolm joined the headquarters staff of the Nation of Islam in Chicago and its leader Elijah Muhammad.

Malcolm was an extremely effective speaker and became the leading spokesman for the Black Muslim movement. He toured the nation recruiting and starting mosques and in 1961 founded the official publication of the Nation of Islam,

Muhammad Speaks. He became minister of a major mosque, Mosque Number Seven in Harlem in New York City.

According to *Britannica Online*, Malcolm X "derided the civil-rights movement* and rejected both integration* and racial equality, calling instead for black separatism, black pride, and black self-dependence." Malcolm advocated violence where necessary for self-protection. His fiery oratory and support of violence along with his call for separatism led to his rejection by most civil rights* leaders. For example, in a 1964 address to a meeting in New York City Malcolm stated: "I'm still a Muslim, but I'm also a nationalist, meaning that my political philosophy is black nationalism, my economic philosophy is black nationalism, my social philosophy is black nationalism. . . . The political philosophy for black nationalism is that which is designed to encourage our people, the black people, to gain complete control over the politics and the politicians of our own people" (*Two Speeches by Malcolm X*, p. 7).

In March 1964 Malcolm X split from the Black Muslims and Elijah Muhammad to form his own Islamic organization. Following a pilgrimage to Mecca in April 1964, Malcolm changed his views and accepted the possibility of goodness in whites and world brotherhood. Malcolm X was assassinated by three Black Muslims at a rally in a Harlem ballroom in 1965, presumably as a result of his conflicts with the main Muslim organization.

Works about: *Britannica Online* (1996); Michael Eric Dyson, *Making Malcolm: The Myth and Meaning of Malcolm X* (New York: Oxford University Press, 1995).

Works by: *By Any Means Necessary* (New York: Pathfinder, 1992); with the assistance of Alex Haley, *The Autobiography of Malcolm X* (New York: Grove Press, 1965); *Two Speeches by Malcolm X* (New York: Pathfinder Press, 1965/1990).

MANDATORY PLAN. A school desegregation plan* in which students and their parents do not have a choice about which school the student will attend. A school desegregation plan may be either a mandatory plan or a voluntary plan.* Mandatory techniques include pairing* and clustering* schools, satellite or pocket zoning, and contiguous rezoning. Mandatory plans usually combine several mandatory techniques, often with voluntary components such as magnet schools,* to form a comprehensive plan. Controlled-choice plans* are generally considered mandatory approaches.

Proponents of busing* for school desegregation* do not like to use the term *mandatory*, pointing out that even with neighborhood schools* assignment is mandatory, that is, students in a specific geographical area are assigned to a particular school. Critics of busing like David Armor* argue that "mandatory busing" was a phrase to label "desegregation plans that changed the basis and purpose of school assignment and busing . . . where the purpose of busing was to attain racial balance* rather than to overcome conditions of geography or distance" (1995:161). Armor also argues that the mandatory/voluntary distinction is important because plans that differ in these ways generate different parental and community responses and have different logistical and cost parameters.

Christine H. Rossell* and Ruth C. Clarke (1987) differentiate between mandatory or voluntary pupil assignment and school-board versus court or Department of Health, Education, and Welfare* (HEW) source of the desegregation plan or order. They are therefore making a distinction between the mandatory imposition of a plan by the court or federal government and the degree of parental choice within a plan, whatever the source of the plan. It is possible to have court-ordered voluntary plans, for example, in Buffalo, Milwaukee, and Houston, and board-ordered mandatory plans, for example, in Berkeley and Seattle.

Contiguous rezoning of attendance areas involves the redrawing of adjacent school attendance boundaries to improve or maximize racial balance. This technique is often used in conjunction with the closing or opening of schools. Thus students in a given geographical area may be reassigned from school A to school B to change the racial composition of the schools. Since redrawing of attendance areas happens with the natural changes of school enrollments over time, and since the reassignment of students is generally to a close school, this approach is less controversial than other mandatory approaches.

In larger school districts, where segregated housing extends over large geographical areas, noncontiguous attendance zones are necessary to achieve racial balance. In these situations desegregation plans involving pairing or clustering schools are often used. For example, in metropolitan plans* a city school serving black students may be clustered with two suburban schools serving white students. Students are then reassigned so that the schools are racially balanced.

There is much dispute over whether mandatory or voluntary plans produce more desegregation. Christine Rossell and David Armor have found that because mandatory plans lead to white enrollment losses, voluntary plans are more successful over the long run in effecting actual school desegregation as measured by an index of interracial exposure.* Mandatory plans do produce more racial balance, but that balance is tied to decreases in interracial exposure as the mandatory elements of the plan lead to white enrollment loss. All agree, however, that having some plan produces more school desegregation than having no plan.

References: Rossell and Armor, ''The Effectiveness of School Desegregation Plans, 1968–1991'' (July 1996); Armor, *Forced Justice* (1995); Fife, *Desegregation in American Schools* (1992); Christine H. Rossell and Ruth C. Clarke, *The Carrot or the Stick in School Desegregation Policy?* Report to the National Institute of Education, ERIC Document 279 781 (1987).

MARGOLD REPORT. The blueprint for the NAACP's strategy against segregation* written by Nathan C. Margold, who was retained in October 1930 by the NAACP to help develop a legal strategy against segregation. The American Fund for Public Service had granted $100,000 to the organization to help launch a nationwide campaign to expand black rights. Margold's report became the basis for the litigation plan to force social change on the nation, the bible of the NAACP's legal effort.

Margold argued that schools had been kept separate but not equal in the South,* and this could be the opening that the NAACP could use to fight segregation. Margold pointed out that in South Carolina expenditures on white students were ten times those for black students and in several other states (Florida, Georgia, Mississippi, and Alabama) the ratio was five to one. He called for bringing suits to challenge not the principle but the reality of the separate but equal* doctrine to force equalization of pupil expenditures. Margold thought that such suits would make the cost of maintaining the dual system* too expensive and encourage other blacks to bring similar suits. When appealed, these cases would then cover a wider area.

The NAACP Legal Defense Fund* modified the Margold strategy and brought suits against separate professional schools rather than elementary and secondary public schools. It would be easier to prove that separate was not equal because in many states no facilities existed for blacks at this level. The threat to states would be less because the expenditures required would not be as massive as those at the elementary and secondary level.

References: Greenberg, *Crusaders in the Courts* (1994); Preer, *Lawyers v. Educators* (1982); Kluger, *Simple Justice* (1975); Nathan C. Margold, *Preliminary Report to the Joint Committee Supervising the Expenditure of the 1930 Appropriation by the American Fund for Public Service to the NAACP, 1931*, in *Judicial Process and Social Change: Constitutional Litigation: Cases and Materials*, by Greenberg (1977), 50–57.

MARSHALL, THURGOOD (born July 2, 1908, Baltimore, Maryland–died January 24, 1993, Bethesda, Maryland). The first black member of the U.S. Supreme Court* (1967–1991), appointed by President Lyndon B. Johnson* after a lifetime of advocacy of school desegregation* and civil rights* for the NAACP Legal Defense and Education Fund.*

Marshall, the great-grandson of a slave and the son of a dining-car waiter and schoolteacher, was a graduate of Pennsylvania's Lincoln University (1930), the only black men's college in the North, and a graduate of Howard Law School* (1933), ranking first in his class. As an undergraduate at Lincoln, Marshall was one of a group of students who sat in the whites-only section of a local (Oxford, Pennsylvania) movie house. While a law student at Howard, he worked with NAACP* lawyers on civil rights cases. His job as an assistant in the Howard Law School library put him in close contact with NAACP* lawyers working on important civil rights cases.

After graduating from Howard Law School, Marshall began a one-man civil and criminal law office in Baltimore in 1933. He traveled throughout Maryland's Eastern Shore counties working for the NAACP investigating lynchings. Through his efforts Baltimore's A and P Stores were forced to hire black clerks. In 1935, working with his Howard professor and mentor, Charles Hamilton Houston,* Marshall was victorious in a suit to compel the University of Maryland's law school to admit a black student (*Pearson v. Maryland** [1936]). Davis and Clark (1994) call this "sweet revenge" because it was this same school that had rejected Marshall's application for law school a few years earlier because of his race.

After a stint as assistant special counsel (1936–1938), Marshall served as the special counsel for the NAACP in New York City from 1938 on. In 1940 Marshall was appointed director-counsel in charge of legal strategy for the newly formed NAACP Legal Defense and Education Fund. Here Marshall built a superb legal staff, calling on friends at Howard Law School. Just ten years out of law school, he successfully argued the *Smith v. Allwright* white-primary suit in front of the U.S. Supreme Court* in 1944, convincing the Court that Texas's "private" Democratic party primaries were unconstitutionally limited to whites only. This was the first of many Supreme Court victories for Marshall.

Thurgood Marshall was instrumental in devising the NAACP's legal strategy at the time. He implemented a strategy to attack segregation* in graduate schools. In 1948 Marshall argued and won the *Shelly v. Kraemer* case in which the Supreme Court struck down restrictive residential housing covenants. Marshall was the lead counsel for the NAACP challenge of school segregation* during the 1950s and was the victorious lead counsel in the *Brown v. Board of Education** (1954) decision. Overall he won 29 of the 32 cases he argued before the U.S. Supreme Court. Marshall's other triumphs included *Sweatt v. Painter** (1950) and *McLaurin v. Oklahoma State Regents** (1950), which limited the use of separate but equal* facilities for graduate and professional students.

Marshall was appointed a U.S. Court of Appeals* judge in the Second Judicial Circuit (New York, Vermont, Connecticut) on September 23, 1961, by President John F. Kennedy.* He was named Solicitor General in July 1965 by President Lyndon B. Johnson.* During his stint as Solicitor General Marshall won 14 of the 19 cases he argued. On June 13, 1967, he was nominated to the U.S. Supreme Court by President Johnson and was confirmed by the Senate on August 30, 1967, by a 69–11 vote. Marshall remained a strong liberal on the Court, advocating for the rights of the nation's minorities. His opinions and dissents in constitutional law cases, including free speech and equal protection issues, were most significant. Marshall was a champion of the less fortunate and a liberal judge.

Marshall received many honorary degrees, including ones from Syracuse University (1956), Brandeis and Princeton universities (1963), and the University of Michigan (1964). Marshall will be remembered as the lead crusader in the courts for school desegregation and equal rights for blacks as well as for being the first black U.S. Supreme Court justice.

Works about: *Britannica Online* (1996); Davis and Clark, *Thurgood Marshall* (1994); Greenberg, *Crusaders in the Courts* (1994); Mark V. Tushnet, *Making Civil Rights Law: Thurgood Marshall and the Supreme Court, 1936–1961* (New York: Oxford University Press, 1994); Carl Thomas Rowan, *Dream Makers, Dream Breakers: The World of Jus-*

tice Thurgood Marshall (Boston: Little, Brown, 1993); *Who's Who in the World, 1971/ 1972*, 610.

MASSACHUSETTS RACIAL IMBALANCE ACT (1965). This act was passed by the Massachusetts state legislature in August 1965 in response to the report of the Advisory Committee on Racial Imbalance and Education to the State Board of Education and made Massachusetts the first state in the nation to enact legislation in support of school desegregation.* This committee in its report, *Because It Is Right, Educationally*, had found that some state communities, including Boston, were in racial imbalance* and that the effect of such imbalance was harmful. Specifically the report indicated that 45 schools in Boston, 8 in Springfield, 1 in Cambridge, and 1 in Medford had black enrollments of over 50 percent. In Boston these schools served three-quarters of the black elementary-school children.

The act stated as a mission for the state "to encourage all school committees to adopt as educational objectives the promotion of racial balance* and the correction of existing racial imbalance in the public schools" (Section 37C). The act called for local school systems to eliminate racial imbalance in any school where the enrollment was more than 50 percent nonwhite. If the district failed to comply, it would lose its state educational aid. Not surprisingly, the act was passed over the strong opposition of Boston's legislators. The act stated that preventing or eliminating racial imbalance should be taken into account when school districts altered or drew school attendance lines and new school sites. The law is still in effect, despite a 1996 questioning of its utility by a state board member that produced a large mobilization that blocked repeal efforts.

References: Marcus and Stickney, *Race and Education* (1981); Bolner and Shanley, *Busing* (1974); James E. Teele, *Evaluating School Busing: Case Study of Boston's Operation Exodus* (New York: Praeger, 1973); Massachusetts Racial Imbalance Act, text reproduced in *Integrated Education*, ed. Weinberg (1968), 214–16.

MASSIVE RESISTANCE. The actions taken by the 11 states of the Old Confederacy to avoid the impacts of the 1954 *Brown v. Board of Education** federal decision. Their tactics included forcing the federal court to issue an injunction against each local school district to force school desegregation* and state laws that led to endless litigation in each of the 3,000 school districts of the South.* In the decade following *Brown*, 1954–1964, only 2 percent of the black children in the former Confederacy were attending integrated schools. State legislatures in the South passed the following types of laws to delay or stop desegregation: pupil placement laws,* abolition of public education, repeal or loosening of requirements to maintain public schools, cutoff of state funds for desegregated schools, resolutions of interposition,* nullification,* or protest against the school desegregation decisions, suspension or modification of compulsory attendance laws, support for pupils to attend private schools to avoid school desegregation, and the closing, leasing, or selling of public schools. Another form of resistance was initiated by white citizens councils* and the Ku Klux Klan,* who acted to disqualify potential litigants by harassing and intimidating the NAACP* and its members or potential members. Senator Harry F. Byrd of Virginia first used the phrase.

For example, Virginia resisted implementing the *Brown* decision through legislative and gubernatorial actions. In a special 27-day session in 1956 the Virginia state legislature passed 23 measures to try to stop school desegregation and get rid of the NAACP. Among the laws passed were a bill to close any school established for one race where a member of another race enrolled and a program to financially assist students in attending private schools with public funds. Schools were closed in Warren County, Charlottesville, and Norfolk by Governor Lindsay Almond. In January 1959 the law permitting the closings was found to be invalid, and the schools were reopened on a desegregated basis, but then the Virginia legislature repealed the compulsory attendance law and provided tuition assistance to those who then went to private school. Prince Edward County then closed its schools and set up six "private" elementary and two high schools to serve the white population, who received grants from the state and county. The most well-known efforts to resist school desegregation court orders occurred in 1957 when Governor Orval Faubus* sent in the Arkansas National Guard to disrupt the start of school desegregation in Little Rock and in 1963 when Governor George Wallace* of Alabama stood in the schoolhouse door in an attempt to block the admission of the first black students to the state university.

The federal courts do not have their own police or army to enforce their orders. They are dependent on the voluntary compliance of individuals and officials and the executive branch of government to ensure compliance with their orders. Therefore resistance poses a threat to the implementation of court orders to desegregate schools.

The Civil Rights Act of 1964* was a major force in the implementation of the *Brown* ruling and related decisions across the South and overcoming resistance. Therefore the period of massive resistance is generally measured from 1954 to 1964. The last resistance collapsed in 1969 when the U.S. Supreme Court* rejected Mississippi's request for a delay in implementing school desegregation. The failure of massive resistance was due to several factors, including the firmness of the federal courts, the commitment of the federal government after the passage of the 1964 Civil Rights Act, the actions of Congress to ensure the desegregation of the South, and the 1960s consensus that the federal government should ensure equal opportunity for blacks, which itself resulted from the civil rights movement.*

See also **Eisenhower, Dwight David;** *Griffin v. School Board of Prince Edward County***; Kennedy, John Fitzgerald**.

References: Marcus and Stickney, *Race and Education* (1981); Wilkinson, *From Brown to Bakke* (1979); Wilhoit, *The Politics of Massive Resistance* (1973); Bartley, *The Rise of Massive Resistance* (1969); Orfield, *The Reconstruction of Southern Education* (1969); Muse, *Ten Years of Prelude* (1964); Greenberg, *Race Relations and American Law* (1959).

MCLAURIN V. OKLAHOMA STATE REGENTS FOR HIGHER EDUCATION, 339 U.S. 637 (1950).

U.S. Supreme Court* decision that established the need for courts to take into account intangible factors, such as interacting with students of other races, in judging whether separate educational facilities were really equal. This decision greatly limited the ability of states to require segregated education at the graduate or professional level and established that universities could not treat students differently based on race after their admission.

George McLaurin was a 68-year-old black educator with a master's degree who applied to the University of Oklahoma's School of Education doctoral program in 1948. When he was not admitted because of his race, he brought suit. The courts held that the state had to provide him with an equal education. The state legislature accepted that if no program for blacks in a field was available, it had to admit the student to the white program, but it did so on a segregated basis. As the *Oxford Companion* (1992) notes, McLaurin attended school in the segregationist state of Oklahoma's version of a plastic bubble. McLaurin had to eat at a separate table, study at a special library desk, and sit in a railed-off area "reserved for colored" at a different time from white students. McLaurin returned to federal court to argue that this segregation placed a "badge of inferiority" on him, but the three-judge panel rejected his appeal. (It should be noted that white students tore down the sign "Reserved for Colored" placed near McLaurin's class seat, and officials had to satisfy themselves with having a special unmarked row for him.)

The issue therefore was only whether segregation was unequal treatment, since McLaurin had access to the same facilities and faculty as the other students. The U.S. Supreme Court unanimously ruled that a black admitted to a white graduate school must be treated like the white students. The opinion, written by Chief Justice Fred Vinson,* indicated that in order to learn his profession, the student had to be able to study and engage in discussions with the other students. This was the companion case to *Sweatt v. Painter** (1950) and applied to graduate education beyond legal education. McLaurin had been admitted to the state university but, according to the Court, was "handicapped in his pursuit of effective graduate instruction" by intangible factors such as "intellectual commingling with other students." He also had access only to very limited tangible facilities such as only certain parts of the library.

McLaurin's health deteriorated, and he did not complete the doctoral program. This case was cited in *Brown I** (1954) as the basis of the impossibility of the separate but equal* doctrine because of the role of intangibles in education. The decision helped to pave the way for the *Brown I* decision ruling separate but equal schools unconstitutional.

References: Greenberg, *Crusaders in the Courts* (1994); Hall, *Oxford Companion* (1992); Yudof et al., *Kirp and Yudof's Educational Policy and the Law* (1987); Marcus and Stickney, *Race and Education* (1981); Kluger, *Simple Justice* (1975).

MEREDITH, JAMES HOWARD (born June 25, 1933, Kosciusko, Mississippi). The first black student to attend the University of Mississippi (1962). James Meredith, a nine-year U.S. Air Force veteran, wanted to transfer from Jackson State College in Mississippi, a historically black college (*see* **Historically Black Colleges and Universities**), to the University of Mississippi in January 1961. The application called for character references from five alumni, but Meredith, knowing none, included five references from five blacks along with the required photograph of himself. The school denied him admission on several grounds and then changed its transfer policies to preclude Jackson State students from transferring to the university. Meredith turned to the NAACP Legal Defense Fund* and Thurgood Marshall.* Although he lost at the U.S. District Court* level, U.S. Court of Appeals* Judge John Minor Wisdom's* decision led to Meredith being ordered admitted to the University of Mississippi on September 13, 1962, by Federal District Court Judge Sidney C. Mize. Because of this, Mississippi's Governor Ross Barnett attacked the federal policy of "racial genocide" that night on a statewide television broadcast. Governor Barnett advocated resistance, citing an 1832 South Carolina Act of Nullification.* This act negated federal laws in violation of state legislation.

On September 20 the governor himself stopped Meredith from registering while a crowd threw rocks at Meredith and the federal marshals. On September 25 the Assistant Attorney General and Chief U.S. Marshal accompanied Meredith to register at the Jackson, Mississippi, federal building, as per previous agreement, but the registrar was not there. They then went to the state legislature, where the Assistant Attorney General addressed the governor in front of television cameras and reporters. The governor referred to interposition* in his defiance. That night an angry Attorney General Robert F. Kennedy, President John F. Kennedy's* brother, called Barnett and told him that Meredith would register. The federal government then moved ahead in contempt procedures against him.

The next day Meredith's third attempt to register was thwarted by the state's lieutenant governor. On September 28 the federal government publicly talked about the use of troops, and the Fifth Circuit Court of Appeals found Barnett guilty of contempt of court. The following day President Kennedy called Barnett to try to work out a deal, but after the deal was made, Barnett backed out. At midnight Kennedy signed a proclamation similar to the one President Dwight D. Eisenhower* signed in the Little Rock crisis (***Cooper v. Aaron*** [1958]) authorizing the use of federal troops.

On Sunday, September 30, 1962, President Kennedy went on television to explain his responsibility under the U.S. Constitution.* The Mississippi High-way Patrol had been almost entirely removed from the university, which left a representative of the Attorney General and 300 marshals surrounded by an angry mob. By 2:15 A.M. federal troops had arrived on campus, but the 5,000 men did not stop the injuries to over one-third of the marshals and the killing of two civilians.

Meredith received his B.A. in political science from the University of Mississippi in August 1963, began law school at Columbia University, and then returned to the South* to participate in civil rights* demonstrations. He was shot on June 5, 1966, but the wound was not serious, and he recovered fully. He returned to Columbia University and went on to earn his J.D. there in 1968. He served as a lecturer on the black race and Africa at several universities. Meredith ran for the Republican nomination for the U.S. Senate from Mississippi in the 1972 primary but lost.

Works about: Greenberg, *Crusaders in the Courts* (1994); *Who's Who in America* (Chicago: Reed Reference Publishing, 1994), 2528; Stern, *Calculating Visions* (1992); Metcalf, *Black Profiles* (1968); Muse, *Ten Years of Prelude* (1964).

Works by: *Three Years in Mississippi* (Bloomington: Indiana University Press, 1966).

METCO (METROPOLITAN COUNCIL FOR EDUCATIONAL OPPOR-TUNITIES).

A voluntary metropolitan school desegregation* program that buses minority students (primarily black) from the city of Boston to suburban schools. METCO, organized by private citizens of Boston and its suburbs, began with 220 students from North Roxbury and Dorchester and the South End of Boston in 1966 and ultimately involved the busing* of over 3,000 black students from Boston to 185 schools in over 30 suburban cities and towns. Over 15,000 students have participated in METCO since its founding. Financial support for METCO has come from a private foundation and state and federal funds.

METCO was the subject of David Armor's* well-known study on the effects of busing on black students. Armor found that METCO, as well as similar programs, did not increase the standardized achievement-test scores, educational aspirations, or self-esteem* of the bused students, but critics charged that the data and methodology of the study were faulty and that the effect of this program was not a good indicator of the potential effects of mandatory busing.

In 1981–1982 enrollments went to 3,280 and have stayed above 3,000 since then. Thirty-two school districts in Greater Boston participate. The total budget in 1995 was $12 million, paid by the state. About 80 percent of the graduates attend college each year, compared to about 60 percent of those graduating from the city schools. In 1995 the race of the new participants was 71 percent black, 24 percent Hispanic, and the rest Asian. In recent years Hispanics and Asians have been given special priority with the goal of having their participation rate equal that of their proportion in the Boston school population. The suburban school districts do screen the applicants, and according to the 1995 *Boston Globe* article, in some districts more than half may be turned down. A newspaper series on METCO in December 1995 claimed that researchers had avoided analyzing the program since David Armor's problems and that the program has served many well-connected and middle-class blacks but few housing-project products. A similar but more limited METCO program is run in the Springfield, Massachusetts, area. In this metropolitan area 170 students participate.

References: Gary Orfield, *City-Suburban Desegregation: Parent and Student Perspectives in Metropolitan Boston*, report by the Harvard Civil Rights Project (Cambridge, MA: Harvard Project on School Desegregation, September 1997); Larry Tye, "High Hopes, Hard Questions: METCO Faces Scrutiny in Era of Education Change," *Boston Sunday Globe*, December 3, 1995, 1, 38–39; Ruth M. Batson and Robert C. Hayden, *A History of METCO* (Boston: Select Publications, 1987); Thomas F. Pettigrew, Elizabeth L. Useem, Clarence Normand, and Michael S. Smith, "Busing: A Review of 'The Evidence,' " *Public Interest*, no. 30 (Winter 1973): 88–118; Armor, "The Evidence on Busing" (1972).

METROPOLITAN PLAN. A school desegregation plan* involving city schools and at least some suburban schools. Such plans can be court ordered or school-district implemented, voluntary plans* or mandatory plans,* and inter- or intradistrict.

The U.S. Supreme Court* placed a major limit on the ordering of metropolitan school desegregation plans with its first *Milliken v. Bradley** (*Milliken I*) decision in 1974. Under this decision metropolitan remedies involving independent central-city school districts and suburban school districts may be ordered by federal courts only when the suburban districts and/or the state have taken actions that caused the segregation* in the city schools. Therefore, in the Detroit case the Court ruled that the Detroit city schools could not be merged with the 53 surrounding suburban school districts, as U.S. District Court* Judge Stephen Roth had originally ordered. Since most metropolitan areas are composed of a predominantly minority city school district, almost exclusively serving minorities, surrounded by multiple predominantly white suburban school districts, the *Milliken I* decision blocked most court-ordered metropolitan desegregation between independent school districts. The vast majority of school districts in the South* are countywide, for example, Dade County and Orlando County, so city-suburban school-district mergers are not necessary for metropolitan school desegregation to be ordered.

Special circumstances have led to court-ordered metropolitan school desegregation plans merging independent school districts. In the Wilmington, Delaware, metropolitan area the U.S. District Court ordered a metropolitan plan in the *Evans v. Buchanan** (1975) case after black parents proved that the state's passage of the Educational Advancement Act in 1968, which allowed the state school board to combine and reorganize all districts except the Wilmington School District, was an obstacle to desegregating the city schools. Eleven school districts were merged into one by order of the court, and 20,000 students were bused across city/suburban lines to fulfill the order. Subsequently the state legislature divided the single district into four smaller districts, each with a section of the city incorporated into a suburban area. In Kentucky the Louisville School District voted itself out of existence to force a merger with the Jefferson County School District (*Newburg Area Council v. Board of Education of Jefferson County, Kentucky** [1974]). Similarly, the Charlotte city schools and the Mecklenburg County school district merged before the *Swann** (1971) busing* decision.

In the case of St. Louis the threat of a possible court order forcing a metropolitan school desegregation plan led to a consent decree* allowing up to 13,000 city students to transfer to suburban school districts. Milwaukee has had over 6,000 minority students a year attending suburban schools in a metropolitan interdistrict transfer plan.

Some metropolitan areas have had successful voluntary metropolitan school desegregation plans. In the Hartford metropolitan area Project Concern* has been responsible for the enrollment of as many as 1,500 minority students per year from the Hartford city schools in the surrounding suburban school districts. In the Boston area METCO* has been responsible for the transfer of students into cooperating school districts in the suburbs since 1966. Metropolitan cooperative plans also existed in Rochester, New York, and New Haven, Connecticut. In such plans the participating school districts maintain their separate identities while cooperating in the transferring of students.

The recent *Sheff v. O'Neill** (1996) decision by the Connecticut State Supreme Court opens the door for state court-ordered metropolitan school desegregation plans. In this case Hartford parents successfully argued that the state had an obligation to ensure equal educational opportunity* for the children of Hartford, and this required a metropolitan school desegregation plan.

In the debate over the degree of white flight* out of cities with school desegregation plans, the one area of agreement has been that metropolitan desegregation plans are likely to be more stable than city-only plans. That is, desegregating city schools merged with suburban schools by mandatory reassignment reduces white flight compared to a city-only district with mandatory reassignment because the percentage of minority students in individual schools is reduced. Some have also argued that such plans also are likely to increase the educational benefits of school desegregation because they maximize the number of higher-achieving middle-class students involved in the plan, students who are more likely to serve as models and whose parents are likely to demand quality education. Metropolitan plans may well be opposed by black leaders who see such plans as a means to dilute black political strength in city school districts and by whites opposed to busing.

Mandatory metropolitan school desegregation plans generally involve school clustering,* often of noncontiguous schools. Thus in the Wilmington plan schools in the city served suburban areas that required students to take a bus ride of 15 miles on the interstate passing through other school districts.

References: Rossell, ''The Convergence of Black and White Attitudes on School Desegregation Issues during the Four Decade Evolution of the Plans'' (January 1995); Varady and Raffel, *Selling Cities* (1995); Jeffrey A. Raffel, *The Politics of School Desegregation: The Metropolitan Remedy in Delaware* (Philadelphia: Temple University Press, 1980); Mary Rashman, *Metropolitan School Desegregation: A Report and Recommendations of the National Task Force on Desegregation Strategies* (Denver: Education Commission of the States, March 1979); U.S. Commission on Civil Rights, *Statement on Metropolitan School Desegregation* (Washington, DC: U.S. Government Printing Office, February 1977); *Milliken v. Bradley: The Implications for Metropolitan Desegregation: Conference before the U.S. Commission on Civil Rights* (Washington, DC: U.S. Government Printing Office, November 9, 1974).

MEXICAN AMERICAN LEGAL DEFENSE AND EDUCATIONAL FUND (MALDEF).

Modeled on the NAACP Legal Defense Fund,* MALDEF received a grant from the Ford Foundation of $2.2 million in 1968 to help it legally challenge the segregation* of Hispanics in the schools. When MALDEF began, the situation for Hispanics in American schools was poor. School segregation was the rule, and few were enrolled in any bilingual education* program. In many schools Hispanic students were placed in the lowest tracks based on English-language tests. Parents generally received communications in English, although the vast majority spoke Spanish at home. While initially MALDEF was engaged in school desegregation* and bilingualism, in the 1970s its attention turned increasingly to the latter. In the Denver *Keyes** (1973) case MALDEF worked to have bilingual programs as a central part of the remedy. In general, its strategy was to have black groups prove that schools were segregated, and then MALDEF would fight for bilingual education for the Hispanics in the district. In the 1990s the fund was based in Los Angeles.

References: Greenberg, *Crusaders in the Courts* (1994); Maurilio Vigil, ''The Ethnic Organization as an Instrument of Political and Social Change: MALDEF, A Case Study,'' *Journal of Ethnic Studies* 18, no. 1 (Spring 1990): 15–31; Guadalupe San Miguel, Jr., *''Let All of Them Take Heed'': Mexican Americans and the Campaign for Educational Equality in Texas, 1910–1981* (Austin: University of Texas Press, 1987); Orfield, *Must We Bus?* (1978).

MILLIKEN V. BRADLEY (MILLIKEN I), 418 U.S. 717 (1974).

Decision by a divided (5–4) U.S. Supreme Court* (Chief Justice Warren Burger* wrote the opinion) establishing the conditions under which suburban school districts could be forced to be involved in remedying city school segregation.* The Court ruled that the 53 suburban school districts surrounding Detroit, Michigan, did not have to be part of a metropolitan school desegregation plan* because they were not responsible for causing the problem of school segregation* in the city, combining the suburban districts would be too complicated, and the state of Michigan had not played a significant role in causing the segregation to warrant being ordered to solve the problem. This decision greatly limited the potential for metropolitan school desegregation* remedies to city segregation.

In September 1971 U.S. District Court* Judge Stephen Roth ruled that the actions of various governmental officials, including school officials, had led to the segregation of schools in the Detroit metropolitan area. The District Court ordered the Detroit Board of Education to submit plans to desegregate the city's schools, but it also ordered state officials to submit plans to desegregate Detroit and the 85 outlying school districts of the metropolitan area. After submission of the plans the District Court concluded that the city-only plan would make the city schools more segregated and that a metropolitan-area plan was therefore appropriate. The court then included 53 of the 85 suburban school districts, in addition to Detroit, in the desegregation area. The Court of Appeals* upheld the decision.

The U.S. Supreme Court, in its 5–4 decision, was concerned about the threat to local control of public schools posed by the remedy. In addition, the practical problems caused by this decision were immense. Besides the logistical problems involved in transporting students across the lines of the 53 school districts, the Court expressed concern with governance and finance issues such as these: "What would be the status and authority of the presently popularly elected school boards? Would the children of Detroit be within the jurisdiction and operating control of a school board elected by parents and residents of other districts?" While the Supreme Court acknowledged that the District Court could work to answer all its questions, it could only do so by becoming a "legislative authority" and then a "school superintendent" for the entire area.

The Court also reasoned that, as stated in *Swann** (1971), "the scope of the remedy is determined by the nature and extent of the constitutional violation." Before a realignment of districts could be ordered, the court must find that a constitutional violation in one district caused segregation in another district. "Without an inter-district violation and inter-district effect, there is no constitutional wrong calling for an inter-district remedy." There was no strong evidence that the suburban districts caused the segregation of the Detroit schools. The Court also rejected the notion that the state's role should lead to a comprehensive remedy. The state had not established school-district lines to segregate schools in Detroit.

Justice Byron White wrote the dissent and was joined by Justices William Douglas, William Brennan,* and Thurgood Marshall.* The dissent noted that there was no disagreement with the District Court's conclusion that a city-only remedy would eventually lead to white flight* from the city and involve the purchase of more buses than a metropolitan plan.* Furthermore, the record did indicate that many agencies of the state had played a role in segregating the Detroit schools. They argued that this decision meant that the constitutional violation would not be remedied, even though a remedy was feasible. Justice Marshall's dissent, which was also signed by the three other judges disagreeing with the majority opinion, emphasized the role that the state played in the segregation of the Detroit schools.

This case has had a major impact on limiting the desegregation of city school districts and was the first clear defeat for civil rights* groups since the *Brown** (1954) decision. Most major U.S. cities lack sufficient white students to deseg-regate the public schools. This decision has made it very difficult to obtain remedies that include suburban school districts with large numbers and per-centages of white (as well as middle-class) students. Thus the courts have re-stricted remedies to de jure segregation* in cities. The criteria established by *Milliken* have been met in the *Evans v. Buchanan** (1975) case in Delaware and the case in Louisville (*Newburg Area Council,** 1974). This decision also is significant because it was the first case in which the U.S. Supreme Court over-turned a lower-court decision favorable to school desegregation.

References: Orfield and Eaton, *Dismantling Desegregation* (1996); Armor, *Forced Jus-tice* (1995); Witt, *Congressional Quarterly's Guide to the U.S. Supreme Court* (1989); Yudof et al., *Kirp and Yudof's Educational Policy and the Law* (1987); Dimond, *Beyond Busing* (1985); Orfield, *Must We Bus?* (1978).

MILLIKEN V. BRADLEY (MILLIKEN II), 433 U.S. 267 (1977). U.S. Su-preme Court* decision concerning the desegregation* of the Detroit schools that established that courts could order state-funded ancillary programs* such as a compensatory education* component, in-service training for teachers, and guid-ance and counseling programs as a component of a school desegregation plan.* Such programs had been challenged on the grounds that the constitutional vio-lation in school desegregation* cases centered on pupil assignments, not edu-cational programs. The Court held, however, that the purpose of a remedy was to restore those who had been wronged to the status they would have held absent the discriminatory act. Thus those children who had been segregated were likely to have suffered consequences that required an educational remedy, that is, one that went beyond equality to compensatory programs. This decision came after the first Detroit school desegregation decision (*Milliken I*),* which had blocked the desegregation of the city schools by combining the city school district with surrounding suburban school districts, thus making city school desegregation infeasible.

Critics have viewed *Milliken II* as a reinstitution of the separate but equal* doctrine as school districts trade off school desegregation for extra money and special programming. Feldman, Kirby, and Eaton's study of four school districts (Detroit, Little Rock, Prince George's County, and Austin) indicated that such compensatory efforts failed to "restore the victims of discriminatory conduct to the position they would have occupied in the absence of such conduct."

References: Orfield and Eaton, *Dismantling Desegregation* (1996); Joseph Feldman, Ed-ward Kirby, and Susan E. Eaton, *Still Separate, Still Unequal: The Limits of Milliken II's Educational Compensation Remedies* (Cambridge, MA: Harvard Project on School Desegregation, April 1994); Yudof et al., *Kirp and Yudof's Educational Policy and the Law* (1987).

MISSOURI EX REL. GAINES V. CANADA, 305 U.S. 337 (1938). First case on segregation of public higher education heard by the U.S. Supreme Court* and thus the first decision by the U.S. Supreme Court to define the meaning of separate but equal* in higher education. This decision was the first case that suggested that attacking the separate but equal doctrine of *Plessy v. Ferguson** (1896) might be successful.

Lloyd Gaines, a 25-year-old graduate of Lincoln University (Missouri) and St. Louis resident, applied to the University of Missouri Law School. There was no black law school in the state at that time. Gaines was rejected by the registrar, S. W. Canada, who told him that blacks were to be educated separately from whites. Gaines was told that he still had an option: the state had a scholarship program for funding blacks in the desegregated schools of any adjacent state in any course of study if that area was not available at a black school in the state. This case was unlike the recently won *Pearson v. Murray** (1936) case in Maryland in that Missouri had tried to make Lincoln University into a quality institution and had funded the scholarship program. The state court upheld Gaines's rejection.

Gaines viewed the Lincoln option and the out-of-state scholarship program as insufficient, and his attorney, Charles Hamilton Houston* of the NAACP Legal Defense Fund* (LDF) filed for admission in state court. The state court sided with the state in agreeing that this program provided Gaines with an equal, although separate, educational opportunity. Gaines appealed again.

At the U.S. Supreme Court level Chief Justice Charles Evans Hughes wrote for the 6–2 majority arguing that the state had to provide an equal educational opportunity,* and such an equal educational opportunity was not met by this funding procedure. The decision did not call for admission to the state school, but only stated that Gaines had to be provided with equal educational opportunity in the state.

In this decision the Court dealt for the first time with the "equal" part of the separate but equal doctrine of *Plessy* in deciding that providing the financing of a service in an adjacent state was not equal treatment. The Court held that the "essence of statehood" required that equal educational opportunity be provided within Missouri. This case represents the first attack of the NAACP* against the *Plessy* decision at the Supreme Court level.

Reacting to the Supreme Court, Missouri protected its all-white law school by requiring Lincoln University to establish a law school with new funds. Other states joined a Southern Regional Education Compact,* originally designed to offer segregated programs for black students so that the states were not forced to offer desegregated programs. Thus the effect of *Gaines* was to indicate that separate but equal meant just that—if blacks were separated, they needed to be given equal opportunities in the state, but did not need to be admitted to "white" schools. In fact, *Gaines* led to the establishment of "overnight law schools": when the separate but equal doctrine was challenged, the state would set up a program at the state's Negro institution virtually overnight.

The NAACP lawyers had started challenging the *Plessy* separate but equal doctrine at the professional-school level because proof of discrimination* was easier, since few professional schools for blacks existed, and because attacks at this level of schooling were less threatening to whites. In addition, the threat of violence was minimal, given the ages and maturity of the students. The lawyers believed that the cost of providing separate but equal facilities would prove too expensive for the South* to maintain.

Lloyd Gaines disappeared and did not enter the law school despite his victory. According to former LDF chief counsel Jack Greenberg,* "Rumors flew about foul play, that he couldn't take the pressure and had run off to Mexico, and so forth. But no one ever discovered anything" (1994:63). This decision was a major victory for the NAACP. The ruling suggested that states had to equalize educational opportunities for blacks in segregated facilities or, if they were unable or unwilling to do so, had to desegregate white educational institutions. This decision became a building block for the *Brown** decision, fought at the elementary and secondary level.

References: Greenberg, *Crusaders in the Courts* (1994); Yudof et al., *Kirp and Yudof's Educational Policy and the Law* (1987); Preer, *Lawyers v. Educators* (1982); Marcus and Stickney, *Race and Education* (1981); Kluger, *Simple Justice* (1975).

MISSOURI V. JENKINS, 115 S. Ct. 2038 (1995). U.S. Supreme Court* decision limiting the funding obligations of the state of Missouri to achieve *Milliken II* (1977) equalization remedies and placing limits on the argument that discrepancies in black and white student achievement* must be eliminated before a school district can be declared a unitary system.* The Court declared the swift return to local school-district control as the primary goal in school desegregation* cases.

The suit was filed in 1977. The Kansas City School District sued the state and the suburban districts in the hopes of creating a metropolitan school desegregation plan,* but the judge decided that the district should be a defendant and would not require the suburban districts to accept city students since these districts had committed no constitutional violation. In 1984 U.S. District Court* Judge Russell G. Clark ruled that the state, since it had segregated schools by law during the pre-*Brown** era, must share in the liability for the remedy. In addition, he found that school segregation* had caused a reduction in the achievement of black students when the Kansas City schools had not been adequately desegregated. In 1986 the Eighth Circuit Court of Appeals* found that the Kansas City School District and the state were liable for the segregation of schools in the district, and it supported Judge Clark's order to make them pay to make a majority (56) of the city's schools into magnet schools* to attract white students from the suburbs, as well as implementing programs to increase student achievement. The magnet schools, which include a school emphasizing classical Greek education and an agricultural school that includes a working farm, can draw pupils from anywhere in the state, although most come from surrounding suburbs. Massive capital improvements, which led to the renovation of 55 schools and the construction of 17 others and the building or purchase of a planetarium, radio and television studios, personal computers, and an Olympic-sized swimming pool, were involved in creating these schools. In 1995, 75.9 percent of the city's 37,000 pupils were minorities. The state had funded the lion's share of the over $1.5 billion of the physical and educational changes through 1995, although the full plan had been in effect only three years. The judge had also ordered a doubling of the city's property tax to help pay for the improvements.

When the state argued that it had fulfilled its burden, the Eighth Circuit Court of Appeals concluded that it was not enough to implement the plan; the plan also had to be successful, and this could be measured in part by the degree of improvement in minority test scores. There was resentment about the remedy since the city has 4.3 percent of the state's public school pupils but has twice as high a proportion of the state's funding.

In June 1995 the U.S. Supreme Court* questioned the lower court's opinion in this case. Federal District Court Judge Russell G. Clark had ruled in 1993 that "the district had not reached anywhere close to its maximum potential because the district is still at or below national norms at many grade levels." Writing for the slim majority (Justices Sandra Day O'Connor, Antonin Scalia, Anthony M. Kennedy, and Clarence Thomas), Chief Justice William H. Rehnquist* concluded that the lower federal courts had improperly ordered the state of Missouri to help pay for the magnet schools and salary increases for teachers and staff in the city schools. The goal of the desegregation plan was to make the majority black Kansas City district so attractive to students in majority white suburbs that students would enroll voluntarily in the city schools. U.S. Solicitor General Drew S. Days III had supported the Kansas City plaintiffs and the school district in the case.

In the 1995 decision Chief Justice Rehnquist reasoned that even with the voluntary elements, the decision violated the *Milliken I** limit on metropolitan school district plans.* There had been no findings that the suburbs had violated the Constitution,* and therefore they did not have to be part of the remedy. There should be no interdistrict solution to an intradistrict problem. The Court also rejected the argument that the failure of minority students in the city to achieve national norms on standardized tests could be used as a rationale to force state funding of the plan. Too many other factors could influence such test scores beyond de jure segregation.* The next step was somewhat ambiguous. The Court suggested that Judge Clark reconsider his ruling taking into account *Freeman v. Pitts** (1992). In May 1996 the attorney general of Missouri asked the District Court to end oversight of the district. A year later Judge Clark decided that court supervision should continue, but state subsidies of the district should end.

This ruling may well help the arguments of districts seeking unitary status* because it rejects a major argument of those trying to maintain orders, that discrepancies on test scores between blacks and whites are due to the perpetuation of school segregation, thus justifying the need to maintain the desegregation order. The significance of this case revolves around the Court's rejection of student achievement as the measure of success of a school desegregation plan. In considering what a unitary or desegregated system is, the Court did not accept the notion that desegregation success should be judged on minority student achievement, a so-called outcomes-based measure.

References: Orfield and Eaton, *Dismantling Desegregation* (1996); Wolters, *Right Turn* (1996); David J. Armor, "Can Desegregation Alone Close the Achievement Gap?" *Education Week* 14, no. 41 (August 2, 1995): 68, 57; Abernathy, *Civil Rights and Constitutional Litigation* (1992); D. Bruce La Pierre, "Voluntary Interdistrict School Desegregation in St. Louis: The Special Master's Tale," in *Justice and School Systems* ed. Flicker (1990), 233–305.

MODIFIED FEEDER PATTERNS. A technique in school desegregation plans* that involves the reassignment of students from different schools to create a desegregated school at the next level. For example, school districts may redraw feeder lines so that a mostly black elementary school and a mostly white elementary school feed into a desegregated middle school.

See also **Rezoning**.

References: Gordon Foster, "Desegregating Urban Schools: A Review of Techniques," *Harvard Educational Review* 43, no. 1 (February 1973): 5–36; Jacob Landers, *Improving Ethnic Distribution of New York City Pupils* (Brooklyn, NY: New York City Board of Education, 1966), ERIC EDO11270.

MORGAN V. HENNIGAN, 379 F. Supp. 410 (1974). U.S. Supreme Court* decision requiring school desegregation* in the city of Boston that was part of a long, bitter, sometimes violent battle over the desegregation of the Boston public schools. In 1974 U.S. District Court* Judge W. Arthur Garrity* found that Boston school authorities had taken intentional action to maintain school segregation* in the Boston public schools. On June 21, 1974, he ordered a school desegregation plan* that included busing* children throughout the city. The Boston School Committee refused to cooperate, and Garrity took over the governance of the school district to enforce the order. Despite protests and the threat of violence from working-class neighborhoods, Garrity steadfastly stuck to his order.

The Massachusetts Racial Imbalance Act* had been passed almost a decade (1965) before Judge Garrity's order and had been ignored by the Boston School Committee for years. In 1965 the Massachusetts Board of Education charged the city district with operating 45 racially imbalanced schools; by 1969, 69 schools were imbalanced. The Boston School Committee denied that the schools were segregated and then challenged the constitutionality of the law. The battles in state court did not move the Boston School Committee to desegregate the city's schools. The Office of Education* in the Department of Health, Education, and Welfare* had also investigated the district, found it wanting, and withheld $25 million in federal aid from it.

The NAACP* filed suit in March 1972 charging that the state and the Boston

School Committee had created and maintained a segregated school system. The NAACP argued that the school board had used pupil assignment policies, attendance zones, and feeder patterns to maintain segregation in the schools. In addition, the school district was charged with engaging in racial discrimination* in the hiring and assignment of teachers and other staff. The Boston School Committee denied these allegations, maintaining that residential segregation and its justifiable neighborhood school* policy were the reasons for any racial imbalance* that might exist.

Judge W. Arthur Garrity, Jr., found that the NAACP's charges were true. For example, the District Court judge found that the school district had let white schools become overcrowded while black schools were maintained with empty seats. The district's open-enrollment* or freedom-of-choice* plan further allowed whites to transfer from schools with high black percentages. Judge Garrity ordered the district to devise a plan to reverse school segregation by September 1974.

Phase I of the plan, which included redistricting and busing components, according to Finch was "accompanied by mob violence and boycotts in certain areas of the city, the worst such incidents occurring during school desegregation in a northern city" (1981:234). The image of Boston as a center of culture and learning was shattered by violence at South Boston and Hyde Park high schools. The opposition to busing, led by city councilwoman Louise Day Hicks,* was strongest in South Boston, an enclave of Irish Catholics with strong community roots. Buses bringing black students from outside South Boston were confronted by angry mobs, and extra policemen and state patrols were required to protect the bused students. The U.S. Commission on Civil Rights* conducted a five-day hearing in June 1975 focused on school desegregation conflict in Boston and a lack of civic leadership.

Phase II of the plan was shaped by four court-appointed experts (including Charles V. Willie*) and included an elaborate educational component. Twenty-one colleges and universities in the metropolitan area were associated with city schools to improve education. A controlled-choice* component was the centerpiece of this phase, implemented in September 1975.

This case is significant for several reasons. First, the violence and opposition to busing focused the nation's attention on the issues of school desegregation, racial prejudice,* and busing. Second, the recalcitrance of the Boston School Committee led to Judge Garrity's increasing involvement in the day-to-day operation of the city's schools, an action that then led to great criticism of Garrity and the federal courts. Finally, the white flight* accompanying the implementation of the desegregation plan certainly raised questions about whether all this conflict was worth it. In 1973 Boston had 94,000 pupils, including 57 percent white pupils. By the time Garrity excused himself from the case, the district had only 57,000 students, and only 27 percent were white.

References: Jennifer J. Beaumont, "Implementation of Court-ordered Desegregation by District-Level School Administrators," in *Beyond Desegregation*, ed. Shujaa (1996), 75–90; Thomas R. Dye, *Understanding Public Policy*, 7th ed. (Englewood Cliffs, NJ: Prentice Hall, 1992); Ronald P. Formisano, *Boston against Busing: Race, Class, and Ethnicity* *in the 1960s and 1970s* (Chapel Hill: University of North Carolina Press, 1991); Robert A. Dentler and Marvin B. Scott, *Schools on Trial: An Inside Account of the Boston Desegregation Case* (Cambridge, MA: Abt Books, 1981); Finch, *The NAACP* (1981); Orfield, *Must We Bus?* (1978).

MORRILL ACT OF 1890 (SECOND MORRILL ACT). This act provided for the establishment and support of black institutions of higher education while it also legitimized the segregation* of land grant colleges and universities. In the 17 segregated states the benefits of the Morrill Act of 1862, the first Morrill Act, had not reached blacks. (The first Morrill Act, named after Vermont Senator Justin Smith Morrill, granted each state and territory 30,000 acres of public land for each congressman and senator. The land would then be sold and the funds used to establish at least one college in each state to teach agriculture and mechanical arts.) There was congressional debate over whether institutions receiving federal land grant funds through the Morrill Act should have to admit blacks or whether separate education for blacks should be required. While the second Morrill Act called for color-blind admissions, the act also stated that "the establishment and maintenance of such colleges separately for white and colored students shall be held to be in compliance with the provisions of this act if the funds . . . be equitably divided." This congressional action predated the *Plessy v. Ferguson** (1896) U.S. Supreme Court* decision by six years. The legislation did result in the creation of at least one black public college in each of the 17 states within a decade, although Congress consistently refused to enforce the "equal" requirement on the states. These schools concentrated on mechanical, industrial, and agricultural education; liberal arts education remained in private schools only. The legislation did not include liberal arts education for black institutions, but rather an emphasis on agricultural, mechanical, and technical education. The scope of these institutions has expanded to include engineering, science, liberal arts, and graduate programs.

According to Jones-Wilson et al. (1996), the current names of these land grant institutions are Alabama A and M University, Huntsville (1875); Alcorn State University, Lorman, Mississippi (1871); University of Arkansas of Pine Bluff, Pine Bluff (1873); Delaware State College, Dover (1891); Florida A and M University, Tallahassee (1887); Fort Valley State College, Fort Valley, Georgia (1895); Kentucky State University, Frankfort (1886); Langston University, Langston, Oklahoma (1897); Lincoln University, Jefferson City, Missouri (1866); University of Maryland Eastern Shore, Princess Anne (1886); North Carolina A and T State University, Greensboro (1891); Prairie View A and M University, Prairie View, Texas (1876); South Carolina State University, Orangeburg (1876); Southern University and A and M College, Baton Rouge, Louisiana (1880); Tennessee State University, Nashville (1912); Tuskegee University, Tuskegee, Alabama (1881); and Virginia State University, Petersburg (1882).

See also **Historically Black Colleges and Universities**.

References: Jones-Wilson et al., *Encyclopedia of African-American Education* (1996) 304–5; Kujovich, "Equal Opportunity in Higher Education" (1992); Preer, *Lawyers v. Educators* (1982); Marcus and Stickney, *Race and Education* (1981).

MULTICULTURAL EDUCATION. "Curricula designed to recognize the integrity, contributions, strengths, and viability of different cultural, language, and social groups in society . . . [which] help students, particularly those from different cultural, social, or language groups, to adjust to the demands of a modern pluralistic society," according to Dejnozka and Kapel (1991:362). Banks and Banks take more of an advocacy view, terming multicultural education a field of study that aims to create equal educational opportunity* for students from all racial, ethnic, social-class, gender, and cultural groups by helping students to acquire the knowledge, skills, and abilities needed to function in a diverse and pluralistic society. Their view in their handbook (1995:xi) is that "multicultural education seeks to reform all aspects of schooling, (*a*) policy and politics; (*b*) the attitudes, perceptions, beliefs, and actions of teachers and professors; (*c*) the formalized curriculum and course of study; (*d*) assessment and testing procedures; (*e*) the languages and dialects sanctioned within educational institutions; (*e*) [*sic*] teaching styles and strategies; and (*f*) instructional materials."

Thus multicultural education may be viewed as an ideal emphasizing the values of freedom, justice, and equality; a reform movement with the goal of equal educational opportunity; or a process aimed at racism* and sexism. American history, culture, and politics, according to multiculturalists, should be viewed from multiple perspectives. Some adherents such as Banks and Banks (267) reject the idea that knowledge is objective, arguing that "knowledge is socially constructed." They believe that America is deeply polarized along racial, ethnic, gender, and class divisions.

Synonyms for multicultural education may include diversity, cultural pluralism, intercultural education, and global education. The field draws from ethnic studies (the study of particular groups), multiethnic education, and women's studies.

Multiculturalism is a 1980s response in part to the failure of school desegregation* to result in equal educational results and frustration with an assimilationist perspective. The multiculturalist perspective calls for the inclusion of materials from the perspective of the nation's racial, ethnic, gender, and other minority groups, broadly defined, to play a central role in the curriculum and to end the domination of the Eurocentric white male perspective. James Banks offers five dimensions of multicultural education (4–5). Content integration refers to the utilization by teachers of examples from various cultures and groups in their classrooms. Knowledge construction focuses on how knowledge is created and influenced by the racial, ethnic, and social-class backgrounds of scientists. Prejudice* reduction is the third component, and equity pedagogy, the use of teaching techniques to facilitate equity, is the fourth. The restructuring of the school's organization and culture to create an "empowering school culture" for those from diverse groups is the final dimension.

The multiculturalist perspective has been criticized (see the review by Sleeter [1995] and individual critiques by Arthur Schlesinger [1991] and Diane Ravitch [1992]) by those with a conservative bent for several reasons, including the potential for divisiveness that may be caused by its excessive emphasis on race and ethnicity and related race-conscious policies. A further criticism revolves on questions about the intellectual rigor of the field. Furthermore, critics have raised questions about the emphasis on self-esteem* building in multicultural education as an inadequate foundation for increasing minority student achievement.* Criticisms from the left have focused on the emphasis on individual mobility rather than structural solutions to inequality.

References: James A. Banks, ed., and Cherry A. McGee Banks, associate ed., *Handbook of Research on Multicultural Education* (New York: Macmillan, 1995), including James A. Banks, "Multicultural Education: Historical Development, Dimensions, and Practice," 3–24, and Christine E. Sleeter, "An Analysis of the Critiques of Multicultural Education," 81–96; Diane Ravitch, "A Culture in Common," *Educational Leadership* 49, no. 4 (1992): 8–11; "Multicultural Education," in *American Educators' Encyclopedia*, by Dejnozka and Kapel (1991), 362; Arthur M. Schlesinger, Jr., *The Disuniting of America: Reflections on a Multicultural Society* (Knoxville, TN: Whittle Direct Books, 1991).

MURRAY V. MARYLAND. See Pearson v. Murray.

MYRDAL, (KARL) GUNNAR (born December 6, 1898, Gustafs, Dalarna, Sweden–died May 17, 1987, Stockholm). Swedish economist who authored the landmark 1944 *An American Dilemma: The Negro Problem and American Democracy*,* an analysis of the conflict between the American ideal of racial equality and the American practice of segregation.* Myrdal was born in a small village in central Sweden. He received his education at Stockholm University and earned a law degree in 1923. He was an impressive student and was immediately hired to teach at the university. After he married Alva Reimer in 1924, he opened a law practice, but the law was not for Myrdal, and he returned to work toward his economics Ph.D. at Stockholm University in 1927. After a tour of England, France, and the United States (on a Rockefeller fellowship in 1929–1930), he accepted a position as a professor in economics. In 1934 he and his wife published a book, *Crisis in the Population Question*, that analyzed his nation's declining birth rate and led to a change in Sweden's policy. Thus by 1938 Myrdal was recognized as an authority on national social problems. During the 1938–1940 period Myrdal, at the invitation of the Carnegie Foundation, which sought a fresh mind, someone who would not be influenced by his own preconceptions or attitudes, to analyze the condition of the American Negro, examined the social and economic problems of blacks in America. At the time of the award Myrdal was a professor of social economy at the University of

Stockholm, an advisor to the national government, and a member of the Swedish Senate. His research, funded by the Carnegie Corporation at the $250,000 level, resulted in a classic book on the status of blacks in the United States. He received assistance for this study from black social scientist Kenneth B. Clark* as well as other prominent black leaders and researchers in the United States. Myrdal's work was cited by the U.S. Supreme Court* in Footnote 11* in the *Brown v. Board of Education** decision.

After World War II Myrdal was Sweden's commerce minister and executive secretary of the United Nations Economic Commission for Europe from 1947 to 1957. Myrdal's wife was named ambassador to India. While there, Gunnar Myrdal wrote *Asian Drama: An Inquiry into the Poverty of Nations* (1968), a three-volume, 2,284-page work funded in part by the Twentieth Century Fund of New York. In 1974 he was awarded the Nobel Prize for economic science, and in 1982 his wife was given the Nobel Peace Prize.

Works about: *Britannica Online* (1996); Grossman, *The ABC-CLIO Companion to the Civil Rights Movement* (1993); *Current Biography Yearbook 1975* (New York: H. W. Wilson Company, 1975), 295–98.

Works by: *Asian Drama: An Inquiry into the Poverty of Nations* (New York: Pantheon Books, 1968); *Challenge to Affluence* (New York: Pantheon Books, 1963); *An American Dilemma: The Negro Problem and American Democracy* (New York: Harper and Brothers, 1944).

N

NAACP LEGAL DEFENSE AND EDUCATIONAL FUND, INC. (LDF).

The legal arm of the NAACP* that led the civil rights movement* in the federal courts and was victorious in the landmark *Brown v. Board of Education** case.

The roots of the LDF were in the early history of the NAACP. After Nathan Margold outlined a strategy for the NAACP in the Margold Report* to systematically challenge segregation,* the NAACP hired Charles Hamilton Houston,* then dean of the Howard Law School,* to be its first full-time legal staff member. Houston filed lawsuits to force southern universities to open their graduate and professional schools to blacks. In 1938 the NAACP had its first victory with *Missouri ex rel. Gaines v. Canada.** In 1939 the NAACP Legal Defense and Educational Fund (later to be called the Legal Defense Fund and then LDF) was incorporated as a separate group so that the LDF could receive tax-exempt charitable donations while the NAACP continued its lobbying activities, which made it ineligible for such tax-exempt deductions. One board of directors directed both organizations.

Houston hired Thurgood Marshall* to help, and by the end of the year Marshall was named the director of the LDF. Marshall led the court battles, building on the success of the *Gaines* case with a victory in *Sweatt v. Painter* (1950),* in which the U.S. Supreme Court* decided that segregated professional-school facilities for blacks had to be equal to those available for whites, which meant that they were likely to be prohibitively expensive. After *Sweatt* the LDF began its battle directly against segregated elementary and secondary schools. This resulted in the victories in 1954 in *Brown v. Board of Education* and *Bolling v. Sharpe.** In the following decade the LDF had to defend itself against southern legislatures, which were passing legislation to attempt to keep the LDF and NAACP from working in their states. In 1963 the Supreme Court concluded that the LDF and NAACP's actions were protected by the First Amendment in *NAACP v. Button.*

By the early 1950s the LDF was developing a separate identity, and in 1952 it moved to a separate facility three blocks from the NAACP home in Freedom House in New York City. The LDF became a separate tax-exempt organization with a distinct board of directors in 1956 after an Internal Revenue Service challenge over the NAACP's tax exemption. The two organizations had been having personality and policy differences. The NAACP added its own legal staff to pursue desegregation in the North, while the LDF concentrated its efforts on the South.* In 1957 both boards passed a resolution ensuring that the boards would be entirely separate and that no member could serve on the two boards simultaneously. In 1961 Thurgood Marshall became a federal judge and was replaced at the LDF by Jack Greenberg.*

The LDF was victorious in several key school desegregation* implementation decisions, including the *Swann** (1971) and *Keyes** (1973) cases. By the end of 1972 the NAACP LDF was working on about 1,200 cases. It concentrated on southern cases since victory in northern cases was so questionable. The LDF employed 24 lawyers in offices in New York, Washington, and Los Angeles. In 1994 the LDF considered dropping the NAACP initials from its name because of the problems at its "father" organization, quite ironically given its battle to keep these initials in 1966 and again in the late 1970s. In 1996 the LDF had a staff of 68 and a budget of just under $9 million to support litigation for defending legal and constitutional rights of minorities not only in education but also in housing, employment, voting, land use, and health care.

The LDF was an early practitioner of public interest law, forging a general strategy to overcome racial segregation* and moving beyond the interests of particular clients. The LDF defeated the white primary election, enforcement of restrictive covenants in housing, and segregation in interstate travel, but it is best known for its legal work in school desegregation cases. The LDF focused on the strategy of ending segregation. For example, the LDF had a continual discussion over whether to attack segregation per se or attack the unequal situation of blacks under *Plessy.**

References: Jaszczak, *Encyclopedia of Associations* (1996); Greenberg, *Crusaders in the Courts* (1994); Gilbert Ware, "The NAACP-Inc. Fund Alliance: Its Strategy, Power, and Destruction," *Journal of Negro Education* 63, no. 3 (1994): 323–35; Hall, *Oxford Companion* (1992); Orfield, *Must We Bus?* (1978); Kluger, *Simple Justice* (1975).

NABRIT, JAMES MADISON, JR. (born September 4, 1900, Atlanta, Georgia–died December 29, 1997, Washington, D.C.). Noted black civil rights* attorney who played a significant role in school desegregation* cases for the NAACP,* including the *Bolling v. Sharpe** case. After graduating from Morehouse College, Nabrit received his law degree from Northwestern University in

1927, where he edited the law review, and then taught at Leland College in Louisiana. In 1928 he was named dean of the Arkansas Agricultural, Mechanical, and Normal College at Pine Bluff. He worked at a black law firm in Houston that specialized in oil wells and real-estate law, but through the firm he met Charles Houston* and William Hastie, who were then making Howard Law School* into a first-rate school for civil rights law. He left private practice in Houston, where he had worked since 1930, upon his appointment in 1936 at Howard Law School, where he served for 24 years. He taught civil rights and constitutional law while working on major civil rights cases for the NAACP Legal Defense Fund.* He became president of Howard University in 1960 and in 1965 was named deputy U.S. representative to the United Nations by President Lyndon B. Johnson.*

Works about: Greenberg, *Crusaders in the Courts* (1994); Grossman, *The ABC-CLIO Companion to the Civil Rights Movement* (1993); Kluger, *Simple Justice* (1975).

NATIONAL ASSOCIATION FOR EQUAL OPPORTUNITY IN HIGHER EDUCATION (NAFEO). A voluntary, independent association of presidents of historically and predominantly black colleges and universities founded in October 1969 to advocate "the need for a higher education system where race, income, and previous education are not determinants of either the quantity or quality of higher education." NAFEO has been opposed to the "disestablishment remedy" in higher education; that is, it is opposed to using the *Green** (1968) approach to public higher education. It favors the preservation of black institutions of higher learning. It seeks increased financial support from federal agencies, philanthropic foundations, and other sources. It sees itself as a voice for historically black colleges and universities* (HBCUs), a clearinghouse of information on black colleges, a coordinator of black education, and a presidential resource. According to its brochure, "NAFEO's aim is to increase the flow of students from minority and economically deprived families, mostly Black, into the mainstream of society." NAFEO holds an annual conference in the nation's capital.

In 1972 NAFEO opposed the NAACP Legal Defense Fund* in the Department of Health, Education, and Welfare* enforcement case (*Adams v. Richardson**), arguing that black colleges need to be maintained and supported to provide equal educational opportunities* for black students. The NAACP Legal Defense Fund had argued in this case that the existence of black and white colleges and universities indicated that state authorities had failed to comply with the legal requirements of the U.S. Constitution.* NAFEO sought to separate the concept of educational opportunity from legal equality.

As of 1995 there were 117 NAFEO institutions, including private two-year and four-year institutions, public two-year and four-year institutions, and graduate and professional schools located in 14 southern states, 6 northern states, 4 midwestern and western states, the Virgin Islands, and the District of Columbia.

These schools had 350,000 enrolled students and graduate one-third of the black students with undergraduate and higher degrees each year.

References: Kujovich, ''Equal Opportunities in Higher Education'' (1992); Myers, *Desegregation in Higher Education* (1989); Preer, *Lawyers v. Educators* (1982).

NATIONAL ASSOCIATION FOR NEIGHBORHOOD SCHOOLS, INC. (NANS). Incorporated in 1976 as a coalition of local groups and individuals opposed to busing* and in favor of neighborhood schools.* NANS has lobbied Congress to pass antibusing legislation and amendments, has held public meetings and appeared in the mass media to present its position, and has attempted to have state and local officials seek release from court oversight of busing court orders. NANS was spearheaded by members of the Positive Action Committee, an antibusing organization formed during the school desegregation* process in the Wilmington, Delaware, metropolitan area.

References: Jost, ''Rethinking School Integration'' (October 18, 1996); *NANS Bulletin* (Cleveland, OH), Summer 1996; Jeffrey A. Raffel, *The Politics of School Desegregation: The Metropolitan Remedy in Delaware* (Philadelphia, PA: Temple University Press, 1980).

NATIONAL ASSOCIATION FOR THE ADVANCEMENT OF COLORED PEOPLE (NAACP). The largest and oldest organizational advocate of black civil rights* and desegregation* in the United States. The NAACP, through NAACP Legal Defense Fund* lawyers Thurgood Marshall* and Robert L. Carter, argued the *Brown v. Board of Education** (1954) case before the U.S. Supreme Court.* It also paid for the litigation and worked to obtain support in the local communities where the suit was based. The NAACP was the spearhead of most of the school desegregation* cases from 1967 to 1990. The NAACP successfully lobbied for the Civil Rights Act of 1957* and the Civil Rights Act of 1964.*

The National Association for the Advancement of Colored People (NAACP) was created in reaction to race riots and a lynching in Springfield, Illinois, Abraham Lincoln's hometown, on the 100th anniversary of Lincoln's birthday, February 12, 1909. The NAACP had its origins in a group of young blacks, begun in 1905 by W.E.B. Du Bois,* who were appalled at the growing violence against blacks throughout the nation. The Niagara Movement* had called for the education of black children. (The group was referred to as the Niagara Movement because the meetings were held on the Canadian side of the falls, where facilities were open equally to blacks.) The group had 400 members. Concerned whites (including a millionaire southern social reformer, William English Walling, and the grandson of abolitionist William Lloyd Garrison, Oswald Garrison Villard, publisher of the *New York Evening Post*) joined with the Niagara Movement to form the NAACP.

The objective of the NAACP at its inception was to spearhead a mass movement of blacks and whites to combat discrimination,* especially with regard to

education. Its specific goals included the abolition of enforced segregation,*
equal educational opportunities* for blacks and whites, enfranchisement of the
Negro, and enforcement of the Fourteenth Amendment* and Fifteenth Amendment.

Du Bois edited the association's publication, *Crisis*. The NAACP won its first
case before the U.S. Supreme Court in 1915 (*Guinn v. United States*). The
"grandfather clause," which had been used to disenfranchise blacks, was outlawed. This case helped to provide the NAACP with growing confidence in a
legal strategy to achieve its goals. But the strategy of fighting school segregation
through the courts had to compete with campaigns against lynching, opposition
to the appointment of racists, and the ad hoc defense of individual blacks.

In 1935 the association appointed Charles Hamilton Houston,* dean of the
Howard Law School* at the time, as its first full-time counsel. In 1939 the
NAACP Legal Defense and Educational Fund, later known as the LDF, was
formed to develop a strategy to challenge segregation through the courts. The
LDF became the spearhead of the NAACP's legal thrust.

The NAACP has worked to defeat several nominees to the U.S. Supreme
Court. In 1930 it helped to defeat John J. Parker's* nomination, and it successfully opposed Clement Haynsworth (1969), G. Harrold Carswell (1970), and
Robert Bork (1987) over their civil rights positions. The NAACP was unsuccessful, however, in blocking the confirmation of Clarence Thomas.

The NAACP is the nation's largest civil rights group, claiming almost 500,000
members (mostly black) in 1994. The NAACP is organized into over 1,700
branches across the nation and in European armed forces bases as well as over
400 youth councils and college chapters. The NAACP views itself as the spo-
kesgroup for black Americans. The NAACP is headquartered in Baltimore (it
moved from New York City in 1986) but maintains a Washington lobbying
office. Many prominent whites have been active in the organization, including
former president Arthur B. Spingarn and Lloyd Garrison, who was chair of the
legal committee. Eleanor Roosevelt was on the board of directors. William
White was the executive secretary of the NAACP up to his death in 1955; Roy
Wilkins succeeded him.

The NAACP became the target of southern legislatures trying to stop school
desegregation after the *Brown* decision. Southern states tried to intimidate the
NAACP and its members. The organization was constantly forced to go to court
to fight this harassment. For example, in Arkansas the attorney general, Bruce
Bennett, an archsegregationist, implemented his "Southern Plan for Peace" by
regularly charging the NAACP with violating one or another law. Then he used
the charge to demand that the NAACP reveal its list of members. This, of course,
would lead to intimidation of individual members that might have resulted in
job loss, physical violence, the denial of credit, or some other form of retaliation.
Similar harassment in Alabama led all the way to the U.S. Supreme Court, which
unanimously concluded that the actions of the state had violated the Fourteenth

Amendment. However, state officials did not comply with the decision, and the NAACP did not operate in the state for years as the appeals dragged on.

In the mid-1990s the NAACP was experiencing many difficulties, including a debt of $3.8 million in 1994, furloughs of staff, charges of fiscal mismanagement, the aftermath of a sexual harassment suit against its former executive director, Benjamin F. Chavis, Jr., and controversy over the organization's relationship with the Nation of Islam and its leader, Louis Farrakhan. Kweisi Mfume, head of the Congressional Black Caucus, was named president in 1995 and shepherded the organization to a projected balanced budget for 1997.

References: Greenberg, *Crusaders in the Courts* (1994); Gilbert Ware, "The NAACP-Inc. Fund Alliance: Its Strategy, Power, and Destruction," *Journal of Negro Education* 63, no. 3 (1994), 323–35; Hall, *Oxford Companion* (1992); Finch, *The NAACP* (1981); Kluger, *Simple Justice* (1975); Peltason, *Fifty-Eight Lonely Men* (1961).

NATIONAL INSTITUTE OF EDUCATION REPORT. The 1984 study titled *School Desegregation and Black Achievement* conducted for the National Institute of Education, then the research arm of the U.S. Department of Education,* which brought together a range of national experts on school desegregation* and methodology. The report is frequently cited in court battles over school segregation* and school desegregation.

Six experts on school desegregation (David Armor,* Robert Crain,* Norman Miller, Walter Stephan, Herbert Walberg, and Paul Wortman) were led by Thomas Cook, a "neutral" methodological specialist. The panel established six criteria for selecting the best studies to analyze, including the existence of a reasonable control or comparison group and a consistent pre- and postdesegregation student achievement* measure. The panel found 19 of 157 empirical studies that met their criteria. The studies had been published from 1966 to 1979. But even here not all the panelists could agree on all the studies, so some included different subsets in their analyses. Not surprisingly, the six experts continued to reach different conclusions about the effect of school desegregation on black achievement.

Thomas Cook, commenting on the analyses of the six experts and his own meta-analysis, found that the mean effect for reading achievement was about six weeks of gain for black students in desegregated versus segregated schools and the median effect was almost a month. The math achievement difference was smaller. Cook concluded that "desegregation does not cause any decrease in black achievement. On the average, desegregation did not cause an increase in achievement in mathematics. Desegregation increased mean reading levels." But Cook concluded that not much is known about how desegregation affects reading, especially given the great variety of effects resulting across the studies.

References: Armor, *Forced Justice* (1995); Janet Ward Schofield, "Review of Research on School Desegregation's Impact on Elementary and Secondary School Students" (1995); Cook et al., *School Desegregation and Black Achievement* (1984).

THE NATURE OF PREJUDICE. An influential work by Gordon Allport* published in 1954 that synthesized the work of social scientists about discrimination* at the time and developed the contact theory* of reducing prejudice.* The theory asserts that contact between members of disparate groups will breed a familiarity and understanding that in turn will lead to reduced prejudice. This prejudice reduction is especially likely where the contact is in a context of equal status and the members of the minority and majority groups are working toward common goals. Where the interaction has the sanction of institutional supports, such as law or custom, the effect of equal-status contact will be even greater.

Schofield's recent review (1996) of peer relations in desegregated schools supports Allport's earlier theory, but Elisabeth Young-Bruehl (1996) argues that there are many causes of the many prejudices that exist and that Allport's assumption that prejudice is a singular characteristic is incorrect. Allport assumed that persons who are prejudiced against blacks will also be prejudiced against other groups such as Jews and Catholics, But Young-Bruehl argues that prejudice is not a generalizable attitude.

References: Janet W. Schofield, "Promoting Positive Peer Relations in Desegregated Schools," in *Beyond Desegregation* ed. Shujaa, (1996), 91–112; Young-Bruehl, *The Anatomy of Prejudices* (1996); Armor, *Forced Justice* (1995); Gordon W. Allport, *The Nature of Prejudice* (Cambridge, MA: Addison-Wesley, 1954).

NEIGHBORHOOD SCHOOL. A school that serves a distinct geographical area defined by a line delimiting neighborhood boundaries around a school, where students are assigned by their residence and not other factors such as race. This concept has been a rallying point for those opposed to busing.* Operationally, neighborhood school refers to the closest school serving a grade level or the school within the attendance area serving a set of students prior to school desegregation.* Neighborhood schools policy associates the choice of residence with the choice of a public school. Ideally, neighborhood schools also offer an anchor point for people, a center of their community and family life. Students walk to school, parents can easily visit their child at school, and student and parental friendships are maintained across the school and neighborhood.

Gordon Foster* notes a number of exaggerated popular notions about the neighborhood school:

1. It is the closest school to a pupil's house.

2. It is a walk-in school with no transportation involved.

3. It is in the geographic center of a small, compact, circular or rectangular attendance area.

4. It enrolls a homogeneous population from families with common interests.

5. It is part of a culturally identifiable community neighborhood with the school, a shopping center, churches, and recreational facilities as components.

6. It is the parents' legal prerogative to send their child to the neighborhood school. (1973: 28)

Foster points out that while some of these may be true in any particular case, or while this may serve as an ideal, in few circumstances are all of these assumptions met. Thus Foster and other critics of the neighborhood school concept view it as an overromanticized view of school assignment policies even outside districts undergoing school desegregation. Advocates of neighborhood schools question the educational wisdom and the constitutionality of busing children away from their neighborhoods and local school for racial balance* objectives.

In a reaction against busing, and to be supportive of neighborhood schools, Congress has enacted legislation demanding that no federally ordered desegregation plan require students to attend a school beyond their neighborhood school. The Esch Amendment* and the Eagleton-Biden Amendment* have provided such limits, but Congress has failed to pass a constitutional amendment to limit the federal courts from ordering busing to overcome a constitutional violation.

See also **Hicks, Louise Day**.

References: Armor, *Forced Justice* (1995); Wilkinson, *From Brown to Bakke* (1979); Gordon Foster, "Desegregating Urban Schools: A Review of Techniques," *Harvard Educational Review* 43, no. 1 (February 1973): 5–36.

NEIGHBORHOOD SCHOOL PLAN. Student assignment plan based on assigning students by their residential location, generally in geographically contained attendance zones served by a single school, usually closest to the student's home. This is the student assignment plan utilized by most U.S. school districts, but generally not used by segregated school districts before *Brown** (1954). In dual systems* two assignment plans were overlaid on the school district, one for whites and one for blacks, so that blacks and whites attended schools only for their race. In the South,* where residential areas were often racially mixed, blacks often had to attend schools far from their neighborhood school,* which enrolled only whites and was closed to blacks. After the *Brown* decisions many southern districts adopted a freedom-of-choice* plan, which allowed students to transfer to their neighborhood school, even if that school had traditionally only enrolled students of the other race. However, black students were not assigned to formerly white neighborhood schools. The 1968 *Green** decision required school districts under desegregation* orders to abandon freedom-of-choice plans, and *Swann** (1971) required school districts to abandon neighborhood school plans and adopt busing* to break the link between segregated housing and segregated schools.

Neighborhood school plans in a different context are viewed as a mechanism for avoiding school desegregation. In school districts where the races are not mixed residentially, assignment to neighborhood schools turns the residential segregation into school segregation.* In Boston, for example, the advocacy of neighborhood schools by Louise Day Hicks* and her supporters was viewed as a not-so-subtle cry for segregated schools. Districts not achieving the status of a unitary system* and no longer having to meet court directives in a desegregation plan are turning to neighborhood school plans.

References: Orfield and Eaton, *Dismantling Desegregation* (1996); Armor, *Forced Justice* (1995); Sondra Astor Stave, *Achieving Racial Balance: Case Studies of Contemporary School Desegregation* (Westport, CT: Greenwood Press, 1995).

NEWBURG AREA COUNCIL V. BOARD OF EDUCATION OF JEFFERSON COUNTY, KENTUCKY, 510 F.2d 1358 (6th Cir. 1974).

The first major metropolitan school desegregation* busing* case involving school-district consolidation, in which the Louisville city schools and surrounding Jefferson County public schools were merged and then desegregated. The circumstances in Louisville/Jefferson County were unique. In Kentucky the county was the basic educational unit. The metropolitan area contained only two school systems, the county district and the Louisville district. As the city district's schools became more segregated because of white movement to the suburbs, the Kentucky Human Rights Commission pressed for a merger of city and suburban schools. The county school district opposed this. When the case was reviewed by the U.S. Court of Appeals* after *Milliken I** (1974), the court found that the Jefferson County schools were guilty of intentional school segregation,* and school-district lines in the state had been ignored to maintain the segregation. A metropolitan plan* was not, therefore, counter to the Detroit decision. When the city board voted itself out of existence, under state law the county had jurisdiction over the schools. In September 1975 Jefferson County implemented a school desegregation plan across city/suburban lines.

References: Gordon, ''The Implementation of Desegregation Plans since *Brown*'' (1994); U.S. Commission on Civil Rights, *School Desegregation in Louisville and Jefferson County, Kentucky* (Washington, DC: U.S. Government Printing Office, 1976); Martin Perley, ''The Louisville Story,'' *Integrated Education* 13, no. 6 (1975): 11–14.

NIAGARA MOVEMENT. Early civil rights* organization begun by W.E.B. Du Bois* in 1905 that was the precursor of the NAACP.* In June 1905 Du Bois called together a group of leading blacks to form a group to work toward ''Negro freedom and growth.'' The group of 29 men met in July in a small hotel in Fort Erie, Ontario, across from Niagara Falls, New York, to plan their efforts for freedom of speech, equal voting rights, and social equality. The group favored civil rights discussions, black history, and improved education for blacks. Its voice was a response, in part, to Booker T. Washington's* more conservative philosophy of accommodation. In 1906 the second meeting was held at Storer College in Harper's Ferry, West Virginia. The third conference was held in Faneuil Hall, Boston. The year following the Springfield, Illinois, race riot of 1908, white liberals and the Niagara Movement's leadership joined to form the NAACP. The delegates had decided that a permanent organization, which became the NAACP, was needed. While the Niagara Movement failed to attract funds for its "radical" program of racial equality, the NAACP had a major impact on civil rights in the United States. In 1910 the Niagara Movement folded and was replaced by the new organization. The Niagara Movement thus served to galvanize black voices for civil rights and counteract Washington's passive approach while laying the foundation for the NAACP, the organization ultimately successful in ending de jure segregation.*

References: *Britannica Online* (1996); Jones-Wilson et al., *Encyclopedia of African-American Education* (1996), 332–34; Grossman, *The ABC-CLIO Companion to the Civil Rights Movement* (1993); Finch, *The NAACP* (1981).

NIXON, RICHARD MILHOUS (born January 9, 1913, Yorba Linda, California–died April 22, 1994, New York City). Thirty-seventh President of the United States, whose Southern Strategy* won him the presidential election and was manifested in his opposition to busing* and civil rights* enforcement during his presidency. Nixon graduated from Whittier College in California in 1934 and received his law degree from Duke University with honors in 1937. He began law practice in Whittier in 1937, served in the Office of Price Administration in Washington, D.C., and joined the U.S. Navy in 1942. He was elected to Congress from the 12th California District in 1947 and to the U.S. Senate in 1950. He served as Vice President of the United States for two terms under Dwight D. Eisenhower* from 1953 to 1961 and ran unsuccessfully for President in 1960 against John F. Kennedy,* losing by only 112,000 of 68 million votes cast. In 1968 he was nominated and elected as President (defeating Hubert H. Humphrey) and was reelected by a landslide over Democratic nominee Senator George S. McGovern in 1972. On August 8, 1974, he resigned the presidency because of the scandal over the cover-up of the burglary and wiretap at the Democratic party's national headquarters in the Watergate complex.

Richard Nixon was an active opponent of busing. In his 1968 campaign he attacked busing and the Warren Court* and promised to move the U.S. Supreme Court* in a more conservative direction. He declared that he favored freedom-of-choice* school desegregation plans* and opposed the threat of federal fund cutoffs to force school desegregation.* Nixon was the first successful presidential candidate to be opposed to civil rights enforcement.

President Nixon followed his Southern Strategy in his political actions, attempting to move the traditionally Democratic South* into the Republican column. Many of his tactics thwarted the furthering of school desegregation. Nixon had his Secretary of the Department of Health, Education, and Welfare* (HEW), Robert Finch, write the Chief Judge of the Fifth Circuit Court of Appeals* stating that immediate desegregation would result in "chaos, confusion, and a catastrophic educational setback." This was the first time in years that the federal government had sided with those resisting school desegregation. Before the end of his administration Nixon's reluctance to implement federal laws supporting equal educational opportunity* and school desegregation led to the *Adams** (1973) suit and a federal court order requiring the administration to enforce the law.

Nixon also tried to appoint conservative judges from the South to the Supreme Court. After Associate Justice Abe Fortas resigned, Nixon nominated Fourth Circuit Judge Clement F. Haynsworth from South Carolina. But questions about Haynsworth's ethical behavior and strong civil rights opposition led to his defeat in November 1969 by a 55–45 vote of the Senate. This was the first rejection of a Supreme Court nominee since 1930. Nixon then nominated another judge in Haynsworth's mold, Fifth Circuit Judge G. Harrold Carswell of Florida. But Carswell's racist record and questionable legal and judicial record, in addition to anti-Nixon political forces, again led to a defeat, 51–45, in April 1970. Nixon's third nomination, Eighth Circuit Judge Harry Blackmun of Minnesota, was confirmed. Given the Carswell and Haynsworth defeats, Nixon had claimed that the Senate would not accept a Southerner on the Court, but the Senate confirmed his nomination of Lewis Powell,* former American Bar Association president from Virginia, in 1971. William Rehnquist,* a conservative Department of Justice* lawyer who had written a memo expressing his support for the separate but equal* doctrine while clerking for Justice Robert Jackson of the Supreme Court during the *Brown** (1954) deliberations, was also named by President Nixon to serve on the Court.

President Nixon did propose a major financial assistance program to help southern school districts make the transition from segregated to desegregated schools. This act became the Emergency School Aid Act of 1972.* The bill passed, but Congress reduced the funding from $1.5 billion to $75 million because of liberal fears that the legislation was not forceful enough in requiring school desegregation and conservative fear of the federal government forcing school desegregation on local school districts.

In 1972, after the Florida presidential primary in which George Wallace* stunned observers by winning over 40 percent of the vote in the Democratic primary, Nixon proposed two pieces of legislation, the Equal Educational Opportunities Act of 1972 and the Student Transportation Moratorium. The Equal Educational Opportunities Act of 1972 affirmed that no state or locality could discriminate in education based on race, color, or national origin and established criteria for what this meant, but it also established priorities for remedies that placed busing as a last resort with strict limitations. The moratorium would have stopped the courts from ordering busing until the Congress considered the busing limitation act. (See Douglas, *School Busing* [1994], for texts of these acts and President Nixon's speech introducing them as well as analyses of their constitutionality.) The Senate killed the bill in 1972. The Equal Educational Opportunities Act of 1974* was passed while he remained in office but with revisions that limited the impact of the bill on court orders.

Works about: *Britannica Online* (1996); O'Reilly, *Nixon's Piano* (1995); Marcus and Stickney, *Race and Education* (1981); Orfield, *Must We Bus?* (1978); Bolner and Shanley, *Busing* (1974); *Who's Who in the World, 1974,* 835; Panetta and Gall, *Bring Us Together* (1971).

Works by: Address to Congress, March 20, 1972 and "A Free and Open Society," 1970, in Douglas, *School Busing* (1994), 121–67; *RN: The Memoirs of Richard Nixon* (New York: Grosset and Dunlap, 1978).

NULLIFICATION. Principle that a state could void a federal requirement within its borders. This principle was first asserted by Virginia and Kentucky in 1798, but its most notable use was by South Carolina in 1832 in its attempt to nullify a federal tariff. Georgia, Alabama, Virginia, and Texas attempted to utilize this principle in fighting the 1954 *Brown** decision, but other southern states did not, viewing nullification as too extreme a position. No state went so far as to call a special state convention to nullify the *Brown* decision. James Kirkpatrick, editor of the *Richmond News Leader*, advocated interposition* and nullification as components of massive resistance* to school desegregation.* Resistance was based on interposition, not nullification.

References: *Dictionary of American History*, revised edition, vol. 5 (New York: Charles Scribner's Sons, 1976), 125–26; Bartley, *The Rise of Massive Resistance* (1969).

O

OFFICE FOR CIVIL RIGHTS (OCR). Established by the Civil Rights Act of 1964* and located in the Department of Education,* the Office for Civil Rights is responsible for enforcing civil rights* statutes that prohibit discrimination* based on race, color, national origin, sex, handicap, or age in programs offered by the Department of Education. The OCR led the legal fight for school-district compliance in school desegregation* in the South* from its creation through Richard Nixon's* election in 1972.

The Office for Civil Rights was created by the 1964 Civil Rights Act as the office responsible for enforcement of this act and subsequent civil rights legislation. OCR is responsible for enforcing Title VI of the Civil Rights Act of 1964 (which prohibits discrimination based on race, color, or national origin), Title IX of the Education Amendments of 1972* (which prohibits discrimination based on sex in educational programs), Section 504 of the Rehabilitation Act of 1973 (which prohibits discrimination based on physical or mental disability), the Age Discrimination Act of 1975 (which prohibits discrimination on the basis of age), and Title II of the Americans with Disabilities Act of 1990 (which prohibits discrimination on the basis of disability). The civil rights laws enforced by OCR cover agencies in the 50 states, the District of Columbia, and U.S. territories and possessions, and the nation's approximately 16,000 school districts, 3,600 postsecondary institutions, 6,800 proprietary schools, and other institutions receiving federal financial aid.

OCR has its administrative offices in Washington and ten regional offices. The latter handle program operations, primarily processing complaints of discrimination. OCR conducts compliance reviews as the need is defined by survey data (discussed later), interest groups, the media, and the general public. Issues that have recently generated compliance reviews include ability grouping* that results in racial segregation* and appropriate identification of special education students. OCR also provides technical assistance to organizations voluntarily complying with civil rights laws.

The Assistant Secretary for Civil Rights manages the OCR and is the principal advisor to the Secretary of Education on civil rights. If the office cannot gain compliance from school districts voluntarily, it can use two methods. It may issue a notice of opportunity for hearing. This initiates a hearing before an administrative law judge. The judge's decision may be reviewed within the department and finally by the Secretary. Alternatively, the OCR may refer a case to the Department of Justice* for court action. One measure of activity by the OCR is the annual number of completed investigations per employee. For example, this decreased from 10.4 in 1980 in the last year of the Carter* administration to 4.4 the next year, the first year of the Reagan* administration.

The OCR has conducted a national school-district survey of civil rights data in even-numbered years since 1974. It had conducted the survey on an annual basis from 1968 until that year. The 1994 survey involved 5,100 school districts, each reporting on school enrollments and assignment to special education and disciplinary action by race. In 1996 the office announced that its 6 percent budget cut would lead to a revamping and delay of the survey. The results of the survey not only had fueled research on changes in school segregation and compliance with desegregation orders, they had helped OCR monitor districts.

OCR has been the spearhead for desegregating higher-education institutions. Its actions have been based on the Fourteenth Amendment* and Title VI of the 1964 Civil Rights Act. OCR has worked to desegregate traditionally white and traditionally black institutions of higher education (historically black colleges and universities*) by adopting policies to change the racial composition of the governing board, administration, faculty, and students at both black and white colleges and universities. OCR has also worked to improve traditionally black colleges and universities by pressing for student recruitment programs, affirmative action* programs for faculty, and unique missions of historically black institutions that are likely to attract white students and vice versa.

In January 1994 the Assistant Secretary for Civil Rights announced a review based on the *United States v. Fordice** (1992) decision of the six states whose higher-education systems are still under scrutiny (Florida, Kentucky, Maryland, Pennsylvania, Texas, and Virginia) and also the eight states declared in compliance under the previous Republican administrations (Arkansas, Delaware, Georgia, Missouri, North Carolina, Oklahoma, South Carolina, and West Virginia). The OCR must consider how it will implement the *United States v. Fordice* decision, emphasizing the need for states to eliminate vestiges of prior segregation across their state systems and doing this without placing a disproportionate burden on black students.

OCR grew from a modest staff in the mid-1960s to 401 in 1970, 872 in 1975, and over 1,000 by 1977 (by 1994 it was reduced to 851), but over time it has shifted its focus from school desegregation to sex discrimination in athletics and developing bilingual/bicultural requirements. During the 1970s OCR's responsibilities were increased to ending discrimination against women and the handicapped. In the 1970s Congress restricted its ability to desegregate schools through the Esch Amendment* and the Eagleton-Biden Amendment.* (It is no longer able to cut off federal funds to discriminatory school districts.)

OCR was viewed as dormant during the Reagan-Bush era but stepped up its activity under the Clinton administration. Funds appropriated by Congress for the OCR fell during the Reagan administration, hit their low point during the Bush administration, and have steadied during the Clinton period.

Under the Nixon administration OCR staff could not provide technical assistance in developing school desegregation plans.* Title IV–funded desegregation assistance centers* could only participate in local desegregation efforts when they could show that local school districts invited their participation. Under President Clinton, however, by November 1994 the OCR had referred two cases to the Justice Department for enforcement, something the previous administrations were unwilling to do. Williams criticizes OCR for its ''limited capacity'' (1988:44).

References: Judith A. Winston, "Fulfilling the Promise of *Brown*," in *Brown v. Board of Education* ed. Lagemann and Miller (1996), 157–66; *Annual Report to Congress, Fiscal Year 1994* (Washington, DC: Office of Civil Rights, Department of Education, 1994); U.S. Department of Education, *Ed Facts: Information about the Office for Civil Rights* (Washington, DC, June 1991); John B. Williams III, *Desegregating America's Colleges and Universities* (1988); Q. Whitfield Ayres, "Racial Desegregation in Higher Education," in *Implementation of Civil Rights Policy*, ed. Charles S. Bullock III and Charles M. Lamb (Monterey, CA: Brooks/Cole, 1984), 118–47; Charles S. Bullock III, "The Office of Civil Rights and Implementation of Desegregation Programs in the Public Schools," *Policy Studies Journal*, 8 (1980): 597–615; Orfield, *Must We Bus?* (1978); Panetta and Gall, *Bring Us Together* (1971).

OFFICE OF EDUCATION. Federal agency created by Congress in 1867 that had its responsibilities assumed by the Department of Education* at its creation as a cabinet department in 1980. The office's principal functions included gathering and reporting statistics and facts on the condition of education in the nation, conducting and funding research on teaching, management, and the organization of education and disseminating relevant information and providing service to local, state, national, and international agencies, and administering federal education grants. The office was directed by the Commissioner of Education. The Office of Education was part of the Department of the Interior (1869–1939), the Federal Security Agency (1939–1953), and the Department of Health, Education, and Welfare* (HEW) (1953–1980). With the passage of the Civil Rights Act of 1964* the Office for Civil Rights* in the Office of Education was established as an enforcement arm of the federal government to ensure that

Title VI of the act was implemented. This title prohibited discrimination based on race, color, or national origin in federally funded programs. With the passage of the Elementary and Secondary Education Act of 1965,* the first comprehensive federal funding bill for local school districts, the Office of Education became the focal point of executive-branch civil rights* activity in the 1960s and 1970s. The office's leadership was rebuffed in its confrontation with Chicago Mayor Richard Daley* in 1965, but in the next decade the office overall successfully led the fight for school desegregation* in the South.* President Richard Nixon* greatly limited its scope and effectiveness in the 1970s, leading to the court challenge of its enforcement work in *Adams v. Richardson** (1973).

References: "United States Office of Education (USOE)," in *American Educators' Encyclopedia*, by Dejnozka and Kapel (1991); Orfield, *Must We Bus?* (1978); Orfield, *The Reconstruction of Southern Education* (1969).

OPEN ADMISSIONS. Postsecondary admissions policy allowing all high-school graduates to be admitted to college. The policy was first established when many of the new land grant colleges founded under the Morrill Act of 1862 offered admission to all high-school graduates. The open-admissions policy was also adopted by the California public higher-education system following World War II. The adoption of open admissions by the City University of New York (CUNY) system in 1969 for the fall of 1970 received widespread national attention because of the open racial and political conflict that generated the abrupt response and the visibility of the large system in New York City. All high-school graduates were guaranteed admission to CUNY. Placement in a community or senior college, however, depended on high-school scores, placement in high-school class, and space available. The system implemented extensive remedial programs and counseling and gave students a "grace period" of their freshman year.

Most community or two-year colleges throughout the United States now have open admissions. The major question surrounding open admissions is what results from the admission of students who are not prepared for college because of inadequate basic academic and social skills. How successful are such students in their studies, what are the costs of providing remedial work, and what effect do such programs have on racial and ethnic diversity? Will access of students who are unequal as they enter college result in equal results?

Open admissions at CUNY resulted from pressure of the black and Puerto Rican communities in New York City for the greater participation of their children in the CUNY system. Few blacks had served on the faculty or staff of CUNY in the decades of the 1930s or 1940s. By 1950 only 5 percent of the total student enrollment was made up of nonwhites, and this small percentage remained unchanged for a decade. While the establishment of community colleges increased the black percentage after their inception in 1955, few blacks attended the senior or four-year colleges.

Open admissions did lead to larger numbers of minorities entering CUNY, and in fact overall enrollments immediately increased by 75 percent. In 1969 the number of blacks was 2,815, but by 1974 this had increased to over 12,000. The number of Puerto Rican students quadrupled from 1,215 to 5,624. The number of black faculty also rose. Open admissions, however, brought with it a large remedial burden, with nearly nine out of every ten students needing such assistance. (It should be noted that Jewish and Catholic students generally outnumbered black and Puerto Rican open-admissions students.) In the mid-1970s CUNY struggled with budget cuts, and the recession made it more difficult for students to attend college.

A 1994 review (reworked as a 1996 book by Lavin and Hyllegard) of the effects of the open-admissions policy at CUNY, by then a 17-campus, 200,000-student system and the largest urban university in the United States, concluded that only 25 percent of CUNY's students graduated within eight years and that open admissions had lowered the quality of the four-year institutions as more and more effort and resources were devoted to remedial work and the distinction between regular and remedial courses became blurred. However, the policy had resulted in not only many more minority college students but also many more minority graduates, tripling the number of blacks and doubling the number of Hispanics earning bachelor's degrees.

References: Karen W. Arenson, "Study Details Success Stories in Open Admissions at CUNY," *New York Times*, May 7, 1996, A1; David E. Lavin and David Hyllegard, *Changing the Odds: Open Admissions and the Life Chances of the Disadvantaged* (New Haven: Yale University Press, 1996); David E. Lavin, Richard D. Alba, and Richard A. Silberstein, "Open Admissions and Equal Access: A Study of Ethnic Groups in the City University of New York," *Readings on Equal Education* (1977–1979), ed. Barnett and Harrington (1984), 298–341; Weinberg, *The Search for Quality Integrated Education* (1983); David Rosen, Seth Brunner, and Steve Fowler, *Open Admissions: The Promise and the Lie of Open Access to American Higher Education* (Lincoln: University of Nebraska, 1973).

OPEN ENROLLMENT. Student assignment technique that permits students to transfer to schools outside of their neighborhood attendance zone where seats are available in order to reduce racial imbalance* or to provide students with school choice. If transportation is necessary, its costs are generally not paid by the school district. Operation Exodus* in Boston, which provided private transportation for black parents wishing to send their children to white schools with empty seats outside of segregated areas but within the Boston School District, was built upon open enrollment. In 1963 the Rochester, New York, Board of Education authorized an open-enrollment plan under which the school district did pay for the transportation of students from 6 inner-city schools who opted to leave their neighborhood schools* for one of 18 receiving schools.

As the basis for voluntary school desegregation plans,* open enrollment suffers from several limitations. First, the number of students who can transfer is limited by the number of available seats in the receiving school. When enrollments are expanding, few seats may be available. Second, open enrollment may allow whites to transfer from schools enrolling blacks to those serving only whites if controls are not part of the plan. Majority-to-minority transfer programs* (M-to-M) do address this problem. A third limitation, as already noted, is that the burden of transportation is generally left to the student and parent. Fourth, with open enrollment the burden of school desegregation* is left to the uncoordinated decisions of individual parents and their children rather than to the actions of a school board or school district. Finally, with open enrollment there are concerns that those who transfer may be "the best and the brightest," leaving the neighborhood school with students with the least motivation.

References: Sondra Astor Stave, *Achieving Racial Balance: Case Studies of Contemporary School Desegregation* (Westport, CT: Greenwood Press, 1995); U.S. Civil Rights Commission, *Racial Isolation in the Public Schools* (Washington, DC: U.S. Government Printing Office, 1967).

OPERATION EXODUS. Program organized by parents in 1965 to send black children from Boston's segregated schools to majority white schools in the city. Following charges by local civil rights* groups that the Boston schools were de facto segregated,* denials by the Boston School Committee that this was true, and subsequent black boycotts of the schools, the North Dorchester–Roxbury Parents Association was formed in 1965. In August 1965 the Massachusetts legislature passed the historic Massachusetts Racial Imbalance Act,* which called for the elimination of racial imbalance* in the public schools. The Boston School Committee ignored this law and instead banned the use of school funds for busing* black children to the 7,000 or so vacant classroom seats throughout the city schools. In addition, the city school superintendent declared that the only way to offset school overcrowding was to go on double session. The parents organized Operation Exodus to send children through the district's open-enrollment* policy to empty seats throughout the district. Thus on September 9, 1965, Operation Exodus began using buses with funds donated by the NAACP,* labor unions, and individuals. (The name of the community group was also changed to Operation Exodus.) About 250 children were in the program initially. By 1967 over 600 were involved. In 1968–1969 this number dropped to about 400 as METCO,* the suburban busing program, and more private-school alternatives siphoned off some children. The program ended in 1970 when its originator, Ellen Jackson, took a position with the state board of education.

References: Jon Hillson, *The Battle of Boston* (New York: Pathfinder Press, 1977); Bolner and Shanley, *Busing* (1974); James E. Teele, *Evaluating School Busing: Case Study of Boston's Operation Exodus* (New York: Praeger, 1973); Clara Mayo, "Quality Education and Integrated Education: A Conflict of Values," paper presented at the Eastern Research Institute for Supervision and Curriculum Development (Philadelphia, PA, April 29, 1970), ERIC ED127377.

ORFIELD, GARY (born September 5, 1941, Minneapolis, Minnesota). Leading social science researcher who is an advocate for school desegregation* and busing,* has testified in over 20 court cases, and has written books supporting the need for school desegregation, even if it necessitates busing. Gary Orfield received his Ph.D. in political science from the University of Chicago. He served as scholar in residence at the U.S. Commission on Civil Rights and as the chair of the National Institute of Education's Desegregation Study Group. He was appointed by the court as an expert in the St. Louis, Los Angeles, Little Rock, and San Francisco cases. He was a professor of political science at the University of Illinois at Urbana. Orfield's school desegregation research has focused on the Civil Rights Act of 1964,* white flight,* and social change in communities undergoing school desegregation. Orfield has also extensively analyzed the relation of school desegregation to housing patterns. In 1993 he launched and became director of the Harvard Project on School Desegregation. Orfield and his staff have studied the movement away from school desegregation. Orfield currently serves as a professor of education and social policy at Harvard University.

Works about: Debra Viadero, "Separate and Unequal: Gary Orfield Wants to Make Sure History Doesn't Repeat Itself," *Education Week* 14, no. 4 (September 28, 1994): 37–38; Harvey Berkman, "Professor Studies, Acts on Equality/Reality Gap," *National Law Journal* 16, no. 38 (May 23, 1994): A12.

Works by: with Susan E. Eaton, *Dismantling Desegregation: The Quiet Reversal of Brown v. Board of Education* (New York: New Press, 1996); *Toward a Strategy for Urban Integration* (New York: Ford Foundation, 1981); *Must We Bus? Segregated Schools and National Policy* (Washington, DC: Brookings Institution, 1978); *The Reconstruction of Southern Education: The Schools and the 1964 Civil Rights Act* (New York: Wiley-Interscience, 1969).

P

PAIRING. A common school desegregation* technique of combining two schools, one white and one minority, so that one school then serves all students in the first subset of grades and the other school serves all students in the second subset of grades. For example, if one school serves all white pupils from kindergarten to sixth grade and another serves black students in the same grades, under pairing pupils are reassigned so that all kindergartners through third graders attend the first school and all fourth through sixth graders attend the second school. Pairing originated in Princeton, New Jersey, in 1948, where two Princeton elementary schools were paired and students were assigned to grades K–5 in one school and 6–8 in the other school. Pairing, therefore, is also referred to as the Princeton Plan. Pairing is differentiated from clustering,* where more than two schools are brought together.

References: Dejnozka and Kapel, *American Educators' Encyclopedia* (1991), 447; Hughes, Gordon, and Hillman, *Desegregating America's Schools* (1980); James M. Laing, *Alternative Methods, Practices, and Concepts for School Desegregation: A Review of the Literature and Annotated Bibliography* (Pleasant Hills, CA: Contra Costa County Department of Education, 1969), ERIC ED041056; Greenberg, *Race Relations and American Law* (1959).

PARKER, JOHN JOHNSTON (born November 20, 1885, Monroe, North Carolina–died March 17, 1958, Washington, D.C.). Key judge on the Fourth Circuit of the U.S. Court of Appeals* during the aftermath and interpretation of the 1954 and 1955 *Brown** decisions whose nomination to the U.S. Supreme Court* by President Herbert Hoover was rejected by the Senate in 1930. Parker was

author of the Court of Appeals *Briggs v. Elliott** decision finding that states had
to desegregate but not integrate or racially balance the schools.

Parker was the grandson of a Confederate soldier and the son of a poor, small-
town merchant. He attended the University of North Carolina, where he was
elected president of his class and to Phi Beta Kappa. Parker practiced law in
North Carolina and in 1910 was nominated by the Republican party for Congress
at the age of 25. In 1916 he ran for attorney general and in 1920 for governor.
While it was difficult to be elected as a Republican in North Carolina, Parker
did receive much praise and was rewarded with a nomination to the U.S. Court
of Appeals, Fourth Circuit, by President Calvin Coolidge in 1925.

President Hoover nominated Parker for the Supreme Court in March 1930,
but the nomination was defeated by a 41–39 vote on May 7, 1930. In an intense
six-week campaign the NAACP* fought the nomination because Parker failed
to repudiate a speech he had made ten years earlier in a gubernatorial campaign
viewing "the participation of the Negro in politics [as] a source of evil and
danger to both races." He was also opposed by the labor movement. Although
considered by other presidents again for a Supreme Court post, he received no
other nominations.

As an appellate judge, Parker authored the 1955 *Briggs v. Elliott** decision.
In this decision Parker concluded that states must stop segregating but had no
obligation to desegregate schools. This view stood in contrast to Judge John
Minor Wisdom's* view that states had the obligation to desegregate to undo the
effects of the segregated system of the past. Parker did, however, oppose massive resistance* and was considered, according to Goings, "a hard-headed,
clear-thinking, relatively enlightened grandson of the Confederacy unafflicted
by the regional fever that so often produced hallucinations over the outcome of
the Civil War" (1990:303). Goings, however, expresses doubts about whether
Parker would have joined a unanimous U.S. Supreme Court in the *Brown* decision if he had been a member.

Works about: Hall, *Oxford Companion* (1992); Kenneth W. Goings, *The NAACP Comes
of Age: The Defeat of Judge John J. Parker* (Bloomington: Indiana University Press,
1990); Kluger, *Simple Justice* (1975).

PASADENA CITY BOARD OF EDUCATION V. SPANGLER, 427 U.S. 424
(1976). U.S. Supreme Court* decision that helped to shape the requirements of
meeting a school desegregation* court order. In this decision the Court concluded that school districts do not need to adjust their school desegregation
plans* annually to maintain a certain degree of school desegregation.

In 1968 a number of black students charged the Pasadena, California, school
board with maintaining a segregated school system; the U.S. District Court*
agreed and ordered the board to submit a plan immediately. In 1970–1971 the
city of Pasadena desegregated its public schools following this successful suit
brought by parents, students, and the federal government. The plan called for
no schools with a majority of minority students. After four years of mandatory

busing* the Pasadena school board, with a number of new members, asked the District Court to permit the adoption of a voluntary plan* with magnet schools* and to end court supervision. The district argued that it had met the requirements for unitary status* as defined by *Green** (1968) and *Swann* (1971).* After a denial of the request by the District Court and an affirming view by the Ninth Circuit Court of Appeals,* the U.S. Supreme Court reversed the lower courts. The Court ruled that annual readjustments of the plan were not necessary to respond to demographic changes. Justice William Rehnquist* wrote the 6–2 majority opinion (Justices William Brennan* and Thurgood Marshall* dissented; Lewis Powell* did not participate). The District Court maintained supervision of the district for three more years, finally relinquishing supervision in 1979 under order from the Court of Appeals. This case continued to signal a more lenient view toward school desegregation by the Supreme Court as first indicated in the *Milliken v. Bradley I** (1974) decision.

References: Armor, *Forced Justice* (1995); Gordon, "The Implementation of Desegregation Plans since *Brown*" (1994); Grossman, *The ABC-CLIO Companion to the Civil Rights Movement* (1993); Hall, *Oxford Companion* (1992).

PEARSON V. MURRAY, 182 A. 590 (Md. 1936). Landmark state court case in Maryland that marked the first successful challenge of the separate but equal* segregationist laws. The case is also referred to as *Murray v. Maryland, Murray v. Pearson*, and *University of Maryland v. Murray.*

Donald Murray, a black resident of Baltimore, Maryland, and a member of a prominent black family in Baltimore, was a graduate of Amherst. He applied to law school at the University of Maryland. At the time Maryland funded two colleges for blacks, a land grant college and a teachers college, but neither offered education at the graduate level. There was a scholarship program to send black students to obtain graduate and professional training, but no funds had been appropriated for this purpose. Murray wrote the president of the University of Maryland inquiring about law-school admission, but President Raymond A. Pearson suggested that Murray look into Princess Anne Academy in-state or Morgan College out-of-state, neither of which had a law school. After his formal application was filed, Murray was rejected by the University of Maryland's law school and told to apply to Howard Law School.* Charles Houston* and Thurgood Marshall* represented Murray. While the state legislature quickly set aside $10,000 for a scholarship for Murray after he brought his suit, in 1936 the Maryland Court of Appeals ruled that the funding was insufficient. The court ordered Murray admitted to the previously all-white law school.

The Maryland court based its decision on the separate but equal* doctrine, ordering Murray admitted after finding that the system was separate but not equal. The NAACP* lawyers had carefully laid the foundation for this ruling by showing how the Maryland law school prepared students for the state's bar exam. They also successfully argued that the U.S. Supreme Court* had left the door open in its *Gong Lum v. Rice** (1927) decision by indicating that its decision might have been different if the Chinese girl had no school in her neighborhood, in contrast to the local colored school, available.

This decision raised the cost of segregation* to the state but did not outlaw it. Maryland tripled its scholarship fund, and several southern states initiated similar programs as a result of this decision. The university decided not to appeal this decision, and thus this case never reached the U.S. Supreme Court.

References: Kujovich, "Equal Opportunity in Higher Education" (1992); Tushnet, *The NAACP's Legal Strategy against Segregated Education, 1925–1950* (1987); Preer, *Lawyers v. Educators* (1982); Marcus and Stickney, *Race and Education* (1981).

PETTIGREW, THOMAS F. (born March 14, 1931, Richmond, Virginia). Leading social psychologist and school desegregation* researcher who has been an advocate of school desegregation. Pettigrew received his bachelor's degree in psychology from the University of Virginia and his M.A. (1952) and Ph.D. (1956) degrees from Harvard University. He was a faculty member at Harvard from 1957 to 1980. Pettigrew consulted for the U.S. Commission on Civil Rights* as well as the U.S. Office of Education* on school desegregation and has served as an expert witness in many court cases. Since 1980 he has served as a professor of social psychology and sociology at the University of California at Santa Cruz. His research interests have focused on race relations.*

Works about: *Who's Who in America, 1997*, 3346.

Works by: *The Sociology of Race Relations: Reflections and Reform* (New York: Free Press, 1980); *Racially Separate or Together?* (New York: McGraw-Hill, 1971); *Profile of the Negro Americans* (Princeton: Van Nostrand, 1964).

PLESSY V. FERGUSON, 163 U.S. 537 (1896). Landmark U.S. Supreme Court* decision in which the Court ruled 7–1 that separate but equal* facilities were constitutional under the U.S. Constitution.* This decision was not overturned by the Court until the 1954 *Brown v. Board of Education** decision over 50 years later.

In 1890 the General Assembly of Louisiana enacted a law requiring all railway companies in the state to provide "equal but separate accommodations for the white, and colored races" and penalties for individuals who did not go to their assigned coach. A test case was sought to challenge the newly enacted Jim Crow* laws in the South* following Reconstruction. In New Orleans a group of Creoles and blacks organized the Citizens' Committee to Test the Constitutionality of the Separate Car Law. Railroad executives were somewhat sympathetic because of the cost of providing dual cars. Homer Adolf Plessy, who appeared to be white but who was seven-eighths Caucasian and one-eighth African, agreed to personalize the challenge and thus on June 7, 1892, refused the conductor's request to enter the coach assigned to the colored race and, instead, sat in the white coach on an East Louisiana Railroad train. When he refused to change coaches, the conductor, with the assistance of a policeman, forcibly removed him from the train. He was then imprisoned for violating the state statute. Plessy's appeal went to the U.S. Supreme Court.

The Court considered the constitutionality of the statute with respect to the Fourteenth Amendment,* focusing on the equal protection clause.* The Court, in an opinion written by Justice Henry Billings Brown, viewed ''the underlying fallacy of the plaintiff's argument to consist in the assumption that the enforced separation of the two races stamps the colored race with a badge of inferiority. If this be so, it is not by reason of anything found in this act, but solely because the colored race chooses to put that construction upon it.'' That is, segregation* does not imply inferiority; it is only the interpretation that one race or another places on such separation that leads to this perception.

While the decision directly dealt with railway coaches and not schools, the Court noted that this law was no more ''unreasonable or more obnoxious'' than the acts of Congress establishing separate schools for colored children or similar acts of other state legislatures. Specifically, the opinion noted that the most common instance of the separation of the races was ''connected with the establishment of separate schools for white and colored children, which has been held to be a valid exercise of the legislative power even by courts of States where the political rights of the colored race have been longest and most earnestly enforced.'' (This referred to the *Roberts v. City of Boston** [1849] case.) Thus the Court forever linked this transportation case with the broader area of schools and education.

The Court's decision was based on the reasoning that segregation of the races, in this case in railway cars, did not harm colored people any more than Caucasian people. The Court viewed the Louisiana law as treating the races equally, despite the history of discrimination* against blacks that led to the law. In the years to follow, this decision provided the foundation for states to continue to separate the races in schools so long as the schools were equal in facilities.

In a dissent Justice John Marshall Harlan* noted that this legal discrimination implied inferiority. ''Everyone knows that the statute in question had its origin in the purpose, not so much to exclude white persons from railroad cars occupied by blacks, as to exclude colored people from coaches occupied or assigned to whites.'' Harlan argued against the decision because ''our Constitution is colorblind and neither knows nor tolerates classes among citizens.''

References: Abraham and Perry, *Freedom and the Court* (1994); Schwartz, *A History of the Supreme Court* (1993); Hall, *Oxford Companion* (1992); Yudof et al., *Kirp and Yudof's Educational Policy and the Law* (1987); Kluger, *Simple Justice* (1975).

PODBERESKY V. KIRWAN, 38 F.3rd 147 (4th Cir. 1994). U.S. Court of Appeals* decision concerning affirmative action* in which the University of Maryland at College Park's African-American scholarship program (Banneker Scholarships) was ruled unconstitutional since the university did not show that the current impact on blacks was from past discrimination* and that the scholarship program was narrowly shaped to remedy such discrimination. The university appealed the decision of the three-judge panel to the entire Fourth Circuit Court of Appeals but this request was denied on May 22, 1995.

Daniel J. Podberesky, a Hispanic student at the University of Maryland at College Park, filed a suit arguing that his civil rights were violated under the Civil Rights Act of 1964* when he was denied a Benjamin Banneker Scholarship Program award. This merit-based scholarship program was restricted to black students. In its first examination of this case the U.S. Court of Appeals remanded the case back to the U.S. District Court* to determine "whether present effects of past discrimination exist and whether the remedy is a narrowly tailored response to such effects." In the second District Court case the university argued that the race-based program was permissible for four reasons: (1) the university's poor reputation among black students, (2) the underrepresentation of blacks in the student population, (3) the low retention and graduation rate of these students, and (4) the perceived hostile atmosphere at the university for such students. The U.S. District Court accepted each of these arguments and ruled against Podberesky.

The Fourth Circuit Court of Appeals concluded that the race-based nature of the Banneker scholarship program required the court to apply a strict scrutiny standard. A two-part analysis was considered. There had to be a "strong basis in evidence for its conclusion that remedial action is necessary," and the remedy must "be narrowly tailored to meet the remedial goal." The appeals court's examination of the university's four reasons for the program led to a conclusion that there was not sufficient evidence that the university's reasons were the effects of past discrimination. That is, the attitudes of blacks toward the University of Maryland at College Park might well be negative, but did they result from past discrimination or other factors such as general societal discrimination? The court also questioned the District Court's reasoning about the applicant-pool statistics on which to compare the need for a scholarship program for black students. Furthermore, the Court of Appeals concluded that "as analyzed by the district court, the program more resembles outright racial balance* than a narrowly tailored remedy program" (160). The court ordered the university to reconsider Podberesky for the scholarship program without the racial restriction.

References: Walter R. Allen, Darnell M. Hunt, and Derrick I. M. Gilbert, "Race-Conscious Academic Policy in Higher Education: The University of Maryland Banneker Scholars Program," *Educational Policy* 11, no. 4 (1997): 443–78; Douglas Lederman, "Split on Racial Preferences," *Chronicle of Higher Education*, April 5, 1996, A25, A29; Panel on Educational Opportunity and Postsecondary Desegregation, *Redeeming the American Promise* (Atlanta, GA: Southern Education Foundation, 1995); David L. Gregory, "The Continuing Vitality of Affirmative Action Diversity Principles in Professional and Graduate School Student Admissions and Faculty Hiring," *Journal of Negro Education* 63, no. 3 (1994): 421–29.

POWELL, LEWIS FRANKLIN, JR. (born November 19, 1907, Suffolk, Virginia). Associate Justice of the U.S. Supreme Court* from 1972 to 1987 whose swing vote and opinion in the *Bakke* case set the standards for affirmative action* plans in colleges and universities. A member of a distinguished Virginia family, Powell attended Washington and Lee College in Lexington, Virginia. He was first in his class and president of the student government. He earned his law degree there in two years rather than the usual three and then went on to Harvard Law School to earn an LL.M. Powell practiced law in Richmond, interspersing a distinguished record as an intelligence officer in World War II within his years as a lawyer. He held numerous civic leadership posts, including Richmond School Board president, membership on the state board of education, and positions in the trial lawyers and bar associations.

Powell was conservative but not a segregationist. He led the opposition to Virginia's massive resistance* approach to the 1954 *Brown** decision. In 1959 as school board president he led the efforts of the Richmond School Board to desegregate* the schools.

Nominated by President Richard M. Nixon,* Powell was sworn in as a Supreme Court justice on January 7, 1972. Powell remained in the Court's center, often casting the decisive vote. The fear of losing his decisive swing vote for civil rights* helped to defeat the nomination of the much more conservative Robert Bork after Powell's retirement. Powell's opinion in *Regents of the University of California v. Bakke** (1978) is one of the most significant and often quoted opinions of the U.S. Supreme Court.

Works about: John C. Jeffries, *Justice Lewis F. Powell, Jr.* (New York: Charles Scribner's Sons, 1994); Hall, *Oxford Companion* (1992); Jacob W. Landynski, "Justice Lewis F. Powell, Jr.: Balance Wheel of the Court," in *The Burger Court: Political and Judicial Profiles*, ed. Lamb and Halpern (1991), 276–314.

PREJUDICE. A stereotyped attitude toward an ethnic group or its individual members. Prejudice is a general belief about an individual based not on knowledge about that individual but rather about all members of the group. The attitudes about the group members are not flexible and are not open to change with new knowledge.

While in *The Nature of Prejudice** Gordon Allport* concluded that prejudice was a generalized attitude, Elisabeth Young-Bruehl argues that there are many prejudices with different causes. In her formulation there are three broad prejudicial character types: the obsessional character who sees "conspiracies of demonic enemies everywhere"; the hysterical character (racists) who sees groups "acting out forbidden sexual or sexually aggressive desires that the person has repressed"; and the narcissistic character (sexists) who "cannot tolerate the idea that there exist people not like them" anatomically (1996:34–35). Prejudice, which is an attitude, may be the foundation for discrimination,* which is an action or behavior.

School desegregation* has been viewed as becoming more feasible as prejudice diminishes, but also as a factor in reducing prejudice and improving race relations.* Unfortunately the research literature does not present strong evidence that school desegregation generally has this positive effect.

References: Janet W. Schofield, "Promoting Positive Peer Relations in Desegregated Schools," in *Beyond Desegregation* ed. Shujaa (1996), 91–112; Young-Bruehl, *The Anatomy of Prejudices* (1996); Marger, *Race and Ethnic Relations* (1991).

PRINCETON PLAN. *See* **Pairing**.

PROJECT CONCERN. A Hartford, Connecticut, voluntary school desegregation* program busing* black students from city to suburban schools, Project Concern was begun in September 1967 with 267 elementary students (88 percent of whom were black) from Hartford to 33 surrounding schools in 5 suburban communities. Support funds have come from private sources as well as city, state, and federal funds. Six thousand students have taken advantage of this program. In 1978, 1,175 students were enrolled in schools in 13 suburban school districts, but in 1996 less than 500 were included in the program. Suburban districts had limited numbers of empty seats, and many black families had moved to the suburbs, forcing some suburban school districts to deal with their own desegregation issues.

References: George Judson, "Hartford to Seek Voluntary Desegregation," *New York Times*, July 11, 1996, B4; Sondra Astor Stave, *Achieving Racial Balance: Case Studies of Contemporary School Desegregation* (Westport, CT: Greenwood Press, 1995); Robert L. Crain, Jennifer A. Hawes, Randi L. Miller, and Janet R. Peichert, *Finding Niches: Desegregated Students 16 Years Later*. Final Report on the Educational Outcomes of Project Concern, Hartford, CT (New York: Institute for Urban and Minority Education, Teachers College, 1992); Armor, "The Evidence on Busing" (1972).

PROPOSITION 209. The California Civil Rights Initiative, California constitutional amendment passed by 54 percent of the state's voters in November 1996 that bars state and local government from using racial or gender preferences in education, as well as employment and contracting. In April 1997 a three-judge panel of the U.S. Court of Appeals* for the Ninth Circuit unanimously overturned the decision of a U.S. District Court* judge who had blocked the amendment from taking effect. This decision was appealed to the full appeals court. The implementation of this measure calls into question affirmative action* programs, including college and professional-school admissions, and voluntary school desegregation plans,* mentoring programs aimed at minority students, and any other program based on race (or sex).

References: Tim Golden, "Federal Appeals Court Upholds California's Ban on Preferences," *New York Times*, April 9, 1997, 1; Mark Walsh, "Calif. Measure Barring Racial Preferences Reinstated," *Education Week* 16, no. 9 (April 1997): 20.

PUERTO RICAN LEGAL DEFENSE AND EDUCATION FUND (PRLDEF). Founded in 1972 to advocate, educate, and litigate to secure and safeguard the rights of the Puerto Rican and Latino community in the nation, the PRLDEF is modeled after the NAACP Legal Defense Fund* (LDF). The PRLDEF has been active in promoting educational rights as well as working in the areas of voting rights, poverty, and economic justice. To that end it has filed hundreds of lawsuits across the nation. Most recently the organization has been involved in the *Sheff v. O'Neill* (1996)* metropolitan school desegregation* case in Hartford and the *Coalition to Save Our Children v. State Board of Education of the State of Delaware* case in Delaware (a case concerning unitary status* begun in 1993 that followed *Evans v. Buchanan** [1975]) and has sought to improve bilingual education* in New York City. The PRLDEF also seeks to increase the number of Latino lawyers. The PRLDEF, with a staff of 20 in 1996, shares a building with the LDF in New York City.

References: Jaszczak, *Encyclopedia of Organizations* (1996), 2071; Greenberg, *Crusaders in the Courts* (1994); Orfield, *Must We Bus?* (1978).

PUPIL PLACEMENT LAWS. Legislation passed by states in the South* resisting the *Brown v. Board of Education** decisions that set the standards of assignment and the methods of review for the assignment of pupils to schools under freedom-of-choice* plans. Review methods varied widely but had in common a lengthy and complicated process. Thus these laws were among the variety of laws passed by southern states offering massive resistance* to implementing the 1954 *Brown** decision. For example, according to NAACP Legal Defense Fund* lawyer Jack Greenberg,* in Alabama the criteria to be utilized in assigning pupils to schools included

available room; teaching capacity; transportation; effect of admission of new pupils on established or proposed academic programs; suitability of established curricula for particular pupils; adequacy of pupils' academic preparation for admission; scholastic aptitude and relative intelligence; mental energy or ability of individual pupil; psychological qualification of pupil for type of teaching and associations involved; effect of admission on academic standards; possibility of threat or friction or disorder among pupils or others; possibility of breaches of the peace or ill will or economic retaliation within the community; home environment of the pupil; maintenance or severance of established social or psychological relationships with other pupils and teachers; choice and interests of the pupil; morals, conduct, health and personal standards of the pupil; request or consent of the parents or guardians and the reasons assigned therefor. (1959:233)

Such laws gave local school boards great discretion in pupil assignment, enough to slow or stop implementation of school desegregation.* According to Wilkinson, these laws were "more popular, more ingenious, and more successful by far than the school closing laws." Ten southern states passed such laws after the *Brown* decision. In theory, these laws helped to implement *Brown*, but in reality they were, according to Wilkinson, "an ideal delaying device, a maze of administrative hearings and appeals through which Negroes on an individual basis had to wind before reaching federal court" (1979:84). Pupil placement laws placed the burden of school desegregation on individual black pupils and their parents.

References: Greenberg, *Crusaders in the Courts* (1994); Marcus and Stickney, *Race and Education* (1981); Wilkinson, *From Brown to Bakke* (1979); Greenberg, *Race Relations and American Law* (1959).

PUPIL PLACEMENT PROGRAM. School desegregation* "plan" used by southern states to implement the *Brown v. Board of Education** (1954 and 1955) decisions; generally considered inadequate by the federal courts because the criteria for school assignment maintained segregated schools. Under pupil placement laws* students were to be placed in schools according to the ability of the school to meet their educational needs or psychological profiles or other vague criteria, such as "health, safety, and general welfare" in North Carolina. Blacks and whites, however, never wound up in the same schools. Procedural obstacles, such as having only one day during working hours when a parent could pick up an appropriate transfer form, limited the actual school changes. The process began with children in the schools they "normally" would have attended. Alabama, Arkansas, Florida, Louisiana, Mississippi, North Carolina, South Carolina, Tennessee, Texas, and Virginia passed pupil placement legislation.

See also **Massive Resistance**.

References: Greenberg, *Crusaders in the Courts* (1994); Marcus and Stickney, *Race and Education* (1981); Wilkinson, *From Brown to Bakke* (1979); Greenberg, *Race Relations and American Law* (1959).

R

***

RACE RELATIONS. The interactions among different racial groups, which may be described as conflictual or harmonious, competitive or cooperative, or dominant or subordinate, or may involve integration* or separation. Race relations are affected by discrimination,* prejudice,* and racism.*

According to Marger (1991), three periods of black-white relations have existed in the United States: slavery, the Jim Crow* era of segregation,* and the contemporary era. To rebut the attacks of abolitionists on slavery from 1830 to 1860, southern slaveholders developed the ideology of racism, that blacks were innately and permanently inferior to whites. While many whites may have previously held a negative view of blacks, such attitudes were generally based on a view that negative characteristics were not innate but rather the result of cultural factors. Segregation during the Jim Crow era reflected the racist ideology of white superiority and black inferiority and was a reaction to the abolishment of slavery, a shift in power and resources to blacks, and the end of paternalism and the beginning of competition between blacks and whites. The Compromise of 1877,* which led to the withdrawal of federal troops from the South,* marked another turning point in race relations. Despite the U.S. Supreme Court's* conclusion in *Plessy v. Ferguson** in 1896 that segregation should not necessarily be viewed as an indictment of either race, white efforts to segregate blacks clearly grew out of a racist ideology of superiority. While many blacks moved north to compete with whites for jobs in the increasingly industrialized cities of the North, segregation of schools, housing, transportation, and a vast array of public and private facilities increased throughout the South. World War II, with the nation's fight against a racist Germany and the return of black as well as white soldiers from the war, helped to provoke a new era in race relations. With government civil rights* activity increasing during the Truman* administration and with the *Brown* decision in 1954, the scene was set for the nonviolent protest of the civil rights movement* and the emergence of black power.* These forces have led to a more competitive situation for blacks and whites in American society.

In the contemporary era a most significant question is whether the status of blacks, which has been increasing in recent years vis-à-vis that of whites, remains unequal primarily because of class or racial factors. That is, is William Julius Wilson (1980) correct that the forces that have led to black-white gaps in economic equality are primarily based on the economic structure of our nation and class factors, or are racism and racial discrimination* the primary explanations for the gaps that remain? While white attitudes toward blacks indicate far more support for racial integration as a principle, and negative stereotypes of blacks are less frequently displayed, white support for concrete actions to further black equality with mechanisms such as busing* and open-housing legislation lags. Blacks are far more likely to explain their unequal condition as the result of social conditions or institutional forms of discrimination, while whites view black disadvantage as a function of individual lack of effort.

School desegregation* may be affected by and have an effect on race relations; many view school desegregation as an important mechanism to improve race relations. Yet the evidence on the effect of school desegregation on race relations is mixed, and the research has even been characterized as "a methodological cesspool" by McConahay (1981:36) because few experiments, as opposed to cross-sectional studies, have been conducted and few studies have analyzed the effects of school desegregation on race relations for more than a year. Gordon Allport* concluded years ago that improved intergroup relations and reduced prejudice are most likely in a setting of equal statuses. But equal status is very hard to achieve in a school desegregation context, for blacks are almost always drawn from lower socioeconomic strata than whites, given the nature of social stratification in the United States.

The status of race relations at traditionally white higher-education institutions has been a concern. Higher black dropout rates, racial incidents of harassment of blacks, self-imposed segregation of blacks, and faculty conflicts over multicultural education* are among the issues that have troubled college campuses. In fact, there is evidence of increasing problems in race relations throughout the nation as manifested in the differential reactions between blacks and whites to the murder trial of O. J. Simpson, the policy of affirmative action,* and the speeches of Louis Farrakhan.

The means by which school desegregation is implemented may well affect its role in changing race relations. Multicultural education,* for example, is offered as an important element of school desegregation efforts aimed at reducing prejudice and improving race relations. Similarly, cooperative learning, which has students work cooperatively in equal-status groups to achieve common academic ends, is also viewed as a positive element of school desegregation. Many desegregated schools have special conflict-management programs to improve race relations. These programs train interested students in how to serve as mediators, and in their role as mediators how to help fellow students express their feelings and listen to others do the same without resorting to violence.

References: Paul A. Winters, ed., *Race Relations: Opposing Viewpoints* (San Diego: Greenhaven Press, 1996); Phillips, "Racial Tension in Schools" (January 7, 1994); Marger, *Race and Ethnic Relations* (1991); John C. McConahay, "Reducing Racial Prejudice in Desegregated Schools," in *Effective School Desegregation*, ed. Hawley (1981), 35–54; William J. Wilson, *The Declining Significance of Race*, 2d ed. (Chicago: University of Chicago Press, 1980).

RACIAL BALANCE. A goal of school desegregation* to have the percentage of minority pupils at each school approximately equal to the percentages in the school district or other defined area. This may be stated as having each school represent the racial composition of a school district within a certain percentage spread. For example, a school district with 60 percent white pupils and 40 percent black pupils may seek to desegregate its schools so that each school has 45–75 percent white and 25–55 percent black students attending each school.

Opponents of racial balance argue that it is a "quota" system, indicating more concern for numbers than students. The U.S. Supreme Court* ruled in *Swann** (1971) that ratios may be used as a guideline but not as an absolute requirement. Thus some schools may be left as predominantly white or predominantly black.

Conservatives have argued that the U.S. Supreme Court made a wrong turn when it changed its standard to judge successful desegregation from the removal of boundaries to school attendance based on race, that is, a color-blind stance, to one that required schools to achieve racial balance, a color-conscious standard, in the 1968 *Green v. County School Board of New Kent County** decision. Those supporting the standard argue that the Court's call for school desegregation plans* to "work," that is, to change segregated schools to schools that serve black and white students, was the appropriate decision, and that the goal of racial balance is the appropriate one.

The primary measure of racial balance used by social scientists is the index of dissimilarity.* The primary measure of racial balance used by the courts is that all schools, or specified schools, must be within a specified range of racial balance, for example, within 15 percentage points or 20 percentage points of the school district's racial composition.

See also **Desegregation; Massachusetts Racial Imbalance Act; Racial Imbalance**.

References: Wolters, *Right Turn* (1996); Armor, *Forced Justice* (1995); Orfield, *Must We Bus?* (1978).

RACIAL IMBALANCE. Racial imbalance exists when the percentage of races across a number of schools varies greatly from the percentage in the general student population of the school district. It is the absence of racial balance.*

School districts that have the affirmative obligation to desegregate their schools because they have been found to be in violation of the U.S. Constitution* must correct racial imbalance in school enrollments. The 1968 *Green** decision of the U.S. Supreme Court* required that school desegregation plans* desegregate the schools, and the 1971 *Swann** decision of the Court allowed the use of enrollment ratios as guides to determine if the schools were desegregated. The amount of racial imbalance tolerated in a district required to desegregate has varied across cases. The specific ratio of blacks and whites allowable at each school in a district, for example, may be within 10 percentage points (e.g., Charlotte-Mecklenburg, Boston, and Norfolk plans) or 15 percentage points (e.g., Denver and Columbus, Ohio, plans). That is, if a district's overall percentage of black students is 30 percent, schools that are 20 to 40 percent black may be considered desegregated in one district and those that are 15 to 45 percent in another. More recently the courts have provided even more latitude, using a range of plus or minus 20 percentage points in Savannah, San Jose, and Yonkers, and some plans have even greater variances permitted. The court allows particular schools with particular circumstances to not be racially balanced, sometimes because there are not enough white students to go around or because the school is quite isolated from the rest of the district's schools. While a majority of school districts with a school desegregation plan used racial balance for defining desegregation,* according to a 1992 federal survey quoted by David Armor,* some use an absolute standard (for example, schools must have enrollments that are half black and half white), and one-third of districts with plans have no explicit racial balance standard.

See also **Massachusetts Racial Imbalance Act; School Segregation**.

References: Wolters, *Right Turn* (1996); Armor, *Forced Justice* (1995); Rossell, "The Convergence of Black and White Attitudes on School Desegregation Issues during the Four Decade Evolution of the Plans" (January 1995); Rossell, *The Carrot or the Stick* (1990); Orfield, *Must We Bus?* (1978).

RACIAL INTEGRATION. *See* **Integration, Racial**.

RACIAL ISOLATION IN THE PUBLIC SCHOOLS. The 1967 Report of the U.S. Commission on Civil Rights* on the effects of school segregation.* This report was prepared in response to President Lyndon B. Johnson's* November 17, 1965, request to "gather the facts and make them available to the nation as rapidly as possible" about school segregation.* The commission focused on the nation's metropolitan areas since two-thirds of the nation lived in these areas and two-thirds of the students attended school there.

The study addressed four questions: (1) the extent of racial isolation in the nation's public schools and gaps in black-white educational achievement; (2)

factors that reinforce segregation; (3) the impact of racial isolation on educational outcomes; and (4) programs available to overcome racial isolation in education. The commission involved numerous consultants to help its staff with this study, held conferences and hearings to collect information, and reanalyzed the data that served as the basis of the Coleman Report.*

The report concluded that racial isolation in public schools was extensive throughout the United States. For example, two-thirds of the black students in first grade surveyed attended schools that had enrollments at least 90 percent black; almost 80 percent of the white students surveyed attended 90 percent white schools. The commission found that such racial isolation was also very severe in central cities, and, at least in northern cities, this isolation was growing. The commission found that the gap between black and white students in academic standing grew as students progressed through the grade span.

The report analyzed reasons why racial isolation was expanding or being maintained, including the decisions of school officials in building new schools in segregated areas and designing geographic attendance areas. The report concluded that "the system of geographic school attendance, imposed upon segregated housing patterns, provides the broad base for racial isolation in Northern schools" (1967:59). But the major reason for racial isolation in city schools, according to the report, was the "social, economic, and racial separation between central cities and suburbs" (70). The commission viewed this separation as a function of housing discrimination,* reinforced by federal policies and increasing disparities in wealth between cities and suburbs. As the wealthy moved to suburbs and the fiscal needs of cities increased, the resources needed to meet such needs declined, thus making escape to suburbs even more attractive to those with resources.

While acknowledging that family background and the social class of students' schoolmates affected educational achievement, the report concluded that racial composition of schools had an independent effect on student achievement.* Racial segregation led to negative social and educational outcomes, for example, lower student achievement, self-esteem,* and aspirations. The commission concluded that black students achieved more in desegregated settings, that is, majority white schools, and that segregation harmed children whatever the cause of it, that is, whether it was de jure* or de facto.* "Negro children who attend predominately Negro schools do not achieve as well as other children, Negro and white" (193). Children in segregated schools were found to have more limited aspirations and lower self-esteem. The commission decided that de facto segregation was also harmful to black children, but recognizing that the federal courts were not about to order school desegregation in de facto segregated schools, the commission called for federal legislation to establish a racial balance* standard of no majority of black students in any school.

Many of the contributors to this report later played leading roles in the school desegregation process. William L. Taylor was staff director. Taylor later was the director of the Center for National Policy Review at Catholic University

School of Law, which focused on school desegregation law, was on the executive committee of the Leadership Conference on Civil Rights, and was staff director for the U.S. Commission on Civil Rights.* M. Carl Holman was deputy staff director. Holman later directed the Community Relations Service* of the Department of Justice.* Thomas F. Pettigrew* was the chief consultant on the Race and Education Study. David Armor* conducted a special analysis of the Coleman data for the commission.

References: Jones-Wilson et al., *Encyclopedia of African-American Education* (1996), 384–86; Armor, *Forced Justice* (1995); St. John, *School Desegregation* (1975); U.S. Commission on Civil Rights, *Racial Isolation in the Public Schools* (Washington, DC: U.S. Government Printing Office, 1967).

RACIAL SEGREGATION. *See* **Segregation, Racial**.

RACIALLY IDENTIFIABLE SCHOOLS. *See* **School Segregation**.

RACISM. Racism is defined by the U.S. Commission on Civil Rights* in the handbook *Racism in America and How to Combat It* (1970) as "attitudes, actions, and institutional structures that subordinate a person or group because of their color." Racism may be divided into individual acts directed at people of color that result in death, injury, or destruction of property, and institutional racism, where the institutional rules and operating policies have negative impacts but are seemingly based on a race-neutral foundation. In schools examples of institutional racism include a lack of role models for minority students based on faulty hiring practices, failure to recognize the achievements of minority individuals in the curricula of the school, and low expectations for minority students. At the higher-education level examples of institutional racism include overt racial conflict against blacks, curricula more relevant to white middle-class students than black students, limited course offerings reflective of minority cultures, and the use of standardized tests for admission. Individual racism, a form of prejudice,* includes the belief that people are divided into distinct groups by heredity, that these groups are innately different in their social behavior and mental capacities, and that the groups can therefore be ranked as superior or inferior. Traits such as intelligence, temperament, and other major characteristics are thus viewed as innate and unchangeable. The failure of groups to succeed is thus viewed as the outgrowth of their genetic inferiority. Bennett (1995) also refers to cultural racism as the "elevation of White Anglo Saxon Protestant cultural heritage to a position of superiority over the cultural experiences of ethnic minority groups" (Bennett, 673, quoting from G. Gay). In the United States racism has traditionally been directed by whites against blacks, although the term *racism* was used to describe the horrors that Adolf Hitler and the Nazis directed against Jews in the 1930s and 1940s. The *Brown** decision was based in part on the effects of racism on black children.

Racism has played a role in U.S. Supreme Court* school segregation* decisions, the most notable being *Plessy v. Ferguson** in 1896. In this decision the Court held that laws requiring separate accommodations for blacks and whites on railroads were not in violation of the Fourteenth Amendment* to the U.S. Constitution.* The Court argued that laws calling for the segregation* of the races were not necessarily stamping blacks with a "badge of inferiority"; "if this be so, it is not by reason of anything found in the act but solely because [the black person] chooses to put that construction on it." In 1954 the Court finally left the *Plessy* decision behind and concluded in *Brown* that separate but equal* had no place in American education. However, implementing its 1955 *Brown II** decision calling for school desegregation with all deliberate speed* proved difficult given the amount of racism existing in the South.* Massive resistance* limited desegregation* for over a decade, even leading one school district, Prince Edward County in Virginia, to close its schools rather than comply.

The U.S. Supreme Court has included racism as a major criterion for action in the school desegregation arena. In *Washington v. Davis** (1976) the Court held that before school desegregation can be ordered, a finding of discriminatory intent* is necessary in addition to a finding of the discriminatory impact of government actions. That is, one must prove not only that a governmental action caused minority-group members harm, but also that the actions were based on intentional discrimination.*

Surveys of the racial attitudes of the American public indicate a decreasing level of racism and increasing support for the principle of desegregation. For example, in the mid-1950s, when the *Brown* decision was made, only about half of Americans supported the principle of blacks and whites attending schools together, but by 1985 support was so widespread that the National Opinion Research Corporation no longer asked the question in its annual surveys. But there is widespread disagreement, even among researchers, over whether school desegregation has reduced the holding of racist views and has improved race relations,* and there is certainly only limited support for implementing desegregation if busing* is the means to achieve this.

See also **Clark, Kenneth Bancroft**.

References: Meyer Weinberg, comp., *Racism in Contemporary America* (Westport, CT: Greenwood Press, 1996); Bennett, "Research on Racial Issues in American Higher Education" (1995); Hawley and Jackson, *Toward a Common Destiny* (1995); Hall, *Oxford Companion* (1992); Marger, *Race and Ethnic Relations* (1991); Joel Williamson, *A Rage for Order: Black/White Relations in the American South since Emancipation* (New York: Oxford University Press, 1986); Newby, *The Development of Segregationist Thought* (1968).

REAGAN, RONALD WILSON (born February 6, 1911, Tampico, Illinois). Fortieth President of the United States and a foe of busing,* racial balance,* and affirmative action* who tried to limit federal activity in the area of civil rights* and school desegregation.* After an extensive acting career, Ronald Reagan won the governorship of California in 1966 and served two terms. In 1980 he won the Republican nomination for President and defeated incumbent Jimmy Carter* in the election by a landslide. During his campaign Reagan promised to "get the federal government off the backs of the American people." Among the areas he felt were burdens were busing, racial balance, and affirmative action. Yet one sympathetic analyst concluded that "no sweeping changes occurred during Reagan's two terms in office," and there was a "general failure to make any substantial reformulation of civil rights policy during the Reagan presidency" (Detlefsen, 1991:3).

Reagan's Department of Justice,* led by Assistant Attorney General for Civil Rights William Bradford Reynolds,* tried to restore fundamentalist Christian Bob Jones University's tax exemption. The university had been denied the exemption because it would not allow black students to date or marry whites and was thus declared to be discriminating. The U.S. Supreme Court* supported the denial of a tax exemption. This was the most controversial civil rights lawsuit of Reagan's first four years as president.

President Reagan was considered a conservative and popular president. He tried to change the members and tone of the U.S. Commission on Civil Rights.* His efforts led to great conflict with Congress and among commission members during his terms in office.

Early in the Reagan administration the Emergency School Aid Act of 1972,* which provided funds to school districts implementing school desegregation plans,* was rescinded, the largest education program cut in the Omnibus Budget Reconciliation Act. Some funds were restored for magnet schools* later on. The administration tried to eliminate desegregation assistance centers,* which helped desegregating school districts deal with educational problems, but while Congress resisted, budget reductions did lead to a reduction in the number of centers by three-fourths. Assistant Attorney General Reynolds argued against busing during this administration, and in 1982 he led the fight to restrict busing in Norfolk, Virginia, in the *Riddick** (1986) case. Reagan appointed Justice William Rehnquist,* an opponent of busing, Chief Justice of the U.S. Supreme Court after Warren Burger's* resignation. In higher education the Reagan administration concentrated on upgrading historically black colleges and universities* (HBCUs) through executive order but did little to desegregate postsecondary institutions.

Wolters (1996) argues that President Reagan was not a racist but believed in the principle of color blindness over color consciousness. Reagan had personally worked to overcome racial discrimination* and intolerance against individuals he knew and had supported Harry Truman's* call for civil rights in 1948. By the mid-1960s Reagan began to question the civil rights movement* as the battle for nondiscrimination became a battle for racial preferences. According to Wolters, Reagan sought equality of opportunity but not equality of results; others have been less charitable in their judgments of President Reagan.

Works about: Orfield and Eaton, *Dismantling Desegregation* (1996); Wolters, *Right Turn* (1996); Greenberg, *Crusaders in the Courts* (1994); Detlefsen, *Civil Rights under Reagan* (1991); Amaker, *Civil Rights and the Reagan Administration* (1988).

REGENTS OF THE UNIVERSITY OF CALIFORNIA V. BAKKE, 438 U.S.

265 (1978). Landmark U.S. Supreme Court* decision on affirmative action* that included six opinions, among them the deciding opinion of Justice Lewis Powell,* resulting in the acceptability of taking race into account in admissions where past discrimination* warrants a remedy and where the remedy is appropriate and does not include quotas.

Allan Bakke majored in mechanical engineering at the University of Minnesota, earning almost a straight A average. To help pay for his education, he joined the Naval Reserve Officers Training Corps. He later fought as a marine captain in Vietnam. In 1967 he earned a master's degree at Stanford and began working as an aerospace engineer at a NASA research center nearby. Married and with three children, Bakke sought to become a doctor, and he enrolled nearly full-time to take the medical prerequisites he needed (e.g., biology, chemistry) to go to medical school. He also worked on a voluntary basis in a hospital room.

At age 33 Bakke applied to 12 medical schools and was rejected by all of them. He was especially upset that his two tries at admission to the medical school of the University of California at Davis had been unsuccessful, and in mid-1974 he sued for admission to the medical school. In 1973 and 1974 there were 2,664 and 3,700 applicants, respectively, for 100 places in the medical school. Bakke's grades and scores were much higher than those of the 16 minority students admitted under a special minority program. Bakke claimed that unconstitutional racial preferences excluded him from this medical school, violating both Title VI of the Civil Rights Act of 1964* and the equal protection clause* of the Fourteenth Amendment* of the U.S. Constitution.*

The special admissions process for the medical school ran parallel to the regular process. Applicants could declare themselves "economically and/or educationally disadvantaged" in 1974 or as "minority group" members (black, Chicano, Asian, American Indian) thereafter. If an applicant did so, her or his application was forwarded to the special committee, which was composed of a majority of minority members. These applicants did not have to meet the 2.5 grade point average cutoff. About one-fifth of these special applicants were interviewed for places in the class. The committee then presented its best candidates to the regular committee, which could reject applicants if they judged them not fully prepared. The number of applicants to be admitted through this special process was prespecified. The university argued that this program was necessary for several reasons, including the need for doctors willing and able to work in minority communities, the need to compensate for previous societal discrimination against minorities, the need to increase the number of minority doctors in the medical profession in which they had been so underrepresented, and the need to diversify the student body of the medical school.

The trial court ruled in Bakke's favor but denied him admission because he had not proved that the special minority program was the cause of his rejection, but on appeal to the California Supreme Court, Bakke won. The court concluded that the medical school could have adopted many other less burdensome procedures to meet its interests. For example, the university could have judged the lower grades of disadvantaged applicants to reflect a greater potential for success due to their previous burdens, or it could have emphasized character of applicants more from personal interviews and other information from the admissions process. The court ordered Bakke admitted.

The university appealed, and the court stayed his admission pending the appeal. This was a very controversial case, with 58 *amicus curiae** (friend of the court) briefs filed. President Carter's* administration had to be convinced to argue for affirmative action but not rigid quotas, according to Jack Greenberg* (1994).

A number of prominent civil rights* lawyers urged the university not to appeal because it had established such a weak case. The university's medical school was new, so it could not base its minority program on the undoing of past discrimination on its grounds. Then what discrimination were its efforts supposed to undo? The reservation of 16 places for minorities was certainly a quota in appearance, if not in fact. Would this not rile the public and threaten more qualitative affirmative action programs? Bakke's credentials were superb, and he was a model plaintiff. Was there really any support for denying a veteran and model student a place in the next class of doctors? Wilkinson (1979) has viewed this case as a conflict over equality and meritocracy. On the one hand was the view that to overcome past discrimination, color-conscious remedies were needed. On the other side were those who argued that such efforts hurt quality and diluted standards.

The U.S. Supreme Court by a 5–4 vote in a set of six opinions totaling 157 pages upheld the use of race as an admissions criterion, but not fixed quotas. But Justices John Paul Stevens, William Rehnquist,* and Potter Stewart and Chief Justice Warren Burger* were opposed to taking race into account at all and concluded that the school had violated Title VI of the Civil Rights Act of 1964, which prohibits racial discrimination in federally funded programs. Justices William Brennan,* Byron White, Thurgood Marshall,* and Harry Blackmun were most supportive of affirmative action; they did not find that the admissions procedure violated the Civil Rights Act of 1964 or the U.S. Constitution. Thus Justice Lewis Powell* was the deciding vote. He joined the Stevens plurality, concluding that the program was invalid because of its strict racial quota, but also joined the Brennan plurality, agreeing that race could be one of many factors taken into account in admissions decisions. Thus a race-sensitive admissions system would be constitutional, but the fixed quota system of the University of California was not. Such a system would only be permissible if the university had been explicitly found in violation of the Constitution. However, according to Justice Powell, schools could take into account a variety of factors such as personal talents and maturity, along with "a history of over-coming disadvantage and ability to communicate with the poor." Bakke was ordered admitted because his exclusion was the result of the quota system.

This case was the first significant test of affirmative action decided by the U.S. Supreme Court. Wilkinson argues that the U.S. Supreme Court recognized the good arguments on both sides of this case and that the final decision was a "brokered judgment" and not a "conclusive outcome" but rather a "Solomonic compromise" (1979:298). Supporters of affirmative action cite this case as a positive one since the role of race-conscious selection was affirmed, but opponents of affirmative action cite it as a case indicating that quotas are not permissible.

References: Greenberg, *Crusaders in the Courts* (1994); Bernard Schwartz, *Behind Bakke: Affirmative Action and the Supreme Court* (New York: New York University Press, 1988); Kaplin, *The Law of Higher Education* (1985); Wilkinson, *From Brown to Bakke* (1979); Sindler, *Bakke, DeFunis, and Minority Admissions* (1978).

REHNQUIST, WILLIAM HUBBS (born October 1, 1924, Milwaukee, Wisconsin). Conservative U.S. Supreme Court* Justice appointed by Richard Nixon* in 1972 as an Associate Justice and named Chief Justice by President Ronald Reagan.* Rehnquist holds a very restrictive interpretation of the *Brown** (1954) decision.

William Rehnquist attended elementary and high school in his hometown of Milwaukee and then attended Stanford University. His college education was interrupted with service in the U.S. Air Force from 1943 to 1946. At Stanford he was elected to Phi Beta Kappa and graduated in 1948. Rehnquist went on to Harvard for a master's in political science and then returned to Stanford for law school. He graduated from law school in 1952, first in his class.

Rehnquist was selected as a clerk to U.S. Supreme Court Justice Robert H. Jackson, a conservative member. During the U.S. Supreme Court's deliberations on *Brown*, Rehnquist wrote a memo supporting the separate but equal* doctrine. After his work in Washington Rehnquist went to work for the Phoenix law firm of Evans, Kitchel, and Jenckes (1953–1956). Thereafter he formed a partnership with another lawyer. At this time Rehnquist also was becoming a strong advocate for conservatism, criticizing Earl Warren,* William O. Douglas, and Hugo Black for their leftist philosophies. He served as state prosecutor, dissolved his law firm, joined another firm, and then formed a new partnership with a former trial lawyer for the Internal Revenue Service. He developed a friendship with two other Arizona conservatives, Senator Barry Goldwater and Richard G. Kleindienst, who had served as national field director for Goldwater's 1964 and Richard Nixon's 1968 presidential campaigns. Kleindienst was named Deputy Attorney General by President Nixon, and in 1969 he in turn named Rehnquist as Assistant Attorney General in charge of the Office of Legal Counsel. In this position he interpreted the Constitution* and governmental statutes for President Nixon and became a leading advocate for the President's policies, especially his "law and order" program. He criticized the Court for having too much sympathy with criminals.

On October 21, 1971, President Nixon nominated Rehnquist and Lewis F. Powell, Jr.,* to fill the Supreme Court seats of Hugo L. Black and John Marshall Harlan, who had resigned. Rehnquist's nomination brought strong criticism. His civil rights* positions became a major focus of these charges. It was charged that he had opposed a nondiscrimination public accommodations law in Arizona in 1964 and a school desegregation plan* for high schools in Phoenix in 1967. He answered the charges before the Senate Judiciary Committee. His memo on the *Brown* case years earlier became an issue, but Rehnquist stated that he had written it for Justice Jackson, not as a statement of his own beliefs. The Senate confirmed his nomination by a 68–26 vote. He was sworn in with Lewis Powell on January 7, 1972.

Orfield and Eaton call Rehnquist "the first clear dissenter on school desegregation in the eighteen years after *Brown*" (1996:10). He was a dissenter on the *Keyes** (1973) case, calling the decision "a drastic extension of *Brown*." Bernard Schwartz reports that in his early years on the Court Rehnquist was given a Lone Ranger doll by his law clerks to symbolize his singular dissenter position (while an Associate Justice Rehnquist set a record by dissenting 54 times), but by the time President Reagan nominated him Chief Justice in 1986, he had become "the most influential member of the Burger Court*" (1993: 364).

Works about: Orfield and Eaton, *Dismantling Desegregation* (1996); Schwartz, *A History of the Supreme Court* (1993); Sue Davis, "Justice William H. Rehnquist: Right-Wing Ideologue or Majoritarian Democrat?" in *The Burger Court*, ed. Lamb and Halpern (1991), 315–42; Kluger, *Simple Justice* (1975); *Current Biography Yearbook* (New York: H. W. Wilson Company, 1972), 359–62.

REHNQUIST COURT. The U.S. Supreme Court* under Chief Justice William Rehnquist* beginning with his appointment as Chief Justice by President Ronald Reagan* in 1986, which has moved the Court's jurisprudence to the right ideologically. In the school desegregation* arena the Rehnquist Court has defined what is necessary for a school district to be declared a unitary system* and thus be relieved of the affirmative obligation to desegregate its schools.

The first members of the Rehnquist Court were the following:

William J. Brennan, Jr.* (1956–1990, appointed by President Dwight D. Eisenhower*)

Byron R. White (1962–1993, appointed by President John F. Kennedy*)

Thurgood Marshall* (1967–1991, appointed by President Lyndon B. Johnson*)

Harry A. Blackmun (1970–1994, appointed by President Richard M. Nixon*)

Lewis F. Powell, Jr.* (1971–1987, appointed by President Nixon)

John Paul Stevens (1975–, appointed by President Gerald Ford)

Sandra Day O'Connor (1981–, appointed by President Ronald Reagan*)

Antonin E. Scalia (1986–, appointed by President Reagan)

Later members were the following:

Anthony Kennedy (1988–, appointed by President Reagan)

David H. Souter (1990–, appointed by President George Bush)

Clarence Thomas (1991–, appointed by President Bush)

References: Arthur L. Galub and George J. Lankevich, *The Rehnquist Court, 1986–1994* (Danbury, CT: Grolier Educational Corporation, 1995); David F. B. Tucker, *The Rehnquist Court and Civil Rights* (Aldershot, England: Dartmouth Publishing Company, 1995); Schwartz, *A History of the Supreme Court* (1993); David G. Savage, *Turning Right: The Making of the Rehnquist Supreme Court* (New York: Wiley, 1992); Sue Davis, *Justice Rehnquist and the Constitution* (Princeton, NJ: Princeton University Press, 1989).

REMEDIES. *See* **School Desegregation Plans**.

REMEDY PHASE. The stage of a school segregation* case after the liability phase* in which the court determines the means necessary, generally a school desegregation plan,* to address the segregation found to be unconstitutional in the liability phase of the case. Remedies must be consistent with the scope of the constitutional violation. Under *Brown II** (1955) remedies are shaped by the U.S. District Court* in school desegregation* cases. Court-ordered remedies may be reviewed by the Court of Appeals* and then the U.S. Supreme Court.*

    See also ***Milliken v. Bradley (Milliken II); Swann v. Charlotte-Mecklenburg Board of Education***.

References: Armor, *Forced Justice* (1995); Kurland, "*Brown v. Board of Education* Was the Beginning" (1994); "Remedy," *The Guide to American Law: Everyone's Legal Encyclopedia* (St. Paul: West Publishing, 1984) vol. 8, 455–56.

RESEGREGATION. The return to racially segregated schools after they have been previously desegregated. Recent U.S. Supreme Court* decisions such as *Riddick v. School Board of the City of Norfolk, Virginia** (1986), *Board of Education of Oklahoma City v. Dowell** (1991), *Freeman v. Pitts** (1992), and *Missouri v. Jenkins** (1995) have made it easier for school districts under school desegregation* court orders to achieve unitary* status, and as such they no longer have the affirmative obligation to desegregate their schools. They may change their student assignment plans to achieve neighborhood schools,* which frequently results in segregating schools again that had been desegregated under the previous student assignment plan. Such resegregation may well be de facto segregation,* not de jure segregation,* in the unitary context. Resegregation may also occur from the effects of white enrollment loss due to white flight* or demographic changes or from second-generation school desegregation problems* such as assignment to special education classes or schools disproportionately by race. School districts dismantling their school desegregation plans have included Denver, Cleveland, and Oklahoma City.

References: Jost, "Rethinking School Integration" (October 18, 1996); Orfield and Eaton, *Dismantling Desegregation* (1996); Armor, *Forced Justice* (1995); Leslie G. Carr,

"Resegregation: The Norfolk Case," *Urban Education* 24, no. 4 (January 1990): 404–13; Meier, Stewart, and England, *Race, Class, and Education* (1989).

REYNOLDS, WILLIAM BRADFORD (born June 21, 1942, Bridgeport, Connecticut). Principal architect of the Reagan* administration's attempt to change the nation's civil rights* policies away from affirmative action* and busing* to race-neutral or color-blind policies. Reynolds was born in the Du Pont family, a descendant of Governor William Bradford, who had traveled to the New World on the *Mayflower*. His father was also a lawyer and head of the patent and trademark division of E. I. Du Pont de Nemours and Company. Reynolds went to the private schools of Tower Hill and Phillips Academy before attending Yale University and the Vanderbilt School of Law. At Vanderbilt he had the second-highest grades in his class and was the law review's editor-in-chief. After serving three years at the prestigious New York City law firm of Sullivan and Cromwell, Reynolds spent three years working for Solicitor General of the United States Erwin Griswold. During this stint he worked on several civil rights cases and argued before the U.S. Supreme Court* 11 times. He then joined a Washington law firm specializing in commercial litigation as a partner.

Reynolds was selected as the Assistant Attorney General for Civil Rights, that is, director of the Civil Rights Division* of the Department of Justice,* under Attorney General William French Smith in the administration of President Ronald Reagan. Because of Reynolds's strong views against racial preferences and his lack of much previous civil rights experience, he was subject to major criticism. When the Reagan administration announced its intention to support Bob Jones University in its fight against the Internal Revenue Service over its racial policies in *Bob Jones University v. United States*,* over 100 of the Civil Rights Division's 176 lawyers signed a protest letter to him. In June 1985 Reynolds's nomination to become Associate Attorney General was thwarted by the Senate Judiciary Committee. Two Republicans joined eight Democrats to oppose the nomination. According to Wolters (1996:11), "Reynolds eventually became [Attorney General] Meese's most trusted advisor and confidant," and Meese named him Counselor to the Attorney General, a designation that did not require another battle with the Senate committee. Reynolds played a significant role in the selection of William Rehnquist to succeed Chief Justice Warren Burger,* as well as other Supreme Court nominations. Wolters concludes that Reynolds became "one of the heroes of the Reagan revolution" (16).

Throughout his tenure in the federal government, Reynolds maintained his opposition to affirmative action and busing. During the first two years of the Reagan administration no school desegregation* suits were filed by the Justice Department. In higher education Reynolds focused on improving historically black colleges and universities* (HBCUs) rather than desegregating historically white schools.

Amaker (1988) argues that Reynolds was opposed to more than mandatory school desegregation plans.* In the St. Louis metropolitan area an agreement was reached to allow suburban students to select a city school and vice versa. While the pressure of a court suit led to the agreement, it did involve voluntary student choice. Yet Reynolds's Justice Department opposed this consent decree* despite its voluntary elements.

Works about: Wolters, *Right Turn* (1996); Amaker, *Civil Rights and the Reagan Administration* (1988); *Current Biography Yearbook 1988* (New York: H. W. Wilson Company, 1988), 476–79.

REZONING. A common school desegregation* technique based on the redrawing of school attendance zones that may be used where residences are racially desegregated or where residential areas housing different races come together or to combine noncontiguous areas of different racial composition together. Rezoning is sometimes called "reverse gerrymandering."

There are two main types of rezoning. Contiguous rezoning changes adjacent attendance areas to increase desegregation, sometimes in conjunction with opening a new school building or closing an old one. Noncontiguous rezoning rearranges nonadjacent attendance areas to increase desegregation and is necessary where residential areas are more segregated and the school district is larger. One technique, combining attendance areas and changing grade structures, may be used in contiguous or noncontiguous rezoning. Pairing* and clustering* recombine the attendance areas of two (pairing or Princeton Plan) or more (clustering) schools and then require students to attend particular grade levels in different schools. For example, two K–6 school attendance areas, one serving whites and one blacks, would be combined, and one school would then serve all students for K–3 grades and the other for 4–6 grades. Two-way busing is the result; over the course of the grade span both minority and majority students travel to desegregated schools out of their neighborhoods. Satellite zoning (or pocket or island zones) is the technique of rezoning where grade structures are not changed and attendance areas are noncontiguous. Here an area with one racial composition is assigned to a school with other noncontiguous areas of a different racial composition. Contiguous rezoning occurs when adjacent school attendance areas are combined without grade changes.

See also **Modified Feeder Patterns**.

References: Armor, *Forced Justice* (1995); Forrest R. White, *"Brown Revisited"* (September 1994); Rossell, "The Classification of School Desegregation Remedies" (1992); Hughes, Gordon, and Hillman, *Desegregating America's Schools* (1980); Gordon Foster, "Desegregating Urban Schools: A Review of Techniques," *Harvard Educational Review* 43, no. 1 (February 1973): 5–36.

RIDDICK V. SCHOOL BOARD OF THE CITY OF NORFOLK, VIRGINIA, 784 F.2d 521 (4th Cir. 1986). The first decision by a federal court that allowed a school district, after being declared unitary,* to undo its school desegregation plan.* Like other schools in Virginia, the Norfolk schools were segregated at the time of the 1954 *Brown** decision. Virginia was the site of massive resistance,* so in 1956 black parents sued the city's school board to obtain desegregated schools. In February 1957 the parents were victorious in court, but the district still refused to accept black applications to white schools. In order to avoid implementing a U.S. Court of Appeals* order to admit all those requesting transfers, Governor J. Lindsay Almond closed the relevant schools. Not until 1972 was a plan that had a major effect on desegregating the schools implemented, a plan based on the 1971 *Swann** decision and employing mandatory school assignments.

In 1975 the school board requested that the school district be judged unitary,* which U.S. District Court* Judge John MacKenzie did. At this time the concept was not well defined. Previously it had meant that only one set of schools was being operated by a school district, not two systems, that is, a dual system.* Here unitary referred to meeting the six criteria raised in the 1968 *Green** decision and therefore eliminating the vestiges of school segregation* in pupil assignments as well as in "faculty, staff, transportation, extracurricular activities and facilities." In 1981 the board began discussing moving from the mandatory plan,* which it did in February 1983 when it approved a plan that would end busing* of elementary-school students. David Armor* had been hired by the district to write a report to document the problems that would arise from continuing with the mandatory plan and the advantages of neighborhood schools*: reversal of white flight* and greater parental involvement in the schools. In 1986 black parents challenged this change by the opening of the *Riddick* case. Judge MacKenzie supported the school board, concluding that since the district was judged to be unitary, the burden of proof* that the district was discriminating now shifted to those bringing suit, and they had not met this burden. The board had argued that the reason for its neighborhood plan was to forestall and perhaps reverse white flight. The U.S. Department of Justice* filed a brief to support the board in the black parents' appeal to the Court of Appeals. The Fourth Circuit accepted the argument that as a unitary district Norfolk could alter its assignment plan for nondiscriminatory reasons, even though the effects might lead to segregation. The U.S. Supreme Court* declined to hear the appeal, so the decision stood.

In 1986 the Norfolk School Board ended its elementary-school assignment plan, and ten nearly all-black and three primarily white schools resulted. This case is thus a significant one because it indicated how a school district could be allowed to alter its school desegregation plan, even if increased segregation was the result, after being judged to be unitary.

References: Orfield and Eaton, *Dismantling Desegregation* (1996); Wolters, *Right Turn* (1996); Armor, *Forced Justice* (1995).

ROBERTS V. CITY OF BOSTON, 5 (Cush.) 198 (1849). Decision of the Massachusetts Supreme Court concerning the first legal attack on school segregation* that established for the first time the principle of separate but equal* and served as a precedent in many other cases, including *Plessy v. Ferguson* (1896). In 1849 Benjamin F. Roberts, on behalf of his five-year-old daughter, Sara, sued the city of Boston. Sara had to walk past five white elementary schools to reach the all-black and run-down Smith School. Roberts asked that his daughter be allowed to attend a white school. Charles Sumner, a distinguished attorney and white abolitionist, assisted by Boston's first black attorney, Robert Morris, argued the case. They argued that all persons were equal before the law and that distinctions based on race were not permissible in Massachusetts. They argued that such racial segregation* branded a whole race as inferior and that classification for purposes of school assignment should be for educational reasons. Further, they contended that a segregated black school could not equal a white school because of the stigma associated with the segregation. (Over 100 years later these arguments were made in the 1954 *Brown* decision.)

In 1849 the Massachusetts Supreme Court in an opinion written by Chief Justice Lemuel Shaw rejected their argument and permitted segregated schools as long as the separate schools were equally provided for. Shaw concluded that the Boston School Committee did have the right to classify and distribute schoolchildren by race, and that this separation benefited both black and white children. This was the first use of the separate but equal doctrine. This case was cited in the *Plessy* decision as support for the segregation ruling, for if even in Massachusetts, where the rights of blacks had been enforced, segregation was considered legal, surely it would be legal in the South.*

Roberts worked toward a law that passed in the Massachusetts legislature in 1855, at the height of abolitionist fever, that prohibited school assignment based on race. The Smith School was closed soon after.

References: Witt, *Congressional Quarterly's Guide to the U.S. Supreme Court* (1989); Duram, *A Moderate among Extremists* (1981); Marcus and Stickney, *Race and Education* (1981); Kluger, *Simple Justice* (1975).

ROSSELL, CHRISTINE HAMILTON (born January 22, 1945, Brooklyn, New York). Social science researcher who has conducted quantitative research on student enrollments and white flight* under various types of school desegregation plans.* Her recent works have found that voluntary school desegregation* plans based on magnet schools* have a greater ability to hold whites and therefore to increase interracial contact than mandatory plans.* Rossell has been an expert witness in several school desegregation cases (e.g., Kansas City, San Jose, St. Louis, Wilmington, Delaware, Yonkers, and Los Angeles) as well as serving as a consultant to the Rand Corporation, the U.S. Office of Education,* and the U.S. Department of Justice.*

Christine Rossell received her A.B. from UCLA in 1967, her M.A. from California State University at Northridge in 1969, and her Ph.D. in political science from the University of Southern California in 1974. She served as an assistant professor at Pitzer College, Claremont, California, from 1973–1974 and then as a research associate at the University of Maryland during 1974–1975. Rossell began an appointment as an assistant professor of political science at Boston University in 1975 and was promoted to associate professor in 1982 and professor in 1989. She chaired the political science department from 1992 to 1995.

Works about: *Who's Who in America* (Chicago: Reed Reference Publishing, 1995), 3168; *Who's Who in American Education, 1994–95*, 4th ed., (New Providence, NJ: Marquis Who's Who, Reed Reference, 1993), 820.

Works by: with David Armor, "The Effectiveness of School Desegregation Plans, 1968–1991," *American Politics Quarterly* 24, no. 3 (July 1996); 267–302; "The Convergence of Black and White Attitudes on School Desegregation Issues during the Four Decade Evolution of Plans," *William and Mary Law Review* 36, no. 2 (January 1995): 613–63; *The Carrot or the Stick for School Desegregation Policy* (Philadelphia: Temple University Press, 1990); with J. Michael Ross, "The Social Science Evidence on Bilingual Education," *Journal of Law and Education* 15, no. 4 (Fall 1986): 385–419; with Willis D. Hawley, eds., *The Consequences of School Desegregation* (Philadelphia: Temple University Press, 1983).

S

SATELLITE ZONING. School desegregation* technique used in mandatory plans* in which schools are clustered but school attendance areas are not contiguous. This technique is used where school desegregation is the objective, where there are large black and white residential areas, and where the pairing* or clustering* only of adjacent schools will not achieve an appropriate racial mix. In satellite zoning an area with one type of racial mix is clustered with a noncontiguous area of a different racial mix. Unlike the pairing or clustering of nonadjacent school attendance areas, in satellite zoning no grade change is involved. This is also called pocket, island, or skip zoning and is used in plans involving busing.* Among the plans that involved satellite zoning are Mobile, Alabama; Riverside, California; Wilmington–New Castle County, Delaware; Boston; Pittsburgh; and Roanoke, Virginia.

References: Armor, *Forced Justice* (1995); Rossell, ''The Convergence of Black and White Attitudes on School Desegregation Issues during the Four Decade Evolution of the Plans'' (January 1995); Rossell, ''The Classification of School Desegregation Remedies'' (January 12, 1992).

SCHOOL DECENTRALIZATION. *See* **Community Control**.

SCHOOL DESEGREGATION. The redistribution of pupils in schools leading to a greater balance of pupils by race. School desegregation can occur because of ''natural'' forces, voluntary actions of school and public officials involving voluntary or mandatory reassignment of students, or mandatory actions ordered by the courts or governmental bodies involving voluntary or mandatory reassignment of students. The definition has changed since the 1954 *Brown v. Board of Education** decision, when school desegregation meant the elimination of state-imposed separation of students in school (school segregation*) because of their race.

School desegregation by ''natural'' forces includes the desegregation* caused by the desegregation of residential housing. As minorities move into a previously majority area, the mix of pupils in an attendance area will change. In some cases, however, white flight* will occur, that is, white families will remove their children from public schools. The process may also be a step in a transition from majority to minority schools as neighborhoods change from white to minority.

School desegregation by voluntary means usually occurs when a school board decides to reassign its pupils to ensure that schools are no longer segregated by race. Such plans may be voluntary or mandatory with respect to student assignments. Berkeley, California, and Seattle, Washington, have voluntarily adopted mandatory assignment plans.* A number of metropolitan areas have voluntarily adopted voluntary assignment plans,* generally called voluntary transfer plans, to desegregate schools. Generally these plans allow city minority students to transfer to predominantly white suburban schools. Hartford (Project Concern*) and Boston (METCO*), for example, have long-standing voluntary metropolitan programs.

Mandatory school desegregation, generally ordered by the federal courts or the Department of Health, Education, and Welfare* to remedy de jure school segregation,* can involve different kinds of reassignment plans. States may require or encourage such desegregation. The Massachusetts Racial Imbalance Act,* for example, has been in effect since 1965. Connecticut, in response to the *Sheff v. O'Neill** (1996) school desegregation suit focused on the Hartford schools, passed legislation in 1993 to encourage planning for school desegregation.

The degree of school desegregation is measured by a number of indexes, including the interracial exposure index,* the index of dissimilarity* or Taueber index, and the index of racial isolation.* According to Armor* in *Forced Justice*, ''the legal definition of school desegregation has undergone significant change over the years since *Brown*** (1995:158). The first definition was the elimination of the laws and practices that compelled segregation of schools. Thus directly after the *Brown* decision school districts complied by either redrawing geographic attendance zones to create neighborhood schools,* instead of schools serving only one race regardless of student residence, or establishing freedom-of-choice* plans, allowing each student to select her or his school. Whatever the remedy, the courts did not insist on racial balance,* just the elimination of forced segregation.

The 1968 *Green** decision recognized that when residential patterns were segregated, neighborhood schools would retain school segregation. Furthermore, some school districts had adopted freedom-of-choice* plans but had discouraged students from "free" choices. The *Green* decision made it clear that school districts had to adjust the racial composition of the formerly segregated schools. That is, school districts that had been de jure segregated now had to move beyond neutrality and take action to desegregate.

The 1971 *Swann* decision expanded the affirmative action* needed to desegregate by including busing,* that is, the mandatory assignment of pupils beyond their neighborhoods, and by specifying the guidelines for racial balance. According to Armor, after the *Swann* decision racial balance became the most frequently used criterion to establish school desegregation. A school is considered desegregated "if its racial composition matches that for the school system as a whole (for a given grade level) within some allowable percentage deviation" (159). In the Charlotte-Mecklenburg case the court set an allowable deviation of plus or minus 10 percentage points from the system average. That is, if the district had a percentage of black pupils of 40 percent at the elementary-school level, individual schools could have 30–50 percent black students and remain in compliance. No specific bands were defined for all cases. According to Armor, while Boston and Norfolk adopted a 10 percentage point band, Denver and Columbus, Ohio, were allowed bands of 15 percentage points, and in one South Carolina case the band was 20 percentage points.

An alternative to the band approach has been used in some majority black districts to avoid defining schools with 90 percent minority students as "desegregated." In several districts an absolute standard of desegregation has been set; for example, in St. Louis and Detroit a desegregated school was defined as one with a 50–50 racial composition. Obviously, in a majority black district not all schools can achieve this ratio, so the courts have specified the number of schools required to be desegregated. A 1992 U.S. Department of Education* survey of desegregation plans found that a majority of districts (55 percent) used a racial balance definition to define a desegregated school, 12 percent used an absolute standard, and the remaining third lacked a specific mathematical standard.

A significant question is the degree to which school desegregation actions have led to minority children studying in desegregated schools and to changes in school desegregation and segregation over time. Gary Orfield* and colleagues have conducted a series of reports for the National School Boards Association Council of Urban Boards of Education to measure changes in patterns of segregation over time. Orfield uses several measures to determine the level of school segregation, including the proportion of black and Latino students in schools with a majority of whites and with 90 percent or more minority students as well as the interracial exposure index, the proportion of whites in the average black or Latino's school. In December 1993 Orfield reported that while the segregation of black students in the South* had decreased from the time of the Civil Rights Act of 1964* through the early 1970s and had held steady through 1988, since that year school segregation had increased. Segregation of Latino students had increased since the 1960s, when data were first collected. Similar trends held across the nation. Orfield's research also indicated that segregation was greatest in big cities, less significant in mid-sized central cities, and least apparent in small towns and rural areas. Orfield cited the 1974 *Milliken** decision as establishing a high barrier for school desegregation that ensured that metropolitan areas with fragmented school districts, typically where the minority proportion in the central city was high and growing, would have the most segregation. Thus Illinois, Michigan, New York, and New Jersey remained intensely segregated states. The states with metropolitan school desegregation plans,* Delaware, North Carolina, and Virginia, were the least segregated states. He concluded that "the civil rights impulse from the 1960s is dead in the water and the ship is floating backward toward the shoals of racial segregation" (1993: 2).

The effects of school desegregation have been widely researched. Most research has focused on student achievement* as measured on standardized tests. Researchers have also tried to determine the effects of school desegregation on race relations* and intergroup attitudes as well as on the long-term integration of black students into society.

The National Institute of Education Report, *School Desegregation and Black Achievement*, carried out in 1984 under the Institute, brought national experts together on school desegregation to try to develop conclusions about the research literature on effects. Six experts on school desegregation of various persuasions (including David Armor* and Robert Crain*) were included along with one "neutral" methodological expert (Thomas Cook). The experts reached agreement on the criteria for including research studies in their analysis:

1. Control or comparison group of contemporaneous black students

2. Existence of pre– and post–school desegregation measures

3. Same standardized test used in pretest and posttest

Nineteen studies met these criteria, but because some studies included testing at more than one grade level, there were 35 observations. The gains from these studies that could be attributed to school desegregation were modest, in the range of four to six weeks of a school year for reading and less for math, according to Cook. Cook's own conclusions stress the range of effects across these studies, that is, the variability of effects.

This study reflects the range of problems in measuring the effect of school desegregation on student achievement. As Daniel U. Levine notes, there are "problems in controlling for the effects of socioeconomic status, in measuring changes that may be relatively small but meaningful over a one- or two-year period, in comparing results for students who participate in different types of desegregation settings (e.g., voluntary transfer programs or mandatory assignment, urban or rural), and in assessing gains in different subject areas such as reading or mathematics" (1994:1483). The most significant problems relate to the variations in the nature of the school desegregation that has occurred. In some school districts there has been great preparation of students, teachers, and parents, but in others, student reassignment has not been supplemented by appropriate in-service training and increased multicultural sensitivity. Given these problems, as well as the ideological charge associated with this topic, it is not surprising that consistency across studies and researchers is not high. In fact, these same factors haunt research on the effects of school desegregation on interracial attitudes and relations, where results have been mixed. Few would expect desegregation to totally eliminate the black-white gap in student achievement, especially given the large socioeconomic gap that remains between white and black students.

Analyses of national longitudinal studies that focus on career attainment indicate that school desegregation leads to participation in desegregated settings in later life. For example, blacks who have been in desegregated elementary and secondary schools are more likely to attend a desegregated college or university. Those who have conducted such research argue that studying the effects of school desegregation only in the short term on standardized achievement tests is insufficient and provides a very incomplete and inaccurate picture of its impact. More research is needed on the effect of school desegregation on the life chances of minorities.

Much research on the methods that are likely to maximize the positive effects of school desegregation has been undertaken. Levine puts forward a number of recommendations and conclusions, including the following: "begin desegregation at as early an age as possible; . . . provide a safe school environment; . . . maintain discipline through clear rules that are consistently and fairly enforced; . . . install a multicultural curriculum" (1485).

See also **Busing; Equal Educational Opportunity; Racial Balance; School Segregation**.

References: Orfield and Eaton, *Dismantling Desegregation* (1996); Armor, *Forced Justice* (1995); Schofield, "Review of Research on School Desegregation's Impact on Elementary and Secondary School Students" (1995); Daniel U. Levine, "Desegregation in Schools," in *The International Encyclopedia of Education*, ed. Husén and Postlethwaite vol. 3 (1994), 1483–86; Wells and Crain, "Perpetuation Theory and Long-Term Effects of School Desegregation" (Winter 1994); Gary Orfield, *The Growth of Segregation in American Schools: Changing Patterns of Separation and Poverty since 1968* (Alexandria, VA: National School Boards Association, December 1993); Kluger, *Simple Justice* (1975).

SCHOOL DESEGREGATION PLANS. Actions to eliminate school segregation* that may be court ordered or voluntarily implemented by a school district, mandatory or voluntary with respect to student assignment to schools (that is, voluntary plans* and mandatory plans*), limited to a single city district or covering a metropolitan area (*see* **Metropolitan Plan**), and involve busing* or not. After *Brown II** (1955) many school districts adopted school desegregation plans to eliminate race as a factor in student assignment through freedom-of-choice* plans, but the effectiveness of these plans was limited since whites did not select formerly black schools and many black parents and students did not change schools because of concerns about safety. Plans allowing for desegregation* one year at a time, in which school districts started at first or twelfth grade and included one more grade each year, were adopted by many school districts. Several legislatures in the South,* led by Virginia, adopted massive resistance* as their response, working to ensure that no school desegregation* would occur. During the period from 1955 to 1963 the U.S. Supreme Court* took only one stand against such resistance or delay. In its *Cooper v. Aaron* decision (1958) the Court criticized Governor Orval Faubus* of Arkansas for interfering with the desegregation of the Little Rock school system. In 1963 the Court concluded that the time for "all deliberate speed*" was over. In *Goss v. Board of Education* (1963) the Court invalidated minority-to-majority transfers in freedom-of-choice plans, that is, students who were whites in the minority at a school could not transfer to a majority white school. The Civil Rights Act of 1964* provided the major mechanism for enforcing the *Brown* decision and desegregating the schools of the South. This legislation gave the Department of Justice* the legal authority to enforce school desegregation, including the power to withhold federal funds. Under this act, coupled with the Elementary and Secondary Education Act,* the first federal general assistance program for local school districts, the federal government had a strong enforcement mechanism, which it used in tandem with the federal courts.

In the 1968 *Green v. County School Board of New Kent County* decision the U.S. Supreme Court required that school desegregation plans "promise realistically to work now," that is, that they eliminate black schools and attain some racial balance.* In *Swann v. Charlotte-Mecklenburg Board of Education* (1971) the Court recognized that racial segregation made plans based on neighborhood schools* ineffective, and the Court required the busing of students to achieve an approximate racial balance* reflecting the majority/minority enrollment in the school district in most district schools. Reaction against such busing has been quite negative. In *Milliken v. Bradley* (1974) the Court set established guidelines for metropolitan school desegregation that greatly limited, but did not eliminate, the chances of a metropolitan interdistrict school desegregation plan.

In the 1990s the Court has focused more on when the obligations of school districts to implement court-ordered plans are completed. A number of Court decisions, including *Board of Education of Oklahoma City v. Dowell* (1991) and *Freeman v. Pitts* (1992), have helped to define when school districts are declared no longer dual systems* and are judged unitary systems.*

Research has indicated that more school desegregation takes place in a school district when a school desegregation plan has been implemented. Rossell* and Armor* examined the extent of school desegregation change as measured by the index of interracial exposure* in large school districts in their sample that had and did not have a plan. In the South they found that while both types of districts experienced a large increase in interracial exposure from 1968 to 1972, the increase was greater among districts with a plan. Rossell and Armor conclude from their research that more desegregation occurs under voluntary plans than mandatory plans because mandatory plans are more likely to lead to white flight.*

Various techniques have been used in desegregation plans, such as majority-to-minority transfers,* rezoning,* magnet schools,* and pairing* or clustering* schools. Most school desegregation plans use a mixture of such techniques.

References: Armor, *Forced Justice* (1995); Fife, *Desegregation in American Schools* (1992); Rossell, *The Carrot or the Stick for School Desegregation Policy* (1990); Henderson, von Euler, and Schneider, "Remedies for Segregation: Some Lessons from Research" (July–August 1981); Gordon Foster, "Desegregating Urban Schools: A Review of Techniques," *Harvard Educational Review* 43, no. 1 (February 1973): 5–36.

SCHOOL DESEGREGATION REMEDIES. *See* **School Desegregation Plans**.

SCHOOL INTEGRATION. Generally considered to be actions to eliminate racial distinctions in the schools or, alternatively, the achieving of successful school desegregation,* this term has a number of more specific meanings. Conservatives view school integration as the affirmative action* to create racial balance* in schools as opposed to desegregation,* the effort to make schools color blind, that is, that schools admit students on a nonracial basis. School integration also may refer to the social integration* and assimilation of minority students into a school where they have equal educational opportunity.* This is generally the definition of those with liberal views. School integration is then referred to as effective school desegregation, where an interracial staff teaches interracial classes with curriculum, policies, and school procedures that treat students from all races in an equal and supportive manner. School desegregation refers to the physical mixing of students from different races.

There is an extensive literature on actions that should lead to effective school desegregation or school integration. Achieving effective school desegregation may be viewed from the perspective of the major players in the school desegregation process. The administrative leadership of a school district, the superintendent and the school board, is advised to exhibit positive leadership rather than delay, resist, or object about the need to desegregate the schools or the preparation and implementation of a school desegregation plan.* Ensuring an administrative staff that reflects the racial composition of the desegregating district is helpful in the process. School principals are usually confronted with dealing with the cultural change that accompanies school desegregation. As students, parents, and teachers from different schools are brought together, principals often have to deal with establishing a new culture and overriding the symbolic and substantive aspects of the previous schools. They must be leaders of the change process, whether the issue is what the mascot of the desegregated high school should be, or what changes in the teaching and learning process are necessary with the widening of students' capabilities and backgrounds. Teachers are generally faced with teaching students from a greater range of abilities and backgrounds and should consider new teaching techniques more appropriate for this situation, such as cooperative learning and curriculum changes to emphasize multicultural education.* Civic leaders must recognize their role in assuring community support for the changes as opposed to lending a hand to opposition and delay. Parents and students have the obligation to meet new people and communicate effectively across racial barriers.

An alternative way to view the achievement of effective school desegregation is as a set of strategies. In his concluding chapter of his edited book on effective school desegregation, Willis Hawley (1981:299–302) lists thirteen such "key strategies":

1. Desegregate students early, in kindergarten, if possible.

2. Encourage substantial interaction among races both in academic settings and extra-curricular activities.

3. Avoid academic competition, rigid forms of tracking, and ability grouping* that draw attention to individual and group achievement differences that are correlated with race.

4. If possible, organize so that schools and classrooms have a "critical mass" of each racial group being desegregated.

5. Minimize the scale of the students' educational experience and decrease the number of students with whom a given teacher has contact.

6. Develop rules and procedures for governing schools that are clear, fair, and consistent and administer them with persistence and equity.

7. Maintain a relatively stable student body over time.

8. Recruit and retain a racially diverse staff of teachers who are unprejudiced, supportive, and insistent on high performance and racial equality.

9. Recruit or retrain principals and other administrators who are supportive of desegregation and exert leadership to that effect.

10. Develop ongoing programs of staff development that emphasize the problems relating to successful desegregation.

11. Involve parents at the classroom level in actual instructional and/or learning activities.

12. When a district has sizable proportions of minority students, incentives for voluntary desegregation should be accompanied by mandatory requirements.

13. School districts should take positive steps to involve and interest the community, especially parents, in the desegregation process and its benefits.

See also **Prejudice.**

References: Wolters, *The Burden of Brown* (1984); Hawley et al., *Strategies for Effective Desegregation* (1983); Chesler, Bryant, and Crowfoot, *Making Desegregation Work* (1981); Hawley, *Effective School Desegregation* (1981); Garlie A. Forehand and Marjorie Ragosta, *A Handbook for Integrated Schooling* (Princeton, NJ: Educational Testing Service, July 1976); Smith, Downs, and Lachman, *Achieving Effective Desegregation* (1973).

SCHOOL SEGREGATION. The isolation of students in schools by race so that schools can be racially identified, for example, a black school or a white school. School segregation generally refers to schools serving one minority or race or predominantly minority students. Segregation may be de facto* or de jure,* that is, caused by individual actions or by governmental actions.

At the time of the *Brown** decision in 1954 the legal definition of what constituted school segregation was clear, namely, state action that explicitly created dual systems* of education, schools for blacks and schools for whites. The removal of legal barriers to blacks and whites attending schools together was thus the focus of the early court decisions. After a decade of massive resistance* and little actual school desegregation, the U.S. Supreme Court* demanded that districts move beyond ''all deliberate speed*'' to plans that worked immediately with the *Green** decision of 1968. In this decision the U.S. Supreme Court indicated that a school district could not be viewed as no longer segregated when its schools reflected the vestiges of the dual segregated system. Such segregation had to be measured not only in enrollments in schools according to race, but also by the district's success in desegregating its faculty and staff and erasing discrimination* in its transportation system, extracurricular activities, and facilities, the so-called *Green* factors. Thus the Court went from defining segregation as explicit laws passed to separate black and white students to a concern for racial balance* in enrollments and the more general treatment of black students in the school system.

The *Keyes** (1973) case, set in Denver, helped to define the meaning of segregation in the North, where states had not enacted laws segregating the races in schools, but many school districts had schools with no or few blacks. In this decision the U.S. Supreme Court concluded that the action of the Denver school board had resulted in the segregation of schools in the Park Hills area of the district, that the board's action was intentionally aimed at discriminating, and that therefore, unless proven otherwise, the presumption was that the school district was guilty of segregating the entire district.

The degree of school segregation in the United States has changed over time. Gary Orfield* and colleagues have conducted a series of reports for the National School Boards Association Council of Urban Boards of Education to measure changes in patterns of school segregation. Orfield reported that while the segregation of black students in the South* had decreased from the time of the Civil Rights Act of 1964* through the early 1970s and had held steady through 1988, since that year school segregation had increased. Segregation of Latino students had increased since the 1960s, and segregation was greatest in big cities. Orfield cited the 1974 *Milliken** decision as establishing a most significant barrier for metropolitan school desegregation.

See also **School Desegregation.**

References: Orfield and Eaton, *Dismantling Desegregation* (1996); Gary Orfield, *The Growth of Segregation in American Schools: Changing Patterns of Segregation and Poverty since 1968* (Alexandria, VA: National School Boards Association, December

1993); Kujovich, "Equal Opportunity in Higher Education" (1992); Dimond, *Beyond Busing* (1985); Kluger, *Simple Justice* (1975).

SECOND-GENERATION PROBLEMS. The policies and practices that maintain school segregation* after a school desegregation plan* is implemented. The first generation of problems is focused on the physical desegregation* of students. Second-generation problems include ability grouping* or tracking and assignment of disproportionate numbers of minority students to special education classes, exclusionary student discipline measures, segregation of faculty and firing of minority teachers, and downgrading of minority administrators. These policies and practices may lead to the resegregation* or continued segregation of a classroom, school, or school district. Meier, Stewart, and England (1989) view second-generation discrimination* as action that impedes integration,* that is, the social process by which minorities receive equal educational opportunity.* They view desegregation as the mechanical process of mixing students. One major issue is whether such policies and practices are purposeful in their effect or are implemented for proper educational as opposed to discriminatory purposes.

According to Meier, Stewart, and England, black educators have been disproportionately affected by school desegregation. Black principals have lost their positions, and the contracts of many black teachers were not renewed as school desegregation was implemented. One estimate was that over 31,000 black teachers in southern and border states were displaced during the process.

Gordon Foster* has called the designation "second generation desegregation problems" inaccurate because "they are usually regular educational concerns which have been exposed for the first time or exacerbated by the desegregation process" (1974:29). For example, the problem of a teacher who is a racist was not caused by a school desegregation plan but becomes a serious problem in the context of school desegregation implementation. The directors of the ten desegregation assistance centers,* through the coordination of the Northwest Regional Educational Lab, have concluded that many school districts have moved beyond second-generation problems and are now in the third generation. This generation includes "the persistent barriers to integration and equity or the attainment of equal education outcomes for all groups of students" (1989:10). That is, even if physical integration is achieved, and equal access is generally assured, there still exist problems that cause unequal student achievement* that need to be addressed. Among the topics that they include as needing to be addressed in the third generation are culturally based learning-style differences, multicultural education,* and culture and gender bias in testing.

References: Meier, Stewart, and England, *Race, Class, and Education* (1989); Northwest Regional Educational Lab, coordinator, *Resegregation of Public Schools: The Third Generation* (Portland, OR: Northwest Regional Educational Lab, June 1989); Gary Orfield, "How to Make Desegregation Work: The Adaptation of Schools to Their Newly-integrated Student Bodies," in The Courts, Social Science, and School Desegregation,

Part 2, *Law and Contemporary Problems* 39, no. 2 (Spring 1975): 314–40; Gordon Foster, "*Milliken v. Bradley*: Implications for Desegregation Centers and Metropolitan Desegregation," in *Milliken v. Bradley: The Implications for Metropolitan Desegregation: Conference before the United States Commission on Civil Rights* (Washington, DC: U.S. Government Printing Office, November 9, 1974).

SECOND MORRILL ACT. *See* **Morrill Act of 1890**.

SEGREGATION, DE FACTO. Racial segregation* resulting from the actions of private individuals or unknown forces, not from governmental action or law. De facto segregation is to be distinguished from de jure segregation,* segregation resulting from governmental action or law. De facto segregation is generally the result of housing patterns, population movements, and economic conditions often reinforced by governmental policies not aimed at segregation but having that effect. For example, most U.S. metropolitan areas have a single central-city school district, serving primarily minority students, surrounded by suburban school districts, serving mostly white students. The U.S. Supreme Court's* first use of this term was in the 1971 *Swann** decision, although the case was considered a de jure case. The Supreme Court has ruled that de facto school segregation need not be remedied through court action.

The distinction between de facto and de jure segregation has been questioned at the top of the nation's legal system. Justice Lewis Powell* concurred with Justice William Douglas in the *Keyes** (1973) case that the difference between de facto and de jure segregation is a distinction without a difference. Douglas argued that indeed many governmental actions, such as restrictive covenants and the actions of urban development agencies, led to so-called de facto segregation. But the Court rejected their argument in *Milliken v. Bradley** (1974), concluding that the courts could not demand a remedy to segregation that did not result from explicit governmental actions. In *Washington v. Davis** (1976) the Court went a step further, deciding that de jure segregation was only unconstitutional if it was the result of "racially discriminatory purpose" by government. In *Crawford v. California* (1982) the Court upheld a California amendment that prohibited state officials from mandating busing* to eliminate de facto segregation. Some have also argued that given enough resources, de jure segregation could be proven in almost every city or school district; that is, when segregation has been labeled as de facto, that racially motivated acts by governmental bodies have led to school segregation in all districts, but such actions are difficult and costly to prove.

References: Armor, *Forced Justice* (1995); Hall, *Oxford Companion* (1992); Yudof et al., *Kirp and Yudof's Educational Policy and the Law* (1987).

SEGREGATION, DE JURE. Racial segregation* resulting from governmental action or law. De jure school segregation is to be distinguished from de facto school segregation,* segregation resulting from the private actions of individuals rather than state-imposed segregation. The U.S. Supreme Court* has ruled that de jure school segregation should be remedied, while de facto segregation does not have to be altered. The latter results from accident or natural phenomena.

In *Plessy v. Ferguson** (1896) the Court ruled that de jure segregation was permissible as long as the facilities were "separate but equal.*" According to the *Oxford Companion* (1992:766), following this decision, "the fifteen former slave states, along with West Virginia and Oklahoma, mandated segregation in most public facilities, while other states allowed, but did not require, localities or state agencies to create de jure segregation." The Court went beyond *Plessy*, however, and also allowed de jure segregation that was not equal. In *Cumming v. Richmond County School Board of Education** (1899), for example, the Court allowed a school district to close a black high school while maintaining high schools for whites, and in *Gong Lum v. Rice** (1927) the Court concluded that the state of Mississippi could segregate Chinese-American students in its schools. Such segregation was the rule in the South* during the Jim Crow* era, not only in schools but in all areas of life.

In 1938 the U.S. Supreme Court changed course in *Missouri ex rel. Gaines v. Canada.** In this decision the Court ruled that graduate and professional schools for blacks could not be both separate and equal, and therefore blacks had to be admitted to white programs and schools. In 1954 the Court finally declared in the landmark *Brown** opinion that "in the field of public education the doctrine of 'separate but equal' has no place" (347 U.S. 495).

Some, including U.S. Supreme Court Justice Lewis Powell,* have questioned the distinction between de jure and de facto school segregation. One view is that given enough resources, plaintiffs or the government can prove that de jure segregation exists in any school segregation situation. A second view is that the function of schooling in American society requires all groups to be taught together (the common-school theory), and thus school segregation, whatever the specific cause, is unconstitutional. Further, the distinction between de jure segregation, found almost exclusively in the South, and de facto segregation, found almost exclusively in the North, has led to different standards in the two regions of the nation, an untenable and unwise outcome.

David Armor* in *Forced Justice* argues that de jure segregation must meet two criteria: "significant segregative effects and discriminatory intent; that is, a policy or action must not only cause a significant degree of segregation, but it also must be motivated by an intent to cause segregation, such as Jim Crow laws of the Old South. A policy or action motivated by a legitimate educational purpose that incidentally causes segregation and has no segregative purpose is not unconstitutional by this rule" (1995:56). But Armor also points out that the standards by which segregative intent are determined are not clear. For example, lower courts had adopted a "foreseeable effects" standard that held that districts that took actions that were obviously going to increase segregation had intentionally segregated. Such a standard reduces the distinction between de jure and de facto segregation.

References: Armor, *Forced Justice* (1995); Hall, *Oxford Companion* (1992); Alexander M. Bickel, "Untangling the Busing Snarl," in *The Great School Bus Controversy*, ed. Mills (1973), 27–37.

SEGREGATION, RACIAL. The separation of people by race. In the field of education, racial segregation refers to the isolation of students by race due to either segregation by law (de jure segregation*) or segregation from actions for which the government is not directly responsible (de facto segregation*). Segregation was the South's* response to Reconstruction and the effort to force equality on that region. Jim Crow* laws were passed segregating blacks from whites in all areas of life, including transportation modes, places of entertainment, and public schools. Advocates of racial segregation preferred the word "separation" to segregation. They asserted that segregation of the races was a way of life in the South that maintained peace and tranquillity among the races.

Galster and Hill conclude that "America's metropolitan areas appear to be more polarized along racial lines than any time since the mid-1960s" (1992:1). The typical pattern, especially for the older, industrialized cities of the Midwest and North, is that of a central city with a majority of minority residents who are poor and not in the economic mainstream surrounded by, but very much separated from, suburbs that are almost entirely white and well off. This pattern is not the result of explicit discriminatory actions by the state or local governments but of a variety of social, economic, and political factors. There is black movement to the suburbs, and the socioeconomic status of blacks in the United States has been rising, but these trends are still working against the backdrop of the "doughnut" phenomenon of white suburbs ringing black cities.

Residential segregation, much linked to the "doughnut" pattern, ensures the segregation of minority students in the dominant American system of city school districts surrounded by smaller suburban school districts. The U.S. Supreme Court's* *Milliken I** (1974) decision established a high barrier to overcome for those seeking to force desegregation of city schools by involving the suburbs. Efforts to desegregate housing in the city by retaining or attracting whites have been tried on a small scale, as Varady and Raffel (1995) demonstrate. Attempts to spread minority citizens throughout the suburbs through recruitment by suburban jurisdictions and federal housing programs to help minority individuals find and fund suburban housing have had some impact on residential segregation.

See also **Integration, Racial**.

References: Varady and Raffel, *Selling Cities* (1995); Safire, *Safire's New Political Dictionary* (1993); Galster and Hill, *The Metropolis in Black and White* (1992); Reynolds Farley, Howard Schuman, Suzanne Bianchi, Diane Colasanto, and Shirley Hatchett, "Chocolate City, Vanilla Suburbs: Will the Trend toward Racially Separate Communities Continue?" *Social Science Quarterly* 7 (1978): 319–44.

SEGREGATIONIST ACADEMIES. The approximately 2,500 private schools (also called private academies or Christian schools) begun in the South* as white-only schools in response to the desegregation* of public schools. The Southern Regional Council estimated that 300,000 students attended such schools in 1969, but by 1970, after the *Alexander v. Holmes County Board of Education* (1969) decision, it estimated that half a million students were in segregationist academies. By 1976 Nevin and Bills estimated that three-quarters of a million students were in over 3,000 such schools. Prince Edward Academy in Prince Edward County, Virginia, opened in 1959 in a school district that was one of the four districts that were in the original *Brown** decision. The Citizens Council, formerly the White Citizens Council,* opened its first school in 1964. This militant segregationist organization opened schools throughout the South. In Memphis, for example, there were 41 private schools in 1970 but 125 five years later; enrollments in these schools almost tripled in the five years.

These schools closely resembled public schools as their parents remembered them—white, authoritarian, and with strong religious and patriotic themes and emphasis on the 3 Rs. Some schools were openly segregationist, while others had a more open policy but no or few blacks attended. Attempts to offer such schools in formerly public schools were stopped by the courts. The fundamentalist churches, however, served as a good foundation for many of these schools since they had classrooms and a financial structure to support the schools.

Since 1972 the Internal Revenue Service has attempted to force segregationist academies to comply with federal nondiscrimination mandates or lose their status as tax-exempt institutions. The U.S. Supreme Court affirmed the IRS's authority to require nondiscrimination in the 1983 *Bob Jones v. United States** decision, which also involved the Goldsboro Christian School in North Carolina. The *Green v. Connally* decision of 1970 was the landmark case on this issue and led to the Internal Revenue Service regulations requiring nondiscrimination to qualify for tax exemption.

References: Marcus and Stickney, *Race and Education* (1981); Nevin and Bills, *The Schools That Fear Built* (1976); Anthony M. Champagne, "The Segregation Academy and the Law," *Journal of Negro Education*, 42, no. 1 (Winter 1973): 58–66.

SEGREGATIONIST STATES. Those 17 states that required the segregation* of the races in public schools: Alabama, Arkansas, Delaware, Florida, Georgia, Kentucky, Louisiana, Maryland, Mississippi, Missouri, North Carolina, Oklahoma, South Carolina, Tennessee, Texas, Virginia, and West Virginia. Congress required school segregation in Washington, D.C. Arizona, Kansas, New Mexico, and Wyoming authorized school segregation by local authorities.

After the 1954 *Brown** decision the 6 border states (Delaware, Kentucky, Maryland, Missouri, Oklahoma, and West Virginia) and the 4 states that had authorized but not required segregation formally complied with the order, as did the District of Columbia. The 11 states of the Old Confederacy met the decision with massive resistance.*

See also **Deep South; South**.

References: Thomas Dye, *Understanding Public Policy*, 7th ed. (Englewood Cliffs, NJ: Prentice Hall, 1992); Wilkinson, *From Brown to Bakke* (1979); Wilhoit, *The Politics of Massive Resistance* (1973); Bartley, *The Rise of Massive Resistance* (1969).

SELF-ESTEEM. Evaluation of an individual about herself or himself; a measure of self-concept. This concept played a key role in the *Brown v. Board of Education** (1954) case.

The studies of Mamie and Kenneth Clark,* using the selection of dolls of one's race as an indirect measure of self-esteem, indicated that black children often preferred white dolls to black dolls and thus exhibited low self-esteem. This was interpreted as indicating the psychological harm resulting from de jure segregation.* The negative social judgment of the majority group or stereotype is fostered on the minority-group members. The findings of the Clarks vis-à-vis school desegregation* have been questioned because, for example, if contact between majority, high-status groups and minority, low-status groups is infrequent, how does the minority person get the negative view?

During the 1960s more extensive research on self-esteem was undertaken. Researchers distinguished between racial self-esteem and personal self-esteem, that is, one's feeling about one's racial group and one's sense of personal worth. Other studies indicated that although white preschoolers prefer to play with white dolls, this is not necessarily related to personal self-esteem. In addition, when personal self-worth is measured directly, blacks generally score higher than or equal to whites. Unfortunately, such studies were not conducted before the 1960s, so we cannot decide if black self-concepts have changed since the *Brown* decision and the Clarks' studies. There is evidence, however, that school desegregation actually lowers black personal self-esteem, perhaps because black students feel academically disadvantaged when placed with white students and/or because of discrimination* they experience in the new setting.

James Coleman's* *Equality of Educational Opportunity* or the Coleman Report* found that the relationship between students' self-concept and sense of control with student achievement* was the strongest of any they examined. To some extent the relation between self-concept and achievement reflects the students' accurate judgment of their own scholastic ability. The sense-of-control variable is less likely to be the result of achievement and more likely to be a cause of doing well. More recent research indicates that blacks have relatively high self-esteem compared to whites, and desegregation has little effect on self-esteem or has no consistent effect on self-esteem, but the research is difficult to summarize because different measures of the variable have been used with different-age students in different settings.

References: Armor, *Forced Justice* (1995); Schofield, "Review of Research on School Desegregation's Impact on Elementary and Secondary School Students" (1995); Edgar G. Epps, "The Impact of School Desegregation on Aspirations, Self-Concepts, and Other

Aspects of Personality,'' in The Courts, Social Science, and School Desegregation, Part 2, *Law and Contemporary Problems* 39, no. 2 (Spring 1975): 300–313; Kenneth Clark, *Prejudice and Your Child* (Boston: Beacon Press, 1955).

SEPARATE BUT EQUAL. Doctrine based on the *Plessy v. Ferguson** (1896) decision, in which the U.S. Supreme Court* established the principle that separate facilities for blacks were not unconstitutional as long as those separate facilities were equal to the facilities for whites. The *Plessy* case dealt with accommodations on railroad passenger cars, but schools were specifically included in the opinion, and the effects of this doctrine became widespread throughout the South* and reinforced existing and resulted in new Jim Crow* laws segregating restaurants, parks, rest rooms, theaters, and a myriad of other facilities. The Court formally extended the separate but equal doctrine to public schools in the *Cumming v. Richmond County Board of Education** (1899) decision. The equal part of this doctrine was a myth, however, as black schools were underfunded, inadequately maintained, and understaffed. Thus the question remains as to whether separate schools (or any other facilities or services) can ever be equal.

The Court turned away from this doctrine as the NAACP Legal Defense Fund* pressed its challenge at the graduate- and professional-school level. Court decisions in *Missouri ex rel. Gaines,* Sipuel,** and *Sweatt** signaled the Court's abandonment of this doctrine in higher education. Finally the Court renounced the separate but equal doctrine in the *Brown v. Board of Education** decision (1954). Writing for a unanimous Court, Chief Justice Earl Warren* held that the separate but equal doctrine violated the equal protection clause* of the Fourteenth Amendment* of the U.S. Constitution.* ''We conclude that in the field of public education, the doctrine of 'separate but equal' has no place. Separate facilities are inherently unequal.''

In Delaware in 1952 Judge Collins Seitz, after personally visiting the schools involved, ruled that the schools established for blacks were separate but not equal in their facilities and educational programs to those established for whites. Thus he ordered the desegregation of the public schools in the state. However, it was not until the *Brown v. Board of Education* decision that the U.S. Supreme Court ruled that separate schools were inherently unequal because they separated and stigmatized the races by law.

References: Hall, *Oxford Companion* (1992); Yudof et al., *Kirp and Yudof's Educational Policy and the Law* (1987); Kluger, *Simple Justice* (1975).

SHEFF V. O'NEILL, 678 A.2d 1267 (Conn. 1996). Metropolitan school desegregation* decision in the Hartford, Connecticut, area in which the Connecticut Supreme Court by a 4–3 vote concluded that the Hartford schools were segregated, and even if the cause of that school segregation* was not intentional, a remedy involving suburban schools must be found. This was the first state court decision that the segregated schools were violating the state, rather than the federal, constitution since a 1975 Los Angeles, California, decision. The hope of desegregation advocates is that this case will be the basis of further school desegregation suits at the state level just as many state school-finance cases (over 40 were filed) succeeded after the failure to win cases based on the U.S. Constitution.*

The lead plaintiff was Hartford student Milo Sheff, whose mother, Elizabeth Horton Sheff, was a Hartford City Council member; the former governor, William A. O'Neill, was the named defendant. The plaintiffs argued that the segregation and ineffective education in Hartford were the state's responsibility to correct, whatever the cause. They had a two-pronged argument. First, they argued that the state had contributed to the segregation of the Hartford schools, and thus the state had the responsibility to remedy the problem. But they also argued that the state constitution required equal education, which necessitated the state remedying de facto* school segregation as well as de jure* school segregation.

The plaintiffs, representing poor minority children in the city of Hartford public schools, asked for an interdistrict metropolitan school desegregation plan* combining the city with 21 suburban school districts. This encompassed 96,000 schoolchildren, including the city's 26,000 children. The defendants did not deny that the schools were segregated (93 percent of the students were minority); rather, the question was the cause of this school segregation and the remedy that should follow, if any. They claimed that the major cause of the problems in the city's schools was poverty.

Under Governor Lowell Weicker's prodding, the state did pass voluntary school desegregation legislation in 1993 to address de facto segregation. However, by October 1994 none of the state's 11 regions had submitted a plan that would substantially desegregate classrooms. Five new magnet schools* in the state were proposed. The most extensive plan was submitted in the Hartford region, where officials recommended expanding Project Concern* from 730 to 6,000 Hartford children to be bused to the suburbs. But this plan called for a slow expansion that would not reach its peak until 2010.

In June 1995 Superior Court Judge Harry Hammer concluded that poverty, not segregation, was the cause of the low achievement of the Hartford students, and since the state was not to blame for the ills in Hartford, a court-ordered school desegregation plan was not appropriate. The plaintiffs appealed the decision to the Connecticut Supreme Court, which held a hearing on the case on September 28, 1995. On July 9, 1996, the Connecticut Supreme Court concluded that the state did have the obligation to desegregate the Hartford schools and ordered the state to do so. The decision ordered the state legislature to develop a remedy but did not set a deadline or offer guidelines to the specifics of any plan. Governor John G. Rowland declared that forced busing* would not be a solution to the problem and indicated that an expansion of recent charter-school legislation might be a component of the response. He appointed a committee of legislators, civil rights* leaders, and local officials to recommend remedies, and in January 1997 the panel made 15 recommendations. These included linking school-construction funding to the effects on racial balance* as well as a state-wide school-choice program and increased state spending on magnet schools.

David Armor* was an expert witness for the defendants, and Gary Orfield* was an expert witness for the plaintiffs. In 1996 Sheff was now a senior in high school; the case had been begun when he was in fourth grade. It is not clear to what extent this decision will be the first of many state challenges to segregation because the Connecticut state constitution has an unusual clause barring segregation that other state constitutions lack. This allowed the state court to conclude that the cause of the segregation, that is, de jure and not de facto, was not significant in this case. In September 1995 a suit similar to *Sheff* was filed in Minnesota. Another rationale based on this case for those in other states is to call on desegregation orders to ensure educational "adequacy," a guaranteed level of education, not just equal educational opportunity.*

References: Christine H. Rossell, "An Analysis of the Court Decisions in *Sheff v. O'Neill* and Possible Remedies for Racial Isolation," *Connecticut Law Review* 29, no. 3 (Spring 1997): 1187–1233; Stephen B. Delaney, "*Milo Sheff et al. v. William A. O'Neill et al.*: April 12, 1995," *Equity and Excellence in Education* 28, no. 2 (September 1995): 14–20; Sondra Astor Stave, *Achieving Racial Balance: Case Studies of Contemporary School Desegregation* (Westport, CT: Greenwood Press, 1995), 85–126; Stephen B. Delaney, "The Battle for School Desegregation in Connecticut," *Equity and Excellence in Education* 27, no. 2 (September 1994): 10–18.

SIPUEL V. OKLAHOMA STATE BOARD OF REGENTS, 332 U.S. 631

(1948). U.S. Supreme Court* decision ruling that Oklahoma could not refuse admission to a student seeking to enter a public institution solely on the basis of race. The decision indicated that black applicants had to be treated equally to white applicants.

Ada Lois Sipuel, 21-year-old daughter of a black clergyman and graduate of the State College for Negroes in Langston, Oklahoma, had applied to law school but had been told to wait until there were enough black citizens applying so that the state would be justified in establishing a black law school. Thurgood Marshall* of the NAACP Legal Defense Fund* (LDF) argued the case before the U.S. Supreme Court. He argued that given the precedent of the 1938 *Missouri ex rel. Gaines** decision, the state must provide an in-state education. But he also argued that Sipuel's education should be at the University of Oklahoma because separate would not be equal. The Court agreed with the first argument but not the second. The state was told that it could admit Sipuel to the white law school or immediately open a black law school. The state then set up a three-professor, ad hoc black law school only for Sipuel, roping off a portion of the state capitol. Sipuel refused to attend and went back to court.

On appeal Thurgood Marshall argued that a legal education is based, in part, on a collegial model; that is, students learn from and with each other as well as from professors. But this was too much for the U.S. Supreme Court to accept, and it returned the case to trial court for reargument about whether Sipuel was being treated equally. In August 1948 the state court again concluded that she was, but by 1949 the Oklahoma legislature enacted a law permitting blacks to attend white graduate and professional schools if such programs were not available in black schools, but on a segregated basis. However, the university admitted Ada Lois Sipuel and then did not segregate her. Sipuel graduated in 1951 and was admitted to Oklahoma's bar.

This was the first case in which the NAACP LDF included social science evidence in its briefs. The lawyers cited the work of Gunnar Myrdal* and the President's (Harry Truman*) Committee on Civil Rights to argue that "the very fact of segregation establishes a feeling of humiliation and deprivation to the group considered to be inferior."

References: Greenberg, *Crusaders in the Courts* (1994); Preer, *Lawyers v. Educators* (1982); Marcus and Stickney, *Race and Education* (1981); George Lynn Cross, *Blacks in White Colleges: Oklahoma's Landmark Cases* (Norman: University of Oklahoma Press, 1975); Kluger, *Simple Justice* (1975).

SLAUGHTERHOUSE CASES, 83 U.S. 36 (1873). While these cases did not directly involve blacks, the U.S. Supreme Court* in these decisions built a distinction between the "privileges and immunities" of U.S. citizens and those of state (in this case Louisiana) citizens. As a result of this decision blacks did not have the protection of the U.S. Civil War amendments, including the Fourteenth Amendment,* as state citizens, a tremendous restriction on their rights since states were far from leaders on civil rights.*

The case involved a 25-year exclusive franchise for butchering in three parishes granted by the Louisiana legislature to a corporation. Rival corporations sued, claiming that they had been deprived of their natural right to earn a living as per the new Fourteenth Amendment.* In a 5–4 vote the U.S. Supreme Court separated the first two sentences of the amendment and thus created a wall between the rights of citizens in the nation versus their rights as citizens of individual states. According to the Court's majority, the first sentence, "All persons born or naturalized in the United States, and subject to the jurisdiction thereof, are citizens of the United States and of the State wherein they reside," established the citizenship rights of Negroes, but the second sentence was interpreted as separating the rights of citizens in states. The second sentence read, "No state shall make or enforce any law which shall abridge the privileges or immunities of citizens of the United States." The Court concluded that "it is quite clear, then, that there is a citizenship of the United States and a citizenship of a State, which are distinct from one another."

References: Abraham and Perry, *Freedom and the Court* (1994); Joseph A. Melusky and Whitman H. Ridgway, *The Bill of Rights: Our Written Legacy* (Malabar, FL: Krieger, 1993); Kluger, *Simple Justice* (1975).

SOUTH. The southeastern region of the United States, distinctive for its climate and long agricultural growing season and plantation system, black agricultural labor, and white-imposed system of segregation.* The South consists of the following 17 states: Alabama, Arkansas, Delaware, Florida, Georgia, Kentucky, Louisiana, Maryland, Mississippi, Missouri, North Carolina, Oklahoma, South Carolina, Tennessee, Texas, Virginia, and West Virginia. The District of Columbia is also included in the South.

The South may be divided into several categories. The Deep South* includes the 5 states of Alabama, Georgia, Louisiana, Mississippi, and South Carolina. Black and Black (1987) call the other 12 southern states the "peripheral South." The 11 states that seceded from the United States of America to form the Confederate States of America include Alabama, Arkansas, Florida, Georgia, Louisiana, Mississippi, North Carolina, South Carolina, Tennessee, Texas, and Virginia. The border states may be considered the southern states that did not secede. Thus Delaware, Kentucky, Maryland, Missouri, Oklahoma, and West Virginia would be included in a list of border states. (Border states may also be considered slave states that bordered on the North. This set would include Delaware, Kentucky, Maryland, Missouri, and Virginia.) Sometimes the official South is referred to in a broader way. Kujovich refers to what herein have been defined as southern states as the "southern and border states . . . the 17 states that maintained a rigid system of segregation in public higher education during the separate but equal era" (1992:30).

The New South generally refers to the reduction of prejudice,* a lessened focus on racial matters, and the end of massive resistance* to school desegregation and the increase of a focus on economic growth and public education for all citizens in southern states. Jimmy Carter,* for example, was viewed as a leader of the New South.

References: Peter Applebome, *Dixie Rising: How the South Is Shaping American Values, Politics, and Culture* (New York: Times Books, 1996); *Britannica Online* (1996); Kujovich, "Equal Opportunity in Higher Education" (1992); Earl Black and Merle Black, *Politics and Society in the South* (Cambridge, MA: Harvard University Press, 1987); Joel Williamson, *A Rage for Order: Black/White Relations in the American South since Emancipation* (New York: Oxford University Press, 1986).

SOUTHERN MANIFESTO. Prosegregation white paper issued on March 12, 1956, by 101 southern congressmen (19 senators, 82 House members) that denounced the *Brown** (1954 and 1955) decisions as a "clear abuse of judicial power [that] climaxes a trend in the federal judiciary undertaking to legislate in derogation of the authority of Congress and to encroach upon the reserved rights of the states and the people." The manifesto lauded "those states which have declared the intention to resist enforced integration by any lawful means." The signatories, almost all elected representatives of the South,* vowed to use all legal means to maintain segregation* and resist desegregation.* (All southern senators except Majority Leader Lyndon B. Johnson* of Texas and Albert Gore and Estes Kefauver of Tennessee signed. Twenty-four southern representatives did not sign.) The statement was drafted by Senator Sam Ervin, although Senator Harry Byrd of Virginia was viewed as the major architect of the manifesto and the first person to use the term massive resistance* in public. The manifesto discouraged President Dwight D. Eisenhower* from taking a strong stand on the Court's decision and gave heart to those planning massive resistance.

Wilhoit lists ten functions of the manifesto, including reasserting a states' rights theory of federalism, trying to convince the South that the *Brown* decision was illegitimate, giving hope to local school-district officials attempting to resist implementing *Brown*, and forcing white moderates to declare against the decision. He concludes that while the manifesto "boosted the morale of the South's segregationists," it did not succeed in "either repealing or discrediting Brown" (1973:54).

References: Marcus and Stickney, *Race and Education* (1981); Wilhoit, *The Politics of Massive Resistance* (1973); Bartley, *The Rise of Massive Resistance* (1969); Muse, *Ten Years of Prelude* (1964).

SOUTHERN REGIONAL COUNCIL. Originally founded by two white ministers and two black leaders and an industrialist as the Commission on Interracial Cooperation in 1919, the Southern Regional Council is a private development and civil rights* agency headquartered in Atlanta. The organization changed its name in 1944. As an interracial, nonpartisan, and nonprofit organization, the council has sought to promote "excellence, opportunity, and democratic principles in education." According to John Egerton (1994:48), "Throughout the 1920s, the commission was just about the only Southern organization with any influence or effectiveness at all in opposing racial violence in the region." While opposed to violence, the organization did not take a position against segregation* until 1952. The council was instrumental in helping with the research that led to Harry S. Ashmore's *The Negro and the Schools*, an analysis of the unequal status of black public schools in the South* prior to the 1954 *Brown v. Board of Education** decision. The council has tried to act as a meeting ground for citizens of all races and backgrounds, to counteract appeals to racism* and prejudice,* and to stimulate local action in support of these objectives. After the 1954 U.S. Supreme Court* decision the council worked to resist racial demagoguery and to preserve the public schools. The council has a variety of programs, including educational initiatives (the Algebra Project) and leadership development (Community Fellows in Public Education). The council has monitored the growth of private schools in the South and the conditions of public education in the South's Black Belt. The council is also involved in voting rights and economic development activities.

References: Southern Regional Council, *Southern Changes* and *Annual Report*; Jaszczak, *Encyclopedia of Associations* (1996), 2072; Egerton, *Speak Now against the Day* (1994); Weldon James, "The South's Own Civil War," in *With All Deliberate Speed*, ed. Shoemaker (1957), 15–35.

SOUTHERN REGIONAL EDUCATION BOARD (SREB). *See* **Southern Regional Education Compact**.

SOUTHERN REGIONAL EDUCATION COMPACT. Agreement on behalf of 14 southern and border states to offer regional education for blacks to maintain their segregated state colleges and universities signed on February 8, 1948, that has developed into a regional educational organization, the Southern Regional Education Board (SREB), offering educational programs helpful to blacks in all situations. The Southern Regional Education Compact was originally designed to circumvent the 1938 *Missouri ex rel. Gaines** decision by offering regional programs for black students. The programs were to be funded by contributions from the states based on population, but over time the compact funded student scholarships as opposed to offering its own programs. The Southern Regional Education Board by 1949 began officially distancing itself from its segregation* origins by intervening for those seeking higher-education desegregation* in Maryland.

By 1996 the board's Web page indicated that "our purpose is to help states improve the quality of education, student opportunity, and student achievement.*" It does this through focusing attention on key educational issues; collecting, compiling, and analyzing comparable data across its member states; and conducting about 40 timely studies annually on topics such as vocational education, technology for schools and colleges, and remedial education. The board's member states are Alabama, Arkansas, Florida, Georgia, Kentucky, Louisiana, Maryland, Mississippi, North Carolina, Oklahoma, South Carolina, Tennessee, Texas, Virginia, and West Virginia. SREB's offices are located in Atlanta, Georgia.

References: http://www.sreb.org; Kujovich, "Equal Opportunity in Higher Education" (1992); Joseph B. Parham, "Halls of Ivy—Southern Exposure," in *With All Deliberate Speed*, ed. Shoemaker (1957), 163–82.

SOUTHERN STRATEGY. President Richard M. Nixon's* attempt to secure favor among voters and politicians in the South* by actions such as the slowing down of civil rights* and school desegregation* enforcement. Safire calls it "an attack phrase attributing racist* or at least political motives toward any position taken on desegregation* or busing* that would be well-received by most Southern whites" (1993:734).

The Democratic party had been troubled by trying to keep the coalition of black voters and southern voters together for decades. President Franklin D. Roosevelt had appealed to both with his New Deal, but the rise in efforts to expand civil rights during the Truman* administration helped to fracture this coalition. The Dixiecrats walked out of the 1948 Democratic convention in protest of President Harry Truman's support of a strong civil rights plank. John F. Kennedy's* campaign for the presidency on the Democratic ticket had been shaped to avoid alienating the South, and his choice of Lyndon B. Johnson*

from Texas as his running mate was an effort to maintain the southern part of the coalition. Kennedy's call of support for Martin Luther King* was also an attempt to maintain black Democratic support. As the civil rights movement* grew stronger, and as President Kennedy grew more sympathetic, southern voters became more restless with the party. The strong civil rights actions of President Johnson, which included the Civil Rights Act of 1964,* the Voting Rights Act of 1965, and the War on Poverty, further attracted blacks to the Democratic party, but at the cost of alienating some southern white voters. Richard Nixon's strategy was to pry the South from the Democratic party by appealing to southern beliefs about race and school desegregation. Nixon was an active opponent of busing. In his 1968 campaign he attacked busing and the Warren Court* and promised to move the U.S. Supreme Court* in a more conservative direction. He declared that he favored freedom-of-choice* school desegregation plans* and opposed the threat of federal fund cutoffs to force school desegregation. Nixon was the first successful presidential candidate to be opposed to civil rights enforcement.

After his election President Nixon slowed down the enforcement of civil rights laws. His administration was sued, and in *Adams v. Richardson** (1973) the courts ordered the administration to implement the law. In the Department of Justice* some lawyers revolted and refused to defend the government's position. Others passed critical information to lawyers on the opposite side.

Safire traces the origin of the term to the strategies and campaign for President of Barry Goldwater in 1964. Goldwater hoped to win the South by building upon Republican gains from the migration of younger businessmen to the region. Safire questions the accuracy of the charge that Nixon had a Southern Strategy based on racism because "to practical politicians, any strategy that wins one region at the expense of all others is nonsensical; however, any national election strategy that seeks to include Southern support is attacked as a 'Southern strategy' because it helps the attacker disaffect the opposition's support elsewhere" (1993, 735).

References: O'Reilly, *Nixon's Piano* (1995); Safire, *Safire's New Political Dictionary* (1993); Wilkinson, *From Brown to Bakke* (1979).

STATUS DIFFERENTIAL. The difference in social class between members of different races. The effects of interracial contact are positive (or at least more positive) when the status differential between the races is minimal, according to the research of Gordon Allport* as described in *The Nature of Prejudice.**

A major argument against school desegregation* by means of busing* is that the status differential between whites and blacks tends to be too great. The difference leads to conflict across the races as opposed to cooperation, according to the critics.

References: Janet W. Schofield, "Promoting Positive Peer Relations in Desegregated Schools," in *Beyond Desegregation*, ed. Shujaa (Thousand Oaks, CA: Corwin Press, 1996), 91–112; Armor, *Forced Justice* (1995); Allport, *The Nature of Prejudice* (1954).

STELL V. BOARD OF PUBLIC EDUCATION, 860 F. Supp. 1563 (S.D. Ga. 1994). U.S. District Court* decision, upheld by the Eleventh Circuit Court of Appeals,* that allowed the first purely voluntary plan,* implemented in Savannah–Chatham County, Georgia, to be declared as unitary. Prior to 1988 the district had a mandatory school desegregation plan* based on school pairing.* In 1988 the district was allowed to adopt a voluntary plan* based on magnet schools* that included neighborhood school* attendance zones and two new schools built in the city's black areas. The district implemented the plan for five years and then asked the court to declare the district a unitary system.* In 1994 U.S. District Court Judge B. Avant Edenfield declared that the school district's "momentous efforts" had been sufficient and ruled that the district was unitary and his supervision of the district could end. This was then upheld by the Court of Appeals.

References: Orfield and Eaton, *Dismantling Desegregation* (1996); Armor, *Forced Justice* (1995).

STUDENT ACHIEVEMENT. The measured educational accomplishments of students. School desegregation* is viewed by some as a means to increase the student achievement of minority students to lessen the gap between whites and blacks and Hispanic students.

The Coleman Report* measured student achievement by standardized achievement tests of verbal and mathematical ability. The Coleman Report established that the gap in student achievement among the races was large and varied over the education span. The findings of Coleman and his colleagues indicated that family background was the strongest factor in explaining student achievement differences. Black students were more affected than white students by the characteristics of the school, and black students in desegregated schools did tend to score better on standardized tests.

The National Assessment of Educational Progress (NAEP) has indicated that black students are closing the gap with white students. From 1971 to 1990 black students' gains on measures of verbal and mathematical achievement were substantial enough to cut the gap by one-half; scores of white students hardly changed during this time period.

In 1984 the National Institute of Education sponsored a special study and asked six experts, including several with known positive and negative views, to come together to study the effects of school desegregation. They reviewed many studies and tried to come to agreement on the best ones to reanalyze. The neutral analyst and chair, Thomas Cook, concluded that the gains from these studies that could be attributed to school desegregation were modest, in the range of four to six weeks of a school year for reading and less for math. Cook's own conclusions stressed the range of effects across these studies, that is, the variability of effects, and that it is not known what it is about school desegregation that causes the effect.

See also **National Institute of Education Report.**

Recent criticisms of standardized tests have led to attempts to develop "authentic assessments," more open-ended examinations that test actual activities that students will have to do in life after their formal schooling ends. To some extent the focus on student achievement in desegregation cases misrepresents the goals of school desegregation. School desegregation in de jure resegregated school districts has been ordered to eliminate racially identifiable schools, for example, black schools and white schools, and to establish "just schools," not identifiable by race. However, recent court cases concerning whether school districts have achieved unitary status* have included the argument that differences in achievement on standardized tests between blacks and whites remain after the implementation of the school desegregation order and that these gaps are evidence of the failure to fully and adequately implement the court order and desegregate the schools. In the Wilmington, Delaware, case U.S. District Court* Judge Sue Robinson rejected this argument, and her decision was upheld by the Third Circuit Court of Appeals.* In *Missouri v. Jenkins** (1995) the U.S. Supreme Court* ruled that many other factors, especially family backgrounds, could have accounted for the failure of blacks to gain vis-à-vis whites on achievement tests. It concluded, as a result, that the school district did not have to close the black-white achievement gap as a condition of unitary status.

Improvements in black student achievement in comparison to whites over the last two decades have led to the conclusion that school desegregation has been a major causal factor in the increase. However, David Armor's* analysis of the black-white achievement gap over time, in which he found segregated black students gaining as much or more than desegregated black students in reading and math on standardized tests, suggests that black social status, not school desegregation, has been the major causal variable.

References: Armor, *Forced Justice* (1995); Schofield, "Review of Research on School Desegregation's Impact on Elementary and Secondary School Students" (1995); Armor, "Why Is Black Achievement Rising?" (Summer 1992); Cook et al., *School Desegregation and Black Achievement* (1984).

SUPERFICIAL TOLERANCE. *See* **Busing**.

SUPREME COURT. *See* **U.S. SUPREME COURT**.

SWANN V. CHARLOTTE-MECKLENBURG BOARD OF EDUCATION, 402 U.S. 1 (1971). Unanimous landmark U.S. Supreme Court* decision (Chief Justice Warren Burger* writing for the Court) that established the acceptability of busing* in school desegregation* remedies. The *Swann* decision followed the 1968 *Green** decision in defining the permissible scope of remedies to constitutional violations as cited in the *Brown** (1954 and 1955) decisions. But while *Green* involved a small rural school district, the *Swann* decision centered on the Charlotte-Mecklenburg school system, the 43rd largest in the country, encompassing 550 square miles. In 1968–1969 the district served over 84,000 students in over 100 schools. Seventy-one percent were white and the remainder were black, but of the 24,000 black students, two-thirds attended schools that were at least 99 percent black in June 1969.

The case focused on student assignment issues: the use of racial balance* or racial quotas, whether all all-black or all-white schools had to be eliminated, limits on the rearrangement of school attendance zones, and, most importantly, the limits on the use of transportation in fashioning a remedy. The U.S. District Court* had ordered an extensive desegregation plan involving a good deal of busing, and the U.S. Court of Appeals* had rejected the plan at the elementary level because of fears that the burdens on pupils would be unreasonable.

The District Court had set a 71–29 ratio of white to black students as an objective for the desegregation plan, a decision called a quota or racial balance requirement by the defendants. The U.S. Supreme Court, however, concluded that this ratio was a "starting point," not an "inflexible requirement," and therefore permissible in a case involving a long failure to desegregate a dual system* of public education. The Court concluded that "the existence of some small number of one-race, or virtually one-race, schools within a district is not in and of itself the mark of a district that still practices segregation by law," but if a district undertaking court-ordered desegregation contemplates some one-race schools, "they have the burden of showing that such school assignments are genuinely nondiscriminatory." That is, the burden of proof* shifts to the school district. In an oft-quoted paragraph, the Court concluded:

Absent a constitutional violation there would be no basis for judicially ordering assignments of students on a racial basis. All things being equal, with no history of discrimination, it might well be desirable to assign pupils to schools nearest their homes. But all things are not equal in a system that has been deliberately constructed and maintained to enforce racial segregation. The remedy for such segregation may be administratively awkward, inconvenient, and even bizarre in some situations and may impose burdens on some; but all awkwardness and inconvenience cannot be avoided in the interim period when remedial adjustments are being made to eliminate the dual school systems.

Thus the Court held that pairing* and clustering* of noncontiguous school attendance areas were allowed as part of a remedy.

The Court concluded that no rigid student transportation guidelines could be set for remedies. It noted that "bus transportation has been an integral part of the public transportation system for years" and then made a pragmatic analysis of the county's situation. The Court stated that the transportation required in the District Court's plan was less burdensome than the past transportation plan in the county under which 32,600 students at all grade levels were bused an average of 15 miles one way for an average trip of more than an hour. (The plan called for elementary-school pupils to be transported for an average of 7 miles and for no longer than 35 minutes.) "Desegregation plans cannot be limited to the walk-in school."

In sum, the Court found the plan to be "reasonable, feasible, and workable."

The Court recognized that school authorities' decisions to build schools in particular areas could affect neighborhood residential patterns. When such patterns were combined with neighborhood school* attendance zones, school segregation* might become locked in.

The decision also defined more specifically the elements of an acceptable desegregation plan, the so-called *Green* factors. Student assignment plans, existing policies and practices with regard to faculty, staff, and transportation, extracurricular activities, and facilities (school construction and abandonment) were cited as important components of such plans; racial distinctions had to be eliminated in all of these areas.

The *Swann* decision had an immediate impact on desegregation plans, for within months its principles were followed in over forty plans. The office of Julius Chambers, who represented the black children in the case, was firebombed. There was also much peaceful opposition to busing, including a rally of 10,000 protesters and thousands of No Forced Busing bumper stickers on cars.

Fiss concludes that the *Swann* decision not only reaffirmed *Green*'s rejection of the view that the equal protection clause* only requires the prohibition of race as a criterion in pupil assignments, but also had four other impacts. First, the decision attacked the use of geographical proximity to assign students in a context where past discrimination* had been practiced and might well have led to segregated residential patterns. Second, the Court placed the burden, and it is a heavy one, of showing that school assignments that resulted in one-race schools were not discriminatory on the school district rather than on those bringing suit. Third, in *Swann* the Court made desegregating the schools the top priority for the district rather than simply one consideration among many for the school board. Finally, Fiss argues that *Swann* "validates the use of race in student assignments when the goal is integration* rather than segregation" (1994:702). Overall, Fiss concludes that this decision moved the Court further toward a results-oriented approach and away from a concern that the process should not use race as a criterion for school assignment.

References: Armor, *Forced Justice* (1995); Owen M. Fiss, "The Charlotte-Mecklenburg Case—Its Significance for Northern School Desegregation," in Douglas, *School Busing* (1994), 279–309; Frye Gaillard, *The Dream Long Deferred* (Chapel Hill: University of North Carolina Press, 1988); Yudof et al., *Kirp and Yudof's Educational Policy and the Law* (1987); Bernard Schwartz, *Swann's Way: The School Busing Case and the Supreme Court* (New York: Oxford University Press, 1986).

SWEATT V. PAINTER, 339 U.S. 629 (1950). U.S. Supreme Court* decision that established the role that intangibles play in comparing separate but equal* law schools. The decision established the need to examine factors such as the quality of the alumni, faculty reputation, and experience of the administration in determining if two schools are indeed equal. This decision thus made it difficult, if not impossible, for states in the South* to legally offer separate but equal graduate and professional education.

Herman Sweatt, a black postman from Texas, applied to the University of Texas Law School in 1945. When he was denied admission, he sued. The U.S. District Court* judge ruled that Sweatt was entitled either to admission to the university law school or to one to be established at Prairie View A and M for blacks. Texas had responded to pressure to offer equal educational opportunity,* as had many other southern and border states. After the 1938 *Missouri ex rel. Gaines** decision the state created an out-of-state scholarship program in 1939 and then appropriated $18,000 to Prairie View State College, the black land grant college, to offer graduate degrees. In 1946 Texas established a Bi-Racial Commission on Negro Education, which in turn recommended that the state legislature build a first-class university for blacks. The legislature responded by appropriating $2 million for the physical plant and $500,000 per year for operating costs. In addition, an integrated board of trustees was appointed. While this case was on appeal, the state allocated $100,000 to establish a new Texas State University for Negroes with a good law school. The state opened the new law school with essentially no library and four part-time faculty from the University of Texas in the basement of a petroleum company in Austin, eight blocks from the nationally recognized law school of the University of Texas. The "school" consisted of four rooms and a leased toilet and had no moot court, no law review, and none of the other "extras" that normally accompany a quality law school. Thus Texas made a major effort to establish separate but equal educational opportunities, but this all was in comparison to one of the leading universities of the South. The state courts, despite the obvious disparities, ruled that the black and white law schools were equal.

Sweatt argued that denying him admission to the all-white law school at the University of Texas in Austin and admitting him to an all-black law school established at the moment violated his constitutional rights. Thurgood Marshall* and James Nabrit* of the NAACP Legal Defense Fund* (LDF) argued that Texas must either provide Sweatt with an equal law school or admit him to the University of Texas school. One hundred and eighty-seven law professors submitted a brief arguing that a separate legal education could not be equal to a regular law school.

In a unanimous decision written by Chief Justice Fred Vinson* the U.S. Supreme Court found that the two law schools were not equal. The university's law school not only had full-time faculty and a far larger library, it also had nationally recognized legal scholars and was ranked nationally. "The law school to which Texas is willing to admit petitioner excludes from its student body members of racial groups which number 85% of the population of the State and include most of the lawyers, witnesses, jurors, judges, and other officials with whom the petitioner will inevitably be dealing when he becomes a member of the Texas Bar." The Court thus decided that segregated law schools for blacks could not provide them with equal educational opportunities. The Court cited intangibles in education such as the reputation of the faculty, the experience of the administration, and the position and influence of the faculty that could not be equal. But the Court did not take on the question of the validity of the separate but equal standard; it only concluded that Sweatt's options were not equal to the University of Texas Law School.

In this decision the Court therefore held that separate was inherently unequal, at least in graduate and professional education. Sweatt was admitted to the law school. However, he never did graduate from law school; he dropped out before the end of his first year.

This case marked a change in strategy for the NAACP LDF from its call for equal opportunity, even if that were fulfilled by separate schools for blacks, to the argument that separate schools were inherently unequal, and thus only the integration* of blacks into white schools was a reasonable remedy. Thus the NAACP attacked segregation head-on. In doing so, however, it had to attack the quality of black institutions of higher education. The U.S. Supreme Court was forced to deal with the existence of a white and a black school for the first time, not just the absence of an alternative for blacks within a state. However, while the U.S. Supreme Court concluded that there did not exist a way to make the two schools separate and equal, the Court did not reject the concept of separate but equal.

References: Kujovich, "Equal Opportunity in Higher Education" (1992); Yudof et al., *Kirp and Yudof's Educational Policy and the Law* (1987); Preer, *Lawyers v. Educators* (1982); Marcus and Stickney, *Race and Education* (1981); Kluger, *Simple Justice* (1975).

SYMBOLIC RACISM. A theory explaining why whites oppose busing* although they favor the principle of school desegregation.* The theory maintains that racism* is formed early in childhood but is not socially acceptable today, so racism is expressed covertly as opposition to busing or preferential treatment for blacks. Thus attitudes on specific policies are related to deep-seated attitudes about the status of blacks in society. Since white opposition to busing is correlated with more direct measures of prejudice* and is not related to having a child in school, some have concluded that it is "not busing but the blacks."

This theory of white opposition to busing has been criticized, however, because opposition to busing is so extensive among whites that one would have to conclude that all whites are racists. Furthermore, this ignores black opposition to busing, also high. A second criticism is that self-interest is being too narrowly defined. The racial divisions and neighborhood instability that busing brings to a community can be counter to one's self-interest, regardless of whether one is a parent.

References: Armor, *Forced Justice* (1995); Rossell, "The Convergence of Black and White Attitudes on School Desegregation Issues during the Four Decade Evolution of the Plans" (January 1995); David O. Sears, "Symbolic Racism," in *Eliminating Racism*, ed. Phyllis A. Katz and Dalmas A. Taylor (New York: Plenum Press, 1988); John B. McConahay, "Self-Interest vs. Racial Attitudes as Correlates of Anti-Busing Attitudes in Louisville: Is It the Buses or the Blacks?" *Journal of Politics* 44 (1982): 692–720.

T

TAEUBER INDEX. *See* **Index of Dissimilarity**.

TIPPING POINT. A specific percentage level of blacks in a school or neighborhood that is the threshold at which the black enrollment or population will continue to increase until the school or neighborhood becomes segregated and black. The tipping point of a school is the percentage of black or minority student enrollment at which whites leave (white flight*) or will not come because they fear that the school will decline or become all black. This term was used more in the 1960s and 1970s than thereafter. In *Forced Justice* David Armor* estimates the tipping point of schools as 50 percent black. Christine Rossell* and Armor also view the degree of flight as a function of where the school is located, the voluntary* versus the mandatory* nature of a school desegregation plan,* and other factors rather than simply as the result of a particular minority percentage of enrollment.

Ottensmann (1995) calls for a "Requiem for the Tipping-Point Hypothesis," at least with respect to residential neighborhood change. The tipping-point hypothesis assumes that racially mixed neighborhoods are inherently unstable, for as the tipping point is reached, whites will leave and/or not move into the area and the percentage of blacks will therefore increase. But studies of the 1980 and 1990 censuses indicate that many neighborhoods remained racially mixed or even increased their percentage of whites during this time period. Ottensmann argues that this change may be due to the greater stability in black population in cities, unlike the previous decades when the black population was greatly increasing and needed to locate somewhere. But whatever the cause, the result challenges the notion of an inevitable change in neighborhoods at a particular racial mix.

References: Rossell and Armor, "The Effectiveness of School Desegregation Plans, 1968–1991," (1996); Armor, *Forced Justice* (1995); John R. Ottensmann, "Requiem for the Tipping-Point Hypothesis," *Journal of Planning Literature* 10, no. 2 (November 1995): 131–41; Michael W. Giles, Everett F. Cataldo, and Douglas S. Gatlin, "White Flight and Percent Black: The Tipping Point Reexamined," *Social Science Quarterly* 56, no. 1 (1975): 85–92; Arthur L. Stinchcombe, "Is There a Racial Tipping Point in Changing Schools?" *Journal of Social Issues* 25, no. 1 (1969): 127–36.

TO SECURE THESE RIGHTS. The 178-page report of the President's Committee on Civil Rights appointed by President Harry S. Truman* issued in 1947 analyzing segregation* and calling for a "cure for the disease as well as treat[ing] its symptoms." The committee called the policy of separate but equal* a failure and recommended the "elimination of segregation, based on race, color, creed, or national origin, from American life." Among the specific recommendations of the commission were a federal antilynching law, abolition of the poll tax, a permanent commission on fair employment, an end to segregation in the military, an end to segregation in public housing and accommodations, and a cutoff of federal funds to recipients that maintained segregation and discrimination.* This was the first U.S. governmental body to reject racial segregation.* President Truman strongly endorsed the committee's recommendations.

References: Egerton, *Speak Now against the Day* (1994); Harry S Truman, *The Truman Administration: Its Principles and Practice* (New York: New York University Press, 1956); *To Secure These Rights: The Report of the President's Committee on Civil Rights* (New York: Simon and Schuster, 1947).

TRACKING. *See* **Ability Grouping**.

TRUMAN, HARRY S. (born May 8, 1884, Lamar, Missouri–died December 26, 1972, Kansas City, Missouri). Thirty-third President of the United States, a strong advocate of civil rights* whose administration exerted leadership in fighting discrimination* and supported the NAACP Legal Defense Fund* in its effort to overturn school desegregation* in the *Brown v. Board of Education** (1954) case. President Truman tried to have Congress pass civil rights legislation but had his greatest impact in this area through executive orders and his administration's support for school desegregation at the U.S. Supreme Court* level.

Son of a mule trader and farmer, and with Confederate ancestors, Truman became a bank clerk after graduating from high school in 1901. He then took over his grandmother's farm and served as the local postmaster and road overseer. Truman was recognized for his leadership in World War I. After the war he returned to Kansas City and became a partner in a haberdashery store, but when the business failed, he entered politics with the help of the Democratic boss of Jackson County, Thomas J. Pendergast. Truman won election as county judge (analogous to a county commissioner) in 1922. Although he lost his re-election bid, in 1926 he was elected as the presiding judge in the county. He served for eight years and established a fine record of good management and honesty.

In 1934 Truman was elected to the U.S. Senate as a supporter of Franklin Roosevelt's New Deal. He was an active senator and won reelection in 1941. His investigation into graft and waste in the procurement of national defense brought him public distinction. President Roosevelt selected him as his running mate in 1944, replacing Vice President Henry A. Wallace. Within 82 days Roosevelt died (April 12, 1945), and Truman became President.

Truman's first term in office was focused on international events, from his decision to drop two atomic bombs on Japan through the start of the Cold War with the Soviet Union and the Truman Doctrine and the Marshall Plan. On the domestic front Truman's Fair Deal included broad social welfare reforms. He supported legislation calling for full employment. In 1946 Truman appointed a large number of distinguished black and white Americans to the President's Committee on Civil Rights; Charles E. Wilson, president of the General Electric Company, was named chairman. The group published the report *To Secure These Rights** in October 1947. The report, relying heavily on Gunnar Myrdal's* book *An American Dilemma,** urged sweeping action to secure equal rights for all Americans. It called for eliminating segregation,* ensuring that federal assistance only went to nondiscriminating agencies, and the granting of equal access to all places of public accommodation. On July 26, 1948, Truman, angered that Congress had failed to include an antidiscrimination provision in the Selective Service Act of 1948, ordered the desegregation* of the armed forces in Executive Order 9981. In June 1947 Truman spoke to 10,000 people on the steps of the Lincoln Memorial assembled for the NAACP* annual conference. He was the first President to address this group. He made an extremely strong speech for ending "insult, intimidation, violence, prejudice,* and intolerance." He called for making the "federal government a friendly, vigilant defender of the rights and equalities of all Americans." Truman's Department of Justice* supported blacks in civil rights cases. Truman established a Fair Employment Board by executive order to see that federal jobs were awarded without regard to "race, color, religion, or national origin." At the 1948 Democratic convention Truman supported the adoption of a civil rights plank to ensure equal opportunity in employment, security from the threat of lynching, and other equal protection actions.

Truman's actions, however, led to anger from the southern wing of the party and fueled the "Dixiecrat" revolt. At the 1948 Democratic National Convention the black-liberal-labor alliance forced a strong civil rights plank into the party platform. Truman objected to this, fearing that this action would divide the party and recognizing that his previous actions had already signaled his commitment to civil rights. The Mississippi delegation, along with half of the Alabama delegation, walked out of the convention. Two days after Truman was nominated, the Dixiecrats met in Birmingham, Alabama, and nominated Governor Strom Thurmond of South Carolina to lead the States' Rights party ticket. They carried Alabama, Georgia, Mississippi, and South Carolina in the general election. Popular wisdom had Truman as a loser to Republican nominee Governor Thomas E. Dewey of New York, but Truman upset Dewey to earn a term in his own right.

Truman's administration supported the desegregation of public schools in the *Brown v. Board of Education* cases. The brief argued that the physical inequalities and psychological harm experienced by black students in the cases before the U.S. Supreme Court* warranted prohibiting school segregation* in the districts. It went beyond attacking the separate but equal* doctrine to argue that "compulsory racial segregation is itself, without more, an unconstitutional discrimination." The administration's *amicus curiae** brief argued that black students could be sent to white schools until equal black schools were built. It also presented the idea that if the Court ruled that separate but equal no longer was appropriate, the case could be returned to the U.S. District Court* judge to define a remedy, and the court could order a gradual or phased approach to school desegregation.

Truman's civil rights positions and actions reflected a number of influences. He was faced with the prospect of holding together a Democratic party joining northern liberals, including many blacks, with white southern conservatives. While President Roosevelt could hold this coalition together during the depression and World War II, President Truman had the more difficult task following the war. But overall, as President, Truman was a strong advocate for equal rights for blacks.

Works about: *Britannica Online* (1996); O'Reilly, *Nixon's Piano* (1995); David G. McCullough, *Truman* (New York: Simon and Schuster, 1992); Stern, *Calculating Visions* (1992); Marcus and Stickney, *Race and Education* (1981); Donald McCoy and Richard T. Reuten, *Quest and Response: Minority Rights and the Truman Administration* (Lawrence: University Press of Kansas, 1973).

Works by: *Memoirs*, 2 vols. (Garden City, NY: Doubleday, 1955–1956).

U

UNITARY SYSTEM. A school system judged by the federal courts to no longer be a dual system,* that is, operating one system for majority and one for minority children; thus the school district has corrected the problem of segregation* and is released from direct monitoring by the federal District Court* of the implementation of the school desegregation plan.* When districts lack unitary status and are under a court order, they must receive approval for all changes to the desegregation plan from the plaintiffs and the court. This could well include changes in attendance areas, the building of a new school or closing of an old school, or changing teacher or student transfer policies. The burden of proof* is on the defendant school district. Unitary school districts, however, have the same constitutional obligations as school districts that have never been under court order. As David Armor* concludes, "No school policy or action can be successfully challenged in court without proving segregative effects and discriminatory purpose on the part of the school board" (1995:214). Thus in unitary districts the burden of proof to show discrimination* shifts back to the plaintiffs, those charging unconstitutional school segregation.*

Armor points out three reasons why districts may prefer to remain under court order rather than be declared unitary. First, school districts under court order who would like to continue their school desegregation plan are protected by the court from political pressures to alter it. Second, court orders help protect staffing plans that spread minority staff throughout the school district. An increasingly significant third reason is to maintain the funding provided under the court order from state and/or federal sources, such as the Magnet Schools Assistance Program.*

School boards seeking unitary status must prove that the district implemented the school desegregation order in good faith, that the plan was effective in eliminating all vestiges of school segregation, as delimited by the *Green** decision, to the extent "practicable," and that they have not violated the U.S. Constitution* subsequent to the original court decision. Armor indicates that the second criterion, the removal of vestiges, is the most complex. Among the vestiges that a federal court is likely to consider are the maintenance of one-race schools from the period prior to the court order through the implementation of the plan, a school faculty racial composition that deviates greatly from the overall district percentage, or inadequate programs to help minorities in predominantly minority schools. If a school that was at one point racially balanced* has since become segregated, the court would consider the extent to which school-district actions or demographics were the cause. In recent cases plaintiffs have called for the elimination of disparities in student achievement,* disciplinary action, and representation in programs for the gifted and special education; they have cited such differences as vestiges of discrimination, but the courts have not definitively ruled favorably on such motions, and the U.S. Supreme Court* has said that a black-white achievement gap by itself is not a barrier to unitary status.

Orfield* and Eaton view recent Supreme Court decisions defining unitary status as leading to the erosion of Court support for school desegregation. According to them, by 1990 unitary status, which under *Green** had meant "discrimination-free, racially integrated education—was no longer the objective; it became merely a method of getting out of racial integration*" (1996:19). The Court no longer supported lasting desegregation and also had abandoned the notion of the parts of a desegregation plan as an inseparable package to move a school district from a dual to a single district. The shift in the burden of proof created a very difficult barrier to proving segregatory intent in an era when officials knew that giving racist reasons for their actions would lead them to court. Practically, moving from dual to unitary status means that acts that were illegal in the former stage are legal in the latter stage. The Court has established a situation where scores of years of discrimination may be "overcome" in a few years of school desegregation. Court cases defining the criteria for unitary status include *Board of Education of Oklahoma City v. Dowell** (1991), *Freeman v. Pitts** (1992), and *Missouri v. Jenkins** (1995).

References: Orfield and Eaton, *Dismantling Desegregation* (1996); Wolters, *Right Turn* (1996); Armor, *Forced Justice* (1995).

UNITED NEGRO COLLEGE FUND (THE COLLEGE FUND/UNCF). An educational assistance organization with 41 private, historically black member colleges and universities established on April 25, 1944, to raise funds to support its member colleges and their students. The United Negro College Fund conducted its first annual campaign in 1944 under the leadership of Frederick D.

Patterson, president of the Tuskegee Institute. The fund drive was aimed at helping 27 black private colleges in the South* that had suffered through the depression and World War II. In the first year $765,000 was collected. This amount was three times the amount raised by these institutions in individual campaigns in the years before.

The 41 member institutions of the United Negro College Fund include Tuskegee University (Alabama), Morehouse and Spelman colleges (Georgia), Wilberforce University (Ohio), Fisk University (Tennessee), and other schools in Arkansas, Louisiana, Mississippi, North Carolina, South Carolina, Texas, and Virginia. The fund provides a wide range of services to member schools and students, including scholarships and curriculum and faculty development. The UNCF's slogan, "A Mind Is a Terrible Thing to Waste," remains a familiar one. The fund has raised over $1 billion since its founding.

References: Jones-Wilson et al., *Encyclopedia of African-American Education* (1996), 485–86; Richette L. Haywood, "UNCF: 50 Years of Making a Difference," *Ebony* 50, no. 2 (December 1994): 36–39; Mark Lowery, "50 Years and Going Strong," *Black Enterprise* 25, no. 2 (September 1994): 132–38; Roebuck and Murty, *Historically Black Colleges and Universities* (1993); Frederick D. Patterson, *Chronicles of Faith: The Autobiography of Frederick D. Patterson* (Tuscaloosa: University of Alabama Press, 1991).

U.S. COMMISSION ON CIVIL RIGHTS. An independent, bipartisan fact-finding agency of the executive branch of the federal government established by the Civil Rights Act of 1957* to, as President Eisenhower* said, "put the facts on the table." The commission was given greater authority by the Civil Rights Act of 1964.* The U.S. Commission on Civil Rights is responsible for investigating allegations that U.S. citizens are being deprived of their right to vote by reason of color, race, religion, sex, age, handicap, or national origin. The commission also studies and collects information about discrimination* and appraises the laws and policies of the federal government with respect to discrimination in areas such as education, housing, employment, transportation, the use of public facilities, and the administration of justice. The commission has the authority to hold hearings and limited subpoena authority. It has statewide advisory committees. In fiscal year 1995 the commission published 11 reports and dealt with approximately 4,500 complaints.

The commission was quite active in the 1960s and 1970s civil rights movement.* The commission's reports and hearings kept the public focused on civil rights,* and its reports and recommendations were often cited by policy makers and courts. Responding to President Lyndon B. Johnson's* request, the commission conducted a study of the effects of de facto segregation* in the nation and possible remedies. Its report was published as *Racial Isolation in the Public Schools* in 1967. The authors used the Coleman Report* and other data to conclude that the negative effects of school segregation* caused by law also applied to school segregation not compelled by law. The commission therefore recommended that the United States establish a racial balance* standard and suggested that it be set so that no school had a majority of black students. The commission also recommended that the federal government provide financial assistance to help states meet this standard. In 1975 and 1976 the commission held hearings on the desegregation process in Louisville, Kentucky; Denver, Colorado; Los Angeles, California; and Boston, Massachusetts.

The Civil Rights Act of 1983 maintained the commission's duties and powers but increased the membership from six to eight, four members appointed by the President and four by Congress. (Previously all six members had been appointed by the President with the advice and consent of the U.S. Senate.) Members serve six-year terms and do not require Senate confirmation.

The activity level of the commission has varied with its membership and the presidential administration's position on school desegregation. Under President Jimmy Carter* the commission played an active role in investigating and describing the problems of school segregation, holding hearings across the United States in cities such as Boston. Under President Ronald Reagan* the commission languished and was accused of mismanagement, spending irregularities, and inaction.

The commission sought an active federal government in civil rights and called for a strong affirmative action* program with the use of racial quotas. This was an anathema to Reagan and his top officials. In 1982 President Reagan tried to change the stance of the commission by replacing its chairman and vice-chairman, Arthur S. Fleming and Stephen Horn, with Clarence M. Pendleton, Jr., and Mary Louise Smith. Reagan tried to replace three other commissioners later in the year, but the nominations never left the Senate Judiciary Committee. A year later President Reagan again tried to replace three members with Democratic nominees who were opposed to busing* and employment quotas. Part of the difficulty was that it was not clear whether the President had the authority to remove commissioners. When the Senate again objected to these nominees, a compromise was reached increasing the number of commissioners from six to eight, four appointed by the President and four by congressional party leaders. The new chair, Clarence Pendleton, was prone to name-calling of civil rights leaders and so angered Reagan appointee John Bunzel that he called for Pendleton's resignation, charging him with clouding a "national debate with an inappropriate bitterness." The chair resigned on December 1, 1986. All the hubbub led to a large reduction in the commission's appropriation from $11.8 to $7.5 million and a reduction in staff from 190 to under 100.

Congress and the Bush administration attempted to revitalize the commission. Two short reauthorization periods were passed, the first in November 1989 for 22 months and the second in November 1991 for three years. The threat of dissolution still hung over the commission's head. In 1993 President Clinton became entangled in a partisan battle over the appointment of the commission's staff director that resulted in a court battle and the appointment of career civil servant Mary Mathews as staff director, but this also had the effect of using up much of the commission's energies on internal matters for most of a year. A reauthorization bill was passed in October 1994 extending the life of the commission for another two years, but Congress failed to reauthorize the commission when this period expired. In 1996 Congress appropriated $8.75 million for the commission to complete its projects. Overall the commission has been an advocate for strong government activity in school desegregation. Its influence has waxed and waned with the administration and the times.

References: John C. Chambers and Bruce P. Waldman, "Interim Report on Performance of the U.S. Commission on Civil Rights during the Clinton Administration," in *New Challenges: The Civil Rights Record of the Clinton Administration Mid-Term*, ed. Corrine M. Yu and William Taylor (Washington, DC: Citizens' Commission on Civil Rights, 1995); Amaker, *Civil Rights and the Reagan Administration* (1988); U.S. Commission on Civil Rights, *Statement on Metropolitan School Desegregation* (Washington, DC: U.S. Government Printing Office, February 1977); U.S. Commission on Civil Rights, *Fulfilling the Letter and Spirit of the Law: Desegregation of the Nation's Public Schools* (Washington, DC: U.S. Government Printing Office, August 1976); U.S. Commission on Civil Rights, *School Desegregation in Louisville and Jefferson County, Kentucky* (Washington, DC: U.S. Government Printing Office, 1976); Foster Rhea Dulles, *The Civil Rights Commission, 1957–1965* (Lansing: Michigan State University Press, 1968).

U.S. CONSTITUTION. Document that is the basis for the government and governance of the United States of America and the basis for school desegregation* law in the United States. The U.S. Constitution, adopted by the federal constitutional convention in Philadelphia on September 17, 1787, and subsequently ratified by the 13 states, is the oldest written constitution in the world. The Constitution provides the legal foundation for the nation's federal system of government and for the three branches of government—executive, legislative, and judicial. Amendments to the Constitution may be proposed by a vote of two-thirds of the House and the Senate or by a convention called by Congress upon the request of two-thirds of the states. Three-fourths of the state legislatures (or state conventions) must ratify any amendment for passage.

The Fourteenth Amendment* to the Constitution, passed after the Civil War, forbids states to deny any individual "life, liberty, or property without due process of law" or to "deny to any person within its jurisdiction the equal protection of the laws." This amendment has been the basis for the establishment of school desegregation law in the United States.

References: John R. Vile, *A Companion to the United States Constitution and Its Amendments* (Westport, CT: Praeger Publishers, 1997); *Britannica Online* (1996); Schwartz, *A History of the Supreme Court* (1993); Yudof et al., *Kirp and Yudof's Educational Policy and the Law* (1987).

U.S. COURTS OF APPEALS. *See* **Courts of Appeals**.

U.S. DEPARTMENT OF EDUCATION. *See* **Department of Education**.

U.S. DEPARTMENT OF HEALTH, EDUCATION, AND WELFARE (DHEW). *See* **Department of Health, Education, and Welfare (HEW).**

U.S. DEPARTMENT OF JUSTICE. *See* **Department of Justice.**

U.S. DISTRICT COURTS. *See* **District Courts.**

U.S. OFFICE OF EDUCATION. *See* **Office of Education.**

U.S. SUPREME COURT. The U.S. Supreme Court is the highest appeals court in the judicial branch of government in the United States, standing above the Courts of Appeals* and District Courts*; the Supreme Court interprets the U.S. Constitution* as well as federal law and regulations. The Court has used its authority to make the final decision on key school segregation* cases heard in lower federal courts such as *Brown v. Board of Education.** The U.S. Supreme Court has played a crucial role in school segregation and school desegregation.* Among its most significant decisions are *Plessy v. Ferguson** (1896), *Brown v. Board of Education* (1954), *Green** (1968), *Swann** (1971), and *Milliken v. Bradley I** (1974) and *II** (1978).

Cases may be brought to the Supreme Court by writ of certiorari and by appeal. The Supreme Court may review a case or decide not to review a case. When it declines to grant the writ, the Court leaves the decision below unaltered.

The Warren Court* unanimously ruled that segregation in public schools was a violation of the equal protection clause* of the Fourteenth Amendment* to the U.S. Constitution and that states should proceed to desegregate their schools "with all deliberate speed.*" The Warren Court, however, did not play an active role in the decade following the *Brown* decisions. The Burger Court* played a major role in setting the parameters for implementation of the *Brown* decisions. Its *Swann* decision led to the busing of students throughout the South* to achieve school desegregation, while its *Milliken I* decision set a major barrier to desegregating city school districts with their suburban counterparts. The Rehnquist Court* has shaped the meaning of unitary system* in indicating what standards school districts must meet to have the school desegregation court order lifted.

The U.S. Constitution* established the Supreme Court as the pinnacle of the third branch of government, adding the judicial branch to the executive and legislative branches. The Court is chaired by the Chief Justice and now has an additional eight associate justices. Congress may determine the number of justices, and the number was increased from five in 1789 through a number of different numbers to eight in 1869. All are nominated by the President and must be confirmed by a majority vote of the Senate. The justices can only be removed by impeachment. A quorum is six justices, and decisions are reached by a majority.

References: Abraham and Perry, *Freedom and the Court* (1994); Lee Epstein, Jeffrey A. Segal, Harold J. Spaeth, and Thomas G. Walker, *The Supreme Court Compendium: Data, Decisions, and Developments* (Washington, DC: Congressional Quarterly, 1994); Schwartz, *A History of the Supreme Court* (1993); Hall, *Oxford Companion* (1992); Witt, *Congressional Quarterly's Guide to the U.S. Supreme Court* (1989); Wasby, D'Amato, and Metrailer, *Desegregation from Brown to Alexander* (1977).

UNITED STATES V. FORDICE, 505 U.S. 717 (1992). U.S. Supreme Court* decision (8–1) that states must eliminate the vestiges of de jure segregation* from their colleges and universities; it is insufficient just to operate a racially neutral system. This was the first higher-education desegregation case to reach the U.S. Supreme Court since *Brown** (1954).

In 1975 a group of blacks in Mississippi (Black Mississippians' Council on Higher Education, Jake Ayers, first plaintiff) sued the state in U.S. District Court* requesting equity in the higher-education system, including more funding for the state's three historically black colleges. The state operated eight higher-education institutions in total, three comprehensive universities (University of Mississippi, Mississippi State University, University of Southern Mississippi), four regional universities (historically black Alcorn State and Mississippi Valley State and historically white Delta State and Mississippi University for Women), and one urban university: (Jackson State). They called for enforcement of Title VI of the Civil Rights Act of 1964,* noting that Mississippi was an "*Adams* State," which had been found to have never desegregated its university system in the *Adams** (1973) decision. Originally titled *Ayers v. Waller*, then the title changed as governors changed: *Ayers v. Allain, Ayers v. Mabus*, and then *Ayers v. Fordice*; the case ultimately became *United States v. Fordice*. The two parties negotiated for 12 years without a final settlement. After a 1987 trial the District Court concluded that no constitutional violation existed because the state's actions were racially neutral, were developed and implemented in good faith, and did not substantially contribute to the racial identification of the schools. The decision was then affirmed by the Fifth Circuit Court of Appeals.*

On appeal to the U.S. Supreme Court the decision was overturned. The Court concluded that the wrong standard had been applied. Since it was possible that race-neutral policies might be reinforcing policies that had been segregative in original intent and effect, these policies also had to be examined. The Court stated, "If policies traceable to the de jure system are still in force and have discriminatory effects, those policies . . . must be reformed to the extent practicable and consistent with sound educational practices." The Court identified four areas where this appeared to be true: admissions policies, program duplication, mission statements, and the number of institutions. It suggested that the state consider closing or merging some of the eight separate institutions that remained from the de jure past. The Court criticized the admissions policies of the state, which emphasized standardized tests that disproportionately excluded blacks from the white colleges and university.

The decision is significant for several reasons. It recognized that segregation continues to play a role in states where colleges and universities were segregated by law. Second, it reinforced the notion that the *Brown* decision also applies to postsecondary education. Third, the Supreme Court rejected race-neutral policies as a sufficient remedy in formerly de jure segregated states. States that had de jure segregated university systems have the affirmative obligation to desegregate their higher-education institutions. Fourth, the decision called for remedies "consistent with sound educational practices," thus giving some leeway to courts and educators. Several issues remained open, however. How can a policy that may be race neutral today be traced back to a policy from past segregation? In 1994 the Department of Education* indicated that this court decision will be used to evaluate the compliance of states that have expired higher education desegregation plans (Florida, Kentucky, Maryland, Pennsylvania, Texas, and Virginia).

There is some fear that this decision imperils historically black colleges and universities.* If the Court applied the same standard to higher-education desegregation that it applied to elementary and secondary education, then HBCUs would be viewed as vestiges of a dual system* and would need to be eliminated, just as black schools were closed after *Brown*. This is viewed as ironic, since HBCUs have remained open to blacks (and whites) and have served as a major institutional force for higher learning for black students who lacked alternatives. Moreover, Jake Ayers and the other plaintiffs sought an upgrading of the three HBCUs, not admission to white schools in the state.

The state responded to the Supreme Court's ruling with a desegregation plan to close one of its three HBCUs and combine another with a predominantly white state university. In May 1994 Mississippi was back in federal court to defend its decision to close the historically black Mississippi Valley State University and merge it with white Delta State University. Mississippi Valley State has 7 whites enrolled among its 2,300 students in its spartan, flat-roofed buildings, while 35 miles away in Delta State University one-quarter of the 4,000 students are black and attend classes on a campus with manicured quadrangles and gabled buildings. Mississippi also advocated merging Mississippi University for Women with Mississippi State University. The return of *United States v. Fordice* was being fought out in Oxford, Mississippi, and a critical issue was the role of HBCUs in the state system.

In March 1995 the federal judge, Neal Biggers, Jr., ruled that the state should not close Mississippi Valley State or historically white universities but should spend $30 million to upgrade the three historically black universities. The judge also ordered that the different admission standards for black and white campuses be changed to one single standard for all of the eight state institutions. The black institutions had lower admissions requirements than the white schools; if the new standards had been in effect in 1994–1995, for example, almost half of Mississippi Valley's students would have fallen into the conditional admissions category. The U.S. Supreme Court has refused to stay Bigger's order or, as per their January 20, 1998 decision, hear an appeal of his order.

References: "The Historically Black Colleges and Universities: A Future in the Balance," report in *Academe* 81, no. 1 (January–February 1995): 49–57 (Washington, DC: American Association of University Professors, Committee L on the Historically Black Institutions and the Status of Minorities in the Profession); *Redeeming the American Promise*, Report of the Panel on Educational Opportunity and Postsecondary Desegregation, (Atlanta, GA: Southern Education Foundation, 1995); Ronald Smothers, "Mississippi's University System Going on Trial," *New York Times*, May 9, 1994, A10; Stefkovich and Leas, "A Legal History of Desegregation in Higher Education" (1994); Leland Ware, "Will There Be a 'Different World' after *Fordice*?" *Academe* 80, no. 3 (May/June 1994): 6–11.

UNITED STATES V. JEFFERSON COUNTY BOARD OF EDUCATION,

372 F.2d 836 (1966). U.S. Fifth Circuit Court of Appeals* decision written by Judge John Minor Wisdom* that had a major effect on the South* and the thinking of the U.S. Supreme Court* and countered the *Briggs** Dictum (1955) made by the Fourth Circuit Court of Appeals. This case consolidated seven cases from Alabama and Louisiana where the school districts had made no progress desegregating the schools 11 years after the 1954 *Brown** decision. (At that time the Fifth Circuit included Texas, Louisiana, Alabama, Georgia, and Florida.) Judge John Minor Wisdom set out new, tough standards for school districts to desegregate based on Department of Health, Education, and Welfare* (HEW) guidelines. His decision was affirmed 8–4 by a panel of judges from the circuit. The key element of his decision was that in states where students had been segregated by law, the court required that a systemwide policy of integration* be established. This decision was a rejection of the *Briggs* Dictum and called for affirmative action* to eliminate racially identifiable schools, that is, "an absolute duty to integrate." Judge Wisdom's holding that "*the only adequate redress for a previously overt system-wide policy of segregation directed against Negroes as a collective entity is a system-wide policy of integration*" was italicized for emphasis. This decision was seen as a turning point or critical case by liberals and conservatives. Wilkinson concludes that "Wisdom transformed the face of school desegregation* law" (1979:111). Thus the courts and the federal government began working in tandem to desegregate the schools of the South.

The early HEW guidelines enforcing the Civil Rights Act of 1964* allowed school districts to offer a court-accepted school desegregation plan* as meeting the requirement for nondiscrimination. Many southern districts had very limited plans, often freedom-of-choice* plans, accepted by the District Court but leading to no real desegregation. This decision required District Courts to require plans that established a pace of school desegregation at least as fast as HEW was now requiring.

The language of the Civil Rights Act of 1964 barring the use of federal funds to pay for racial balance* was interpreted as banning the use of such funds for overcoming racial imbalance* not righting a constitutional wrong of de jure* segregated schools. Thus this decision offered a rationale for the federal courts to order desegregation plans that did more than establish race-neutral, and often ineffective, desegregation plans. In doing so it changed the power of the courts.

References: Armor, *Forced Justice* (1995); Wolters, *The Burden of Brown* (1984); Wilkinson, *From Brown to Bakke* (1979); Orfield, *Must We Bus?* (1978); Frank T. Read, "Judicial Evolution of the Law of School Integration since *Brown v. Board of Education*," in *The Courts, Social Science, and School Desegregation*, Part 1, ed. Betsy Levin and Willis D. Hawley, School of Law, Duke University, 39 (Winter 1975): 7–49.

UNITED STATES V. LOUISIANA, 692 F. Supp. 642 (1988); C.A. No. 80–3300 (1994). Negotiated settlement of the higher-education desegregation* case in Louisiana and the first post-*Fordice** (1992) remedy outside of Mississippi. The settlement includes $65 million in previously deferred capital improvements to be spent on historically black college and university* campuses; up to $58 million for new programs at HBCUs in the next ten years; additional recruitment of minorities, especially at the graduate level, by traditionally white institutions; altering admissions criteria; the establishment of a new community college that would have articulation agreements with the present four-year institutions; and the consideration of possible reduction in program duplication by geographically close, previously segregated institutions. Thus the agreement addresses both the concern for the maintenance and enhancement of HBCUs and the desegregation of previously segregated institutions.

The case began in 1969 when the U.S. Department of Health, Education, and Welfare* (HEW) tried to force the state to end its dual system* of higher education. Having failed to negotiate a satisfactory plan, five years later HEW turned the case over to the Department of Justice* to bring suit. In September 1981 the state and the Justice Department agreed to a consent decree* that maintained the state's HBCUs but did try to increase the number of whites at HBCUs and blacks at white higher-education institutions. But at the end of the term of the six-year agreement segregation had, if anything, increased. The case went back to court, and after the Fifth Circuit Court of Appeals* reviewed the problems with the consent decree, the District Court* ordered the merger of Louisiana State Law School and Southern University Law School as well as the consolidation of the state's three boards of higher education. In November 1994, however, the parties to the suit agreed to a settlement, as outlined previously, that maintained the three governing boards (one for the historically black Southern University System, one for the Louisiana State University System, and a third for all other state institutions).

References: "Consent Decrees," in *Encyclopedia of African-American Education* ed. Jones-Wilson et al. (1996), 117–19; Panel on Educational Opportunity and Postsecondary Desegregation, *Redeeming the American Promise* (Atlanta, GA: Southern Education Foundation, 1995); James J. Presage and Jewel L. Presage, "The Consent Decree as a

Tool for Desegregation in Higher Education," in *Black Education*, ed. Smith and Chunn (1989), 158–75; Raphael Cassimere, Jr., *"Plessy* Revisited: Louisiana's Separate and Unequal University System," *Equity and Excellence* 24, no. 1 (Fall 1988): 12–21.

UNITED STATES V. SCOTLAND NECK BOARD OF EDUCATION, 407
U.S. 484 (1972). U.S. Supreme Court* decision that disallowed the formation of a new school district from part of a desegregating school district to avoid school desegregation.* Halifax County, North Carolina, was under a school desegregation order, but by 1968, 99 percent of whites attended all-white schools and 97 percent of the black students were attending all-black schools. The federal government called upon the county to take a more vigorous approach to school desegregation in 1968. In January 1969 the state legislature passed a bill allowing Scotland Neck to withdraw from the Halifax County school district to form an all-white district. The U.S. Supreme Court unanimously decided that the plan was unconstitutional because it interfered with the desegregation* of the county schools.

References: Nowak and Rotunda, *Constitutional Law* (1995); Zirkel, Richardson, and Goldberg, *A Digest of Supreme Court Decisions Affecting Education* (1995); Grossman, *The ABC-CLIO Companion to the Civil Rights Movement* (1993); Witt, *Congressional Quarterly's Guide to the U.S. Supreme Court* (1989).

UNITED STATES V. YONKERS BOARD OF EDUCATION, 837 F.2d 1181
(2nd Cir. 1987). U.S. Court of Appeals* decision upholding U.S. District Court* Judge Leonard B. Sand's ruling linking housing and school segregation* in Yonkers, New York. The U.S. District Court had accepted the argument of the Yonkers NAACP* and the U.S. Department of Justice* that the concentration of public housing segregation in one area of Yonkers had led to school segregation within the Yonkers School District. As a result, the Yonkers City Council was ordered to build publicly subsidized housing in other areas of the city, and the school district was required to desegregate its schools.

Located north of New York City, in 1980 Yonkers was New York's fourth-largest city, with a population of almost 200,000. In 1980 blacks accounted for 18.8 percent of the city's population and over one-third of the city's school enrollment. In the 1970s the city had built subsidized housing projects in one of three distinct sections of the city, the "Southwest," near a declining downtown harmed by suburban shopping malls. In the years ahead more than 80 percent of the tenants who chose to live in this housing were black. During the same period the white population of this area declined. The school district had maintained a neighborhood school plan,* and the disparate racial composition across the city was therefore tied to a great disparity in the percentage of blacks and whites across the schools.

On December 1, 1980, the Civil Rights Division* of the Department of Justice* under President Jimmy Carter,* who had recently been defeated for reelection, filed its first suit linking housing and school discrimination.* The suit was a response to a Yonkers NAACP complaint filed earlier in the year charging that the city had intentionally segregated its public housing and schools. U.S. District Court Judge Leonard B. Sand, in a detailed 665-page opinion, held that the city had "illegally and intentionally" maintained segregated public housing projects as well as segregated public schools. The judge found that the siting of the public housing had helped to cause segregated schools. Twenty-seven housing projects for families were approved during the time period in question, all but one in a mile-and-a-half-square section in the southwest area of the city. The concern for "political feasibility" of siting helped to maintain segregated housing, which was reinforced by the school board's desire to maintain segregated schools. Included in the evidence was the admission from city council members representing the white areas of the city that their constituents sought to keep their schools free from too many minority children. In December 1987 the three-judge panel from the Second Circuit Court of Appeals affirmed Sand's judgment, and the U.S. Supreme Court* refused to hear an appeal in its June 14, 1988, ruling.

The remedy Judge Sand required included both a public housing component, the building of 200 low-income housing units initially in east Yonkers and plans for 800 more units over time, and a schools component, a plan that would change attendance zones, close some schools and require the building of others, and create or expand twenty magnet-school* programs. The two plans met with strong white resistance. By 1993 the white enrollment in Yonkers had been halved. The first 200 housing units were not opened until 1992, and the additional 800 units remained in legal limbo. The Yonkers case is most significant because it was the first time that a federal court accepted the argument that housing segregation had led to school segregation.

References: "*U.S. v. Yonkers Board of Education,*" in *Encyclopedia of African-American Education,* ed. Jones-Wilson et al. (1996), 489–90; Wolters, *Right Turn* (1996); Judith L. Failer, Anna Harvey, and Jennifer Hochschild, "Only One Oar in the Water: The Political Failure of Desegregation in Yonkers, New York," *Educational Policy* 7, no. 3 (September 1993): 276–96; Marcia Marker Feld, "The Yonkers Case and Its Implications for the Teaching and Practice of Planning," *Journal of Planning Education and Research* 8, no. 3 (Summer 1989): 169–75.

UNIVERSITY OF MARYLAND V. MURRAY. *See Pearson v. Murray.*

V

VINSON, FREDERICK MOORE (born January 22, 1890, Louisa, Kentucky–
died September 8, 1953, Washington, D.C.). Thirteenth Chief Justice of the U.S.
Supreme Court* who authored the Court's unanimous *McLaurin** (1950) and
Sweatt* (1950) decisions that led to the admittance of blacks to graduate and
professional schools and established that equality had to be real if separation
was required, but did not directly change the separate but equal doctrine* of
Plessy v. Ferguson* (1896). Nominated by President Harry Truman* while he
served as Secretary of the Treasury, Vinson died suddenly after the Court had
heard arguments on the *Brown* (1954 and 1955) cases but before the scheduled
reargument on the history of the Fourteenth Amendment.*

Vinson was the son of a small-town jailkeeper and was actually born in the
jail building that housed his parents' apartment. He completed his undergraduate
and law-school work at Centre College while showing a flair for math. He
practiced law for a decade in and around his hometown. In 1924 he was elected
to Congress as a Democrat and served a total of six terms. In Congress he was
recognized for his legislative skills and common sense as well as his support
for labor. Vinson was appointed to the U.S. Court of Appeals* in 1938 and then
served as chief judge of an emergency appeals court reviewing the decisions of
the wartime Office of Price Administration. He did his job so well that the
President, Franklin Delano Roosevelt, asked him to serve as Director of Economic Stabilization, "about the toughest job in town," according to Kluger
(1975:245). He served President Truman as an advisor and cabinet secretary.
Truman named Vinson to replace Chief Justice Harlan Stone when he died,
hoping that Vinson would restore tranquillity to the Court, which had been the

subject of tremendous political pressure and conflict under President Franklin Delano Roosevelt. But the Court remained split, and many saw Vinson as too close to government and too unconcerned about civil liberties.

Works about: *Britannica Online* (1996); Kluger, *Simple Justice* (1975); *Current Biography 1943* (New York: H. W. Wilson Company, 1944), 793–96.

VOLUNTARY PLAN. A school desegregation plan* under which students and their parents have a choice about where the student will attend school. A school desegregation plan may be either a mandatory plan* or a voluntary plan. School desegregation plans vary by the extent of parent choice over the school assignment, including whether the parent may keep his or her child in a neighborhood school.* This definition refers to parental choice and not the source of the plan, that is, whether it is court ordered or developed by a school board.

Voluntary plans normally allow pupils to remain in their neighborhood school or to transfer out if space is available in the alternative school and if the move does not hurt the racial balance* at the alternative school. Several techniques utilized in voluntary plans are open enrollment,* freedom of choice,* majority-to-minority transfers,* and magnet schools.* Under open enrollment, students can transfer to any school with available space. Plans based on this technique have not been viewed favorably by the courts because of questions about their effectiveness in achieving school desegregation.* Majority-to-minority (M-to-M) transfers allow a student to transfer from a school where the student is in the majority to one where the student is in the minority. Voluntary plans based on magnet schools allow and encourage students to move from their neighborhood schools* to take advantage of specialized curricula, smaller class sizes, and extra resource teachers at magnet schools. Voluntary plans usually combine these techniques, sometimes with limited mandatory techniques such as clustering,* to achieve a comprehensive plan. Controlled-choice plans* have a voluntary component with a mandatory backup.

School desegregation plans may also be voluntary in the sense that they are not court ordered, that is, they are voluntarily adopted by a school board. School districts such as Berkeley, California, and Seattle, Washington, have adopted school desegregation plans voluntarily, but the plans have mandatory student assignments.

References: Rossell, ''The Convergence of Black and White Attitudes on School Desegregation Issues during the Four Decade Evolution of the Plans'' (January 1995); Fife, *Desegregation in American Schools* (1992); Rossell, *The Carrot or the Stick for School Desegregation Policy* (1990).

W

WALLACE, GEORGE CORLEY (born August 25, 1919, Clio, Alabama). Governor of Alabama for four terms who first received national attention for "standing in the schoolhouse door" in Alabama in 1963 in an attempt to halt the implementation of the desegregation* of the University of Alabama. Wallace was a farmer's son who worked his way through the University of Alabama Law School and earned an LL.B. in 1942. After serving in World War II, Wallace became the assistant attorney general of the state of Alabama in 1946 and was then elected for two terms to the state legislature. As judge of the Third Judicial Circuit of Alabama from 1953 to 1959, Wallace earned a reputation as the "Fighting Judge" for defying the U.S. Commission on Civil Rights'* investigation of black voting rights.

In 1948 Wallace led the fight against a strong civil rights* plank at the Democratic National Convention, receiving national exposure. He was in solo legal practice from 1958 to 1962. He ran unsuccessfully for the Alabama governorship in 1958, but was victorious in his second attempt in 1962, focusing on segregation* and economic issues.

In his inauguration speech on January 14, 1963, Governor Wallace declared, "In the name of the greatest people that ever trod the earth, I draw the line in the dust and toss the gauntlet before the feet of tyranny . . . and I say . . . segregation now . . . segregation tomorrow . . . segregation forever." Within a year of his victory (June 13, 1963) he kept his pledge to "stand in the schoolhouse door" to stop black students from enrolling at the University of Alabama, and thus "stand in the doorway" became a symbol of southern resistance to the

*Brown** school desegregation decision and federal enforcement. In February 1956 Autherine Lucy started at the University of Alabama but was suspended "for her own safety" when a mob of 1,000 congregated. A federal judge ordered her readmitted, but she was expelled after she accused the university of complicity in the mob action. In June 1963 President John F. Kennedy* issued a proclamation ordering Governor Wallace to obey a court order to admit two black students (Vivian Malone and James A. Hood) to the University of Alabama. Deputy Assistant Attorney General Nicholas Katzenbach accompanied the two students. Governor Wallace blocked the doorway as the two students tried to enter the university building. President Kennedy federalized the Alabama National Guard. Later in the day the students returned with 100 guardsmen. Wallace again stood in the doorway, read a protest statement, but then stepped aside. Wallace also closed the Tuskegee High School to stop public school desegregation.*

In 1968 George Wallace ran for President on the American Independent party ticket and won 46 electoral votes. He campaigned again four years later, this time for the Democratic nomination. Running against busing,* Wallace won the Florida Democratic primary with 42 percent of the vote, "sending a message" to Congress and the President about the public's concern about busing. On May 15, 1972, Wallace was paralyzed and confined to a wheelchair after an assassination attempt in Laurel, Maryland. He campaigned for the Democratic party nomination in 1976. In 1982 Wallace, despite once exclaiming, "Segregation now, segregation tomorrow, segregation forever," renounced his previous segregationist policies and won a fourth term with substantial support from black voters. Thus Wallace served as governor for four terms (1963–1966, 1971–1974, 1975–1978, and 1983–1986). In 1966, when George Wallace was ineligible to run for governor, Lurleen, his wife, won election. She died in 1968 without completing her term.

In 1987 Wallace's poor health forced him to retire from politics. He then served as the chair of the public administration program at Troy State University, Montgomery, from 1987 to 1992. In October 1996 Wallace apologized to Vivian Malone Jones, who with James Hood had been one of the two black students Wallace had tried to prevent from registering at the University of Alabama 33 years earlier. Wallace, suffering from Parkinson's disease and paralysis, presented the Lurleen B. Wallace Award of Courage, named after his wife, to Jones, a recent Environmental Protection Agency retiree. The award recognizes women who have made improvements in the state. Wilhoit (1978) describes Wallace as a "charismatic demagogue," like an old "hell-fire" evangelist who railed against not sin and the devil but the NAACP,* bureaucrats, integrationists, and pseudointellectuals who "couldn't park a bicycle."

Works about: *Britannica Online* (1996); Stephen Lesher, *George Wallace: American Populist* (Reading, MA: Addison-Wesley, 1994); *Who's Who in America* (Chicago: Reed Reference Publishing, 1994), 3823; E. Culpepper Clark, *The Schoolhouse Door: Segre-*

gation's Last Stand at the University of Alabama (New York: Oxford University Press, (1993); Marcus and Stickney, Race and Education (1981); Wilhoit, The Politics of Massive Resistance (1973); Marshall Frady, Wallace (New York: World Publishing, 1968).

WARREN, EARL (born May 19, 1891, Los Angeles, California–died July 9, 1974, Washington, D.C.). Fourteenth Chief Justice of the U.S. Supreme Court* during the period of major changes in constitutional law in race relations* and school desegregation*; author of the 1954 and 1955 Brown v. Board of Education* decisions.

The son of a railroad worker, Warren worked his way through the University of California at Berkeley, graduating in 1912, and then earned a law degree in 1914 from its law school. Thereafter he practiced law and became vice president of the Alameda County Bar Association. Warren was drafted as a private in the infantry during World War I and exited as a first lieutenant, although he never left the United States. Warren became deputy city attorney in Oakland in 1919 and then deputy district attorney of Alameda County (in which Oakland is located). By 1925 he was elected district attorney, and he held this position until 1938. He led an anticorruption campaign responsible for annoying the Ku Klux Klan* and removing the mayor of Oakland and all but one city councilman from office. For this he received much national publicity, including an article in the Saturday Evening Post.

Warren became active in Republican party affairs, serving as a delegate to the Republican National Convention in 1932, chairman of the Republican State Central Committee from 1934 to 1936, and Republican National Committeeman until 1940. In 1938 he was elected state attorney general on the Republican ticket, despite the Democratic victory in the governorship race. His stint as attorney general got mixed reviews as he led efforts to prosecute saboteurs and suggested that the Japanese population on the West Coast was a menace to aircraft plants while blocking the nomination of a distinguished international scholar to the state Supreme Court.

Warren ran in both primaries of both parties in the race for governor in 1942, winning the Republican but just missing out on the Democratic nomination. He won the state office despite the almost 2–1 Democratic ratio in registrations. As governor, Warren was able to reduce taxes, carry out campaign pledges, and appoint good people from both parties. Ironically, while he was governor, Warren made clear his opposition to centralization of power in the U.S. government; he was anxious to protect states' rights and favored the return of private enterprise. In 1944 he ruled himself out for the vice-presidential nomination under Republican nominee Thomas E. Dewey. He did make the keynote speech at the convention.

Warren was appointed by President Dwight D. Eisenhower* to be the Chief Justice in 1953 and was confirmed by the Senate on March 1, 1954. He presided over the Court when it opened its term in the fall of 1953. As Chief Justice of the U.S. Supreme Court, Warren forged a consensus to outlaw school segregation* in the court's 1954 *Brown v. Board of Education* decision and reject the separate but equal* principle from the 1896 *Plessy** decision on which the Court had relied for over half a century. He began by quizzing his fellow jurists about the issues the cases raised but remaining circumspect about his own opinions. He stressed the need to reach a unanimous position on important cases and worked to avoid even concurring opinions on this case. He gave special attention to the three justices on the Supreme Court who represented states with segregated school systems: Justices Hugo Black of Alabama, Stanley Reed of Kentucky, and Tom Clark of Texas. According to White (1982), when he did state his views, he linked support for *Plessy* to a belief that blacks were inferior to whites. Thus he was discreetly challenging any justices who supported segregation* to deal with the issue of racial prejudice.* He also sought an opinion that would not establish blame but only change. Chief Justice Warren also separated the principle at stake in the decision from the implementation of the decision to convince the reluctant justices to support a unanimous opinion. He was quite concerned about how a court decision to eliminate segregated schools could be implemented.

At 12:52 P.M. on May 17, 1954, Chief Justice Earl Warren read the 11-page opinion to the hushed courtroom. "We unanimously conclude that in the field of public education the doctrine of 'separate but equal' has no place." One year later he read the implementation decision, that school desegregation must be carried out with "all deliberate speed.*"

In November 1963 President Lyndon B. Johnson* named Warren chairman of a commission to investigate the assassination of President John F. Kennedy.* Warren retired from the Court in 1969.

Earl Warren wrote or took part in landmark decisions beyond the *Brown* decisions, including establishing rights of defendants in criminal cases and mandating legislative reapportionment consistent with the "one man, one vote" principle. His leadership is generally recognized as critical to the unanimous *Brown* decision, the Warren Court,* and the nation, but he also received much criticism for his judicial activism.

Works about: Hall, *Oxford Companion* (1992); G. Edward White, *Earl Warren: A Public Life* (1982); Pollack, *Earl Warren* (1979); John Downing Weaver, *Warren, the Man, the Court, the Era* (Boston: Little, Brown, 1967); *Current Biography Yearbook 1944*, 716–719, and *1974*, 471 (New York: H. W. Wilson Company).

Works by: *The Memoirs of Earl Warren* (Garden City, NY: Doubleday, 1977).

WARREN COURT. The U.S. Supreme Court* under the leadership of Chief Justice Earl Warren* from 1953 to 1969 that declared school segregation* unconstitutional in the *Brown v. Board of Education** decision in 1954. The Warren Court was a liberal and activist court, rejecting the concepts of judicial restraint and deference to the legislature while strongly enforcing personal rights and equality. The Warren Court made landmark decisions not only on school desegregation* but also on reapportionment of state legislatures and criminal justice procedure.

According to Tushnet (1993:2), "The Warren Court implemented the modern liberal agenda, enforcing norms of fair treatment and racial equality that, in their core meanings, are no longer contested in American society." The Court under Chief Justice Fred Vinson* had postponed deciding *Brown* and the related cases and would have split in any decision. Under Warren, who replaced Chief Justice Vinson after his death on September 8, 1953, the Court made the critical decision and did so unanimously as Warren forged a consensus. Warren, a moderate conservative politician and governor of California, was not a legal scholar, but he was a superb leader of the Court. As Bernard Schwartz (1993) has written, his legacy was in his decisions, not his opinions. But during the period from 1954 to 1962 the Warren Court was not very active or liberal. The *Cooper v. Aaron* (1958) decision was the only school desegregation case decided by the Court from 1955 to 1963. The Court was constrained by Justices Felix Frankfurter, a strong advocate of judicial restraint, and Charles E. Whittaker, and it was not until they were both replaced (by Arthur Goldberg and Byron White) that the Court took on a different cast. Thus Tushnet argues that the "real" Warren Court spans the years from 1962 to 1969, when Earl Warren retired from the Court. Tushnet reasons that the Warren Court actually lasted after Earl Warren retired from the office of Chief Justice.

The members of the Warren Court included the following justices in 1954, the year of the historic *Brown* decision:

Hugo L. Black (1937–1971, appointed by President Franklin D. Roosevelt)

Stanley F. Reed (1938–1957, appointed by President Roosevelt)

Felix Frankfurter (1939–1962, appointed by President Roosevelt)

William O. Douglas (1939–1975, appointed by President Roosevelt)

Robert H. Jackson (1941–1954, appointed by President Roosevelt)

Harold H. Burton (1945–1958, appointed by President Harry S. Truman*)

Tom C. Clark (1949–1967, appointed by President Truman)

Sherman Minton (1949–1956, appointed by President Truman)

Before Warren's retirement in 1969 the following justices also served:

John Marshall Harlan (1955–1971, appointed by President Dwight D. Eisenhower*)

William J. Brennan, Jr.* (1956–1990, appointed by President Eisenhower)

Charles E. Whittaker (1957–1962, appointed by President Eisenhower)

Potter Stewart (1958–1981, appointed by President Eisenhower)

Byron R. White (1962–1993, appointed by President John F. Kennedy*)

Arthur J. Goldberg (1962–1965, appointed by President Kennedy)

Abe Fortas (1965–1969, appointed by President Lyndon B. Johnson*)

Thurgood Marshall* (1967–1991, appointed by President Johnson)

In his comprehensive history of the Supreme Court Bernard Schwartz calls the time of the Warren Court "the second great creative period" in American public law, joining the time of the Marshall Court (1801–1835). The Warren Court was followed by the Burger Court.*

References: Arnold S. Rice, *The Warren Court, 1954–1969* (Danbury, CT: Grolier Educational Corporation, 1995); Schwartz, *A History of the Supreme Court* (1993); Tushnet, *The Warren Court in Historical and Political Perspective* (1993); Leonard Williams Levy, ed., *The Supreme Court under Earl Warren* (New York: Quadrangle Books, 1972); H. C. Hudgins, Jr., *The Warren Court and the Public Schools: An Analysis of Landmark Supreme Court Decisions* (Danville, IL: Interstate Printers and Publishers, 1970).

WASHINGTON, BOOKER TALIAFERRO (born April 5, 1856, Franklin County, Virginia–died November 14, 1915, Tuskegee, Alabama). The most influential spokesman for blacks from 1895 to 1915; major advocate of industrial education for blacks and the first president and principal developer of the Tuskegee Institute, which he led for 34 years. Booker T. Washington was born as a slave in rural Virginia five years before the Civil War began. By age nine he was no longer a slave and was working in a salt furnace and then a salt mine. He attended the Hampton Normal and Agricultural Institute at age 16, working as a janitor to pay his way. At Hampton he was influenced by the school's founder, General Samuel C. Armstrong, a white New Englander who became a father figure to Washington. Armstrong believed that it was the responsibility of the superior white race to rule the inferior darker races until they became civilized. At Hampton, Armstrong sought to build strong moral and Christian principles in his students, and therefore the curriculum stressed the dignity of human labor, a personal sense of responsibility in each student, and manual training. Washington graduated in 1875, having adopted these principles.

Washington attended Wayland Seminary in Washington, D.C., in 1878. In 1879 he went back to Hampton to teach night school. In May 1881 Armstrong recommended Washington to head a new school in Tuskegee, Alabama. Washington modeled the Tuskegee Normal and Industrial Institute after Hampton. Students were required to work making bricks, building buildings, and raising food for the school. Their studies included a trade as well as academic subjects. Washington was able to raise an endowment from local white leaders and through speaking tours.

Washington professed what whites wanted to hear and therefore became a popular speaker in the South.* At a speech before the Cotton States and International Exposition held in Atlanta in 1895 (delivered on September 18, 1895, and later called the Atlanta Compromise Address* by its critics), Washington stated, "It is at the bottom of life we must begin, and not at the top." Progress would come not from agitation but from severe and constant struggle. He called upon blacks to accept segregation* in return for progress in economic opportunity. He appealed to whites on the basis of self-interest, reminding them that one-third of the South's population was black and the region's prosperity depended in part on their condition. He believed in "the values of patience, enterprise, and thrift" (*Britannica Online*) and in education as a utilitarian venture.

In 1901 Washington published *Up from Slavery*, further enhancing his popularity with whites. While he became one of the most powerful men in the region as others sought his advice, his visit to the White House in 1901 was greeted by some with protest. His ideas were opposed by W.E.B. Du Bois* and other black leaders, who in 1905 formed the Niagara Movement* as an alternative to Washington's leadership.

While Washington influenced the philosophy and practice of black education, helped to develop and support black institutions, and developed Tuskegee, his legacy is mixed. Some view him as selling out to the white oppression of the times and accommodating too much to racism* and segregation, while others see him as a leader in black nationalism,* self-help ideology, and black institutions. He received honorary degrees from Harvard University (1896) and Dartmouth College (1901).

Works about: Jones-Wilson et al., *Encyclopedia of African-American Education* (1996); *Britannica Online* (1996); Michael W. Williams, *The African American Encyclopedia* (1993), 1656–57; Marcus and Stickney, *Race and Education* (1981).

Works by: *The Future of the American Negro* (Boston: Small, Maynard, and Co., 1899); *Up from Slavery* (Garden City, NY: Sun Dial Press, 1937 [1901]); *A New Negro for a New Century* (New York: Arno Press, 1969 [1900]).

WASHINGTON V. DAVIS, 426 U.S. 229 (1976). U.S. Supreme Court* ruling that policies must be intentionally discriminatory and have a racially disproportionate impact in order to be unconstitutional. The case concerned police department personnel tests but has been applied to school desegregation* cases.

This case focused on discrimination* in police employment. The verbal-skills test ("Test 21") to screen applicants to the Metropolitan Police Department in the city of Washington, D.C., was challenged by two unsuccessful black applicants on the grounds that the test was discriminatory and therefore a violation of the equal protection clause* of the Fourteenth Amendment.* The plaintiffs claimed that blacks failed the test at a higher rate than whites. (Four times as many blacks as whites failed the test.) They made no claim about the intent of the test.

The U.S. District Court* held for the police department, concluding that the differential failure rates shifted the burden of proof* on the reasons for the test to the defendants. But, given this finding, the District Court found the test to be job related and to have no discriminatory purpose. The court concluded that the test was constitutional. The U.S. Court of Appeals* reversed the decision on the grounds that Title VII of the Civil Rights Act of 1964* does not require proof of discriminatory intent; the test had a racially discriminatory impact, and the police department had failed to justify its use.

A majority of the U.S. Supreme Court (the opinion was written by Justice White, who was joined by Chief Justice Burger* and Justices Blackmun,

Powell,* Rehnquist,* Stevens and Stewart for a 7–2 vote) decided that a racially disparate outcome is insufficient to lead to a finding of constitutional violation. The Court concluded that the requirements to find unconstitutional racial discrimination are different under the Constitution* than under the Civil Rights Act; more than a racially disproportionate impact is required to lead to a finding of a violation of the Fourteenth Amendment. The Court decision stated:

The school desegregation cases have also adhered to the basic equal protection principle that the invidious quality of the law claimed to be racially discriminatory must ultimately be traced to a racially discriminatory purpose. That there are both predominantly black and predominantly white schools in a community is not alone a violation of the Equal Protection Clause.

Dissenters Thurgood Marshall* and William J. Brennan* argued that the Metropolitan Police Department had not shown that the test was appropriately related to the job requirements of a police officer.

Thus this case reaffirmed a difference between de facto* and de jure school segregation.* De jure school segregation requires discriminatory intent. The decision has been criticized for several reasons (see Hall, *Oxford Companion*, 1992). First, the Court did not make clear how discriminatory intent can be shown. Must minutes of a school board reflect discrimination; can one argue that actions of a school board that clearly will result in increased school segregation* show intent? Related to this criticism is the linkage between discriminatory intent and effects. If racially discriminatory effects are an indicator of racially discriminatory intent, the two standards become difficult to distinguish. Finally, the decision does not acknowledge that past discrimination can mean that a nondiscriminatory action leads to discrepancies in results as wide as discriminatory acts. "For example, if Test 21 was intended to discriminate, and four times as many blacks failed it as whites, it would be unconstitutional, but if there was no such intent, and the result were identical because of a history of school segregation that was still being felt, no constitutional violation would occur" (1992:919).

References: Armor, *Forced Justice* (1995); Hall, *Oxford Companion* (1992); Yudof et al., *Kirp and Yudof's Educational Policy and the Law* (1987).

WEINBERG, MEYER (born December 16, 1920, New York City). Professor emeritus of Afro-American studies at the University of Massachusetts at Amherst and consultant, writer, and researcher of integrated education. Weinberg has written 18 books and numerous articles on the topic of education and race. Weinberg received his B.A. (1942) and M.A. (1945) from the University of Chicago and served on the history faculty at Chicago City College from 1947 to 1967, reaching the rank of professor of history at Loop College from 1971 to 1978. He was an active participant in the civil rights movement* in Chicago in the 1960s and 1970s. In 1963 he founded and became the editor of *Integrated Education*,* a journal that focused on civil rights* and education (since 1986 published as *Equity and Excellence* and later *Equity and Excellence in Education* by the School of Education, University of Massachusetts at Amherst). Weinberg directed the Horace Mann Bond Center for Equal Education at the University of Massachusetts from 1978 to 1992, a national clearinghouse of research and information on educational inequality. In 1990 he was named professor emeritus. From 1992 through 1994 Weinberg served as the initial holder of the Veffie Milstead Jones Endowed Chair in multicultural education* at California State University at Long Beach. His works include *The Search for Quality Integrated Education* and *Racism in the United States*, a bibliography of over 3,000 works. Weinberg has served as a consultant to many governmental and nonprofit agencies, such as the United States Office of Education,* the United States Commission on Civil Rights,* the NAACP Legal Defense Fund,* and the Educational Commission of the States, as well as numerous local school districts and state departments of education.

Works about: http://www.csulb.edu/~bookstor/author/weinberg.html (July 29, 1997); *Who's Who in America, 1997*, 4497; Josie Johnson, "Meyer Weinberg: Scholar, Teacher, Friend," *Equity and Excellence* 22, nos. 2–4 (Summer 1986): 108–10.

Works by: *A Chance to Learn: The History of Race and Education in the United States*, expanded edition (Long Beach: University Press of California State University, 1995); *Racism in Contemporary America* (Westport, CT: Greenwood Press, 1996); *Racism in the United States* (Westport, CT: Greenwood Press, 1990); *The Search for Quality Integrated Education: Policy and Research on Minority Students in School and College* (Westport, CT: Greenwood Press, 1983); *School Integration: A Comprehensive Classified Biography of 3,100 References* (Chicago: Integrated Education Associates, 1967).

WHITE ACADEMIES. *See* **Segregationist Academies**.

WHITE CITIZENS COUNCILS. Community groups established in reaction to the *Brown** decision to fight school desegregation* and to preserve the racial status quo in the South.* Citizens councils existed in Alabama, Arkansas, Florida, Louisiana, Mississippi, South Carolina, Tennessee, Texas, and Virginia, while allied groups existed in North Carolina (Patriots) and Georgia (States' Rights Council).

The first such council was established within two months of the *Brown* decision in Indianola, Mississippi, on July 11, 1954. The 14 original members soon spread to about 100, and within six weeks councils had been established in 17 counties. Within three years these councils could boast 80,000 members in Mississippi and 100,000 in Alabama, including many of the leading citizens of the communities. In early 1955 U.S. Senator James O. Eastland of Mississippi helped to organize a meeting to coordinate these councils across state lines.

The white citizens councils' literature was often inflammatory and anti-Semitic, although the organizations claimed nonviolent objectives of information and education, political action, and legal activity. For example, the Association of Citizens Councils pamphlet "Why Does Your Community Need a Citizens Council" (no date) argued, "The fate of our great nation may well rest in the hands of the Southern white people today. If we submit to this unconstitutional, judge-made integration law, the malignant powers of atheism, communism and mongrelization will surely follow, not only in our Southland but throughout our nation. . . . The white people of the South will again stand fast and preserve an unsullied race as our forefathers did eighty years ago.'' One observer, Weldon James, termed white citizens councils ''the community action arm of all segregationists'' (1957:19). Their number one target was the NAACP,* and the councils led the fight to harass this spearhead of the black legal fight against school segregation.* Among the groups were the States' Rights Councils in Florida and Georgia; the Patriots of North Carolina, Inc.; the Defenders of State Sovereignty and Individual Liberties in Virginia; the National Association for the Advancement of White People in Delaware; the Tennessee Federation for Constitutional Government, the Pro-Southerners, and the Tennessee Society to Maintain Segregation in Tennessee; and Southern Gentlemen, Inc., in Louisiana.

Circuit Judge Tom P. Brady played a key role in the development of these councils in Mississippi. Brady wrote the pamphlet *Black Monday*,* the handbook of the movement. By the end of 1956 the Mississippi Association of White Citizens Councils claimed 85,000 members in chapters in 65 of the state's 82 counties, and their national membership has been estimated at 250,000 at their zenith. Ross R. Barnett, a longtime member of the Mississippi council, was elected the state's governor in 1960. Bartley (1969) has detailed the activity of these councils across the individual states of the South. The tactics of the movement varied greatly by state. Florida's councils pressured Florida State University to expel ''pro-integrationist students,'' in New Orleans the councils rallied parents against ''subversive'' history books to be adopted for school use, and in Texas the councils picketed liberals and racial moderates. The strongest councils were in the Black Belt areas of the South.

The councils, unlike the Ku Klux Klan,* had a middle-class foundation in small towns, with bankers, lawyers, doctors, judges, and congressmen among their membership, although in cities the councils were more likely to attract working-class members. Thus white citizens councils have been called the ''white-collar Klan,'' ''uptown Klan,'' ''button-down Klan,'' and ''country club Klan,'' and they maintained a relatively high degree of respectability in the Deep South.* The councils rejected violence and instead used the weapons of pressure-group politics, economic harassment, and mass-media propaganda. Council members drafted or inspired much of the segregationist legislation during the period of massive resistance.*

References: Marcus and Stickney, *Race and Education* (1981); Wilhoit, *The Politics of Massive Resistance* (1973); Bartley, *The Rise of Massive Resistance* (1969); Weldon James, ''The South's Own Civil War,'' In *With All Deliberate Speed*, ed. Shoemaker (1957), 15–23.

WHITE FLIGHT. Generally, the withdrawal of whites from desegregating institutions such as schools, school districts, or residential communities; in the school context, the loss of white students in a desegregated school or school district because of the consideration and implementation of a school desegregation plan.* The concept is a controversial one, for while the loss of white pupils in a school district is fairly easy to document, the reasons for the decline are generally not easy to identify and isolate. City school districts in the 1960s and 1970s lost a large percentage of their white pupils. The primary reason for the loss was white flight according to busing* opponents and researchers such as David Armor* and James S. Coleman.* White families' opposition to school desegregation* and busing motivates them to escape to private or parochial schools or move from the city to the suburbs. To desegregation advocates and researchers such as Gary Orfield* and Thomas Pettigrew* the loss in enrollment was due to historical trends of suburbanization and demographic factors, especially the drop in the white birthrate. In a series of point-counterpoint academic articles, these researchers battled over the causes of enrollment drops. While agreement was never reached on the causes of the decreases, the researchers did agree that metropolitan plans* for school desegregation, because they included the white suburbs, offered the best hope of minimizing white flight.

In a 1975 study of school desegregation trends James S. Coleman and colleagues reported the results of their study of racial enrollment trends from 1968 to 1973 in the 67 largest central-city school districts in the nation. These researchers concluded that whites were fleeing central cities not only for demographic reasons (percentage of blacks, size of the school district) but also because of school desegregation, and thus school desegregation plans were increasing city-suburban segregation. (White parents express concern about declining educational quality, racial conflict, violence, value conflicts, and general disruption in the desegregation process.) This study generated a host of follow-up analyses, including critical analyses by Reynolds Farley, Christine Rossell,* and Thomas Pettigrew as summarized in Robin and Bosco (1976).

Much quantitative empirical research on white flight has been undertaken since this mid-1970s outbreak of social science conflict. One type of analysis, called "no-show" analysis, compares the actual white enrollment after the implementation of a desegregation plan to the projected white enrollment. For example, in her article on the Sheff v. O'Neill* case based on her court testimony, Rossell (1997) reports that "no-show" rates in Boston were 45 percent, 42 percent in Savannah–Chatham County, 52 percent in Baton Rouge, and 56 percent in California where whites were assigned to formerly minority schools. That is, about half of whites assigned to "black" schools do not remain in the public school system immediately after the implementation of a school desegregation plan. Rossell concludes that minority percentage, not whether the plan involves a metropolitan area or a city district, is the major factor affecting the extent of white flight.

Analyzing a national probability sample of 600 school districts, Rossell and Armor (1996) found that school districts that had a mandatory school desegregation plan lost one-third more white students than those that never had a plan.

Those districts that had a voluntary-only plan* experienced less than 3 percent white enrollment loss, which was not statistically significant. Controlled-choice plans* had flight almost as high as mandatory plans.*

Researchers have questioned whether flight should be characterized as simply "white" or as middle class, that is, including black middle-class flight. They have also tried to explain why whites may flee school desegregation when in surveys they indicate support for the principle of school desegregation. Various theories for this contradiction have been offered, including symbolic racism.*

While whites have increasingly accepted the principle of desegregation, many white parents do not want to send their children to schools with a majority of black students. Armor in *Forced Justice* (1995) reports that respondents in national surveys have been asked whether black and white students should attend the same or separate schools for decades. In 1942 about one-third of the white respondents answered "same schools." This percentage has been increasing over time: 50 percent in 1956, 75 percent in 1970, and 90 percent in 1980. Armor reports that surveys in the 1990s in individual cities could identify fewer than 5 percent of white parents who selected the segregated schools option. Similarly, national respondents have been asked whether they would object to sending their children to a school where different percentages of black children were enrolled. The percentage of whites not objecting to sending their children to a school where half of the pupils were white and half black increased from 50 to over 75 percent from 1958 to 1983. The percentage of whites not objecting to sending their children to a majority black school has risen from the low 30 percentile to the high 30s. In the eyes of many white parents, a majority black school is not desegregated, whatever the racial balance* of the school district.

The passage of more than two decades since the original social science conflict over white flight has not led to consensus on its causes. Gary Orfield and Susan Eaton's (1996) summary of the literature on white flight offers a counterpoint to Rossell's and Armor's work. They argue that since whites abandoned cities that did not have desegregation orders, such as Atlanta, New York, Chicago, and Houston, one cannot view school desegregation orders as the basis of flight. Nor have whites returned or stayed when mandatory school desegregation has been eliminated. They do accept, however, that some school desegregation plans are more likely to accelerate flight than others; metropolitan school desegregation plans are viewed as the most stable. Rossell's statistical reanalysis of Orfield's data, as reported in the *Connecticut Law Review* (1997), indicates that voluntary plans produce less white flight than mandatory plans, regardless of whether the plans are metropolitan in scope.

See also **Tipping Point**.

References: Christine H. Rossell, "An Analysis of the Court Decisions in *Sheff v. O'Neill* and Possible Remedies for Racial Isolation," *Connecticut Law Review* 29, no. 3 (Spring 1997): 1187–1233; Orfield and Eaton, *Dismantling Desegregation* (1996); Rossell and Armor, "The Effectiveness of School Desegregation Plans, 1968–1991" (July 1996); Armor, *Forced Justice* (1995); Rossell, *The Carrot or the Stick for Desegregation*

Policy (1990); Thomas F. Pettigrew and Robert L. Green, "School Desegregation in Large Cities: A Critique of the Coleman 'White Flight' Thesis," *Harvard Educational Review* 46, no. 1 (February 1976): 1–53; Stanley S. Robin and James J. Bosco, "Coleman's Desegregation Research and Policy Recommendations," in *School Desegregation* ed. Levinsohn and Wright (1976), 46–57; Coleman, Kelly, and Moore, *Trends in School Segregation, 1968–1973* (1975).

WHITE HOUSE INITIATIVE ON HISTORICALLY BLACK COLLEGES AND UNIVERSITIES. An effort directing federal agencies and requesting the private sector to enhance historically black colleges and universities* (HBCUs). This action was first established by Executive Order 12232 of President Jimmy Carter* on August, 8, 1980; Presidents Ronald Reagan,* George Bush, and Bill Clinton have also signed executive orders to continue this program. The initiative seeks "to strengthen the capacity of historically black colleges and universities to provide excellence in education." The goals of this initiative include ensuring that the HBCU perspective is included in policy making affecting higher education and to strengthen these institutions. In practice the initiative seeks to ensure that HBCUs receive access to federally funded programs. President Bush's order included the establishment of a Presidential Advisory Board on HBCUs appointed by the President, which advises the President and Secretary of the Department of Education* and issues an annual report, and President Clinton's Executive Order 12876 requires that 27 federal agencies set goals for the amount of their funds to be awarded to these institutions, that senior officials in each agency have oversight over this effort, and that the Office of Management and Budget monitor the implementation of his order. Each agency must produce an annual plan for assisting HBCUs and an annual performance report on its success. The Department of Education has the obligation to seek private-sector support for HBCUs under this order. The initiative's organizational location is in the U.S. Department of Education.

References: President's Board of Advisors on Historically Black Colleges and Universities, *A Century of Success: Historically Black Colleges and Universities, America's National Treasure* (Washington, DC: Author, September 1996); *White House Initiative on Historically Black Colleges and Universities* (Washington, DC: U.S. Department of Education, 1994); Myers, *Desegregation in Higher Education* (1989).

WILLIE, CHARLES VERT (born October 8, 1927, Dallas, Texas). Leading researcher and academic whose works have supported school desegregation;* architect of controlled-choice* school desegregation plans.* Charles Willie graduated with his B.A. from Morehouse College in 1948 and received his M.A. from Atlanta University the next year. He received his Ph.D. from Syracuse University in 1957. He stayed at Syracuse, moving up the academic ladder from instructor status to assistant professor, associate professor, and professor in 1968. He chaired the Sociology Department from 1967 to 1971 and was a vice president of the university from 1972 through 1974. In 1974 Willie moved to the Harvard Graduate School of Education, where he became the first black to hold a tenured professorship in the school.

Judge W. Arthur Garrity* named Willie as a master in the Boston school desegregation case in 1975, in which he helped to develop the controlled-choice phase II desegregation plan. Willie also worked with the schools in Cambridge in the development of controlled-choice desegregation plans and has served as an expert witness in school desegregation cases, including the Dallas, Texas, case.

Willie has received many awards and much recognition across the nation, including honorary degrees from Morehouse, Syracuse, Berkeley, and Harvard. He served as president of the Eastern Sociological Society, a member of the Council of the American Sociological Society, and a member of the board of the Social Science Research Council.

Works about: *Who's Who in America, 1996,* 4491.

Works by: *School Desegregation Plans That Work* (Westport, CT: Greenwood Press, 1984); with Susan Greenblatt, *Community Politics and Educational Change: Ten School Districts under Court Order* (New York: Longman, 1981).

WISDOM, JOHN MINOR (born May 17, 1905, New Orleans). John Minor Wisdom wrote three key opinions in school desegregation* following *Brown,** including *United States v. Jefferson County Board of Education** (1966) after his appointment to the Fifth Circuit Court of Appeals* in July 1957 by President Dwight D. Eisenhower.* His opinions reflected the premise that school officials had an affirmative obligation to desegregate the schools, not merely to halt school segregation.* The elimination of racial factors in pupil assignment was insufficient. As Wilkinson states, Wisdom believed that "what the state had done, it must now undo" (1979:112). Wisdom judged that remedies must eliminate the system of past school segregation and undo its effects.

Wisdom was a graduate of Washington and Lee University (1925) and received his law degree from Tulane University (1929). He was a partner in a law firm in New Orleans from 1929 until his appointment to the Court of Appeals in 1957. He was the presiding judge of the Fifth Circuit from 1975 to 1986. Wisdom has been the recipient of numerous awards, including honorary law degrees from Tulane, Oberlin, Haverford, Middlebury, and Harvard University.

Works about: *Who's Who in American Law?* (New Providence, NJ: Marquis Who's Who, Reed Reference, 1994), 999; *Who's Who in America, 1996,* 4518; Hall, *Oxford Companion* (1992); Wilkinson, *From Brown to Bakke* (1979).

WRIGHT V. COUNCIL OF THE CITY OF EMPORIA, 407 U.S. 451 (1972). The first U.S. Supreme Court* decision on school desegregation* that placed emphasis on the effect rather than the reason for the actions of public officials in deciding school desegregation cases and limited the right of public officials to reconstitute school districts to hinder school desegregation. Two weeks after the U.S. District Court* ordered the pairing* of Emporia's schools to replace a freedom-of-choice* plan disallowed by the *Green** (1968) decision, the city of Emporia, Virginia, sought to leave the county school system and run its own schools. The plaintiffs argued that this separation would increase the concentration of black students in the county schools as the city removed its white students from the overall mix of students. The 5–4 Supreme Court majority concluded that the effect, not the purpose, of the act was most significant and thus ruled that no matter whether the city's motive was acceptable or not, the effect of the separation would be to hinder the implementation of the school desegregation plan.* The majority thus ruled that the city's action was unacceptable. The minority, while agreeing with the principles stated by the majority, disputed the facts in arguing that the effect on racial balance* would be minimal.

References: Nowak and Rotunda, *Constitutional Law* (1995); Kurland, "*Brown v. Board of Education* Was the Beginning" (1994); Witt, *Congressional Quarterly's Guide to the U.S. Supreme Court* (1989).

Y

YICK WO V. HOPKINS, 118 U.S. 356 (1886). Unanimous U.S. Supreme Court* decision invalidating a San Francisco ordinance prohibiting laundries in wooden (but not brick) buildings, presumably for safety reasons, but viewed as racially discriminatory against Chinese-owned businesses. The law was challenged by Yick Wo, who had been in the laundry business for 22 years. Wo claimed that the ordinance violated his Fourteenth Amendment* rights because of its discriminatory effects. The U.S. Supreme Court agreed, but this decision had little immediate impact because the composition of the Court soon changed and this decision had not overturned *Plessy** (1896), despite the similarities. However, the Court had viewed a law equal on its face as discriminatory in practice, thus setting the stage for challenges concerning the equal component of *Plessy*'s separate but equal* principle.

References: Greenberg, *Crusaders in the Courts* (1994); Nathan C. Margold, *Preliminary Report to the Joint Committee Supervising the Expenditure of the 1930 Appropriation by the American Fund for the Public Service to the NAACP* in Greenberg, *Judicial Process and Social Change: Constitutional Litigation Cases and Materials* (1977), 50–57; Kluger, *Simple Justice* (1975).

BIBLIOGRAPHICAL ESSAY

If you have the time or inclination to read only one book on the topic of school segregation and desegregation, you would certainly receive the same recommendation from almost everyone in the field: read *Simple Justice* by Richard Kluger (1975). This readable and fascinating book traces the history of school segregation and desegregation from the 1800s to *Brown* (1954) and its immediate aftermath. Other readable historical presentations that are both helpful and interesting are former NAACP Legal Defense Fund Special Counsel Jack Greenberg's *Crusaders in the Courts* (1994), social scientist Gary Orfield's *The Reconstruction of Southern Education* (1969), John Egerton's *Speak Now against the Day: The Generation before the Civil Rights Movement in the South* (1994), and Gil Kujovich's (1992) lengthy article on the history of black education in the United States, "Equal Opportunity in Higher Education and the Black Public College." For comprehensive discussions of the early history of school desegregation I recommend J. Harvie Wilkinson, *From Brown to Bakke* (1979), and George R. Metcalf, *From Little Rock to Boston* (1983).

As of the writing of this book, the two most up-to-date and comprehensive analyses of school segregation and desegregation are David Armor's *Forced Justice* (1995) and Gary Orfield and Susan Eaton's *Dismantling Desegregation* (1996). Armor has been a consistent skeptic about mandatory busing and has testified on the antibusing side for years, but does support voluntary desegregation plans. He has written a valuable book, filled with empirical analysis, that everyone interested in this topic must read. On the other side of the topic of mandatory busing, and with a very different style (less quantitative but more readable), Gary Orfield's works are supportive of school desegregation and busing (e.g., *Must We Bus?*, 1978) while being comprehensive and interesting. In these opposing books Armor explains why the release of school districts from desegregation orders is a good thing and Orfield and Eaton why dismantling school desegregation is wrong.

Legal decisions and analysis play a very large role in the history of school segregation and desegregation. There are a number of excellent references that focus on a legal perspective, including Henry J. Abraham and Barbara A. Perry, *Freedom and the Court: Civil Rights and Liberties in the United States*, 6th edition (1994). *The Oxford Companion to the Supreme Court of the United States*, edited by Kermit L. Hall (1992), is an excellent dictionary of legal terms, cases, and people. Perry A. Zirkel, Sharon Nalbone Richardson, and Steven S. Goldberg, *A Digest of Supreme Court Decisions Affecting Education*, 3d edition (1995), includes excellent brief summaries of the key court cases (and some less important cases). The most substantive resource on the legal issues surrounding school segregation and desegregation is Mark G. Yudof, David L. Kirp, Tyll Van Geel, and Betsy Levin, *Kirp and Yudof's Educational Policy and the Law*, 2d edition (1987). The third edition (1992) by Mark G. Yudof, David L. Kirp, and Betsy Levin, *Educational Policy and the Law*, updates the material. Other helpful law books include Charles F. Abernathy, *Civil Rights and Constitutional Litigation; Cases and Materials*, 2d edition (1992), John E. Nowak and Ronald D. Rotunda, *Constitutional Law*, 5th edition (1995), and Ronald D. Rotunda, *Modern Constitutional Law: Cases and Notes*, 4th edition (1993). The latter book contains many of the most significant court decisions in school desegregation law. Jack Greenberg, *Judicial Process and Social Change* (1977), is an excellent case book covering many of the older court decisions from *Plessy* (1896) through *Brown* (1954).

Davison M. Douglas, *School Busing: Constitutional and Political Developments* (1994), is a marvelous source book that provides original material on the topic of school segregation and desegregation with a focus on busing. The two volumes include Armor's famous article "The Evidence on Busing," a selection from the Coleman Report, the full text of several key busing decisions such as *Swann* (1971), and legislation such as the Civil Rights Act of 1964, as well as speeches by notables such as President Richard M. Nixon on busing. In addition, noted constitutional scholar Philip B. Kurland provides an excellent review and analysis of the major court decisions on school desegregation from 1954 to 1979. I therefore recommend these volumes highly. Peter B. Levy, *Documentary History of the Modern Civil Rights Movement* (1992), is also an excellent compendium of original material. *The Encyclopedia of African-American Education* (1996), edited by Faustine C. Jones-Wilson and others, is certainly a complement to the present dictionary and of major interest to those interested in segregation and desegregation.

For the reader concerned about how to design a school desegregation plan in the 1990s, the works of Christine Rossell and David Armor, particularly for their descriptions of unpublished plans, are the place to begin. There are a host of writings on the pre–magnet-school desegregation plans of the 1960s and 1970s. Gordon Foster's classic article "Desegregating Urban Schools: A Review of Techniques," *Harvard Educational Review*, 43, no. 1 (February 1973): 5–36, is a must for those interested in the plans of these decades. Three of his students, Larry W. Hughes, William M. Gordon, and Larry W. Hillman, wrote a helpful desegregation-planning text, *Desegregating America's Schools* (1980). Those wanting more information on how to implement a school desegregation plan that is more likely to lead to community acceptance, increased student achievement, and integration should read Al Smith, Anthony Downs, and M. Leanne Lachman, *Achieving Effective School Desegregation* (1973); Willis Hawley, *Effective School Desegregation* (1981); Hawley and others, *Strategies for Effective Desegregation* (1983); and Mark A. Chesler, Bunyan I. Bryant, and James E. Crowfoot, *Making Desegregation Work* (1981).

Those interested in the effects of school desegregation should consider a number of reviews of this subject. Certainly Nancy H. St. John, *School Desegregation: Outcomes for Children* (1975), is an excellent place to start. St. John presents the mid-1970s evidence on desegregation and academic achievement, self-confidence, and racial prejudice. Rossell and Hawley's edited volume *The Consequences of School Desegregation* is an excellent summary of the literature on desegregation effects through its publication date of 1983. Jennifer L. Hochschild, *The New American Dilemma* (1984), presents a helpful review of the effects of school desegregation that result from different school desegregation plans. Amy Stuart Wells and Robert L. Crain's 1994 article "Perpetuation Theory and the Long-Term Effects of School Desegregation" will be helpful to those seeking greater understanding of the impact of school desegregation. David Armor, *Forced Justice* (1995), provides an analysis from the perspective of the 1990s, as does Janet Ward Schofield, "Review of Research on School Desegregation's Impact on Elementary and Secondary School Students" (1995). Those who seek empirical analyses of the effects of school desegregation on racial balance and exposure to students of other races, the "numbers game," should read the works of Christine Rossell. Rossell's research is careful, comprehensive, significant for policy makers, and social science at its best. Among her best works is *The Carrot or the Stick for Desegregation Policy* (1990). The most significant debate now focuses on whether mandatory school desegregation plans are more or less effective than voluntary plans. Rossell and Armor's 1996 article, "The Effectiveness of School Desegregation Plans, 1968–1991" not only engages this issue, but also provides the reader with helpful long-term examinations of the amount of school desegregation that has occurred in the nation over time.

One topic that offers fascinating insights into the history of school segregation and desegregation is presidential politics. Mark Stern, *Calculating Visions: Kennedy, Johnson, and Civil Rights* (1992), is an excellent book that probably should be joined on the bookshelf by Kenneth O'Reilly, *Nixon's Piano: Presidents and Racial Politics from Washington to Clinton* (1995). The latter may have the most interesting title of all the books that I read in writing this book. O'Reilly describes the scene at the annual Gridiron Club in Washington, D.C., on March 14, 1970, when President Nixon, after being roasted about his Southern Strategy and recent failed Supreme Court nominations of two southern judges, appeared at twin pianos with Vice President Spiro Agnew. Nixon asked Agnew about his southern strategy, and Agnew responded in dialect, "Ah agree with you completely on yoah southern strategy." While Nixon played the favorite song of each of the last few presidents, in turn Agnew drowned out the President with Dixie. At the end of their bit President Nixon led the audience of 500 men in "God Bless America" and "Auld Lang Syne." O'Reilly relates this incident to highlight Nixon's cynical division of the nation along racial lines to win election, the respect of those in power for his exploitation of the racial issue, and the long line of American presidents who have deliberately fanned the flames of racism and ignored racial problems at best. "Simply put, [his] southern strategy worked" (7). The reader is also advised to consider Leon Panetta and Peter Gall, *Bring Us Together* (1971), Panetta's first-person account of his years on the Nixon civil rights team. For a political analysis from a more technical viewpoint, Stephen L. Wasby's 1993 article "A Transformed Triangle: Court, Congress, and Presidency in Civil Rights" is helpful, as is James Bolner and Robert Shanley, *Busing: The Political and Judicial Process* (1974). The clearest analysis of the role of Congress and the President in busing is found in Edward Keynes and Randall K. Miller, *The Court vs. Congress* (1989). Edward G. Carmines and James A. Stimson, *Issue Evolution: Race and the Transformation of American Politics* (1989), also belongs on the politics-of-race bookshelf.

There are many collections of school desegregation cases that would prove helpful to those seeking to understand the history of school segregation and desegregation. The most clever research design was developed by my colleague at the University of Delaware, Thomas Muncy Keith Professor of History Raymond Wolters, who, for the 30th anniversary of the *Brown v. Board of Education* and *Bolling v. Sharpe* (1954) decisions, returned to the original sites of the cases included in the *Brown* decision: New Castle County, Delaware, Clarendon County, South Carolina, Topeka, Kansas, Prince Edward County, Virginia, and Washington, D.C. He simply asked what had happened after the decisions in each venue. While Wolters's conservatism leads him to see the five glasses half empty, he certainly is asking the right questions and presents the reader with significant material in *The Burden of Brown* (1984). Readers may also be interested in his latest book, which has a significant focus on school desegregation policy under President Ronald Reagan, *Right Turn* (1996). Charles Willie and Susan Greenblatt's collection of ten communities that desegregated their schools, *Community Politics and Educational Change* (1981), is an interesting and helpful volume for the reader who seeks to understand the process of school desegregation at the local level. The geographical bibliography included in the present book includes several other such collections for the interested reader. Some readers may want to supplement the present dictionary with Meyer Weinberg's bibliography compiled in *Racism in Contemporary America* (Westport, CT: Greenwood Press, 1996) for its geographical bibliography, which includes newspaper articles and dissertations organized by state. Finally, excellent case studies may be found in *Integrated Education* (now *Equity and Excellence in Education*), the *Southern Education Report*, published by the Southern Education Reporting Service, and reports of the U.S. Commission on Civil Rights.

The literature on segregation and desegregation at the college and university level is not very extensive. Several collections of essays on this topic are helpful, including Jean L. Preer, *Lawyers v. Educators* (1982), Laurence R. Marcus and Benjamin D. Stickney, *Race and Education* (1981), and Julian B. Roebuck and Komanduri S. Murty, *Historically Black Colleges and Universities* (1993).

On the occasion of the 40th anniversary of the *Brown v. Board of Education* decision, a number of anthologies were published. The volumes edited by Mwalimu J. Shujaa, *Beyond Desegregation* (1996), and Ellen Condliffe Lagemann and Lamar P. Miller, *Brown v. Board of Education* (1996), are good compendiums.

Those who would like to keep current on school desegregation should follow *Education Week* for the latest news in elementary and secondary education and the *Chronicle of Higher Education* for the higher-education version of relevant news. The journal *Equity and Excellence in Education* (formerly *Integrated Education*), edited by the School of Education at the University of Massachusetts, has a steady flow of helpful articles about school desegregation. For those who want to check on facts, I suggest *Facts on File* and *Britannica Online*, which I also found very helpful in compiling individual biographies. *The African American Education Data Book* (1997), compiled by Michael T. Nettles and Laura W. Perna, became available as I was putting the finishing touches on this volume; it should prove valuable to those seeking quantitative data on the status of blacks in elementary, secondary, and higher education, for it includes chapters with myriads of tables on enrollment, student achievement, and even drug and alcohol use. In short, the reader interested in school segregation and desegregation will find a wealth of historical and current material on the subject.

GENERAL
BIBLIOGRAPHY

Abernathy, Charles F. *Civil Rights and Constitutional Litigation: Cases and Materials*. 2d ed. St. Paul: West Publishing, 1992.

Abraham, Henry J., and Barbara A. Perry. *Freedom and the Court: Civil Rights and Liberties in the United States*. 6th ed. New York: Oxford University Press, 1994.

Alkin, Marvin C., editor in chief. *Encyclopedia of Educational Research*. 6th ed. New York: Macmillan, 1992.

Allport, Gordon W. *The Nature of Prejudice*. Cambridge, MA: Addison-Wesley, 1954.

Altbach, Philip G., and Kofi Lomotey, eds. *The Racial Crisis in American Higher Education*. Albany: State University of New York Press, 1991.

Amaker, Norman C. *Civil Rights and the Reagan Administration*. Washington, DC: Urban Institute Press, 1988.

Armor, David J. "The Evidence on Busing." *Public Interest*, no. 28 (Summer 1972): 90–126.

Armor, David J. *Forced Justice: School Desegregation and the Law*. New York: Oxford University Press, 1995.

Armor, David J. "Why Is Black Achievement Rising?" *Public Interest*, no. 108 (Summer 1992): 65–80.

Banks, James A., ed., and Cheryl A. McGee Banks, associate ed. *Handbook of Research on Multicultural Education*. New York: Macmillan, 1995.

Barnett, Marguerite Ross, and Charles C. Harrington, eds. *Readings on Equal Education* 7 (1977–1979). New York: AMS Press, 1984.

Bartley, Numan V. *The Rise of Massive Resistance: Race and Politics in the South during the 1950's*. Baton Rouge: Louisiana State University Press, 1969.

Bell, Derrick A. *Faces at the Bottom of the Well: The Permanence of Racism*. New York: Basic Books, 1992.

Bell, Derrick A. *Race, Racism, and American Law*. Boston: Little, Brown, 1973.

Bell, Derrick A., ed. *Shades of Brown: New Perspectives on School Desegregation*. New
    York: Teachers College Press, 1980.
Bennett, Christine I. "Research on Racial Issues in American Higher Education." In
    Handbook of Research on Multicultural Education, ed. James A. Banks. associate
    ed. Cheryl A. McGee Banks. New York: Macmillan, 1995. 663–82.
Bickel, Alexander. *The Least Dangerous Branch: The Supreme Court at the Bar of
    Politics*. Indianapolis: Bobbs-Merrill, 1962, 1986.
Biles, Roger. *Richard J. Daley: Politics, Race, and the Governing of Chicago*. DeKalb:
    Northern Illinois University Press, 1995.
Blasi, Vincent, ed. *The Burger Court: The Counter-revolution That Wasn't*. New Haven:
    Yale University Press, 1983.
Bolner, James, and Robert Shanley. *Busing: The Political and Judicial Process*. New
    York: Praeger, 1974.
Britannica Online. http://www.eb.com (Encyclopedia Britannica, 1995, 1996).
Brown, Kevin. "Revisiting the Supreme Court's Opinion in *Brown v. Board of Education*
    from a Multiculturalist Perspective." In *Brown v. Board of Education: The Chal-
    lenge for Today's Schools*, ed. Ellen Condliffe Lagemann and Lamar P. Miller.
    New York: Teachers College Press, 1996. 44–53.
Butler, Grace L. "Legal and Policy Issues in Higher Education." *Journal of Negro
    Education* 63, no. 3 (1994): 451–59.
Carmines, Edward G., and James A. Stimson. *Issue Evolution: Race and the Transfor-
    mation of American Politics*. Princeton: Princeton University Press, 1989.
Carter, Robert L. "The Unending Struggle for Equal Educational Opportunity." In
    Brown v. Board of Education: The Challenge for Today's Schools, ed. Ellen
    Condliffe Lagemann and Lamar P. Miller. New York: Teachers College Press,
    1996. 19–26.
Cashman, Sean Dennis. *African-Americans and the Quest for Civil Rights, 1900–1990*.
    New York: New York University Press, 1991.
Catalog of Federal Domestic Assistance, 1996. Washington, DC: U.S. Government Print-
    ing Office, 1996.
Chesler, Mark A., Bunyan I. Bryant, and James E. Crowfoot. *Making Desegregation
    Work: A Professional's Guide to Effecting Change*. Beverly Hills, CA: Sage,
    1981.
Coleman, James S., Ernest Q. Campbell, Carol J. Hobson, James McPartland, Alexander
    M. Mood, Frederic D. Weinfield, and Robert L. York. *Equality of Educational
    Opportunity*. Washington, DC: U.S. Government Printing Office, 1996.
Coleman, James S., Sara D. Kelly, and John A. Moore. *Trends in School Segregation,
    1968–73*. Washington, DC: Urban Institute, August 1975.
Contreras, A. Reynaldo, and Leonard A. Valverde. "The Impact of *Brown* on the Edu-
    cation of Latinos." *Journal of Negro Education* 63, no. 3 (1994): 470–81.
Cook, Thomas, David Armor, Robert Crain, Norman Miller, Walter Stephan, Herbert
    Walberg, and Paul Wortman. *School Desegregation and Black Achievement*.
    Washington, DC: National Institute of Education, U.S. Department of Education,
    1984.
Crain, Robert L. *The Politics of School Desegregation: Comparative Case Studies of
    Community Structure and Policy-making*. Chicago: Aldine, 1968.
Darden, Joe T., Joshua G. Bagaka's, and Sameh M. Kamel. "Historically Black Insti-

tutions and Desegregation: The Dilemma Revisited." *Equity and Excellence in Education* 29, no. 2 (September 1996): 56–68.

Davis, Michael D., and Hunter R. Clark. *Thurgood Marshall: Warrior at the Bar, Rebel on the Bench.* updated and revised edition. Secaucus, NJ: Carol Publishing, 1994.

Dawkins, Marvin P., and Jomills Henry Braddock II. "The Continuing Significance of Desegregation: School Racial Composition and African American Inclusion in American Society." *Journal of Negro Education* 63, no. 3 (1994): 394–405.

Dejnozka, Edward L., and David E. Kapel. *American Educators' Encyclopedia.* Rev. ed. by David E. Kapel, Charles S. Gifford, and Marilyn B. Kapel. New York: Greenwood Press, 1991.

Dentler, Robert A., D. Catherine Baltzell, and Daniel J. Sullivan. *University on Trial: The Case of the University of North Carolina.* Cambridge, MA: Abt Books, 1983.

Deskbook Encyclopedia of American School Law 1996. Rosemount, MN: Data Research, 1996.

Detlefsen, Robert R. *Civil Rights under Reagan.* San Francisco: Institute for Contemporary Studies Press, 1991.

Dimond, Paul R. *Beyond Busing: Inside the Challenge to Urban Segregation.* Ann Arbor: University of Michigan Press, 1985.

Douglas, Davison M., ed. *School Busing: Constitutional and Political Developments.* 2 vols. New York: Garland, 1994.

Duram, James C. *A Moderate among Extremists: Dwight D. Eisenhower and the School Desegregation Crisis.* Chicago: Nelson-Hall, 1981.

Egerton, John. *Speak Now against the Day: The Generation before the Civil Rights Movement in the South.* New York: Alfred A. Knopf, 1994.

Fife, Brian L. *Desegregation in American Schools: Comparative Intervention Strategies.* Westport, CT: Praeger, 1992.

Finch, Minnie. *The NAACP: Its Fight for Justice.* Metuchen, NJ: Scarecrow Press, 1981.

Flicker, Barbara, ed. *Justice and School Systems: The Role of the Courts in Education Litigation.* Philadelphia: Temple University Press, 1990.

Friedelbaum, Stanley H. "Justice William J. Brennan, Jr.: Policy-Making in the Judicial Thicket." In *The Burger Court: Political and Judicial Profiles,* ed. Charles M. Lamb and Stephen C. Halpern. Urbana: University of Illinois Press, 1991. 100–128.

Galster, George C., and Edward W. Hill, eds. *The Metropolis in Black and White: Place, Power, and Polarization.* New Brunswick, NJ: Center for Urban Policy Research, 1992.

Gatti, Richard D., and Daniel J. Gatti. *New Encyclopedic Dictionary of School Law.* West Nyack, NY: Parker, 1983.

Gordon, William M. "The Implementation of Desegregation Plans since *Brown.*" *Journal of Negro Education* 63, no. 3 (1994): 310–22.

Graglia, Lino A. *Disaster by Decree: The Supreme Court Decisions on Race and the Schools.* Ithaca: Cornell University Press, 1976.

Graham, Judith. *Current Biography Yearbook.* New York: H. W. Wilson Company, 1993, 1994, 1995.

Green, Robert L., ed. *Metropolitan Desegregation.* New York: Plenum Press, 1985.

Greenberg, Jack. *Crusaders in the Courts.* New York: Basic Books, 1994.

Greenberg, Jack. *Judicial Process and Social Change: Constitutional Litigation, Cases, and Materials.* St. Paul: West Publishing, 1977.

Greenberg, Jack. *Race Relations and American Law*. New York: Columbia University Press, 1959.

Grossman, Mark. *The ABC-CLIO Companion to the Civil Rights Movement*. Santa Barbara, CA: ABC-CLIO, 1993.

Gurwitt, Rob. "Getting off the Bus." *Governing* 5, no. 8 (May 1992): 30–36.

Hall, Kermit L., editor-in-chief. *The Oxford Companion to the Supreme Court of the United States*. New York: Oxford University Press, 1992.

Hawley, Willis D., ed. *Effective School Desegregation: Equity, Quality, and Feasibility*. Beverly Hills, CA: Sage Publications, 1981.

Hawley, Willis D., Robert L. Crain, Christine H. Rossell, Mark A. Smylie, Ricardo R. Fernández, Janet W. Schofield, Rachel Tompkins, William T. Trent, and Marilyn S. Zlotnik. *Strategies for Effective Desegregation*. Lexington, MA: Lexington Books, 1983.

Hawley, Willis D., and Anthony W. Jackson, eds. *Toward a Common Destiny: Improving Race and Ethnic Relations in America*. San Francisco: Jossey-Bass, 1995.

Henderson, Ronald D., Nancy M. Greenberg, Jeffrey M. Schneider, Oscar Uribe, Jr., and Richard R. Verdugo. "High-quality Schooling for African American Students." In *Beyond Desegregation: The Politics of Quality in African American Schooling*, ed. Mwalimu J. Shujaa. Thousand Oaks, CA: Corwin Press, 1996. 162–84.

Henderson, Ronald D., Mary von Euler, and Jeffrey M. Schneider. "Remedies for Segregation: Some Lessons from Research." *Educational Evaluation and Policy Analysis* 3, no. 4 (July/August 1981): 67–76.

Hochschild, Jennifer L. *The New American Dilemma: Liberal Democracy and School Desegregation*. New Haven:Yale University Press, 1984.

Holmes, Steven A. "Education Gap between Races Closes."*New York Times*, September 6, A18.

Hornsby, Alton, Jr. *Milestones in 20th-Century African-American History*. Detroit:Visible Ink Press, 1993.

Hughes, Larry W., William M. Gordon, and Larry W. Hillman. *Desegregating America's Schools*. New York: Longman, 1980.

Husén, Torsten and T. Neville Postlethwaite, editor-in-chief. *The International Encyclopedia of Education*. 2d ed. Oxford, England: Pergamon, 1994.

Jaszczak, Sandra, ed. *Encyclopedia of Associations*. 31st ed. Vol. 1, *National Organizations of the U.S.* Detroit: Gale Research, 1996.

Jones, Leon. *From Brown to Boston: Desegregation in Education, 1954–1974*. Metuchen, NJ: Scarecrow Press, 1979.

Jones-Wilson, Faustine C., Charles A. Asbury, Margo Okazawa-Rey, D. Kamili Anderson, Sylvia M. Jacobs, and Michael Fulltz, eds. *Encyclopedia of African-American Education*. Westport, CT: Greenwood Press, 1996.

Jost, Kenneth. "Rethinking Affirmative Action." *CQ Researcher* 5, no. 16 (April 28, 1995): 369–92.

Jost, Kenneth. "Rethinking School Integration." *CQ Researcher* 6, no. 39 (October 18, 1996): 913–36.

Kalodner, Howard I., and James J. Fishman, eds. *Limits of Justice: The Courts' Role in School Desegregation*. Cambridge, MA: Ballinger, 1978.

Kaplin, William A. *The Law of Higher Education: A Comprehensive Guide to Legal Implications of Administrative Decision Making*. 2d ed. San Francisco: Jossey-Bass, 1985.

Keynes, Edward, with Randall K. Miller. *The Court vs. Congress: Prayer, Busing, and Abortion*. Durham, NC: Duke University Press, 1989.

Kluger, Richard. *Simple Justice: The History of Brown v. Board of Education and Black America's Struggle for Equality*. New York: Vintage Books, 1975.

Kujovich, Gil. "Equal Opportunity in Higher Education and the Black Public College: The Era of Separate But Equal." In *Race, Law, and American History, 1700–1990: The African-American Experience*. Paul Finkelman. Vol. 7, pt. 2, *The Struggle for Equal Education*. New York: Garland, 1992. 217–360.

Kunen, James S. "The End of Integration." *Time*, April 29, 1996, 39–45.

Kurland, Philip B. "*Brown v. Board of Education* Was the Beginning." In *School Busing: Constitutional and Political Developments*, ed. Davison M. Douglas. Vol. 1. New York: Garland, 1994. 420–484.

Lagemann, Ellen Condliffe, and Lamar P. Miller, eds. *Brown v. Board of Education: The Challenge for Today's Schools*. New York: Teachers College Press, 1996.

Lamb, Charles M., and Stephen C. Halpern, eds. *The Burger Court: Political and Judicial Profiles*. Urbana: University of Illinois Press, 1991.

Lee, Francis Graham, ed. *Neither Conservative nor Liberal: The Burger Court on Civil Rights and Liberties*. Malabar, FL: Robert E. Krieger, 1983.

Levinsohn, Florence H., and Benjamin D. Wright, eds. *School Desegregation: Shadow and Substance*. Chicago: University of Chicago Press, 1976.

Levy, Peter B., ed. *Documentary History of the Modern Civil Rights Movement*. New York: Greenwood Press, 1992.

Lewis, Dan A., and Kathryn Nakagawa. *Race and Educational Reform in the American Metropolis: A Study of School Desegregation*. Albany: State University of New York Press, 1995.

Marcus, Laurence R., and Benjamin D. Stickney. *Race and Education: The Unending Controversy*. Springfield, IL: Charles C. Thomas, 1981.

Marger, Martin N. *Race and Ethnic Relations: American and Global Perspectives*. 2d ed. Belmont, CA: Wadsworth, 1991.

Mayer, Robert R., Charles E. King, Anne Borders-Patterson, and James S. McCullough. *The Impact of School Desegregation in a Southern City: A Case Study in the Analysis of Educational Policy*. Lexington, MA: Lexington Books, 1974.

Meier, Kenneth J., Joseph Stewart, Jr., and Robert E. England. *Race, Class, and Education: The Politics of Second-Generation Discrimination*. Madison: University of Wisconsin Press, 1989.

Metcalf, George R. *Black Profiles*. New York: McGraw-Hill, 1968.

Metcalf, George R. *From Little Rock to Boston: The History of School Desegregation*. Westport, CT: Greenwood Press, 1983.

Mills, Nicolaus, ed. *The Great School Bus Controversy*. New York: Teachers College Press, 1973.

Muse, Benjamin. *Ten Years of Prelude: The Story of Integration since the Supreme Court's 1954 Decision*. New York: Viking Press, 1964.

Muse, Benjamin. *Virginia's Massive Resistance*. Bloomington: Indiana University Press, 1961.

Myers, Samuel L., Sr., ed. *Desegregation in Higher Education*. Lanham, MD: NAFEO Research Institute, University Press of America, 1989.

Myrdal, Gunnar. *An American Dilemma: The Negro Problem and Modern Democracy*. New York: Harper and Brothers, 1944.

Nettles, Michael T., and Laura W. Perna. *The African American Education Data Book.* Vol. 1, *Higher and Adult Education*; Vol. 2, *Preschool through High School Education.* Fairfax, VA: Frederick D. Patterson Research Institute of the College Fund/UNCF, 1997.

Neuborne, Burt. "Brown at Forty: Six Visions." In *Brown v. Board of Education: The Challenge for Today's Schools*, ed. Ellen Condliffe Lagemann and Lamar P. Miller. New York: Teachers College Press, 1996. 199–205.

Nevin, David, and Robert E. Bills. *The Schools That Fear Built: Segregationist Academies in the South.* Washington, DC: Acropolis Books, 1976.

Newby, I. A., ed. *The Development of Segregationist Thought.* Homewood, IL: Dorsey Press, 1968.

Nowak, John E., and Ronald D. Rotunda. *Constitutional Law.* 5th ed. St. Paul: West Publishing, 1995.

Oakes, Jeannie. *Keeping Track: How Schools Structure Inequality.* New Haven: Yale University Press, 1985.

O'Reilly, Kenneth. *Nixon's Piano: Presidents and Racial Politics from Washington to Clinton.* New York: Free Press, 1995.

Orfield, Gary. *Congressional Power: Congress and Social Change.* New York: Harcourt Brace Jovanovich, 1975.

Orfield, Gary. *The Growth of Segregation in American Schools: Changing Patterns of Separation and Poverty since 1968.* Alexandria, VA: National School Boards Association, 1993.

Orfield, Gary. *Must We Bus? Segregated Schools and National Policy.* Washington, DC: Brookings Institution, 1978.

Orfield, Gary. *The Reconstruction of Southern Education: The Schools and the 1964 Civil Rights Act.* New York: Wiley-Interscience, 1969.

Orfield, Gary, and Susan E. Eaton. *Dismantling Desegregation: The Quiet Reversal of Brown v. Board of Education.* New York: New Press, 1996.

Panetta, Leon E., and Peter Gall. *Bring Us Together: The Nixon Team and the Civil Rights Retreat.* Philadelphia: J. B. Lippincott, 1971.

Peltason, Jack W. *Fifty-eight Lonely Men: Southern Federal Judges and School Desegregation.* New York: Harcourt, Brace, and World, 1961.

Phillips, Susan. "Racial Tensions in Schools." *CQ Researcher* 4, no. 1 (January 7, 1994): 1–24.

Pollack, Jack Harrison. *Earl Warren: The Judge Who Changed America.* Englewood Cliffs, NJ: Prentice-Hall, 1979.

Preer, Jean L. *Lawyers v. Educators: Black Colleges and Desegregation in Public Higher Education.* Westport, CT: Greenwood Press, 1982.

Roebuck, Julian B., and Komanduri S. Murty. *Historically Black Colleges and Universities: Their Place in American Higher Education.* Westport, CT: Praeger, 1993.

Rossell, Christine H. *The Carrot or the Stick for School Desegregation Policy.* Philadelphia: Temple University Press, 1990.

Rossell, Christine H. "The Classification of School Segregation Remedies." Unpublished paper, Boston University, January 12, 1992.

Rossell, Christine H. "The Convergence of Black and White Attitudes on School Desegregation Issues during the Four Decade Evolution of Plans." *William and Mary Law Review* 36, no. 2 (January 1995): 613–63.

Rossell, Christine H., and David Armor. "The Effectiveness of School Desegregation Plans, 1968–1991." *American Politics Quarterly* 24, no. 3 (July 1996): 267–302.

Rossell, Christine H., and Willis D. Hawley, eds. *The Consequences of School Desegregation*. Philadelphia: Temple University Press, 1983.

Rotunda, Ronald D. *Modern Constitutional Law: Cases and Notes*. 4th ed. St. Paul: West Publishing, 1993.

Safire, William. *Safire's New Political Dictionary: The Definitive Guide to the New Language of Politics*. New York: Random House, 1993.

St. John, Nancy H. *School Desegregation: Outcomes for Children*. New York: John Wiley and Sons, 1975.

Schofield, Janet Ward. "Review of Research on School Desegregation's Impact on Elementary and Secondary School Students." In *Handbook of Research on Multicultural Education*, ed. James A. Banks, associate ed. Cheryl A. McGee Banks. New York: Macmillan, 1995. 597–616.

Schwartz, Bernard. *A History of the Supreme Court*. New York: Oxford University Press, 1993.

Shoemaker, Don, ed. *With All Deliberate Speed: Segregation-Desegregation in Southern Schools*. New York: Harper and Brothers, 1957.

Shujaa, Mwalimu J., ed. *Beyond Desegregation: The Politics of Quality in African American Schooling*. Thousand Oaks, CA: Corwin Press, 1996.

Sindler, Allan P. *Bakke, DeFunis, and Minority Admissions: The Quest for Equal Opportunity*. New York: Longman, 1978.

Smith, Al, Anthony Downs, and M. Leanne Lachman. *Achieving Effective Desegregation*. Lexington, MA: Lexington Books, 1973.

Smith, Jeff E., ed. *The Impact of Desegregation on Higher Education*. Raleigh, NC: Institute on Desegregation, North Carolina Central University, 1979.

Smith, Willy DeMarcell, and Eva Wells Chunn, eds. *Black Education: A Quest for Equity and Excellence*. New Brunswick, NJ: Transaction Publishers, 1989.

Steel, Lauri, and Roger Levine. *Educational Innovation in Multiracial Contexts: The Growth of Magnet Schools in American Education*. Palo Alto, CA: American Institutes for Research, 1994.

Stefkovich, Jacqueline A., and Terrence Leas. "A Legal History of Desegregation in Higher Education." *Journal of Negro Education* 63, no. 3 (1994): 406–20.

Stern, Mark. *Calculating Visions: Kennedy, Johnson, and Civil Rights*. New Brunswick, NJ: Rutgers University Press, 1992.

Stern, Mark. "Eisenhower and Kennedy: A Comparison of Confrontations at Little Rock and Ole Miss." *Policy Studies Journal* 21, no. 3 (1993): 575–88.

Thompson, Carolyn J. "African American Student Leadership: Implications for Quality in College Achievement in the 21st Century." In *Beyond Desegregation: The Politics of Quality in African American Schooling*, ed. Mwalimu J. Shujaa. Thousand Oaks, CA: Corwin Press, 1996. 185–206.

Tushnet, Mark. *The NAACP's Legal Strategy against Segregated Education, 1925–1950*. Chapel Hill: University of North Carolina Press, 1987.

Tushnet, Mark, ed. *The Warren Court in Historical and Political Perspective*. Charlottesville: University Press of Virginia, 1993.

U.S. Commission on Civil Rights. *Funding Federal Civil Rights Enforcement*. Washington, DC: U.S. Government Printing Office, June 1995.

U.S. Congress. House. Subcommittee on Civil and Constitutional Rights of the Committee on the Judiciary. *School Desegregation Hearings*. 97th Cong., 1st Session. Washington, DC: U.S. Government Printing Office, 1982.

Varady, David P., and Jeffrey A. Raffel. *Selling Cities: Attracting Homebuyers through Schools and Housing Programs*. Albany: State University of New York Press, 1995.

Wasby, Stephen L. "A Transformed Triangle: Court, Congress, and Presidency in Civil Rights." *Policy Studies Journal* 21, no. 3 (1993): 565–74.

Wasby, Stephen L., Anthony A. D'Amato, and Rosemary Metrailer. *Desegregation from Brown to Alexander: An Exploration of Supreme Court Strategies*. Carbondale: Southern Illinois University Press, 1977.

Weinberg, Meyer, ed. *Integrated Education: A Reader*. Beverly Hills, CA: Glencoe Press, 1968.

Weinberg, Meyer. *The Search for Quality Integrated Education: Policy and Research on Minority Students in School and College*. Westport, CT: Greenwood Press, 1983.

Wells, Amy Stuart, and Crain, Robert L. "Perpetuation Theory and the Long-Term Effects of School Desegregation." *Review of Educational Research* 64, no. 4 (Winter 1994): 531–55.

Wheelock, Anne. *Crossing the Tracks: How "Untracking" Can Save America's Schools*. New York: New Press, 1992.

White, Forrest R. "*Brown* Revisited." *Phi Delta Kappan* 76, no. 1 (September 1994): 13–20.

White, G. Edward. *Earl Warren: A Public Life*. New York: Oxford University Press, 1982.

Wicker, Tom. *Tragic Failure: Racial Integration in America*. New York: William Morrow, 1996.

Wilhoit, Francis M. *The Politics of Massive Resistance*. New York: George Braziller, 1973.

Wilkins, Roger. "Dream Deferred But Not Defeated." In *Brown v. Board of Education: The Challenge for Today's Schools*, ed. Ellen Condliffe Lagemann and Lamar P. Miller. New York: Teachers College Press, 1996. 14–18.

Wilkinson, J. Harvie, III. *From Brown to Bakke: The Supreme Court and School Integration, 1954–1978*. Oxford: Oxford University Press, 1979.

Williams, John B., III, ed. *Desegregating America's Colleges and Universities: Title VI Regulation of Higher Education*. New York: Teachers College Press, 1988.

Williams, Michael W., ed. *The African American Encyclopedia*. 6 vols. New York: Marshall Cavendish Corporation, 1993.

Willie, Charles V. "The Intended and Unintended Benefits of School Desegregation." In *Black Education: A Quest for Equity and Excellence*, ed. Willy DeMarcell Smith and Eva Wells Chunn. New Brunswick: Transaction Publishers, 1989. 127–35.

Willie, Charles V. *The Ivory and Ebony Towers: Race Relations and Higher Education*. Lexington, MA: Lexington Books, 1981.

Willie, Charles V. *School Desegregation Plans That Work*. Westport, CT: Greenwood Press, 1984.

Willie, Charles V., Antoine M. Garibaldi, and Wornie L. Reed, eds. *The Education of African-Americans*. New York: Auburn House, 1991.

Willie, Charles V., and Susan L. Greenblatt. *Community Politics and Educational Change: Ten School Systems under Court Order.* New York: Longman, 1981.

Wirt, Frederick M. *"We Ain't What We Was": Civil Rights in the New South.* Durham: Duke University Press, 1997.

Witt, Elder. *Congressional Quarterly's Guide to the U.S. Supreme Court.* 2d ed. Washington, DC: Congressional Quarterly, 1989.

Wolters, Raymond. *The Burden of Brown: Thirty Years of School Desegregation.* Knoxville: University of Tennessee Press, 1984.

Wolters, Raymond. *Right Turn: William Bradford Reynolds, the Reagan Administration, and Black Civil Rights.* New Brunswick, NJ: Transaction Publishers, 1996.

Young-Bruehl, Elisabeth. *The Anatomy of Prejudices.* Cambridge, MA: Harvard University Press, 1996.

Yudof, Mark G., David L. Kirp, and Betsy Levin. *Educational Policy and the Law.* 3d ed. St. Paul: West Publishing, 1992.

Yudof, Mark G., David L. Kirp, Tyll Van Geel, and Betsy Levin. *Kirp and Yudof's Educational Policy and the Law: Cases and Materials.* 2d ed. Berkeley, CA: McCutchan, 1987.

Zirkel, Perry A., Sharon Nalbone Richardson, and Steven S. Goldberg. *A Digest of Supreme Court Decisions Affecting Education.* 3d ed. Bloomington, IN: Phi Delta Kappa Educational Foundation, 1995.

GEOGRAPHICAL
BIBLIOGRAPHY

ATLANTA, GEORGIA

Crim, Alonzo A., and Nancy J. Emmons. "Desegregation in the Atlanta Public Schools: A Historical Overview." In *School Desegregation Plans That Work*, by Charles Vert Willie. Westport, CT: Greenwood Press, 1984. 149–162.

Hornsby, Alton, Jr. "Black Public Education in Atlanta, Georgia, 1954–1973: From Segregation to Segregation." *Journal of Negro History* 76 (1991): 21–47.

Orfield, Gary, and Carole Ashkinaze. *The Closing Door: Conservative Policy and Black Opportunity*. Chicago: University of Chicago Press, 1991.

AUSTIN, TEXAS

Eaton, Susan E., Joseph Feldman, and Edward Kirby. "Still Separate, Still Unequal: The Limits of *Milliken II*'s Monetary Compensation to Segregated Schools." in *Dismantling Desegregation: The Quiet Reversal of Brown v. Board of Education*, by Gary Orfield and Susan Eaton. New York: New Press, 1996. 143–78.

BAKERSFIELD, CALIFORNIA

Wolters, Raymond. *Right Turn: William Bradford Reynolds, the Reagan Administration, and Black Civil Rights*. New Brunswick, NJ: Transaction Publishers, 1996.

BALTIMORE, MARYLAND

Crain, Robert L. *The Politics of School Desegregation: Comparative Case Studies of Community Structure and Policy-Making*. Chicago: Aldine, 1968. 72–80.

BERKELEY, CALIFORNIA

Kirp, David L. *Just Schools: The Idea of Racial Equality in American Education*. Berkeley: University of California Press, 1982.
Sullivan, Neil V., with Evelyn S. Stewart. *Now Is the Time: Integration in the Berkeley Schools*. Bloomington: Indiana University Press, 1969.

BOSTON, MASSACHUSETTS

Beaumont, Jennifer J. "Implementation of Court-ordered Desegregation by District-Level Administrators." In *Beyond Desegregation: The Politics of Quality in African American Schooling*, ed. Mwalimu J. Shujaa. Thousand Oaks, CA: Corwin Press, 1996. 75–90.
Bullard, Pamela, Joyce Grant, and Julia Stoia. "The Northeast: Boston, Massachusetts: Ethnic Resistance to a Comprehensive Plan." In *Community Politics and Educational Change: Ten School Systems under Court Order*, by Charles V. Willie and Susan L. Greenblatt. New York: Longman, 1981. 31–63.
Case, Charles W. "History of the Desegregation Plan in Boston." In *The Future of Big-City Schools*, ed. Daniel U. Levine and Robert J. Havighurst. Berkeley, CA: McCutchan, 1977. 153–76.
Dentler, Robert A. "The Boston School Desegregation Plan." In *School Desegregation Plans That Work*, by Charles Vert Willie. Westport, CT: Greenwood Press, 1984. 59–80.
Dentler, Robert A. "Educational Implications of Desegregation in Boston." In *The Future of Big-City Schools*, ed. Daniel U. Levine and Robert J. Havighurst. Berkeley, CA: McCutchan, 1977. 177–91.
Dentler, Robert A., and Marvin B. Scott, *Schools on Trial: An Inside Account of the Boston Desegregation Case*. Cambridge, MA: Abt Books, 1981.
Formisano, Ronald P. *Boston against Busing: Race, Class, and Ethnicity in the 1960s and 1970s*. Chapel Hill: University of North Carolina Press, 1991.
Hillson, Jon. *The Battle of Boston*. New York: Pathfinder Press, 1977.
Lukas, J. Anthony. *Common Ground: A Turbulent Decade in the Lives of Three American Families*. New York: Alfred A. Knopf, 1985.
Lupo, Alan. *Liberty's Chosen Home: The Politics of Violence in Boston*. Boston: Little, Brown, 1977.
Rossell, Christine H. "Boston's Desegregation and White Flight." *Integrated Education* 15, no. 1 (January–February 1977): 36–39.
Rossell, Christine H. "The Mayor's Role in School Desegregation Implementation." *Urban Education* 12 (Fall 1977): 247–70.
Smith, Ralph R. "Two Centuries and Twenty-Four Months: A Chronicle of the Struggle to Desegregate the Boston Public Schools." In *Limits of Justice: The Courts' Role in School Desegregation*, ed. Howard I. Kalodner and James J. Fishman. Cambridge, MA: Ballinger, 1978. 25–114.
Taylor, D. Garth. *Public Opinion and Collective Action: The Boston School Desegregation Conflict*. Chicago: University of Chicago Press, 1986.
U.S. Commission on Civil Rights. *Desegregating the Boston Public Schools: A Crisis in Civic Responsibility*. Washington, DC: U.S. Government Printing Office, 1975.

BUFFALO, NEW YORK

Crain, Robert L. *The Politics of School Desegregation: Comparative Case Studies of Community Structure and Policy-Making*. Chicago: Aldine, 1968. 59–71.

CHARLOTTE-MECKLENBURG, NORTH CAROLINA

Douglas, Davison M. *Reading, Writing, and Race*. Chapel Hill: University of North Carolina Press, 1995.

Gaillard, Frye. *The Dream Long Deferred*. Chapel Hill: University of North Carolina Press, 1988.

Morantz, Alison. "Desegregation at Risk: Threat and Reaffirmation in Charlotte." In *Dismantling Desegregation: The Quiet Reversal of Brown v. Board of Education*, by Gary Orfield and Susan Eaton. New York: New Press, 1996. 179–206.

Schwartz, Bernard. *Swann's Way: The School Busing Case and the Supreme Court*. New York: Oxford University Press, 1986.

Smith, Stephen Samuel. "Hugh Governs? Regime and Education Policy in Charlotte, North Carolina." *Journal of Urban Affairs* 19, no. 3 (1997): 247–75.

CHARLOTTESVILLE, VIRGINIA

Holden, Anna. "Charlottesville, Virginia: A Southern City's Struggle to Achieve Racial Balance." In *The Bus Stops Here: A Study of School Desegregation in Three Cities*. New York: Agathon Press, 1974. 1–126.

CHICAGO, ILLINOIS

Remsberg, Charles, and Bonnie Remsberg. "Chicago Voices: Tales Told out of School." In *Our Children's Burden: Studies of Desegregation in Nine American Communities*, ed. Raymond W. Mack. New York: Random House, 1968. 273–386.

Wolters, Raymond. *Right Turn: William Bradford Reynolds, the Reagan Administration, and Black Civil Rights*. New Brunswick, NJ: Transaction Publishers, 1996.

CINCINNATI, OHIO

Felix, Joseph L., and James N. Jacobs. "Issues in Implementing and Evaluating Alternative Programs in Cincinnati." In *The Future of Big-City Schools*, ed. Daniel U. Levine and Robert J. Havighurst. Berkeley, CA: McCutchan, 1977. 105–15.

Griffin, Virginia K. "Desegregation in Cincinnati: The Legal Background." In *The Future of Big-City Schools*, ed. Daniel U. Levine and Robert J. Havighurst. Berkeley, CA: McCutchan, 1977. 87–94.

Holm, Duane. "The Metropolitan Context for Reducing Racial Isolation." In *The Future of Big-City Schools*, ed. Daniel U. Levine and Robert J. Havighurst. Berkeley, CA: McCutchan, 1977. 116–23.

Varady, David P., and Jeffrey A. Raffel. *Selling Cities: Attracting Homebuyers through*

Schools and Housing Programs. Albany: State University of New York Press, 1995.

Waldrip, Donald R. "Alternative Programs in Cincinnati; or, 'What Did You Learn on the River Today?' " In *The Future of Big-City Schools*, ed. Daniel U. Levine and Robert J. Havighurst. Berkeley, CA: McCutchan, 1977. 95–104.

CLARENDON COUNTY, SOUTH CAROLINA

Wolters, Raymond. *The Burden of Brown: Thirty Years of School Desegregation*. Knoxville: University of Tennessee Press, 1984. 129–74.

CLEVELAND, OHIO

Gurwitt, Rob. "Getting off the Bus." *Governing* 5, no. 8 (May 1992): 30–36.

COLUMBUS, OHIO

Dimond, Paul R. *Beyond Busing: Inside the Challenge to Urban Segregation*. Ann Arbor: University of Michigan Press, 1985.

CORPUS CHRISTI, TEXAS

Cirilo-Medina, Amelia, and Ross Purdy. "The South and Southwest: Corpus Christi, Texas: A Tri-ethnic Experience in School Desegregation." In *Community Politics and Educational Change: Ten School Systems under Court Order*, by Charles V. Willie and Susan L. Greenblatt. New York: Longman, 1981. 129–54.

DALLAS, TEXAS

Albert, Geoffrey P., H. Ron White, and Paul Geisel. "Dallas, Texas: The Intervention of Business Leaders." In *Community Politics and Educational Change: Ten School Systems under Court Order*, by Charles V. Willie and Susan L. Greenblatt. New York: Longman, 1981. 155–73.

Levine, Daniel U., and Nolan Estes. "Desegregation and Educational Reconstruction in the Dallas Public Schools." *Phi Delta Kappan* 59, no. 3 (1977): 163–67, 221.

Schultze, Jim. *The Accommodation: The Politics of Race in an American City*. Secaucus, NJ: Citadel Press, 1986.

DAYTON, OHIO

Dimond, Paul R. *Beyond Busing: Inside the Challenge to Urban Segregation*. Ann Arbor: University of Michigan Press, 1985.

Stave, Sondra Astor. *Achieving Racial Balance: Case Studies of Contemporary School Desegregation*. Westport, CT: Greenwood Press, 1995. 5–22.

DENVER, COLORADO

Pearson, Jessica, and Jeffrey Pearson. "Keyes v. School District No. 1." In *Limits of Justice: The Courts' Role in School Desegregation*, ed. Howard I. Kalodner and James J. Fishman. Cambridge, MA: Ballinger, 1978. 167–222.

Wood, Robert, ed. *Remedial Law: When Courts Become Administrators*. Amherst: University of Massachusetts Press, 1990.

DETROIT, MICHIGAN

Dimond, Paul R. *Beyond Busing: Inside the Challenge to Urban Segregation*. Ann Arbor: University of Michigan Press, 1985.

Eaton, Susan E., Joseph Feldman, and Edward Kirby. "Still Separate, Still Unequal: The Limits of *Milliken II*'s Monetary Compensation to Segregated Schools." In *Dismantling Desegregation: The Quiet Reversal of Brown v. Board of Education*, by Gary Orfield and Susan Eaton. New York: New Press, 1996. 143–78.

Hain, Edward. "Sealing Off the City: School Desegregation in Detroit." In *Limits of Justice: The Courts' Role in School Desegregation*, ed. Howard I. Kalodner and James J. Fishman. Cambridge, MA: Ballinger, 1978. 223–308.

Wolf, Eleanor P. *Trial and Error: The Detroit School Segregation Case*. Detroit: Wayne State University Press, 1981.

ERIE, PENNSYLVANIA

Iutcovich, Joyce Miller, and Elaine Clyburn. "Erie, Pennsylvania: The Effect of State Initiative." In *Community Politics and Educational Change: Ten School Systems under Court Order*, by Charles V. Willie and Susan L. Greenblatt. New York: Longman, 1981. 64–81.

GOLDSBORO, NORTH CAROLINA

Mayer, Robert R., Charles E. King, Anne Borders-Patterson, and James S. McCullough. *The Impact of School Desegregation in a Southern City: A Case Study in the Analysis of Educational Policy*. Lexington, MA: Lexington Books, 1974.

GREENVILLE, SOUTH CAROLINA

Merritt, S. Russell. "The Success of Greenville County, South Carolina, in Avoiding Public School Resegregation, 1970–1990." *Equity and Excellence in Education* 28, no. 3 (December 1995): 50–56.

HARTFORD, CONNECTICUT

Delaney, Stephen B. "*Milo Sheff et al. v. William A. O'Neill et al.*: April 12, 1995." *Equity and Excellence in Education* 28, no. 2 (September 1995): 14–20.

Fuerst, J. S. "School Desegregation in the Hartford, Connecticut, Area." *Urban Education* 22 (1987): 73–84.

Rossell, Christine H. "An Analysis of the Court Decisions in *Sheff v. O'Neill* and Possible Remedies for Racial Isolation." *Connecticut Law Review* 29, no. 3 (Spring 1997): 1187–1233.

Stave, Sondra Astor. *Achieving Racial Balance: Case Studies of Contemporary School Desegregation.* Westport, CT: Greenwood Press, 1995. 85–126.

HEMPSTEAD, NEW YORK

Dworkin, Rosalind J. "Segregation and Suburbia." In *Our Children's Burden: Studies of Desegregation in Nine American Communities*, ed. Raymond W. Mack. New York: Random House, 1968. 190–234.

HOUSTON, TEXAS

Campbell, Connie, and John Brandstetter. "The Magnet School Plan in Houston." In *The Future of Big-City Schools*, ed. Daniel U. Levine and Robert J. Havighurst. Berkeley, CA: McCutchan, 1977. 124–38.

Trombley, William. "Houston." *Integrated Education* 15, no. 6 (1977): 92–94.

INDIANAPOLIS, INDIANA

Marsh, William E. "*United States v. Board of Commissioners.*" In *Limits of Justice: The Courts' Role in School Desegregation*, ed. Howard I. Kalodner and James J. Fishman. Cambridge, MA: Ballinger, 1978. 309–58.

KALAMAZOO, MICHIGAN

Pease, John. "Desegregation in the Midwest: The Case of Kalamazoo." In *Our Children's Burden: Studies of Desegregation in Nine American Communities*, ed. Raymond W. Mack. New York: Random House, 1968. 235–72.

KANSAS CITY, MISSOURI

Morantz, Alison. "Money and Choice in Kansas City: Major Investments with Modest Returns." In *Dismantling Desegregation: The Quiet Reversal of Brown v. Board of Education*, by Gary Orfield and Susan Eaton. New York: New Press, 1996. 241–63.

Wolters, Raymond. *Right Turn: William Bradford Reynolds, the Reagan Administration, and Black Civil Rights.* New Brunswick, NJ: Transaction Publishers, 1996.

LITTLE ROCK, ARKANSAS

Bates, Daisy. *The Long Shadow of Little Rock: A Memoir.* New York: David McKay, 1962.

Beals, Melba. *Warriors Don't Cry: A Searing Memoir of the Battle to Integrate Little Rock's Central High.* New York: Pocket Books, 1994.

Eaton, Susan E., Joseph Feldman, and Edward Kirby. "Still Separate, Still Unequal: The

Limits of *Milliken II*'s Monetary Compensation to Segregated Schools." In *Dismantling Desegregation: The Quiet Reversal of Brown v. Board of Education*, by Gary Orfield and Susan Eaton. New York: New Press, 1996. 143–78.

Freyer, Tony Allan. *The Little Rock Crisis: A Constitutional Interpretation*. Westport, CT: Greenwood Press, 1984.

Huckaby, Elizabeth. *Crisis at Central High, Little Rock, 1957–58*. Baton Rouge: Louisiana State University Press, 1980.

LOS ANGELES, CALIFORNIA

Dworkin, Anthony Gary. "No Siesta Manana: The Mexican American in Los Angeles." In *Our Children's Burden: Studies of Desegregation in Nine American Communities*, ed. Raymond W. Mack. New York: Random House, 1968. 387–440.

Orfield, Gary. "Lessons of the Los Angeles Desegregation Case." *Education and Urban Society* 16 (May 1984): 338–53.

LOUISVILLE/JEFFERSON COUNTY, KENTUCKY

Perley, Martin. "The Louisville Story." *Integrated Education* 13, no. 6 (1975): 11–14.

U.S. Commission on Civil Rights. *School Desegregation in Louisville and Jefferson County, Kentucky*. Washington, DC: U.S. Government Printing Office, 1976.

MEMPHIS, TENNESSEE

Ailes, Roger. "A Bittersweet Victory: Public School Desegregation in Memphis." *Journal of Negro Education* 55 (1986): 470–83.

MILWAUKEE, WISCONSIN

Barndt, Michael, Rick Janka, and Harold Rose. "The West and Midwest: Milwaukee, Wisconsin: Mobilization for School and Community Cooperation." In *Community Politics and Educational Change: Ten School Systems under Court Order*, by Charles V. Willie and Susan L. Greenblatt. New York: Longman, 1981. 237–59.

Bednarek, David I. "Milwaukee." *Integrated Education* 15, no. 6 (1977): 36–37.

Bennett, David A. "A Plan for Increasing Educational Opportunities and Improving Racial Balance in Milwaukee." In *School Desegregation Plans That Work*, by Charles Vert Willie. Westport, CT: Greenwood Press, 1984. 81–118.

Faltz, Christine J., and Donald O. Leake. "The All-Black School: Inherently Unequal or a Culture-based Alternative?" In *Beyond Desegregation: The Politics of Quality in African American Schooling*, ed. Mwalimu J. Shujaa. Thousand Oaks, CA: Corwin Press, 1996. 227–52.

MOBILE, ALABAMA

Foley, Albert S. "Mobile, Alabama: The Demise of State-sanctioned Resistance." In *Community Politics and Educational Change: Ten School Systems under Court*

Order, by Charles V. Willie and Susan L. Greenblatt. New York: Longman, 1981. 174–207.

MONTGOMERY COUNTY, MARYLAND

Eaton, Susan E. "Slipping toward Segregation: Local Control and Eroding Desegregation in Montgomery County." In *Dismantling Desegregation: The Quiet Reversal of Brown v. Board of Education*, by Gary Orfield and Susan Eaton. New York: New Press, 1996. 207–39.
Henig, Jeffrey. "Choice in Public Schools: An Analysis of Transfer Requests among Magnet Schools." *Social Science Quarterly* 71, no. 1 (1990): 69–82.

MOUNT VERNON, NEW YORK

Fishman, James J., Laura Ross, and Steven R. Trost. "With All Deliberate Delay: School Desegregation in Mount Vernon." In *Limits of Justice: The Courts' Role in School Desegregation*, ed. Howard I. Kalodner and James J. Fishman. Cambridge, MA: Ballinger, 1978. 359–410.

NASHVILLE, TENNESSEE

Pride, Richard A., and J. David Woodard. *The Burden of Busing: The Politics of Desegregation in Nashville, Tennessee*. Knoxville: University of Tennessee Press, 1985.

NEW ORLEANS, LOUISIANA

Baker, Liva. *The Second Battle of New Orleans: The Hundred-Year Struggle to Integrate the Schools*. New York: HarperCollins, 1996.
Crain, Robert L. *The Politics of School Desegregation: Comparative Case Studies of Community Structure and Policy-Making*. Chicago: Aldine, 1968. 237–305.

NEW YORK CITY, NEW YORK

Fishman, James J. "The Limits of Remedial Power: *Hart v. Community School Board 21*." In *Limits of Justice: The Courts' Role in School Desegregation*, ed. Howard I. Kalodner and James J. Fishman. Cambridge, MA: Ballinger, 1978. 115–66.

NEWARK, DELAWARE

Barringer, Herbert R. "Integration in Newark, Delaware: Whatever Happened to Jim Crow?" In *Our Children's Burden: Studies of Desegregation in Nine American Communities*, ed. Raymond W. Mack. New York: Random House, 1968. 141–89.

NEWARK, NEW JERSEY

Crain, Robert L. *The Politics of School Desegregation: Comparative Case Studies of Community Structure and Policy-Making.* Chicago: Aldine, 1968. 51–58.

NORFOLK, VIRGINIA

Carr, Leslie G. "Resegregation: The Norfolk Case." *Urban Education* 24 (January 1990): 404–13.

Eaton, Susan E., and Christina Meldrum. "Broken Promises: Resegregation in Norfolk, Virginia." In *Dismantling Desegregation: The Quiet Reversal of Brown v. Board of Education,* by Gary Orfield and Susan Eaton. New York: New Press, 1996. 115–41.

White, Forrest R. *Pride and Prejudice: School Desegregation and Urban Renewal in Norfolk, 1950–1959.* Westport, CT: Praeger, 1992.

Wolters, Raymond. *Right Turn: William Bradford Reynolds, the Reagan Administration, and Black Civil Rights.* New Brunswick, NJ: Transaction Publishers, 1996.

OAKLAND, CALIFORNIA

Kirp, David L. *Just Schools: The Idea of Racial Equality in American Education.* Berkeley: University of California Press, 1982.

OKLAHOMA CITY, OKLAHOMA

Wolters, Raymond. *Right Turn: William Bradford Reynolds, the Reagan Administration, and Black Civil Rights.* New Brunswick, NJ: Transaction Publishers, 1996.

OMAHA, NEBRASKA

Mihelich, Dennis N., and Ashton Wesley Welch. "Omaha, Nebraska: Positive Planning for Peaceful Integration." In *Community Politics and Educational Change: Ten School Systems under Court Order,* by Charles V. Willie and Susan L. Greenblatt. New York: Longman, 1981. 260–97.

PANOLA, MISSISSIPPI

Wirt, Frederick M. *Politics of Southern Equality: Law and Social Change in a Mississippi County.* Chicago: Aldine, 1971.

Wirt, Frederick M. *"We Ain't What We Was": Civil Rights in the New South.* Durham: Duke University Press, 1997.

PITTSBURGH, PENNSYLVANIA

Crain, Robert L. *The Politics of School Desegregation: Comparative Case Studies of Community Structure and Policy-Making.* Chicago: Aldine, 1968. 95–105.

PORTLAND, OREGON

U.S. Commission on Civil Rights. *School Desegregation in Portland, Oregon*. Washington, DC: U.S. Government Printing Office, 1977.

PRINCE EDWARD COUNTY, VIRGINIA

Smith, Robert Collins. *They Closed Their Schools: Prince Edward County, Virginia, 1951–1964*. Chapel Hill: University of North Carolina Press, 1965.

PRINCE GEORGE'S COUNTY, MARYLAND

Eaton, Susan E., and Elizabeth Crutcher. "Magnets, Media, and Mirages: Prince George's County's 'Miracle' Cure." In *Dismantling Desegregation: The Quiet Reversal of Brown v. Board of Education*, by Gary Orfield and Susan Eaton. New York: New Press, 1996. 265–89.

Eaton, Susan E., Joseph Feldman, and Edward Kirby. "Still Separate, Still Unequal: The Limits of *Milliken II*'s Monetary Compensation to Segregated Schools." In *Dismantling Desegregation: The Quiet Reversal of Brown v. Board of Education*, by Gary Orfield and Susan Eaton. New York: New Press, 1996. 143–78.

PROVIDENCE, RHODE ISLAND

Holden, Anna. "Providence, Rhode Island: White and Black Power and Citywide Dispersal of Blacks in Public Schools." In *The Bus Stops Here: A Study of School Desegregation in Three Cities*. New York: Agathon Press, 1974. 127–278.

RACINE, WISCONSIN

U.S. Commission on Civil Rights. *School Desegregation in Racine, Wisconsin*. Washington, DC: U.S. Government Printing Office, 1977.

RICHMOND, VIRGINIA

Pratt, Robert A. *The Color of Their Skin: Education and Race in Richmond, Virginia, 1954–89*. Charlottesville: University Press of Virginia, 1992.

Sartain, James A., and Rutledge M. Dennis. "Richmond, Virginia: Massive Resistance without Violence." In *Community Politics and Educational Change: Ten School Systems under Court Order*, by Charles V. Willie and Susan L. Greenblatt. New York: Longman, 1981. 208–36.

RICHMOND UNIFIED SCHOOL DISTRICT, CALIFORNIA

Kirp, David L. *Just Schools: The Idea of Racial Equality in American Education*. Berkeley: University of California Press, 1982.

Rubin, Lillian B. *Busing and Backlash: White against White in a California School District*. Berkeley: University of California Press, 1972.

RIVERSIDE, CALIFORNIA

Duster, Troy. "Violence and Civic Responsibility: Combinations of 'Fear' and 'Right.' " In *Our Children's Burden: Studies of Desegregation in Nine American Communities*, ed. Raymond W. Mack. New York: Random House, 1968. 1–40.

ROCHESTER, NEW YORK

Stave, Sondra Astor. *Achieving Racial Balance: Case Studies of Contemporary School Desegregation*. Westport, CT: Greenwood Press, 1995. 23–44.

SACRAMENTO, CALIFORNIA

Holden, Anna. "Sacramento, California: Partial Desegregation in a Racially Imbalanced, Multiethnic School District." In *The Bus Stops Here: A Study of School Desegregation in Three Cities*. New York: Agathon Press, 1974. 279–434.

ST. LOUIS, MISSOURI

Crain, Robert L. *The Politics of School Desegregation: Comparative Case Studies of Community Structure and Policy-Making*. Chicago: Aldine, 1968. 13–27.

Grady, Michael K., and Charles V. Willie. *Metropolitan School Desegregation: A Case Study of the Saint Louis Area Voluntary Transfer Program*. Bristol, IN: Wyndham Hall Press, 1986.

Monti, Daniel J. *A Semblance of Justice: St. Louis School Desegregation and Order in Urban America*. Columbia: University of Missouri Press, 1985.

Wells, Amy Stuart, and Robert L. Crain. *Stepping over the Color Line: African-American Students in White Suburban Schools*. New Haven: Yale University Press, 1997.

Wolters, Raymond. *Right Turn: William Bradford Reynolds, the Reagan Administration, and Black Civil Rights*. New Brunswick, NJ: Transaction Publishers, 1996.

SAN BERNARDINO, CALIFORNIA

Trombley, William. "San Bernardino." *Integrated Education* 15, no. 6 (1977): 103–4.

SAN FRANCISCO, CALIFORNIA

Crain, Robert L. *The Politics of School Desegregation: Comparative Case Studies of Community Structure and Policy-Making*. Chicago: Aldine, 1968. 81–94.

Kirp, David L. *Just Schools: The Idea of Racial Equality in American Education*. Berkeley: University of California Press, 1982.

Kirp, David L. "Multitudes in the Valley of Indecision: The Desegregation of San Francisco's Schools." In *Limits of Justice: The Courts' Role in School Desegregation*, ed. Howard I. Kalodner and James J. Fishman. Cambridge, MA: Ballinger, 1978. 411–92.

Kirp, David L. "Race, Politics, and the Courts: School Desegregation in San Francisco." *Harvard Educational Review* 46, no. 4 (November 1976): 572–611.

SAUSALITO, CALIFORNIA

Kirp, David L. *Just Schools: The Idea of Racial Equality in American Education*. Berkeley: University of California Press, 1982.

SAVANNAH, GEORGIA

Simms, Ruth P. "The Savannah Story: Education and Desegregation." In *Our Children's Burden: Studies of Desegregation in Nine American Communities*, ed. Raymond W. Mack. New York: Random House, 1968. 109–40.

SEATTLE, WASHINGTON

Maynard, William. "The Seattle Plan for Eliminating Racial Imbalance." In *School Desegregation Plans That Work*, by Charles Vert Willie. Westport, CT: Greenwood Press, 1984. 119–48.

Siqueland, Ann LaGrelius. *Without a Court Order: The Desegregation of Seattle's Schools*. Seattle: Madrona Publishers, 1981.

STOCKTON, CALIFORNIA

Muskal, Fred, and Donna Treadwell. "Stockton, California: Education and Coalition Politics." In *Community Politics and Educational Change: Ten School Systems under Court Order*, by Charles V. Willie and Susan L. Greenblatt. New York: Longman, 1981. 298–316.

TACOMA, WASHINGTON

U.S. Commission on Civil Rights. *School Desegregation in Tacoma, Washington*. Washington, DC: U.S. Government Printing Office, 1979.

TOPEKA, KANSAS

Wolters, Raymond. *The Burden of Brown: Thirty Years of School Desegregation*. Knoxville: University of Tennessee Press, 1984. 253–71.

TRENTON, NEW JERSEY

Stave, Sondra Astor. *Achieving Racial Balance: Case Studies of Contemporary School Desegregation*. Westport, CT: Greenwood Press, 1995. 45–66.

TULSA, OKLAHOMA

U.S. Commission on Civil Rights. *School Desegregation in Tulsa, Oklahoma.* Washington, DC: U.S. Government Printing Office, 1977.

WASHINGTON, D.C.

Wolters, Raymond. *The Burden of Brown: Thirty Years of School Desegregation.* Knoxville: University of Tennessee Press, 1984. 9–63.

WILMINGTON, DELAWARE

Dimond, Paul R. *Beyond Busing: Inside the Challenge to Urban Segregation.* Ann Arbor: University of Michigan Press, 1985.

Green, Robert L., ed. *Metropolitan Desegregation.* New York: Plenum Press, 1985.

Raffel, Jeffrey A. *The Politics of School Desegregation: The Metropolitan Remedy in Delaware.* Philadelphia: Temple University Press, 1980.

Raffel, Jeffrey A., and Barry R. Morstain, "Wilmington, Delaware: Merging City and Suburban School Systems." In *Community Politics and Educational Change: Ten School Systems under Court Order*, by Charles V. Willie and Susan L. Greenblatt. New York: Longman, 1981. 82–128.

Stave, Sondra Astor. *Achieving Racial Balance: Case Studies of Contemporary School Desegregation.* Westport, CT: Greenwood Press, 1995. 67–84.

Varady, David P., and Jeffrey A. Raffel. *Selling Cities: Attracting Homebuyers through Schools and Housing Programs.* Albany: State University of New York Press, 1995.

Wolters, Raymond. *The Burden of Brown: Thirty Years of School Desegregation.* Knoxville: University of Tennessee Press, 1984. 175–251.

Wolters, Raymond. "The Consent Order as Sweetheart Deal: The Case of School Desegregation in New Castle County, Delaware." *Temple Political and Civil Rights Law Review.* 4, no. 2 (Spring 1995): 271–99.

WINSTON-SALEM, NORTH CAROLINA

Lauerman, Henry C. "The Role of the Judiciary in the Desegregation of the Winston-Salem/Forsyth County Schools, 1968–1975." In *Limits of Justice: The Courts' Role in School Desegregation*, ed. Howard I. Kalodner and James J. Fishman. Cambridge, MA: Ballinger, 1978. 493–568.

YONKERS, NEW YORK

Failer, Judith L., Anna Harvey, and Jennifer Hochschild. "Only One Oar in the Water: The Political Failure of School Desegregation in Yonkers, New York." *Educational Policy* 7, no. 3 (September 1993): 276–96.

Feld, Marcia Marker. "The Yonkers Case and Its Implications for the Teaching and

Practice of Planning." *Journal of Planning Education and Research* 8, no. 3 (Summer 1989): 169–75.

Wolters, Raymond. *Right Turn: William Bradford Reynolds, the Reagan Administration, and Black Civil Rights*. New Brunswick, NJ: Transaction Publishers, 1996.

INDEX

Note: main entry page numbers are set in **boldfaced** type.

About the Author

JEFFREY A. RAFFEL is Professor and Director of the School of Urban Affairs and Public Policy at the University of Delaware and has served as a researcher, scholar, expert witness, practitioner, community leader, and parent in the school desegregation process. He has published three previous books, and his articles have appeared in journals such as *Harvard Educational Review*, *Educational Evaluation and Policy Analysis*, *Phi Delta Kappan*, *Urban Affairs Quarterly*, *Journal of Urban Affairs*, and *Urban Education*. From 1974 through 1978 he served as executive director of the Delaware Committee on the School Decision, which worked toward the desegregation of Delaware's schools.

ISBN 0-313-29502-6

HARDCOVER BAR CODE